Sardinia

Duncan Garwood

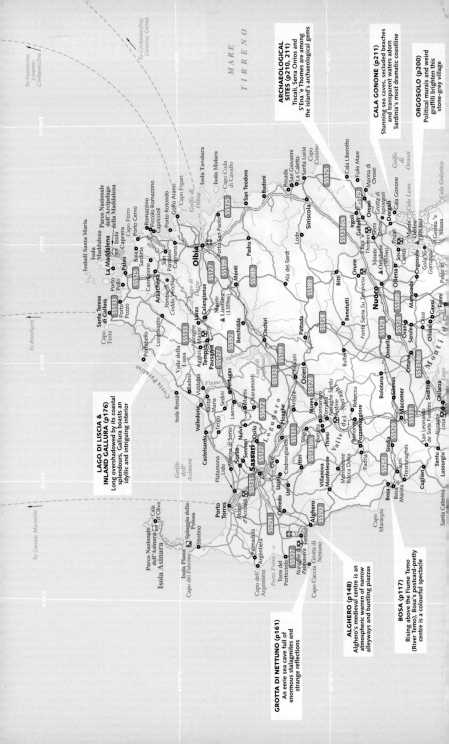

ARCHAEOLOGICAL SITES (p210, 211)
Tiscali, Serra Orrios and S'Ena 'e Thomes are among the island's archaeological gems

CALA GONONE (p211)
Stunning sea caves, secluded beaches and transparent waters adorn Sardinia's most dramatic coastline

ORGOSOLO (p200)
Political murals and weird graffiti brighten this stone-grey village

LAGO DI LISCIA & INLAND GALLURA (p176)
Long overshadowed by its coastal splendours, Gallura boasts an idyllic and intriguing interior

GROTTA DI NETTUNO (p161)
An eerie sea cave full of enormous stalagmites and strange reflections

ALGHERO (p148)
Alghero's medieval centre is an atmospheric warren of narrow alleyways and bustling piazzas

BOSA (p117)
Rising above the Fiume Temo (River Temo), Bosa's postcard-pretty centre is a colourful spectacle

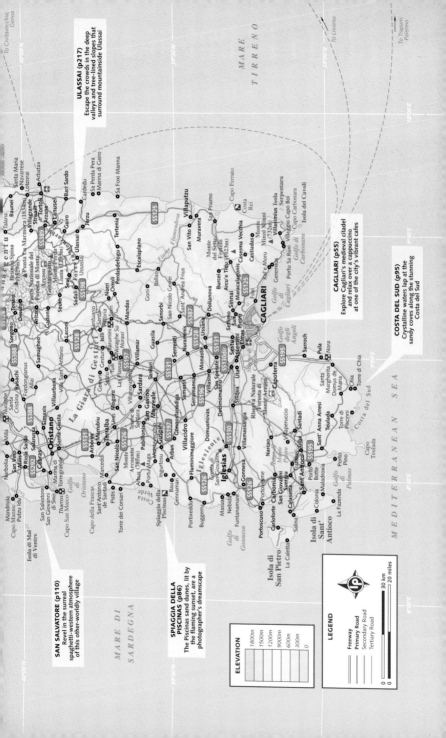

SAN SALVATORE (p110)
Revel in the surreal spaghetti-western atmosphere of this other-worldly village

SPIAGGIA DELLA PISCINAS (p86)
The Piscinas sand dunes, lit by the flaming sunset, are a photographer's dreamscape

ULASSAI (p217)
Escape the crowds in the deep valleys and tree-lined slopes that surround mountainside Ulassai

CAGLIARI (p55)
Explore Cagliari's medieval citadel and relax over a cappuccino at one of the city's vibrant cafes

COSTA DEL SUD (p95)
Crystalline waters lap at the sandy coves along the stunning Costa del Sud

ELEVATION
1800m
1500m
1200m
900m
600m
300m
0

LEGEND
Freeway
Primary Road
Secondary Road
Tertiary Road

0 — 30 km
0 — 20 miles

Sardinia Highlights

In a country where every nook and cranny appears to have been explored, experienced and exhausted, Sardinia is a charming reminder that some of travel's best-kept secrets lie right beneath our noses. It's renowned for its stunning beaches, laissez-faire atmosphere, rustic cuisine and authentic festivals, so here are some top tips from travellers.

ANDREW PEAC

1 BEACH-HOPPING ALONG THE GOLFO DI OROSEI

Cala Gonone (p211) was stupendous. I loved the caves. We visited the Grotta del Bue Marino (p213) and took a boat excursion down the coast, stopping off at the most fabulous beaches. The sea was stunning, really beautiful and crystal clear.

Stefania Masella, Traveller, Italy

WADE EAKLE

2 ARCHAEOLOGICAL DELIGHTS

There's so much of archaeological interest in Sardinia. Serra Orrios and S'Ena 'e Thomes (p210) are both fascinating sites. Nobody was there when we were at Serra Orrios and it was absolutely wonderful. Another superb site was Tiscali (p211), although you really need a guide to get there.

Alan Paddison, Traveller, UK

ULASSAI

It took us ages to drive to Ulassai (p217), but the scenery was absolutely amazing. In three hours of driving we only passed about five other cars as we twisted through huge valleys blanketed in silence and covered by sweeping forests. Overhead, huge slabs of rocks sat baking in the boiling sun. I've never felt so cut off from the rest of the world. It really felt like we were the only people on earth.

Lidia Salvati, Traveller, Italy

ANDREW PEACOCK

3

DAMIEN SIMONIS

4 ALGHERO

Wandering through Alghero's old town (p148) was like stepping back in time. You can easily slip down a cobbled alleyway to get away from the bustle, and it was there that we stumbled across locals drying laundry and wanting to chat.

Paul Griffin, Traveller, UK

KAYAKING ALONG THE RIVER TEMO

We hired kayaks and went paddling on the Fiume Temo (River Temo) amid the tall, scratchy reeds. It was so quiet gliding through the countryside, but best of all was our return to Bosa (p117) in the early evening, when the town houses glowed a burnished gold in the sunset.

Sandra Haywood, Traveller, UK

DOUG MCKINLAY

CAGLIARI

For me the best thing was just strolling round the cobbled streets of Il Castello (p57) in Cagliari, finding unexpected corners and old art studios. There's also a fantastic fish and food market called the Mercato di San Benedetto (p69) in the Villanova district.

Alice Grigg, Traveller, UK

DALLAS STRIBLEY

RICCARDO SPILA / SIME/4CORNERS IMAGES

SPIAGGIA DELLA PISCINAS

The sand dunes on the Spiaggia della Piscinas (p86) are fabulous. You can take the most incredible photos, especially at sunset, when the light is stunning.

Luca Antonelli, Traveller, Italy

EXPLORING SEA CAVES AT THE GROTTA DI NETTUNO

We boarded a boat in Alghero and sped across the turquoise water to the Grotta di Nettuno (p161). Climbing through these enormous sea caves was breathtaking. Stalagmites spiralled up to the ceiling and were reflected in still pools of water. At times, it felt like a cathedral, at others it felt more like the moon.

Korina Miller, Lonely Planet Author, Canada

WAYNE WALTON

WAYNE WALTON

8

9 SINIS PENINSULA

I loved the surreal, almost tropical feel of the Sinis Peninsula (p109), with its white sands, Tharros ruins (p110) and low-lying lagoons. When I went to San Salvatore (p110), I drove straight past the entrance the first time. I couldn't believe that the tiny, sandy track was the village's main entrance. Everything about it was strange – the odd little pilgrim houses, the dusty piazza. I even had to ask where the main church was and I was staring straight at it.

Duncan Garwood, Lonely Planet Author, Italy

DALLAS STRIBLEY

10 TANTALISING TASTES

The food was so yummy. I ate pasta and cheese that tasted smoky, and lots of sorbet. My favourite dinner was a big plate of pasta that we ate sitting right over the sea.

Simone Griffin, Traveller, Age Four

INTO THE INTERIOR

We tore ourselves away from the beach and drove into the interior, where we enjoyed spectacular views of the coast and had a picnic on neolithic stones amid fields of wildflowers.

Caroline Haywood, Traveller, UK

ORGOSOLO

I knew there were murals in Orgosolo (p200), but I never imagined that the whole village was a canvas for some of the weirdest graffiti I've ever seen. Social commentary, politics, international news and 'end-of-the-world' prophecy all make an appearance on the shabby exteriors of houses and cafes. It was the strangest experience, especially when we came upon images of the Twin Towers and the fall of Baghdad, which seemed a world away from this small mountain village.

Paula Hardy, Lonely Planet Staff

COSTA DEL SUD BEACHES

Sardinia's beaches are really beautiful. You've just got to get out and see them, especially those along the Costa del Sud (p95) on the southwestern coast.

Hema Mistry, Traveller, UK

Contents

Regional Map Contents

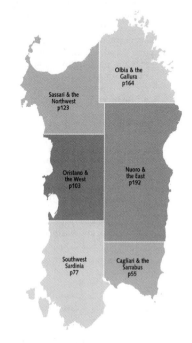

Olbia & the
Gallura
p164

Sassari & the
Northwest
p123

Oristano &
the West
p103

Nuoro &
the East
p192

Southwest
Sardinia
p77

Cagliari & the
Sarrabus
p55

Destination Sardinia

Despite its celebrity as a holiday destination, Sardinia remains remarkably enigmatic. Hidden behind the golden facade of swanky coastal resorts and spectacular beaches is an altogether different Sardinia, an island of untamed nature and proud tradition, of dark granite peaks, dizzying valleys and endless forests, all shrouded in an eerie coat of silence. Almost 7000 *nuraghi* (stone towers) lie strewn about the countryside, a reminder of prehistoric life on the island.

This beautiful Celtic landscape has fostered an isolated lifestyle still evident today. Although access is now assured by modern roads, for centuries many inland communities were cut off from the outside world by Sardinia's mountainous terrain. As a result inlanders, though unfailingly polite and helpful, can be diffident towards outsiders, and many towns bear the hallmarks of a difficult existence.

To address the traditional scourges of rural life, the regional authorities are aggressively promoting Sardinia as a year-round holiday destination. The island's fabulous outdoors potential means that hiking, biking and climbing are becoming popular activities for visitors. Regional festivals – not only great spectacles but genuine expressions of local pride – are drawing tourists seduced by Sardinia's folkloristic appeal and unique gastronomic traditions.

The Sardinian coast, however, continues to attract most of the attention and most of the visitors. An increase in low-cost flights into Alghero and Olbia has seen tourist numbers rising in recent years, and the Costa Smeralda (Emerald Coast) remains the destination of choice for oligarchs, captains of industry and media moguls.

But while tourism thrives, the rest of the economy struggles. After two years of expansion, industrial growth slowed going into 2008 – exports of oil, chemical and metal products fell – and with the spectre of recession hanging in the air, the economic outlook looks grim. Further exacerbating the situation is the EU's decision to reduce funding to the region – up until 2007 the EU considered Sardinia a backward region and financed it accordingly.

The man with the job of balancing the books is regional president Ugo Cappellacci. Elected on a centre-right ticket in February 2009, Cappellacci took the reins of power from Renato Soru, an unflinching character whose four-year tenure sparked controversy and division. Central to much debate was a coastal building ban and a tax on holiday homes and super-yachts, which Soru had introduced as part of a wide-ranging plan (the *piano paesaggistico*, or landscape plan) to regulate development on the island. But the political pendulum has swung right again and with Soru out of the way, the path is clear for Cappellacci to set his own agenda. The new president has highlighted poverty and unemployment as priorities, and has promised to modify Soru's landscape plan.

FAST FACTS

Population: 1.65 million

Area: 24,090 sq km

Italy's GDP: €1.4 trillion

Sardinia's GDP per head: €18,570

GDP growth: 1.3%

Inflation: 4.75%

Unemployment rate: 11.8%

Population density: 68 per sq km

Number of sheep: 3 million

Getting Started

Sardinia may be an island, but it's a big one. Even with your own transport, you may be surprised how long it can take to get from A to B. In many inland places the tourist infrastructure is also very basic and it really pays to come prepared. If time is limited, consider trying to organise trekking, climbing and diving activities before you arrive. Also be aware that changeable weather in the autumn and spring can play havoc with carefully laid plans.

Undoubtedly the most popular (and expensive) areas are the Costa Smeralda, Alghero and Cagliari, but for the independent traveller there is much to discover away from these hot spots. Although the island is well serviced by European airlines and ferries, a potential problem is Sardinia's popularity during summer. You will need to book a long way in advance if you're travelling in July and August. In general the only way to really see Sardinia is to hire your own vehicle; train and bus services are reliable but can be limited in the interior, especially outside of high season.

WHEN TO GO

Sardinia is famous for its seven-month summer and in a good year you could be happily stretched out on the beaches from April till as late as October, when temperatures still hover around 20°C. Touring the interior is best between March and June, when many towns celebrate their patron saints' day (see p17). It's great fun to visit during these festivals, but you'll have to book well in advance.

Average temperatures are 25°C in summer (a little hotter inland) and around 8°C to 10°C in winter (a little colder inland, naturally decreasing with altitude). Rain falls mainly in spring and autumn, and the mountainous interior receives the bulk of it, which falls as snow on the higher peaks; the plains and coastal areas in the east and south are significantly drier. The ideal time for walking in the Gennargentu is between March and June, when the wildflowers are in bloom and the countryside is at its greenest.

See Climate Charts (p223) for more information.

From mid-July all of Italy thunders to the sound of millions hitting the holiday roads – and Sardinia is one of their primary objectives. Hundreds of thousands pour in daily until the end of August, when the flood starts to flow in the opposite direction. It's a bad time to join in, as accommodation can be hard to find, prices reach for the sky and the summer heat can become unbearable.

Another thing to bear in mind are varying costs between the high season – Easter and from mid-June to early September – and the rest of the year, when

---

DON'T LEAVE HOME WITHOUT...

- Travel insurance that covers everything you hope to do, especially if planning to dive, cycle, climb etc (p227)
- Your ID card or passport and visa if required (p231)
- Driving licence and car documents if driving, along with appropriate car insurance (p242)
- An adaptor for electrical appliances
- Some wet-weather gear, a warm sweater or fleece and sturdy, waterproof walking boots if you plan on trekking (p138)
- A set of smart clothes for those nights on the Costa Smeralda

even the busiest resorts drop their prices. Between November and February some places close altogether (especially campsites), so do your research first if you plan to travel during this period.

COSTS & MONEY

HOW MUCH?

City bus fare €1

International newspaper €2.50 to €3

Coffee and *cornetto* €2.50 to €3

Bowl of pasta €6 to €8

Gelato €2.50 to €4

How much you spend in Sardinia depends on where you go and when. Staying at the top resorts in July and August can be bank-breakingly expensive, but visit the island out of season and you'll be surprised at how cheap it can be. Certainly, the island compares favourably with mainland Italy, which is generally more expensive. See the Directory's Accommodation (p219) and Food (p225) sections for detailed information on the pricing system we've used in this book.

A prudent backpacker might scrape by on €50 per day by staying in cheap *pensioni*/hostels, buying food at supermarkets and eating in pizzerias. Realistically, though, a traveller wanting to stay in a comfortable midrange hotel, eat two square meals per day, hire a car and not feel restricted to one site per day should reckon on a daily average of about €120 to €150.

TRAVEL LITERATURE

Despite the island's striking beauty and rich, rural past, there is relatively little travel literature to recommend. Sardinia's most famous commentator was DH Lawrence, whose sharply drawn portrait of the island is the only real travel book of its kind.

Sea and Sardinia (DH Lawrence) Lawrence's classic Sardinian travelogue was written after he'd grumped his way around the island for six days in 1921. His empathy with the rural essence of the island tempers his acerbic, and often hilarious, tantrums at the inadequate accommodation and food.

The Lead Goat Veered Off: A Bicycling Adventure on Sardinia (Neil Anderson) This witty, light-hearted read follows Anderson and his partner Sharon as they pedal their way round Sardinia, meeting eccentric locals and sleeping in out-of-the-way spots. There are no great revelations, but if you've always fancied cycling but don't have the thighs, it's the ideal substitute.

Grazia Deledda: A Legendary Life (Martha King) The biography of Sardinia's greatest female novelist, this concise volume reveals much about the Nuorese society in which Deledda grew up and the boundaries she had to break in order to write.

The Bandit on the Billiard Table (Alan Ross) A waistcoat-straight account of Sardinia in the 1950s. Alan Ross has the tone of a schoolmaster and he takes the island to task in a masterly way, with anecdotal stories and some sensitive insights.

La civiltà dei Sardi (The Civilisation of the Sards; Giovanni Lilliu) Unfortunately only printed in Italian, Lilliu's magnum opus is the definitive book on the history, archaeology and culture of the island.

INTERNET RESOURCES

Get Around Sardinia (www.getaroundsardinia.com) Great for practical advice on travelling Sardinia by public transport. Has links to bus companies, notes on major towns and plenty of useful tips.

Lonely Planet (www.lonelyplanet.com) Check out the Cagliari destination guide and exchange Sardinia info on the Thorn Tree forum.

Mare Nostrum (www.marenostrum.it) A fantastic Sardinian portal listing events, exhibitions, festivals, hotels, restaurants and much more, as well as all the latest news.

Sardegna Turismo (www.sardegnaturismo.it) Sardinia's official tourism site is comprehensive, easy to navigate and packed with background and practical information.

Sardinia Hike and Bike (www.sardiniahikeandbike.com) A great route planner for hikers and bikers. You can download trail maps and read up about routes, divided by area and level of difficulty.

Sardinia Point (www.sardiniapoint.it, in Italian) Here you will find oodles of cultural information, from what's on right now to recipes and accommodation.

Sarnow (www.sarnow.com) A magazine website with well-written features on the island and plenty of itinerary suggestions.

TOP **PICKS**

SARDINIA
(ITALY)

◦ Rome

TOP CONSERVATION AREAS

Sardinia's compelling landscape has largely escaped the ravages wrought by development. But conservation is an issue and here we highlight the island's most beautiful protected areas.

- The **Parco Nazionale del Golfo di Orosei e del Gennargentu** (p200) encompasses the mountainous Supramonte (p198) and Golfo di Orosei (p207).

- The **Parco Nazionale dell'Arcipelago di La Maddalena** (p178) comprises seven islands and some 40 islets.

- The **Parco Nazionale dell'Asinara** (p147) is home to a population of pint-size albino donkeys.

- **Isola Tavolara** (p169) boasts translucent waters and great views.

- Just off the Sinis Peninsula, **Isola di Mal di Ventre** (p111) features a windswept landscape and sandy beaches.

- The woods of the **Riserva Naturale Foresta di Monte Arcosu** (p98) are roamed by the *cervo sardo* (Sardinian deer)

- The **olivastri millenari** (p176) are a group of thousand-year-old olive trees overlooking **Lago di Liscia** (p176).

- Said to have been created by St George, the **Scala di San Giorgio** (p218) is a picturesque gorge near Ulassai.

MUST-HAVE MUSIC

Cultural isolation has made Sardinia a mecca for ethnomusicologists. These CDs provide a good introduction to the original and sometimes strange sounds; see p36 for more on Sardinian music.

- *Suoni di Un'Isola* (2003) A compilation of traditional *tenores* (vocal songs).

- *Intonos* (2000) and *Caminos De Pache* (2005), Tenores di Bitti. Vocal music from Sardinia's most famous *tenores* outfit.

- *Launeddas* (2002), Efisio Melis and Antonio Lara. Historic recordings of the *launeddas*, Sardinia's unique woodwind instrument.

- *Alguimia* (2003), Franca Masu. A homage to Alghero's musical traditions, sung in the local Catalan dialect.

- *Organittos* (1999), Totore Chessa. Guitar renditions of traditional Sardinian folk music.

- *Forse il Mare* (1986), Ritmia. Innovative Sardinian folk music.

- *Sonos* (1988), Elena Ledda. A popular singer and friends' take on Sardinian folk.

- *Launeddas* (2003), Franco Melis. Traditional *launeddas* music from a modern master.

- *Sardegna Canta* (1970), Maria Carta. The first album by Sardinia's legendary folk musician.

TOP BOOKS

Sardinia has more of an oral storytelling tradition than a written one. However, the post-WWI years have proved fruitful and Sardinia is now well established on the literary map. See p38 for more.

- *Sardinia Blues* (2008), Flavio Soriga

- *Canne al Vento* (Reeds in the Wind; 1913), Grazia Deledda

- *Sardinian Brigade* (1938), Emilio Lussu

- *Il Giorno del Giudizio* (The Day of Judgement; 1975), Salvatore Satta

- *Padre Padrone* (1975), Gavino Ledda

- *Il Figlio di Bakunin* (Bakunin's Son; 1991), Sergio Atzeni

- *Cosima* (1937), Grazia Deledda

- *Diario di una Maestrina* (Diary of a Schoolteacher; 1957), Maria Giacobbe

- *Il Disertore* (The Deserter; 1961), Giuseppe Dessi

TRAVELLING RESPONSIBLY

In a 2006 *National Geographic* survey of the environments of 111 island-holiday destinations Sardinia came 31st. It was commended for its beaches and unspoilt coastline but marked down for its poor transport networks and underdevelopment of tourist facilities. This summarises the situation pretty well. Sardinia is largely unspoilt and the transport network is inadequate, although to claim that tourist facilities are underdeveloped is debatable. Certainly in some areas, particularly inland, they are almost nonexistent, but in the big coastal resorts they are second to none. The challenge facing travellers today is how to get the best out of Sardinia while contributing to the island's welfare, or at the very least not damaging it.

For sustainable-tourism listings, see the GreenDex on p270.

Your choice of accommodation can make a difference. Many of the big resorts are owned by international companies which contribute surprisingly little to the island economy. There are, however, a growing number of locally run B&Bs and *agriturismi* (farm-stay accommodation). These rarely offer the facilities guaranteed by the big hotels but they're generally cheaper, they're often in beautiful locations and many serve superb food. Useful websites include www.agriturismodisardegna.it, which has lists of *agriturismi* with prices, and www.bed-and-breakfast.it.

Restaurants recommended by the **Italian Slow Food** (www.slowfood.it) organisation – look out for stickers bearing its snail logo – will usually use local ingredients and serve traditional food. Another way of supporting island food producers is to visit markets and local food festivals.

Transport is a tricky one, and there's really no escaping the fact that if you want to get off the beaten track, you'll have to hire a car. Unless, of course, you cycle (or walk). Bike hire is available in most big towns and there are an increasing number of local operators offering cycling and hiking tours. Many of these take you into parts of the island that you'd be unlikely to visit under your own steam.

Similarly, there are a whole range of locally run cooperatives offering excursions and outdoor activities (trekking, climbing, caving, kayaking etc). Even if you loathe the idea of a guided tour, don't dismiss these guys out of hand. The Sardinian wilderness can be challenging and if you venture into unchartered territory, there's a real danger of getting lost. For further details see the Tours section, p244.

Common sense rules should also be applied wherever you go: don't waste water; keep to marked paths; respect barriers; don't pick wildflowers; don't light fires in unauthorised areas; and give way to sheep on the roads.

Festivals Calendar

Sardinia's festival calendar comprises everything from saints' day celebrations and religious festivities to costumed processions, insane horse races and jazz jamborees. For information on food festivals see p46.

JANUARY

FESTA DI SANT'ANTONIO ABATE   16 Jan
With the winter solstice passed, many villages in Nuoro province celebrate the arrival of spring with great bonfires. You'll be sure to find raging conflagrations in Orosei, Orgosolo, Sedilo and Paulilatino.

FESTA DI SANT'ANTONIO ABATE – MAMUTHONES   16-17 Jan
An eerie pagan festival celebrated in Mamoiada. A dozen townspeople don hairy costumes with a half-human, half-animal allure. Ritually chasing them are eight *issokadores,* in the guise of outmoded gendarmes.

FESTA DI SAN SEBASTIANO   19 Jan
Similar to the festival of Sant'Antonio. Towns all over the island set up their winter bonfires for San Sebastiano.

FEBRUARY

CARNEVALE   Period up to Ash Wed
Many towns stage carnival festivities. Highlights include the burning of an effigy of a French soldier in Alghero; the sinister *mamuthones* in Mamoiada; costumed displays in Ottana; and the townsfolk of Bosa inspecting each others' groins.

SA SARTIGLIA   Shrove Tues & preceding Sun
Oristano stages a medieval tournament of horsemen in masquerade involving bright processions and knightly challenges. More anarchic horse races take place at Santu Lussurgiu and Sedilo.

MARCH/APRIL

PASQUA   Easter
Holy Week in Sardinia is a big deal and is marked by solemn processions and Passion plays all over the island. The celebrations in Alghero, Castelsardo, Cagliari, Iglesias and Tempio Pausania are particularly evocative.

FESTA DI SANT'ANTIOCO   2nd Sun after Easter
Costumed parades, dancing, concerts and fireworks are held over four days in Sant'Antioco to celebrate the town's patron saint.

MAY

FESTA DI SANT'EFISIO   1-4 May
On 1 May a wooden statue of St Ephisius is paraded around Cagliari on a bullock-drawn carriage amid colourful costumed celebrations. The saint is carried to Nora, from where he returns on 4 May accompanied by yet more festivities.

FESTA DI SANTA GIUSTA   14-18 May
Held in the town of the same name just south of Oristano, the festival involves parades and music over four days.

CAVALCATA SARDA   2nd-last Sun in May
Hundreds of Sardinians in traditional costume gather at Sassari to mark victory over the Saracens in AD 1000. They are followed by horsemen who make a spirited charge through the streets at the end of the parade.

JUNE

FESTA DELLA MADONNA DEI MARTIRI
Mon after the 1st Sun of Jun
The people of Fonni dress in traditional costume and stage a procession with a revered image of the Virgin Mary, starting at the town's grand basilica.

JULY

S'ARDIA   6-7 Jul
This impressive and ferocious horse race celebrates the victory of Roman Emperor Constantine over Maxentius in AD 312. An unruly pack of skilled horsemen race around the chapel at Sedilo erected in Constantine's name.

L'ISOLA DELLE STORIE, FESTIVAL LETTERARIO DELLA SARDEGNA
1st week of Jul
Gavoi's three-day literature festival has enjoyed enormous success since it was inaugurated in 2006. Readings, author Q&A sessions and concerts are held in and around the pretty Barbagia lake town.

FESTA DELLA MADONNA DEL NAUFRAGO
2nd Sun of Jul

This procession takes place off the coast of Villasimius, where a statue of the Virgin Mary lies on the seabed in honour of shipwrecked sailors.

ISOLA TAVOLARA CINEMA FESTIVAL
Mid-late Jul

Outdoor screenings are staged against an atmospheric backdrop of bare rocky peaks on the Isola Tavolara.

NARCAO BLUES FESTIVAL
Last week of Jul

The otherwise unexceptional town of Narcao hosts Sardinia's top blues festival, attracting big-name international artists and passionate crowds.

AUGUST

ESTATE MUSICALE INTERNAZIONALE DI ALGHERO
Jul & Aug

Alghero's medieval centre comes alive with the sound of classical music as concerts are staged across town.

FESTA DI SANTA MARIA DEL MARE
1st Sun of Aug

Bosa's fishermen pay homage to the Virgin Mary with a river parade of boats bearing her image. Town celebrations continue for four days.

MATRIMONIO MAUREDDINO
1st Sun of Aug

Santadi's costumed townsfolk reenact a Moorish wedding in the central piazza. The grinning bride and groom are carried in on a traditional carriage drawn by a hefty bull.

I CANDELIERI
14 Aug

Sassari's great annual festival. The traditional high point is the *faradda*, when the city's nine trade guilds, along with drummers and pipers, parade giant timber 'candles' through the streets.

FESTA DELL'ASSUNTA
15 Aug

Held in Orgosolo, this is one of the most important festivals in the Barbagia. The event is marked by processions of religious fraternities and the colourful local costumes worn by the women.

ESTATE MEDIOEVALE IGLESIENTE
Mid-Aug

Since the mid-1990s Iglesias has hosted a popular 'medieval summer', the high point of which is the *Corteo Storico Medioevale* (Historic Medieval Parade), a grand costumed affair.

TIME IN JAZZ
Mid-Aug

A big music fest with jazz jams, dance happenings, dawn concerts and wine tastings. Centre of operations is Berchidda, but concerts are also staged at Olbia, Tempio Pausania, Oschiri and Ozieri.

FESTA DEL REDENTORE
2nd-last or last Sun of Aug

Sardinia's grandest costumed parade is accompanied by horsemen and dancers. A torch-lit procession winds through Nuoro on 28 August and an early-morning pilgrimage to the statue of Christ the Redeemer on Monte Ortobene takes place the following day.

SEPTEMBER

FESTA DI SAN SALVATORE
1st Sun of Sep

Several hundred young fellows clothed in white set off from Cabras on the Corsa degli Scalzi (Barefoot Race), an 8km run to the hamlet and sanctuary of San Salvatore.

FESTA DI NOSTRA SIGNORA DI REGNOS ALTOS
Mid-Sep

The people of the old town of Bosa decorate their streets with huge palm fronds, flowers and *altarittos* (votive altars) in honour of the Virgin Mary.

DECEMBER

NATALE
Christmas

In the run up to Christmas processions and religious events are held. Many churches set up elaborate cribs or nativity scenes, known as *presepi*. The day itself is a quiet family affair.

Itineraries
CLASSIC ROUTES

SEVEN ROYAL CITIES
Two Weeks / Cagliari to Castelsardo

Kick off in **Cagliari** (p55), Sardinia's down-to-earth capital. Take a couple of days to explore the labyrinthine **Il Castello** (p57) and the jumble of the **Marina** district (p62). You must visit the **Museo Archeologico Nazionale** (p59), with its wonderful bronze figurines, while kids will enjoy **Poetto Beach** (p64).

Travel west to **Iglesias** (p78), the heart of Sardinia's mining country. Take in the enormous **Grotta di San Giovanni** (p82) on the way. Dawdle along the beautiful **Costa Verde** (p84) and marvel at the dunes of the **Spiaggia della Piscinas** (p86) before arriving in **Oristano** (p103). Nearby are the Phoenician ruins of **Tharros** (p110).

Head inland to see the nuraghic complex of **Santa Cristina** (p114) and the **Nuraghe Losa** (p115). Detour to **Santu Lussurgiu** (p113), where you can eat well, before arriving in medieval **Bosa** (p117). Beyond is salty **Alghero** (p148), with its distinct Catalan flavour. Tackle the cliff-side steps of **Capo Caccia** (p161), which descend to the enormous sea cave of the **Grotta di Nettuno** (p161).

Continue on to Sardinia's second city, **Sassari** (p123). Check out the **Duomo di San Nicola** (p127) and the archaeological museum, **Museo Nazionale Sanna** (p126). Finally, hit Sardinia's north coast at scenic **Castelsardo** (p135), perched on a rocky bluff above the sea.

This 285km itinerary will take you through Sardinia's seven royal cities, its most famous archaeological museums and along some lovely coastline. Two weeks is enough to cover this route, but with an extra week you could really savour the Costa Verde beaches and explore the area around Oristano. Trains and buses serve all these towns.

PAST MEETS PRESENT   One to Two Weeks / Alghero to the Costa Smeralda

Fancy a swim in Caribbean-blue seas or a walk in an ancient cork forest? Whether you want to mingle with celebs or meditate in Sardinia's Romanesque churches, the north of the island is a smorgasbord of delights.

Start gently in picturesque **Alghero** (p148) with its cobbled lanes and honey-coloured walls. Day trip to the dramatic cliffs of **Capo Caccia** (p161) and dine in some of the island's most stylish restaurants (p154).

Meander north to isolated **Stintino** (p146) to laze on one of the island's best beaches, **Spiaggia della Pelosa** (p147), or visit the strange **Parco Nazionale dell'Asinara** (p147). Then duck inland to gritty **Sassari** (p123) for its city atmosphere and excellent dining. Tour the Pisan Romanesque churches of the tranquil Logudoro valley – **Basilica della Santissima Trinita di Saccargia** (p132), **Chiesa di San Michele e Sant'Antonio di Salvenero** (p132), **Chiesa di Santa Maria del Regno** (p132), **Chiesa di Sant'Antioco di Bisarcio** (p132) and the **Chiesa di Nostra Signora di Castro** (p132) on the shores of Lago di Coghinas.

Jump on to the SS127 and head northeast to **Tempio Pausania** (p185), deep in verdant cork forests. Shop in **Aggius** (p188), which produces nearly 80% of Sardinia's carpets and rugs, explore the weird landscape of the **Valle della Luna** (p188) and drive to the peak of **Monte Limbara** (p187)

To the northeast the country is rich with prehistoric sites, especially around **Arzachena** (p174), beyond which the bright lights of **Porto Cervo** (p171) beckon. Armed with a fistful of dollars, enjoy the high life along the Costa Smeralda before heading on to island-hop around the **Parco Nazionale dell'Arcipelago di La Maddalena** (p178).

A week is enough to cover this 265km itinerary, but if you want to kick back on the beaches and explore the woody slopes around Tempio Pausania you could easily fill a fortnight. It's preferable to have your own wheels, although you can get to the main towns on public transport.

SARDINIA'S GRANITE CORE　　　　　Two Weeks / Nuoro to Tortoli

Encompassing some of Sardinia's most spectacular scenery, this route takes you through the Parco Nazionale del Golfo di Orosei e del Gennargentu, the island's uncompromising granite heartland.

Start in **Nuoro** (p191), capital of the Barbagia hill country and birthplace of the island's most celebrated writer, Grazia Deledda. Check out the **Museo Deleddiano** (p193) and the **Museo della Vita e delle Tradizioni Sarde** (p191), before hitting the road for **Oliena** (p198), famous for its red wine.

Some 20km to the east, the bustling town of **Dorgali** (p209) makes an excellent base for exploring the surrounding wilderness. From here you can visit the **Grotta di Ispinigoli** (p210), home to the world's second-tallest stalagmite, and the nuraghic village of **Serra Orrios** (p210).

From Dorgali, it's a roller-coaster ride down to **Cala Gonone** (p211), a popular resort on the **Golfo di Orosei** (p207). This is Sardinia's most dramatic coastline, harbouring some superb beaches, such as **Cala Luna** (p213) and the sublime **Cala Mariolu** (p213), as well as the purple sea cave of **Grotta del Bue Marino** (p213). To get to these places you'll need to jump on a boat.

Continuing south, the SS125 rises through a spectacular granite landscape to the Genna 'e Silana pass. In the wilds to the west of the road you can trek to the nuraghic village of **Tiscali** (p211), and the **Gola Su Gorruppu** (p210), a vast rock chasm dubbed the Grand Canyon of Europe.

Back on the main road, you'll need to pass through the nondescript town of Baunei to reach the **Altopiano del Golgo** (p217), a weird highland plateau. A couple of restaurants make it a memorable place to lunch.

At the end of the road is **Tortoli** (p214), a resort town with a brassy atmosphere that will bring you back to earth with a bump.

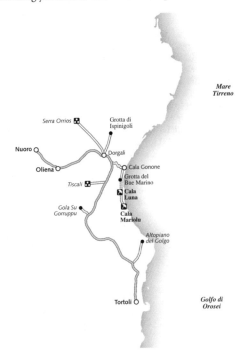

On this 180km trip you'll discover hidden gorges, prehistoric villages, a stunning stretch of pristine coastline and beautiful, secluded beaches. Two weeks is enough to cover it, as long as you have your own transport.

TAILORED TRIPS

THRILLS & SPILLS

Sardinia's 1849km coastline and untamed interior provide superb outdoor opportunities, ranging from hard-core trekking and mountain biking to climbing, diving, caving and windsurfing.

Windsurfers are spoilt for choice but the top spot is **Porto Pollo** (p178), where winds are funnelled through the Bocche di Bonifacio, the strait that divides Sardinia from Corsica. Here you can also try kitesurfing, sailing and diving. Other hot spots include **Capo del Falcone** (p147) and the **Sinis Peninsula** (p111).

Divers will love Sardinia's waters. You can trawl shipwrecks in the **Golfo di Cagliari** (p65); dive off the coast of **Alghero** (p148) and explore the Grotta di Nettuno, the Mediterranean's largest sea cave; visit an underwater mountain on the **Capo Carbonara** (p73) and Roman ruins at **Pula** (p96).

On terra firma, the choices are endless. There's superb trekking in the **Supramonte** (p198), where grottoes provide endless fun for cavers, and the magnificent **Golfo di Orosei** (p207), whose 45km *selvaggio blu* is reckoned to be the toughest trek in Italy. The sheer rock faces around **Ulassai** (p217) and **Cala Gonone** (p211) are a mecca for climbers.

Cyclists are well catered to, although the largely mountainous terrain sets some tough challenges. One of the more accessible routes is the scenic coastal run from **Bosa** (p117) up to Alghero.

Horse riding is also popular. The biggest school is the **Horse Country Resort** (p109), near Arborea, where you can arrange treks along the Piscinas dunes. Another good riding school is **Mandra Edera** (p116), near Abbasanta.

THE SARDINIAN TABLE

Sardinian cuisine is a weird and wonderful experience. If you arrive in **Cagliari** (p55) or **Alghero** (p148) you'll enjoy lots of seafood, in particular red and grey mullet, rock lobster, sardines and Spanish-inspired paella. Other seafood hot spots include **Carloforte** (p89) for its tuna- and saffron-flavoured *casca* (couscous); **Cabras** (p109) for mullet, *bottarga* (mullet roe) and smoked eel; and **Olbia** (p164) for stuffed squid and smoked cuttlefish, along with a range

of Gallurese dishes such as *suppa cuata* (cheese and bread broth). Spanish and Genoese accents are to be found in **Sassari** (p123), where you can sample *panadas* (pies filled with meat and game) and *fainè* (a pizzalike snack), but Sardinia's most ancient culinary roots are in the mountains of Barbagia. In villages such as **Orgosolo** (p200) you can buy world-class *pecorino*, and in towns like **Oliena** (p198) you'll find fragrant honey. Other specialist products are the velvety *bue rosso* beef, peppery olive oil – produced around **Seneghe** (p112) – and the sweet Malvasia wine of **Bosa** (p117). Round it all off with a selection of honey-drenched treats or almond-flavoured biscuits, best sampled in **Durke** (p71) in Cagliari.

History

For much of its messy history, Sardinia has been little more than an after-thought in the tactical and territorial battles of the Mediterranean's great powers. Its mineral reserves and strategic position ensured a constant stream of unwanted visitors. But foreign colonialists never had it easy. Endemic malaria and the island's granite core made Sardinia a tough deployment for outsiders. In more recent times, banditry and tourism have kept the island in the limelight.

THE MYSTERY OF PREHISTORIC SARDINIA

Sardinia as Atlantis? In his 2002 book *Le Colonne d'Ercole. Un' inchiesta* (The Pillars of Hercules. An investigation), Italian journalist Sergio Frau stakes a claim for Sardinia as the lost civilisation of Atlantis. As theories go, it's a tough one to prove, but the fact that it's up for debate is symptomatic of an island whose origins lie well beyond the reach of traditional history.

When the first islanders arrived and where they came from are questions that have been puzzling researchers for centuries. The most likely hypothesis is that they landed on Sardinia's northern shores in the lower Palaeolithic period (Old Stone Age). When flint tools were found at Perfugas in 1979, archaeologists muttered excitedly about primitive humans crossing from mainland Italy as far back as 350,000 BC. It's thought they came from Tuscany, although it's possible other waves arrived from North Africa and the Iberian Peninsula via the Balearic Islands. Geneticists have attempted to solve the riddle by researching the island's curious genetic make-up – in certain parts of the interior a particular gene mutation is found in concentrations only otherwise present in Scandinavia, Bosnia & Hercegovina and Croatia. However, they seem just as puzzled as the rest of us.

Check out www.sarnow.com for a good introduction to Sardinia's prehistory, with fascinating features explaining the historical context of local arts, crafts and culture.

Neolithic Paradise

Wherever the early settlers came from, they were apparently happy with what they found, for by the neolithic period (8000 BC to 3000 BC), Sardinia was home to several thriving tribal communities. The island would have been perfect for the average neolithic family – it was covered with dense forests full of animals, there were caves for shelter and land for grazing and cultivation. Underlying everything were rich veins of obsidian, a volcanic black stone that was used for making tools and arrow tips. This black gold became the Mediterranean's most coveted commodity, and was traded across the area – shards of Sardinian obsidian have been found as far away as France.

Most of what we know of this period, known as the Ozieri (or San Michele) culture, comes from findings unearthed in caves around Ozieri. Fragments of

TIMELINE

350,000 BC	4000–2700 BC	1800–500 BC
Fragments of basic flint tools indicate the first traces of human culture on the island. No one knows where the early islanders came from, although theories point to Tuscany or the Iberian Peninsula.	Thriving Copper Age communities formed around the town of Ozieri. Copper was smelted into ingots and traded, and the first *domus de janas* (rock tombs) appear. Archaeologists use the term 'Ozieri culture' to describe this lifestyle.	The nuraghic period: most of the stone ruins that litter Sardinia date back to this time. Some 30,000 fortified stone towers were built, most to serve as military watchtowers.

ceramics, tools and copper ingots attest to knowledge of smelting techniques and artistic awareness, while early *domus de janas* (literally 'fairy houses'; tombs cut into rock) tell of complex funerary rituals.

It's All in the Rocks

To the untrained eye, the strange stone circles that litter much of Sardinia's interior are mysterious and incomprehensible. But to archaeologists, they are a veritable encyclopaedia of ancient life. And in the absence of any written records – a fact that has led scholars to assume that the early Sards never had a written language – they provide one of the few windows into the dark world of the nuraghic society.

There are said to be up to 7000 *nuraghi* (stone towers) across the island, most built between 1800 and 500 BC. No one is quite sure what they were used for, or indeed how they were built, but suspicion falls on the usual suspect: the military. By the 2nd millennium BC, metal weapons were widespread and violent contact between settlements was becoming more frequent.

Early *nuraghi* were simple free-standing structures with internal chambers. Over time, they became bigger – the Nuraghe Santu Antine (p132) is the tallest remaining *nuraghe*, at 25m – and increasingly complex with elaborate rooms and labyrinthine passages. Walls were raised around the grand watchtowers and villagers began to cluster within the walls' protective embrace. The most spectacular example of this is the beehive complex of the Nuraghe Su Nuraxi (p100), near Barumini.

The discovery of Mycenaean ceramics in Sardinia and nuraghic pottery in Crete suggest an early trade in tableware and contact with other cultures. Evidence of pagan religious practices are provided by *pozzi sacri* (well temples). Built from around 1000 BC, these were often constructed so as to capture light at the yearly equinoxes, hinting at a naturalistic religion as well as sophisticated building techniques. The well temple at Santa Cristina (p114) is a prime example.

But perhaps the most revealing insights into nuraghic culture come from the *bronzetti* (bronze figurines) which populate many of Sardinia's archaeological museums, most notably those in Cagliari (p59) and Sassari (p126). Scholars reckon that these primitive depictions of shepherd kings, warriors, farmers and sailors were used as decorative offerings in nuraghic temples.

A PAWN IN OTHER PEOPLE'S GAMES

Sardinia's strategic position and its rich natural resources (silver and lead reserves) and fertile arable land have long made the island a victim of the Mediterranean's big powers.

The first foreigners on the scene were the Phoenicians (from modern-day Lebanon). The master mariners of their day, they were primarily interested in Sardinia as a staging post – they had colonies on Sicily, Malta, Cyprus,

Some historians argue that the nuraghic populace of Sardinia were the Shardana, a piratical seafaring people who appear in early Egyptian inscriptions.

La Civiltà dei Sardi (The Civilisation of the Sards) by Giovanni Lilliu is the definitive book about Sardinia's mysterious *nuraghe* builders.

1100 BC	227 BC	AD 456
The Phoenicians establish the town of Nora on the southwest coast. Now largely underwater, it was one of a series of important trading posts along with Karalis (Cagliari) and Tharros.	Sardinia becomes a Roman province, although it's not until 216 BC that the Carthaginians are defeated. The Romans build roads and develop centres at Karalis (Cagliari), Nora, Sulcis, Tharros, Olbia and Turris Libisonis (Porto Torres).	In wake of the fall of the Roman Empire, the Vandals land on Sardinia. Byzantine chroniclers, not the most objective, record the 80 years of Vandal rule as a time of misery for islanders.

Corsica – and so Sardinia was an obvious addition. The exact date of their arrival is unclear, although Semitic inscriptions suggest that Spain-based Phoenicians may have set up at Nora, on the south coast of Sardinia, as early as 1100 BC.

In the early days, the Phoenicians lived in relative harmony with the local nuraghic people, who seemed happy enough to leave the newcomers to their coastal settlements – Karalis (Cagliari), Bithia (near modern Chia), Sulci (modern Sant'Antioco), Tharros and Bosa. However, when the outsiders ventured inland and took over the lucrative silver and lead mines in the southwest, the locals took umbrage. Clashes ensued and the Phoenicians built their first inland fortress on Monte Sirai in 650 BC. This proved wise, as disgruntled Sardinians attacked several Phoenician bases in 509 BC.

Against the ropes, the Phoenicians appealed to Carthage for aid. The Carthaginians were happy to oblige and joined Phoenician forces in conquering most of the island. Most, though, not all. As the Carthaginians found out to their cost and the Romans would discover to theirs, the tough, mountainous area now known as the Barbagia didn't take kindly to foreign intrusion.

Carthage vs Rome

It was the Carthaginians, rather than the Phoenicians, who first dragged Sardinia into the Mediterranean's territorial disputes. By the 6th century BC, Greek dominion over the Mediterranean was being challenged by the North African Carthaginians. So when the Greeks established a base on Corsica, the Carthaginians were happy to accept Phoenician invitations to help them subdue the by-now rebellious islanders. It was the foot in the door that the Carthaginians needed to take control of the island and boost their defences against the growing threat from Rome.

The ambitious Roman Republic faced two main challenges to their desire to control the southern Mediterranean: the Greeks and the Carthaginians. The Romans saw off the Greeks first, and then, in 241 BC, turned their attention to Carthaginian-controlled Sardinia.

The Romans arrived in Sardinia buoyed by victory over Carthage in the First Punic War (264–261 BC). But if the legionnaires thought they were in for an easy ride, they were in for a shock. The new team of the Sards and their former enemies, the Carthaginians, were in no mood for warm welcomes. The Romans found themselves frequently battling insurgents, especially in the mountainous Gennargentu area, which they dubbed Barbaria in reluctant homage to the sheer bloody-minded courage of the region's shepherd inhabitants.

In 215 BC Sardinian tribesmen, under their chieftain Ampsicora, joined the Carthaginians in the Second Punic War and revolted against their Roman masters. But it was a short-lived rebellion, and the following year the rebels were crushed at the second battle of Cornus (see p114).

Sardinian histories tend to be weighty and academic, and *Archaeology and History in Sardinia from the Stone Age to the Middle Ages: Shepherds, Sailors and Conquerors* by Stephen L Dyson and Robert J Rowland is no exception.

AD 600	1000–1400	1015
Christianity is finally imposed on the Barbagia region, the last to succumb to Byzantine proselytising. Its ancient pagan rites have not been forgotten and are still celebrated in modern-day festivals.	Sardinia is divided into four *giudicati* (provinces), the most famous being the Giudicato d'Arborea, centred on Oristano and led by its talismanic heroine Eleonora d'Arborea. The *giudicati* are eventually incorporated into Pisan and Genoese spheres.	Pisan and Genoan navies help Sardinia defeat Arab forces from Mallorca. Pisa and Genoa begin their long struggle for control of the island. By the late 13th century, the mainlanders control three-quarters of the island.

Once they had Sardinia in their hands, the Romans set about shaping it to suit their own needs. Despite endemic malaria and frequent harassment from locals, they expanded the Carthaginian cities, built a road network to facilitate communications, and organised a hugely efficient agricultural system. The Romans also severely decreased the island's population – in 177 BC around 12,000 Sardinians died and as many as 50,000 were sent to Rome as slaves. Many noble families managed to survive and gain Roman-citizen status and came to speak Latin, but on the whole, the island remained an underdeveloped and overexploited subject territory.

Pisa vs Genoa

By the 9th century, the Arabs had emerged as a major force in the Mediterranean. They had conquered much of Spain, North Africa and Sicily, and were intent on further expansion. Sardinia, with its rich natural resources and absentee Byzantine rulers, made for an inviting target and the island was repeatedly raided in the 9th and 10th centuries. But as Arab power began to wane in the early 11th century, so Christian ambition flourished, and in 1015 Pope Benedict VIII asked the republics of Pisa and Genoa to lend Sardinia a hand against the common Islamic enemy. The ambitious princes of Pisa and Genoa were quick to sniff an opportunity and gladly acquiesced to the pope's requests.

At the time Sardinia was split into four self-governing *giudicati* (provinces), but for much of the 300-year period between the 11th and 14th centuries, the island was fought over by the rival mainlanders. Initially the Pisans had the upper hand in the north of the island, while the Genoese curried favour in the south, particularly around Cagliari. But Genoese influence was also strong in Porto Torres, and the *giudicati* swapped allegiances at the drop of a hat. Against this background of intrigue and rivalry, the period was strangely prosperous. The island absorbed the cultural mores of medieval Europe, and powerful monasteries ensured that islanders received the message of Roman Christianity loud and clear. The Pisan Romanesque churches of the northwest remain a striking legacy of the period.

Spain & the Savoys

Sardinia's Spanish chapter makes grim reading. Spanish involvement in Sardinia dates back to the early 14th century. In 1297 Pope Boniface VIII created the Regnum Sardiniae e Corsicae (Kingdom of Sardinia and Corsica) and granted it to the Catalan-Aragonese as an inducement to the Spaniards to give up their claims on Sicily. Unfortunately, however, the kingdom only existed on paper and the Aragonese were forced to wrench control of Sardinia from its stubborn islanders. In 1323 the Aragonese invaded the southwest coast, the first act in a chapter that was to last some 400 years.

1297	1392	1400–1500
In the face of Catalan pressure, Pope Boniface VIII creates the Regnum Sardiniae et Corsicae (Kingdom of Sardinia and Corsica) and declares Jaume II of Aragon its king, thus handing him control of the island.	Sardinia's great heroine and ruler of the Giudicato d'Arborea, Eleonora d'Arborea, publishes the Carta de Logu, the island's first code of common law. It tackles land use, women's rights and property issues.	Under Catalan-Aragonese control, absentee landlords impose devastating taxes and leave the rural population to struggle against famine and plagues, which claim 50% of the island's population.

Under the Catalan-Aragonese and Spanish, the desperately poor Sardinian population was largely abandoned to itself – albeit on the crippling condition that it pay its taxes – and the island remained underdeveloped. But Spanish power faded in the latter half of the 17th century and the death of the heirless Habsburg ruler Carlos II in 1700 once again put Sardinia up for grabs. His death triggered off the War of the Spanish Succession, which set pro-Habsburg Austrian forces against pro-Bourbon French factions in a battle for the spoils of the Habsburg empire. In 1708 Austrian forces backed by English warships occupied Sardinia. There followed a period of intense politicking as the island was repeatedly passed back and forth between the Austrians and the Spanish, before ending up in the hands of the Duchy of Savoy.

Piedmontese rule (from 1720, until Italian unification in 1861) was no bed of roses, either, but in contrast to their Spanish predecessors the Savoy authorities did actually visit the areas they were governing. The island was ruled by a viceroy who by and large managed to maintain control.

In 1847 the island's status as a separate entity ruled through a viceroy came to an end. Tempted by reforms introduced in the Savoys' mainland territories, a delegation requested the 'perfect union' of the Kingdom of Sardinia with Piedmont, in the hope of acquiring more equitable rule. The request was granted. At the same time events were moving quickly elsewhere on the Italian peninsula. In a series of daring military campaigns led by Giuseppe Garibaldi (see p181 for more info) and encouraged by King Carlo Emanuele, Sardinia managed to annexe the Italian mainland to create the united Kingdom of Italy in 1861.

FIGHTING SPIRIT

Fuelled by ferocious pride, Sardinia's fighting spirit runs deep and for much of its history the island has played David to an ever-changing cast of Goliaths.

The Lone Province

The talismanic figure of Sardinia's medieval history, Eleonora d'Arborea (1340–1404) embodies the islanders' deep-rooted fighting soul. Queen of the Giudicato d'Arborea, one of four *giudicati* – the others were Cagliari, Logudoro (or Torres) in the northwest and Gallura in the northeast – into which the island had been divided, she became a symbol of Sardinian resistance for her unyielding opposition to the Pisans, Genoese and Catalan-Aragonese.

By the end of the 13th century, Arborea was the only *giudicato* not in the hands of the Pisans and Genoese. The Arboreans, however, toughed it out and actually increased their sphere of influence. At its height under King Marianus IV (1329–1376) and Eleonora, the kingdom encompassed all of the modern-day provinces of Oristano and Medio Campidano, as well as much of the Barbagia mountain country.

Italy's revolutionary hero, Giuseppe Garibaldi, died on 2 June 1882 on the Isola Caprera, his private island in the Arcipelago di La Maddalena.

1478	1708	1720
On 19 May, Sardinian resistance to Aragonese control is crushed at the Battle of Macomer. Led by the Marquis of Oristano, Leonardo de Alagon, Sard forces prove no match for the Iberian army.	English and Austrian forces seize Sardinia from King Felipe V of Spain during the War of the Spanish Succession, a European-wide scramble for the spoils of the rudderless Habsburg Empire.	Duke Vittorio Amedeo II of Savoy becomes King of Piedmont and Sardinia after the island is yo-yoed between competing powers: first Austria, then Spain, Austria again, Spain for a second time, and finally the Savoys.

JUSTICE & EQUALITY FOR ALL

Throughout the island's long and sorry history one person stands head and shoulders above the rest: Eleonora d'Arborea (1340–1404). Described as Sardinia's Boudicca or Joan of Arc, she was the island's most inspirational ruler, remembered for her wisdom, moderation and enlightened humanity.

Eleonora became Giudicessa of Arborea in 1383, when her venal brother, Hugo III, was murdered along with his daughter. Surrounded by enemies within and without (her husband was imprisoned in Aragon), she silenced the rebels and for the next 20 years worked to maintain Arborea's independence in an uncertain world.

Her greatest legacy was the Carta de Logu, which she published in 1392. This progressive code, based on Roman law, was far ahead of the social legislation of the period. The code was drafted by her father, Mariano, but Eleonora revised and completed it. To the delight of the islanders, it was published in Sardinian, thus forming the cornerstone of a nascent national consciousness. For the first time the big issues of land use and the right to appeal were codified, and women were granted a whole raft of rights, including the right to refuse marriage and – significantly in a rural society – property rights. Alfonso V was so impressed that he extended its laws throughout the island in 1421, and this remained so until 1871.

Eleonora never saw how influential her Carta de Logu became. She died of the plague in 1404, and the Aragonese took control of Arborea only 16 years after her death. Eleonora remains the most respected historical figure on the island.

Initially Arborea had supported the Catalan-Aragonese in their conquering of Cagliari and Iglesias, but when they realised that their allies were bent on controlling the whole island, their support for the foreigners quickly dried up. From 1383 to 1404, Eleonora bitterly opposed the Catalan-Aragonese. But she couldn't live forever and her death paved the way for defeat. In 1409, the Sardinians were defeated at the Battle of Sanluri, in 1410 Oristano fell, and in 1420 the *giudicato*'s exhausted Arborean rulers gave in to the inevitable and sold their provinces to the Catalans.

Bravery & Banditry

Between 1960 and 1992, 621 people were kidnapped in Italy, 178 of them in Sardinia.

Sardinia's martial spirit found recognition on a wider stage in the early 20th century. The island's contributions to Italy's campaigns in WWI are legendary. In 1915 the Brigata Sassari (see p126 for more info) was formed and immediately dispatched to the northeastern Alps. The regiment was manned entirely by Sards, who quickly distinguished themselves in the merciless slaughter of the trenches. It is reckoned that Sardinia lost more young men per capita on the front than any other Italian region, and the regiment was decorated with four gold medals.

A less salubrious chapter is the island's tradition of banditry, which had reached epidemic proportions by the late 19th century. In May 1899 the

1795–1799	1823	1847
After Piedmontese authorities deny requests for greater self-rule, talk turns to revolution and angry mobs take to the streets of Cagliari, killing senior Savoy administrators. By 1799 the revolutionary flame has burnt itself out.	Intended to promote land ownership among the rural poor, the Enclosures Act sees the sale of centuries-old communal land and the abolition of communal rights. It's not popular and riots result.	Requests that the Kingdom of Sardinia, up to this point a separate entity ruled by a viceroy, be merged with the Kingdom of Piedmont are granted. From this point on, Sardinia is governed from Turin.

SARDINIA'S REGIONAL AWAKENING

WWI was a watershed for Sardinia. Not only in terms of lives lost and horrors endured, but also as a political awakening. When Sardinian soldiers returned from the fighting in 1918, they were changed men. They had departed as illiterate farmers and returned as a politically conscious force. Many joined the new Partito Sardo d'Azione (PSd'Az; Sardinian Action Party), whose central policy was administrative autonomy on the island.

Founded in Oristano in 1921 by Emilio Lussu and fellow veterans of the Brigata Sassari (the Sardinian regiment that served in WWI), the PSd'Az tapped into this emerging political awareness, embracing the burgeoning sense of regional identity that was spreading through the island. Sardinians had long been a proud people but until they were thrown together in the trenches they had rarely fought a common island-wide cause together. This led many to start viewing Sardinia as a region with its own distinct culture, aspirations and identity.

But a call for autonomy was just one of the cornerstones of the party's political manifesto. Combining socialist themes (a call for social justice and development of agricultural cooperatives) with free-market ideology (the need for economic liberalism and the removal of state protectionism), it created a distinct brand of Sardinian social-democratic thought.

Some 90 years on, the party is still in existence (no mean feat for an Italian political party!) and still active. It was a minor member of Renato Soru's 2004-2008 regional government, and it stood independently in the 2008 general election, winning 1.5% of the Sardinian vote.

New York Times reported: 'The Italian Government is at last realizing that the increase of brigandage in certain parts of Sardinia, and especially in the Province of Sassari, is becoming serious, and steps are being taken by the authorities to bring the bandits to justice.' It was a crusade the government was destined to lose as poverty and an inhospitable environment fuelled banditry throughout the 20th century. The town of Orgosolo, deep in Barbagia hill country, earned a reputation as a hotbed of lawlessness, and as recently as the 1990s gangs of kidnappers were operating in its impenetrable countryside.

MALARIA, THE GREAT ENEMY

Sardinia has endured millennia of invasion and foreign control, but until 1946 the island's single-most dangerous enemy was malaria.

Although scientists reckon that the disease was probably present in prehistoric times – some maintain that *nuraghi* were built as defence against weak-flying mosquitoes – it became a serious problem with the arrival of the Carthaginians in the 5th century BC. Keen to exploit the island's agricultural potential, the colonists cut down swaths of lowland forest to free land for wheat cultivation. One of the effects of this was to increase flooding and create areas of free-standing water, ideal habitats for mosquitoes. The problem was exacerbated by the arrival of imported soldiers from North Africa, many of whom were infected.

Vittorio de Seta's 1961 classic film, *Banditi a Orgosolo* (Bandits of Orgosolo), brilliantly captures the harsh realities of rural life in mid-20th-century Sardinia.

1915	1921	1928–38
The Brigata Sassari (Sassari Brigade) is founded and sent straight into WWI action in the northeastern Alps. Its Sardinian soldiers earn a reputation for valour and suffer heavy losses – 2164 deaths, 12,858 wounded or lost.	The Partito Sardo d'Azione (Sardinian Action Party) is formed by veterans of the Brigata Sassari. It aims to pursue regional autonomy and politicise the Sardinian public.	As part of Mussolini's plans to make Italy economically self-sufficient, Sardinia is given a makeover. Large-scale irrigation, infrastructure and land-reclamation projects are launched and new towns are established.

By the time the Romans took control of the island in the 3rd century BC, Sardinia was a malarial hothouse, its *mal aria* (bad air) thought to bring certain death. Despite this the Romans followed the Carthaginian lead and continued to exploit the island's fertile terrain. The Campidano plain became, along with Sicily and occupied North Africa, the granary of the entire Roman Empire.

Neglect & the Poverty Trap

Over the centuries malaria has been one, although not the only, reason for Sardinia's lack of development. Another was straightforward neglect. During the island's Spanish period (14th–18th centuries), most of the island was owned by absentee aristocrats who didn't give a peseta for the place as long as they got their taxes. As a result the Sards who actually worked the land were left free to pursue their traditional subsistence lifestyle (agriculture in the lowlands, pastoralism in the highlands), with very little interference from outside. Technological innovation was not something that troubled most islanders.

Even when feudalism was banned by the island's Piedmontese rulers in 1835, little changed. Legislation was introduced to reform land ownership but it failed to change very much. The poor simply couldn't afford the taxes on their newly acquired land and were forced to sell it back to the very people who had sold it to them. The Enclosures Act of 1823, aimed at turning over common land to private ownership, may have been motivated by laudable economic thinking but it inevitably excluded poor Sardinian farmers and shepherds, who lost the use of common land.

Against this background of poverty, malaria flourished. Attempts were made to eradicate it in the years following Italian unification (1861), but these were unsuccessful.

In the 1940s 60% of Sardinians suffered from malaria.

The Sardinia Project & Eradication

Until the late 19th century, it had been assumed that malaria was an airborne disease. The poor rural population had no idea that the mosquitoes that thrived in their dark, airless houses were the real carriers. As late as 1946, people were still questioning whether killing off the island's mosquitoes would eradicate the disease.

The Sardinia Project, financed by the US Rockefeller Foundation and hailed as the greatest campaign ever waged against malaria, was launched in 1946. Over four years, 10,000 tonnes of DDT were sprayed over the island by 32,000 operators. The effect was immediate: in 1946, 75,000 cases of malaria were reported; in 1951 this had dropped to nine.

However, the project was not without its critics, and even today researchers are examining the effects of such massive exposure to DDT. In 2005 a report published in the US journal *Cancer Research* concluded that there was no link between exposure to DDT and several forms of cancer.

1948	1946–1951	1950–70
Sardinia becomes a semiautonomous region with a regional assembly, the Giunta Consultativa Sarda. The regional government has control over agriculture, forestry, town planning, tourism and the police.	The sinister-sounding Sardinia Project finally rids the island of malaria. The US Army, financed by the Rockefeller Foundation, sprays 10,000 tons of DDT over the countryside. The effects are still being researched.	Sardinia becomes one of the principal beneficiaries of the Cassa per il Mezzogiorno, a development fund for southern Italy. But improvements in agriculture, education, industry, transport and banking can not prevent widespread emigration.

BURIED TREASURES

Although all but extinct, Sardinia's mining industry has played a significant role in the island's history. Southwest Sardinia is riddled with empty mine shafts and abandoned mine works, hollow reminders of a once-booming sector.

Sardinia's rich mineral reserves were being tapped as far back as the 6th millennium BC. Obsidian was a major earner for early Ozieri communities and a much sought-after commodity. Later, the Romans and Pisans tapped into rich veins of lead and silver in the Iglesias and Sarrabus areas.

Boom Years

The history of Sardinian mining really took off in the mid-19th century. In 1840 legislation was introduced that gave the state (the ruling Savoys) control of underground resources, while allowing surface land to remain in private hands. This, combined with an increased demand for raw materials fuelled by European industrial expansion, started a mining boom on the island.

By the late 1860s there were 467 lead, iron and zinc mines in Sardinia, and at its peak the island was producing up to 10% of the world's zinc.

Inward investment had spillover effects. The birth of new towns, the introduction of electricity, construction of schools and hospitals – these were all made possible thanks to mining money.

But however much material conditions improved, the life of a miner was still desperately hard, and labour unrest was not uncommon – strikes were recorded in southwest Sardinia at Montevecchio in 1903, and a year later at Buggerru. The burgeoning post-WWI socialist movement attempted to further politicise Sardinia's mine workers, but without any great success.

Fascism & Failure

Following the worldwide recession sparked off by the 1929 Wall Street Crash, the Sardinian mining industry enjoyed something of a boom under the Fascists. Production was increased at Montevecchio, and the Sulcis coalmines were set to maximum output. In 1938, the town of Carbonia in southwest Sardinia was built to house workers from the Sirai-Serbariu coalfield.

Mining output remained high throughout Italy's post-WWII boom, but demand started to decline rapidly in the years that followed. Regular injections of public money couldn't stop the rot, which was further exacerbated by high production costs, the poor quality of the minerals, and falling metal prices. One by one the mines were closed and, as of 2008, Sardinia's only operative mine was Nuraxi Figus, near Carbonia.

Written by an Oristano teacher, www .minesofsardinia.com provides an unusual take on Sardinian history by focusing on its mines and mining areas.

Iglesiente miners only went on strike in September, when the wild prickly pear came into fruit. This meant their families would have something to eat while the miners weren't earning a wage.

SELF-RULE

In 1994 *L'Unione Sarda* went online, the first European newspaper to do so.

The Sardinians have rarely been left alone to direct their own affairs, but since 1948, the island has enjoyed an autonomy shared by only four other Italian regions.

WWII left Sardinia shattered. The island was never actually invaded, but Allied bombing raids in 1943 destroyed three-quarters of Cagliari. Worse still, war meant that the island was isolated. The ferry between the mainland and Olbia was knocked out of action and did not return to daily operation until 1947.

As a result of this and the political upheavals that rocked Italy in the aftermath of the war – in a 1946 referendum the nation voted to dump the monarchy and create a parliamentary republic – Sardinia was granted autonomy in 1948. This came in the form of a regional parliament and a degree of local policy-making latitude. Yet there was a limit to what local government could achieve on its own, and outside intervention continued.

Students of Marxism can bone up on Sardinian Antonio Gramsci's ideas in *Selections from the Prison Notebooks*, written whilst serving time in Turin.

In 1950 Sardinia was nominated as one of the main beneficiaries of the Cassa per il Mezzogiorno, a development fund intended to kick-start the pitiful economy of Italy's south. In subsequent decades billions of lire were pumped into the island's economy, although poor administration meant that it was not always well spent. The oil and petrochemical plants at Porto Torres, Portovesme and Sarroch, for example, failed to provide the local jobs required and now stand as belching white elephants. The collapse of the industry in the 1970s, due to the OPEC oil wars, saw much of the workforce laid off, causing an island-wide recession. Rubbing salt into the wounds, the Iglesiente mines also went into decline and finally shut down in the mid-1990s.

Agricultural and administrative reforms were also slow in coming. The net result was that, although the quality of life in Sardinia gradually rose from the 1950s to the 1980s, serious problems remained. The most eloquent expression of this was the wave of emigration that hit the island from the late 1940s. The arrival of TV and greater awareness that life *could* be better led increasing numbers of young men to leave. In the 1960s 10% of the population left Sardinia for the Italian mainland or Western Europe.

In 1921, DH Lawrence spent six days travelling from Cagliari to Olbia. The result was *Sea and Sardinia*, his celebrated travelogue full of amusing and grumpy musings.

TOURISM & THE SARDINIAN BILL GATES

Tourism has put Sardinia on the map. Until malaria was eradicated in the mid-20th century, visitors (at least those with peaceful intent) were few and far between. DH Lawrence famously grumped his way round the island in 1921, and his words paint a fairly depressing picture of poverty and isolation. Were he to return today he'd find a very different island. Poverty still exists, particularly in the rural interior, and unemployment remains a serious issue (in 2008 it stood at 11.8%), but the island has changed almost beyond recognition.

2004	2008	2008
Renato Soru, founder of internet service provider Tiscali and self-made billionaire, is elected president of Sardinia. He sets the cat among the pigeons by banning building within 2km of the coast and taxing holiday homes and mega-yachts.	After a 36-year sojourn, the US Navy withdraws from the Arcipelago di La Maddalena. Its presence had long divided opinion: friends highlighted the money it brought; critics spotlighted the risks of hosting atomic submarines.	Sardinia becomes the first Italian region to switch to digital TV. As of November 2008 islanders could only receive channels of RAI, the Italian national broadcaster, through a digital decoder.

Before it was 'discovered' in the late 1950s and developed by a consortium of international high rollers, Gallura's northeastern coast was a rocky backwater, barely capable of supporting the few shepherds who lived there. Now the Costa Smeralda (Emerald Coast) is one of the world's glitziest destinations, its beaches a playground for Russian oligarchs, VIPs and bling-laden football players. Over on the northwestern coast, Alghero has become a popular resort served by a fleet of low-cost European airlines.

But development has not been painless, and although most would argue that tourism has been beneficial, there are those who question its long-term sustainability. In its current form, Sardinian tourism is largely a summer business and mostly confined to the coast, leaving out much of the long-neglected interior of the island. The impact on the environment is also a concern, as observers warn that there's a real danger of defacing the nature for which the tourists come. It's an argument that regional president Renato Soru seemed to take on board in 2004 when he introduced a ban on new buildings within 2km of the coast.

The Soru Years

Dubbed the Sardinian Bill Gates, self-made billionaire Renato Soru is the central character in the island's recent past. Born in 1957 in Sanluri, the son of a school caretaker and a grocery store owner, he founded the internet company Tiscali in 1998, and went on to become one of Italy's richest men. In 2003 Soru entered politics and a year later was voted regional president, a position he held until February 2009.

Used to the fast-moving world of the web, Soru was not afraid to ruffle feathers, and he soon had critics lined up against him. In addition to a ban on coastal development (see the boxed text, p53, for more on this), he introduced a 'luxury' tax, slapping tariffs onto everything from yachts and private planes to holiday homes and hotel stays. His intention, he stated, was to protect the landscape by limiting visitor numbers. Critics countered that it would simply drive tourists away.

But away from these controversies, what will Soru be remembered for? Certainly, one of his most lasting achievements was to oversee the withdrawal of US atomic naval forces from the environmentally sensitive Arcipelago di La Maddalena after a presence of 35 years. This divided local opinion, with environmentalists and Soru fans applauding the move, and business owners mourning the loss of free-spending American sailors. Soru was, however, able to soften the economic blow by announcing that the Isola Maddalena had been selected to host the 2009 G8 summit.

Soru's internet background had led to hopes that Sardinia might become the Mediterranean's Silicon Valley. But very little of this dream seems to have materialised.

According to newspaper *La Nuova Sardegna*, Italian Prime Minister Silvio Berlusconi paid €50,000 tax on his main Porto Rotondo residence after the introduction of the 'luxury' tax.

Of Italy's 20 regions, five have autonomous powers: Sardinia, Sicily, and the Alpine regions of Valle d'Aosta, Trentino-Alto-Adige, and Friuli-Venezia Giulia.

In 2003 the US nuclear-powered submarine USS *Hartford* ran aground in shallow waters near its base in the Arcipelago di La Maddalena.

The Culture

When DH Lawrence described Sardinia as 'lost between Europe and Africa, and belonging to nowhere' he was missing the point. Sardinia belongs to the Sardinians. History might suggest otherwise, but centuries of colonial oppression have done little to dent the islanders' fierce natural pride and their patient, melancholic resolve. On the surface, Sardinians display none of the exuberance usually associated with mainland Italians, nor their malleability or lightness of heart. They come across as friendly and hospitable, but serious and quietly reserved. Unlike other islanders, they don't look outwards, longing for escape and opportunity; instead they appear becalmed in the past, gripped by an inward-looking intensity.

A strong sense of fraternity, respect for tradition, and passion for a good *festa* – these are what unite Sardinians. But to speak of a regional identity is to overlook the island's geography.

ISOLATION & INTROSPECTION

In 2007 Italy's oldest woman, Rafaella Monni, died in Arzana in the province of Ogliastra, at 109. Five years earlier the then oldest man in the world, 112-year-old Antonio Todde, had died in Tiana, province of Nuoro.

'We never knew the sea, even if it was only about 150km away by the roads of those days,' says Maria Antonietta Goddi, a Cagliaritana by adoption who spent her early childhood in Bitti, a dusty inland town north of Nuoro. By modern roads, Bitti is only about 50km from the sea, but until relatively recently it was a world unto itself, cut off from the rest of the island by inhospitable mountains and a lack of infrastructure.

The same could be said of any one of hundreds of inland communities, left to fend for themselves by island authorities unable or unwilling to reach them. Such isolation nurtured introspection and a diffidence towards outsiders, whilst also preserving local traditions – many towns speak their own dialects, cook their own recipes and celebrate their own festivals that have been developed without any outside interference. It also exacerbated the ever-increasing divide between coast and interior. The advent of tourism and industrial development has had a far greater impact on coastal towns than on the island's hinterland, and there's a world of difference between the modern-minded cities of Alghero, Sassari, Olbia and Cagliari and the traditional lifestyles of inland villages.

However, to stereotype the differences can be misleading. According to Maria Antoinetta Goddi, in the centre of Sardinia there's a lot less male chauvinism than in the rest of Sardinia, and inland women impose themselves and make other people value them, which some people see as being a more balanced society.

Sixty-seven dialects make up the island's native language, Sardo.

Yet for all the hardship isolation has inflicted on the islanders, it has left Sardinia with some unique qualities. In recent years, researchers have been falling over themselves to study the island's uncontaminated gene pool (see boxed text, opposite), and musicologists have long appreciated the island's strange and unique musical traditions. Linguists study Sardo (or Sardu), Sardinia's mother tongue and also the largest minority language in Italy. Originally derived from the Latin brought over by the Romans in the 3rd century BC, it has four main dialects: Logudorese (in the northwest), Campidanese (in the south), Gallurese (in the northeast) and Sassarese (in the Sassari area). These dialects are further complicated by the incorporation of distinct local influences, so in Alghero residents speak a variation of Catalan, and on the Isola di San Pietro locals parlay in a 16th-century version of Genoese. The Gallura and Sassari dialects also reflect the proximity of Corsica.

THE SECRET OF A LONG LIFE – IT'S ALL IN THE GENES

Inhabitants of the mountainous province of Ogliastra have long been undisturbed by the outside world. As a result intermarriage has produced a remarkably pure gene pool, a veritable goldmine of genetic raw material.

In recent years three big genetic projects have been launched in the province: the Shardna programme to research genetic influences on diseases such as kidney stones, asthma and diabetes; the ProgeNIA initiative to study genes associated with heart disease in old age; and a University of Sassari project to examine genetic factors associated with longevity.

Sardinia boasts some 150 centenarians out of a population of 1.6 million, about twice the normal ratio. Of these, five live in the tiny village of Ovadda (population 1700). Previous studies have highlighted environmental and lifestyle factors (local Cannonau wines are rich in procyanidins, chemicals that contribute to red wine's heart-protecting qualities) as the main reasons for this longevity, but researchers from the University of Sassari remain convinced that there's a fundamental genetic element.

A research team, led by Professor Luca Deiana, has identified a number of genetic characteristics shared by Ovadda's centenarians, and although it's too early to tell where they fit into the puzzle, researchers are confident that they will shed some light on the secret of long life.

As a footnote, in February 2008, Sardinian scientists announced that they had discovered the gene responsible for male-pattern baldness. So there might yet be hope for us slap-tops.

ECONOMIC REALITIES

Until the 1950s Sardinia was a poor, disenfranchised part of Italy. Tourism had yet to discover the island and malaria had only just been eradicated; island society was overwhelmingly rural and 22% of the population was illiterate. Many people lived as they always had, eking out a tough living in small farming communities. Injections of development money in the immediate postwar years did much to transform the landscape but little to resolve the fundamental scourges of island life.

Poverty has been a constant of Sardinia's history and although it's not as apparent today as it once was, it is still an issue. Figures released in August 2008 showed that the average income in Sardinia was actually decreasing, that it was 2.9% less in 2007 than it had been in 1999. In the period between 1999 and 2007 islanders earned on average €13,286 per year, €3000 less than the national average.

Bearing the brunt of this downturn are the island's agricultural workers, who have struggled to compete in the global economy. In late 2007 a group of disillusioned farmers, shepherds and fishermen went on hunger strike to draw attention to their increasingly precarious plight. Their immediate concern was the paying back of a series of cheap loans that the Sardinian government had issued in 1988, and that the EU had subsequently condemned as unlawful subsidies. At the time of the strike Italian courts had just given the go-ahead for auctions of land put up as collateral.

Sardinians have long learned to rely on no one but themselves, and the family remains central to island society. Attitudes are changing, but many families still live according to the classic family model, with the women staying at home and the men going out to earn a crust. These clearly defined gender roles were originally dictated by the practical division of labour – with the men away from home pasturing their flocks, women were left running the house and raising the children – although nowadays they're as much about tradition and social convention as practical necessity.

Sardinian children, along with their mainland cousins, tend to fly the nest later than many northern Europeans, typically not until they marry. This is the subject of much ridicule, yet it is largely an economic decision – many young people, particularly if unemployed, simply can't afford to leave home. Unless, of course, it's to emigrate.

There are said to be around 500,000 Sards dispersed around the world. Many left between the 1950s and 1980s, most to northern Italy, but up to 150,000 to other European countries. It is not such a problem these days, although many inland towns still lose their young to summer work on the coast and seasonal jobs in Italian ski resorts.

FEASTING, FASTING & FOLKLORE

Conservative and for much of the year politely reserved, Sardinians let go with a bang during their great festivals. These boisterous and spectacular occasions reveal much about the islanders' long-held beliefs, mixing myth with faith and folklore.

Religious belief has deep roots in Sardinia. The presence of *sacri pozzi* (well temples) in nuraghic settlements attests to naturalistic religious practices dating to the 2nd millennium BC. Christianity arrived in the 6th century, brought over by the Byzantines, and quickly established itself as the religion of choice. Today Sardinian faith finds form in street parties as much as church services, and many of the island's biggest festivities are dedicated to much-loved saints. The greatest of them all, St Ephisius, an early Christian martyr and Sardinia's patron saint, is the star of Cagliari's huge May day carnival.

Elsewhere in the island, you'll find a number of *chiese novenari*, small countryside chapels that are only opened for several days of the year to host saints' day celebrations. These churches are often surrounded by *cumbessias* (also known as *muristenes*), simple lodgings to house the pilgrims who come to venerate the saint honoured in the church.

Easter is an important event in Sardinia, marked by island-wide celebrations, many of which reflect a Spanish influence. Castelsardo, Iglesias and Tempio Pausania all put on solemn night processions featuring ominously hooded members of religious brotherhoods more readily associated with Spain.

Religion, though, is only part of the story. Beliefs shaped by centuries of rural life take shape in many of the more memorable festival characters. Most dramatic of all are the *mamuthones* and *issokadores* of Mamoiada (p202), and Ottana's *boes* and *merdules* (p202). These mystical representations of ancient fears and pagan lore are thought to date to prehistoric times, yet their annual apparition is a much-waited-for event. Sardinian folklore, for all its superstitions and pagan mythology, is not simply the product of a poor underclass but is seen by all levels of society as a common cultural heritage.

For the visitor, observing a Sardinian festival holds the key to a deeper understanding of the people themselves. The striking costumes and jewellery of the women show a profound appreciation of skilled handicraft. Traditional pastimes such as horse racing and wrestling and competitive games like the Jocu de Sa Murra (see the boxed text, p203) allow men the opportunity to display their courage, nerve and skill.

THE ARTS
Music

Shielded from outside influences, the island's musical traditions sound like nothing else on the planet and they fuel a contemporary fusion scene of vibrant beauty.

The mainstay of traditional Sardinian music is male harmony singing. The *canto a tenores*, one of the oldest known forms of vocal polyphany, is performed by a four-part male choir, the *tenores*, made up of *sa oghe*, the soloist and lead voice, *su bassu* (bass), *sa contra* (contralto) and *sa*

Salvatore Mereu's 2008 film *Sonetàula* tells of a young boy's descent into brigandage and vendetta in the rocky heart of the island.

The Art-Culture section of www.marenostrum.it details all the up-and-coming cultural events and festivals, including art retrospectives and cinema shows.

Each of the 370 villages and towns on the island has its own traditional costume.

SA FEMMINA ACCABADORA

Bridging the gap between folklore and reality is the figure of *sa femmina accabadora* (also spelt *agabbadora*). This was the woman whose job it was to bring *'la dolce morte'* (sweet death) to people suffering from terminal illnesses in remote country villages. Unofficial euthanasia was an accepted part of rural life for centuries, and even if the authorities (and church) never condoned its practice, they never intervened to stop it. The last recorded cases were in Luras in 1929 and in Orgosolo in 1952.

After being 'commissioned' by the patient's family, *sa femmina* would arrive at the appointed house in the dead of night. Dressed in black and with her face covered, she would enter through a door which had been left open for her, and silently dispatch the patient with *sa mazzola*, a rudimentary hammer shaped out of olive wood. She would leave without speaking to or seeing a soul. She was never paid for her work, as to pay for death was considered a violation of accepted religious and superstitious norms.

You'll find a chilling example of a *mazzola* at the Museo Etnografico Galluras in Luras (p188).

mesu oghe (countertenor). Little is known of the canto's origins but it's thought that the voices were originally inspired by the sounds of nature – the *contra* based on a sheep's bleat, the *bassu* on a cow's moo, and the *mesu oghe* on the sound of the wind.

Canto a tenores is most popular in the centre and north of the island, with most of the best-known groups coming from the Barbagia region. The most famous is the Tenores di Bitti, which has recorded on Peter Gabriel's Real World record label and performed at Womad festivals. Other well-known choirs hail from Oniferi, Orune and Orgosolo.

Read up about Sardinia's best-known traditional group and listen to them in action at www .tenoresdibitti.com.

A similar style, although more liturgical in nature, is the *canto a cuncordu*, again performed by four-part male groups. To hear this head for Castelsardo, Orosei and Santu Lussurgiu.

Sardinia has also produced some fine female vocalists, most notably Maria Carta, a 20th-century island legend. Franca Masu is the diva of the Catalan enclave, Alghero, although the folksy tunes of Elena Ledda are probably more widely known. Solo singing was traditionally accompanied by *launeddas* in the south and by guitar in the north.

The *launeddas* is Sardinia's trademark musical instrument (see the boxed text, p38). A rudimentary wind instrument made of three reed canes, it is particularly popular at village festivals in the south. If you can't attend a festival, buy the legendary recordings *Launeddas,* by Efisio Melis and Antonio Lara. Other names to look out for on the *launeddas* circuit are Franco Melis, Luigi Lai, Andria Pisu and Franco Orlando Mascia.

For an interesting insight into Sardinian music, listen to Andy Kershaw's exploration of Sardinian (and Corsican) music at www.bbc.co.uk/radio3 /worldmusic/onlocation/corsica.shtml. The Sardinian tourist website www .sardegnaturismo.it also has recordings of traditional island music.

Poetry

Like many of the island's art forms, Sardinian poetry is not, and never has been, the preserve of the chattering classes. It is a much-felt part of local culture which in the 19th century gave rise to an early form of rap duelling, the so-called *gare poetiche* (poetry duels). At village festivals, villagers would gather to watch two verbal adversaries improvise rhyming repartee that was sarcastic, ironic or simply insulting. The audience loved it and would chime in with their own improvised shooting! Little of this was ever written down, but you can find CDs featuring a classic duo from the mid-20th century, Remundo Piras and Peppe Sozu.

Bardic contests still take place in the mountain villages and there are two important poetry competitions, Ozieri's Premio di Ozieri (p131) and the Settembre dei Poeti in Seneghe (p112).

Sardinia's most famous poet is Sebastiano Satta (1867–1914), who celebrated the wild beauty of the island in his poetry *Versi Ribelli* and *Canti Barbaricini*.

Get the lowdown on Sardinia's top literary event, Gavoi's Festa Letterario di Sardegna, at www .isoladellestorie.it.

Dance

A staple of festivals up and down the island, traditional folk dancing, generically referred to as *ballo sardo* (Sardinian dancing) or *su ballu tundu* (dancing in the round), is hugely popular. There are hundreds of variations, but most involve circular formations or complex line-dancing routines. There has been much speculation on the connections between *ballo sardo* and the similar *sardana* (circular folk dance) of Catalonia in northeastern Spain.

Literature

Sardinia's rural society had no great literary tradition, but the early 20th century marked a watershed. Grazia Deledda (1871–1936) won the 1926 Nobel Prize and a series of talented scribes began to emerge from the shadows. Their work provides an unsentimental picture of island life, as well as a fascinating insight into how the islander's saw, and see, themselves.

In the 1930s the Fascists banned the Sardinian *cantadores* (poets), whose attacks on church and state they deemed dangerous and subversive.

Taking inspiration from the petty jealousies and harsh realities of the Nuoro society in which she grew up, Grazia Deledda towers above the world of Sardinian literature. Her best-known novel is *Canne al vento* (Reeds in the Wind), which recounts the slide into poverty of the aristocratic Pintor family, but all her works share a strong local flavour.

Also Nuoro born, Salvatore Satta (1902–75) is best known for *Il giorno del giudizio* (The Day of Judgement), a biting portrayal of small-town life which is often compared to Giuseppe di Lampedusa's Sicilian classic *Il gattopardo* (The Leopard).

A contemporary of Satta, Giuseppe Dessì (1909–77) found fame with *Il disertore*, the story of a shepherd who deserts his WWI army unit and returns to his native Sardinia where he finds himself caught between a sense of duty and his own moral code.

One of the most famous works to have emerged from postwar Sardinia is *Padre Padrone*, Gavino Ledda's bleak autobiographical depiction of his early life as a shepherd. Later made into a critically acclaimed but unpopular film by the Taviani brothers, it paints a harrowing picture of the relentlessness of poverty and the hardships it provokes.

THE LAUNEDDAS *Barnaby Brown*

Although thisintriguing bagpipe-like instrument appears carved on 10th-century Irish and Scottish stones, its vibrant trance-inducing music survives only in Sardinia, connecting the listener directly with the Bronze Age.

In the past, *launeddas*-playing was a profession that required superhuman determination to pursue. Teaching was wilfully ineffective, so students were forced to travel from festival to festival, stealing the music that their masters so jealously guarded. The only reason the tradition is so healthy today is thanks to recordings made by a young Dane between 1957 and 1962.

Until the 1930s each village had its own *launeddas* player, and bachelors paid handsomely to keep the best players attached to their villages. This was because the Sunday *ballu* in the piazza was how single Sardinians met, but, sadly, Mussolini's reforms put an end to all that.

Barnaby Brown is a triplepipe player.

WRITING ON THE WALL

A precursor of graffiti art, Sardinia's *murales* (murals) emerged as a popular art from in the 1970s. Born of the students' and workers' unrest of 1968, they were often political in nature, although they were also used to celebrate the island's earthy culture. The most famous *murales* centre is Orgosolo (p201), the walls of which are covered with more than 150 murals, many of them executed by local students. They expound the most pressing social issues, from land reform and unemployment to the big questions of famine, warfare and terrorism. The town of San Sperate, just outside Cagliari, is another place worth checking out.

The intractability of political and social life in postwar Italy is the central theme of *Il figlio di Bakunin* (Bakunin's Son), the one translated work of Sergio Atzeni (1952–95). One of the giants of Sardinia's recent literary past, Atzeni, like Deledda before him, depicts a society that resists the simple reductions of comfortable moral and political assumptions.

In recent times, Sardinia has produced a good crop of noir writers, including the latest to hit the scene, Flavio Soriga (born 1975), whose *Diavoli di Nuraio* (The Devil from Nuraio) won the Premio Italo Calvino prize in 2000. His latest work, *Sardinia Blues* (2008), is set in a modern milieu of graduate unemployment, disco nights and lost ambitions, an environment recognisable to thousands of young Italians.

Traditional Crafts

As befits an agricultural island, Sardinia has a long tradition of craftwork. But where objects were originally made for practical, everyday use, they are now largely made for decoration. Local ironworkers around Santu Lussurgiu, for example, have adapted to the modern market by replacing agricultural tools, the mainstay of their traditional income, with decorative lamps, gates and bedsteads. Similarly carpet weavers in Castelsardo and knife producers in Arbus now sell their wares as souvenirs rather than as functional tools.

Quality still remains high, however, and you can find some excellent buys. Cagliari and Alghero are good for filigree jewellery, the latter famous for its red coral work, while Ulassai is a good place to pick up locally made tapestries. For ceramic work head to the Oristano area where local potters use methods honed over centuries. For more on where to shop, see p229.

Grazia Deledda's semiautobiographical novel *Cosima* offers a real insight into the life of a Sardinian mountain town in the late 19th to early 20th century.

Food & Drink

Unique but unmistakably Italian, Sardinia's earthy cuisine is a curious mix of tradition and adopted tastes. The focus is on meat, particularly inland, where until fairly recently communities were cut off from the coast and dishes developed according to the needs of shepherds. Pork and lamb were spit roasted over juniper fires to save on equipment; bread was baked light so shepherds could carry it; *pecorino* cheese was made hard to last. The relative poverty of the island ensured that nothing went to waste: donkey sausages, tripe sandwiches, horse carpaccio and black pudding were all common delicacies.

But it's not all about meat. You'll also enjoy Sardinia's wonderful seafood. Local specialities abound: tuna on the Isola di San Pietro; *bottarga* (mullet roe) in the lagoon town of Cabras, *aragosta alla catalana* (Catalan lobster) in Alghero. Alghero's Catalan-inspired cuisine is a classic case of culinary colonisation (the town was for centuries ruled by the Aragonese and Spanish), although not the only one. *Cascà* served on the Isola San Pietro is derived from the North African couscous, and the local *farinata*, pizza-style flatbread, is Genoese in origin. Many island sweets reveal Arab influences.

Yet imported or home-grown, Sardinia's cuisine relies on its incomparable raw materials. Fruit, vegetables, grain and meat – they're all produced on the island and they're all delicious.

ANTIPASTI

Antipasti have never been a feature of the Sardinian table, but other Italian cuisines have influenced local habits. *Antipasto di terra* (antipasto of the earth) will consist of homemade bread, preserved meats, smoked sausage, cheese, olives, mushrooms and a range of cooked, raw and marinated vegetables.

Along the coast you'll find seafood antipasti, such as thinly sliced *bottarga* drizzled with olive oil and Cagliari's famous *burrida* (marinated dogfish). There is also *frittelle di zucchine,* an omelette stuffed with zucchini (courgettes), breadcrumbs and cheese.

TOP TEN AGRITURISMI

The best way to taste real authentic Sardinian food is to eat at an *agriturismo* (farm-stay accommodation). There are hundreds dotted around the island, but these are our faves:

- **Arcuentu** (p85) Break your journey with lunch in the wilds of the Costa Verde.
- **Su Pranu** (p110) Dine on freshly roasted *porceddu* on the Sinis Peninsula.
- **Porticciolo** (p162) A friendly farm near Alghero.
- **Rena** (p175) Escape the Costa Smeralda hordes at this rural spot.
- **Romanzesu** (p198) They don't come any more authentic than this hideaway north of Bitti.
- **Guthiddai** (p199) A delightful whitewashed retreat in the granite Supramonte.
- **Nuraghe Mannu** (p213) Look over the spectacular Orosei coast at this terraced jewel.
- **Li Licci** (p176) Hidden among oak trees in Gallura's green heartland.
- **Su Boschettu** (p100) Feast on fresh cheese in Sardinia's agricultural heartland
- **Tenuta Lochiri** (p189) An elegant restaurant surrounded by silence.

BREAD

Using durum wheat of the best quality and age-old kneading techniques, Sardinians have come up with literally hundreds of types of bread, each one particular to its region and town.

The most famous is the shepherd's bread *pane carasau,* also known as *carta da musica* (music paper). It was introduced by the Arabs in the 9th century and is vaguely reminiscent of Indian poppadams. Wafer-thin and long-lasting, *pane carasau* was ideal for shepherds out in the pasture. It predominates in the Gallura, Logudoro and Nuoro regions.

Brushed with olive oil and sprinkled with salt, *pane carasau* becomes a moreish snack known as *pane guttiau.* A fancier version often served as a first course is *pane frattau,* where *pane carasau* is topped with tomato sauce, grated *pecorino* and *uovo in camicia* (soft-boiled egg).

Originally from the Campidano region, the commonly seen *civraxiu* (sivra-ksyu) is a thick, circular loaf with a crispy crust and a soft white interior. The *tundu* is similar. Another common bread is the *spianata* or *spianada,* which is a little like Middle Eastern pitta. In Sassari snack bars you'll discover *fainè,* the chickpea-flour *farinata* flat bread imported centuries ago by Ligurians from northwestern Italy.

The Spaniards contributed *panadas,* scrumptious little pies that can be filled with anything from minced lamb or pork to eel.

CHEESE

Sardinia is an island of shepherds, so it's hardly surprising that islanders have cheese-making down to a fine art. Cheese has been produced here for nearly 5000 years, and the island now makes about 80% of Italy's *pecorino.* Gourmands will delight in all the flavours and textures, from hard, tangy *pecorino sardo* to smoked varieties, creamy goat's cheeses (such as *ircano* and *caprino*), ricottas and speciality cheeses like *canestrati,* flavoured with peppercorns and herbs.

Fiora sarda, a centuries-old cheese recipe, is eaten fresh, smoked or roasted and packs a fair punch. It is traditionally made from ewe's milk, but varieties such as *fresa* and *peretta* are made from cow's milk. The most popular goat's cheese is *caprino,* and the soft *crema del Gerrei* is a combination of goat's milk and ricotta.

Only the bravest connoisseurs will want to sample *formaggio marcio* or *casu marzu,* quite literally a 'rotten cheese' alive with maggots!

The Foods of Sicily & Sardinia is a highly illustrated cookery book by Giuliano Bugialli featuring some of the best traditional Sardinian recipes.

SOUPS

You'll find that Sardinian cooks specialise in soups and meat-based broths more than any other region of Italy. It is in these dishes that the island's legumes and grains are utilised to their best advantage, particularly when combined with at least one defining flavour such as fennel bulbs, fava beans, chickpeas or spinach. The important difference between *suppa* (or *zuppa*; soup) and *minestra* (broth) is that the latter uses short pasta instead of bread.

Sardinian soups are often substantial, hearty meals in themselves, requiring little in the way of a side dish. One example is the Herculean *pecora in cappotto,* a broth of boiled mutton, potatoes, onions and dried tomatoes made in Barbagia. In Gallura, the gut-busting *suppa cuata* consists of layers of bread and cheese drowned in a tasty meaty broth and then oven-baked to create a thin, golden crust on top.

Minestra varieties include *gallina* (chicken), *piselli con ricotta* (peas and ricotta), *ceci* (chickpeas) and *lenticchie* (lentils). Other soups might be fennel- or endive-based.

Celebrate all that's odd about Sardinian cooking in Sweet Myrtle & Bitter Honey: The Mediterranean Flavours of Sardinia, a lavish cookbook by Efisio Farris.

PASTA

Sardinia generally has an individual way of doing things, and the island's pasta is no different.

Malloreddus, dense shell-shaped pasta made of semolina and flavoured with saffron, is usually served with *salsa alla campidanese* (sausage and tomato sauce) and is sometimes called *gnocchetti sardi.* Another uniquely Sardinian creation is *fregola,* a granular pasta similar to couscous, which is often served in soups and broths.

Another popular pasta is *culurgiones* (spelt in various ways), a type of ravioli. Typically it has a ricotta or *pecorino* filling and is coated in a tomato and herb sauce. *Culurgiones de l'Ogliastra,* made in Nuoro province, is stuffed with potato purée and sometimes meat and onions. A little *pecorino,* olive oil, garlic and mint are added, and a tomato sauce is the usual accompaniment.

Maccarones furriaos are strips of pasta folded and topped with a sauce (often tomato-based) and melted cheese. *Maccarones de busa,* or just plain *busa,* is shaped by wrapping the pasta around knitting needles.

Other pastas you may come across are *pillus,* a small ribbon pasta, and *filindeu,* a threadlike noodle usually served in soups.

> For a good selection of hearty recipes, try to pick up *Gastronomia in Sardegna,* by Gian Paolo Caredda. He covers all the basics of the Sardinian kitchen.

MEAT

Sardinia's carnivorous heart beats to its own unique drum. Three specialities stand out: *porceddu* (suckling pig), *agnello* (lamb) and *capretto* (kid). These dishes are flavoured with Mediterranean herbs and spit-roasted.

The most famous of this culinary triumvirate is the *porceddu* (also spelt *porcheddu*) which is slow roasted until the skin crackles and then left to stand on a bed of myrtle leaves.

Agnello is particularly popular around December, although it's served year-round. A country classic is *carne a carrarglu* (literally 'meat in a hole') – the meat is compressed between two layers of hot stones, covered in myrtle and left to cook in a hole dug in the ground. Sardinians say you can still come across country folk who will prepare this, but it is a rarity.

Capretto is harder to find on menus, but it gets more common up in the mountains, where it is flavoured with thyme.

Sards also have a penchant for game birds, rabbit and wild boar. A wonderful local sauce for any meat dish is *al mirto* – made with red myrtle, it is a tangy addition.

There is an impressive range of offal-based recipes, but few restaurants will serve them to tourists (see the boxed text, opposite).

> To hide evidence of their crime, bandits would slow roast stolen pigs in underground holes under bonfires. The technique is known as *carraxiu.*

FISH & SEAFOOD

Sardinians point out that they are by tradition *pastori, non pescatori* (shepherds, not fishermen). There is some tradition of seafood in Cagliari, Alghero and other coastal towns, but elsewhere the phenomenon has arrived from beyond Sardinia.

At the top end of the scale, lobster (legally in season from March to August) is *the* local speciality, particularly in Alghero, where it's served as *aragosta alla catalana* with tomato and onion. *Muggine* (mullet) is popular on the Oristano coast, and *tonno* (tuna) dishes abound around the Isola di San Pietro. *Cassola* is a tasty fish soup, while *zuppa alla castellanese,* a Castelsardo speciality, is similar but with a distinct tomato edge.

Cagliari also has a long tradition of seafood recipes that run the gamut from sea bream to bass, although the most famous is based on the local *gattucio di mare* (dogfish). Clams, cockles, octopus and crab also feature, as do eels around the marshes of Cabras. You can also try *orziadas* (sea-anemone tentacles rolled in semolina and deep-fried).

WE DARE YOU TO TRY...

- *Cordula* – Lamb tripe grilled, fried or stewed with peas.
- *Granelle* – Calf's testicles sliced, covered in batter and lightly fried.
- Horsemeat or donkey sausages.
- *Tataliu* or *trattalia* – A mix of kidney, liver and intestines stewed or grilled on skewers. The dish is made with veal, lamb, kid or suckling pig.
- *Zimino russo* – A selection of roasted offal, usually from a calf, including the heart, diaphragm, liver, kidney and other red innards.
- *Zurrette* – A black pudding made of sheep's blood cooked, like haggis, in a sheep's stomach with herbs and fennel.

SWEETS & DESSERTS

Unlike Sicily, where sugary, creamy desserts reign supreme, Sardinia's sweet trolley has always been constrained by the natural flavours of the island. Take the recipe for *amarettes* (almond biscuits): there are just three ingredients – almonds, sugar and eggs – but the biscuits are delightfully fluffy and moist. In Quartu Sant'Elena the recipe is a little more complex for *mustazzolus* (it includes flour and vanilla), a biscuit vaguely reminiscent of German *Lebkuchen*.

Other sweets and biscuits are strictly seasonal. *Ossus de mortu* (dead men's bones) are served on All Saints' Day in November, and the curd-based *pardulas* (ricotta-filled biscuits flavoured with saffron) are traditionally an Easter recipe. After the grape harvest you'll start to see things like *papassinos de Vitzi* (an almond and sultana biscuit) and the rich *pabassinas cun saba,* little sultana patties mixed with almonds, honey and candied fruit moulded together with grape must. One of the most delicious confections is *coffettura,* tiny baskets of finely shaved orange peel and almonds drenched in honey. They're usually served at weddings.

The island's most famous dessert, however, is the *seadas* (or *sebadas*). It consists of a delightfully light pastry (vaguely like a turnover) stuffed with bran, orange peel and ricotta or sour cheese and then drenched in *miele amaro* (bitter honey). The only other widely served dessert is *crema catalana,* a local version of crème caramel.

The other way to end a meal is with a platter of Sardinian cheese and a glass of local liqueur.

Sardinia's most sought-after honey is made with pollen from *corbezzolo*, an autumnal plant similar to wild strawberry.

WINE

Although on the menu for thousands of years, Sardinian wine is relatively unknown outside its home country. This is changing, however, as vintners push for a higher profile and quality improves. Contemporary producers have started taming the mighty alcoholic content of their traditional blends and are now producing some light, dry whites and more sophisticated reds.

The best known and most successful of Sardinia's wines are the Vermentino whites, made primarily in the northeast, and the Monica, Carignano and Cannonau reds.

On the whole Sardinian wine is very reasonably priced, with quality labels often available from around €10 to €15 per bottle. You can buy wine directly from the producer or from a *cantina sociale* (wine-producers' cooperative). Lots of these organisations offer a *degustazione* (tasting).

Many *agriturismi* also produce their own wine, much of which is surprisingly good value.

In a restaurant, the cost of a bottle of decent wine depends on where you are: in the more expensive parts (Alghero, Costa Smeralda etc) you could be looking at €15 and upwards, while in cheaper areas you can easily find something for around €10. A litre of *vino della casa* (house wine) costs around €5 to €8.

Like all Italian wines, Sardinian wines are subject to strict classification by the authorities. There are four main classification types: DOCG *(denominazione di origine controllata e garantita;* produced in a specific area according to specific rules and evaluated by a designational committee before being bottled); DOC *(denominazione di origine controllata;* produced in a specific area according to specific rules), IGT *(indicazione geografica typica;* produced in a specific area) and *vino da tavola* (table wine). Each wine's classifcation must be marked clearly on the bottle. The winemakers of Sardinia currently produce one DOCG (Vermentino di Gallura) and 19 DOCs.

Dry and authoritative, www.winecountry.it provides technical details for all of Sardinia's major wines.

Vermentino Leads the Whites

Introduced to Sardinia in the 18th century, the vermentino grape flourishes on the sandy granite-based soil in the northeast. The area's best wine is the Vermentino di Gallura, Sardinia's only DOCG. A crisp aromatic white with a slightly bitter almond aftertaste, it's best drunk young as an aperitif or with fish.

But Vermentino is not confined to the Gallura DOCG area, although the Vermentino di Sardegna produced elsewhere only carries the DOC rating. You'll find an excellent assortment of this highly drinkable wine at the Cantina del Vermentino (p188), in the small village of Monti, about halfway between Olbia and Tempio Pausania. Another quality Vermentino producer is the award-winning Cantine Argiolas (p73). Cantine Argiolas also makes some excellent Nuragus di Cagliari under the Selegas label. This ancient dry white, said to have been introduced by the Phoenicians, is one of the most popular tipples on the island.

A good bottle of 1998 Turriga will set you back around €60.

A SWEET FOR EVERY TOWN

Sweets, tarts, cakes and biscuits – Sardinia's dessert menu is rich and varied. Alongside the island staples, there's a never-ending list of local specialities.

'Every town has its own recipes,' explains Maria Antonietta Goddi, one of four sisters who along with their mother, the formidable Signora Maurizia, run Durke, a traditional sweet shop in Cagliari's Marina district.

'For example, there's a *dolce* (sweet) called *papassino* (from papassa, which means raisin) that's made all over Sardinia, but there are lots of local variations. So you have variations from Torralba, Benetutti, Bitti and Selargius in the province of Cagliari. The version from Selargius uses cinnamon and *vino cotto* (mulled wine).'

Such variations often reflect an area's history, incorporating foreign influences into traditional recipes. 'In the centre and the south of Sardinia, the Arab influence is very strong – orange blossom, cinnamon and vanilla are used a lot. In the north they use a lot of *vino cotto* and *vino selvatico* (wine from wild plants). In the centre they also use *pecorino* to make *casatinas*, which have a much stronger taste. Here in Cagliari we use a lot of ricotta, often with saffron.

'Then there's *torrone* (nougat), a *dolce* that is made in Sicily as well, but is made in Sardinia without the addition of sugar, so with honey, egg whites, almonds and walnuts.'

For more info on Durke, see p71.

A DROP OF THE HARD STUFF? *Duncan Garwood*

It's 10am and I've just been offered a *mirto*. I smile and politely refuse, not wanting to offend but not wanting to get into the hard stuff right now. *Mirto* is Sardinia's national drink, a smooth, powerful liqueur distilled from the fragrant purple fruit of the myrtle bush. In its most common form it's a purplish berry-red, although a less common white version is also made.

But *mirto* is just the tip of the iceberg. Islanders have developed a range of local firewaters using easily found ingredients such as *corbezzolo* (an autumnal plant similar to wild strawberry), prickly pears and basil. There's even a local form of *limoncello*, a sweet lemon-based tipple, similar to the better known Amalfi Coast drink.

The strangely named *filu e ferru* (the iron wire) provides quite a kick. Similar to grappa, it is made from a distillate of grape skins and positively roars down the throat – the alcohol content hovers around 40%, with some home brews reaching an eye-watering 60%.

Zedda Piras is a reliable brand of *mirto* and *filu e ferru*.

Live Life to the Full with the Reds

The island's best-known reds are made from the Cannonau vine. This is cultivated across the island, although it's particularly widespread on the mountains around Oliena (p198) and Jerzu (p217). Especially good with roast meats, it's a rich heavy drop that has been sustaining locals for centuries. Research has revealed that Cannonau wines are particularly rich in procyanidins, one of the chemicals that is reputed to give red wine its heart-protecting qualities, which may go some way to explaining the exceptional longevity of people in the Nuoro province; see the boxed text, p35.

The Antichi Poderi (p217), Jerzu's local cantina, is a good place to get to grips with Nepente di Oliena, a robust red (14.5%) which was praised by poet Gabriele D'Annunzio. For a lighter note try a more modern blend such as Dule.

One of the most lauded Cannonau wines is Argiola's Turriga, an intense full-bodied wine which regularly wins awards. Other excellent reds produced by Argiolas include a silky-smooth Perdera Monica and the spicy Costera.

Right at the heart of the southwestern Sulcis district, the Cantina Santadi (p88) produces some strong Carignano wines. Two good buys are Roccia Rubia and Grotta Rossa, both available at the cantina and both ideal with hearty meat dishes.

Sardinia's flagship vintner is Sella e Mosca (p159) near Alghero. It makes a huge range of wines including the renowned Marchese di Villamarina and a fruity, palatable Capocaccia. Its Torbato Terre Bianche sparkling wine is another fine buy.

Also worth tasting are wines made from the Nebbiolo grape, introduced by the Piedmontese in the 18th century.

Get Your Sweet Desserts

Produced since Roman times on the alluvial plains around Oristano, Vernaccia is one of Sardinia's most famous wines. It's best known as an amber sherrylike drop usually taken as an aperitif or to accompany pastries like *mustazzolus*. However, there are nine Vernaccia wines, ranging from dry still whites to aged fortified wines. The best place to experiment is the Cantina Sociale della Vernaccia (p107), just outside Oristano.

Another excellent tipple, Malvasia (Malmsey) is most commonly associated with Bosa, where it's produced in the surrounding Planaragia hills, but it's also made around Cagliari (Malvasia di Cagliari). The Malvasia di Bosa, a delicious honey-coloured dessert wine, is widely available in the Bosa area.

Italian Wines, published by Gambero Rosso and Slow Food Editore, is the definitive annual guide to Italian wines. Producers and their labels are reviewed in encyclopaedic detail.

To avoid taxes Sardinians hid their homemade *acquavita*. They'd mark the hideout with an iron wire (the *filu e ferru*), from which the drink derives its name.

PARTY LIKE IT'S...

Sardinians need little excuse to let their hair down. A history of poverty and rural isolation has led to a fierce pride in local traditions, many of which find form in extravagant celebrations and food-based *sagre* (festivals dedicated to a particular food). Traditionally these were based on the farming calendar and provided a rare occasion for villagers to meet up, show off their most splendid costumes and prepare their finest recipes. They're cheery events, with food stalls, drinks, and often live music.

Sardinia's party calendar spans the whole year, although the biggest festivals centre on Carnevale (the period leading up to Ash Wednesday, the first day of Lent), Pasqua (Easter) and Natale (Christmas).

Lovers of seafood can get the year off to a good start by heading to Alghero for the Sagra del Bogamarì (p153), a celebration of the humble yet delicious *riccio* (sea urchin), held between the end of January and February. Two festivals celebrate all things tuna related: Carloforte's Girotonno festival (p90), in late May, and the Sagra del Tonno (Tuna Fair) at Portoscuso (p87), in June.

For something sweeter, the town of Tonara, in the Barbagia di Belvi, pays tribute to nougat during the Sagra del Torrone, an annual event since 1979. It's held in March.

Still in the Barbagia, the lively mountain resort of Aritzo (p205) was for centuries Sardinia's ice supplier. To taste its celebrated lemon sorbet, get along to the Festa de San Carapigna, staged in mid-August. Later in the year, on the last Sunday of October, people flock to the town to munch on chestnuts at the Sagra delle Castagne (Chestnut Fair).

Wine is sniffed, tasted, discussed and sold at the Rassegna del Vino Novello (Festival of Young Wine), Sardinia's most important wine event held at Milis (p112) every November.

To discover the nuances of Sardinian cuisine, consult www.sarnow.com, which gives a great overview of the specialities of each region.

COOKING COURSES

Sardinia is not as well served with cooking schools as many Italian regions, but there are a number of places offering cooking courses. These include the Cooperativa Gorropu (p211), based in the highlands around Dorgali; Lu Aldareddu (p165), a lovely B&B near Olbia; and Hotel Lucrezia (p112), in the flatlands north of Oristano.

There are a number of specialist operators selling cooking holidays to Sardinia. One such is **Ciao Laura** (www.cialaura.com), an American outfit that arranges culinary stays in Orosei (p208), on the east coast. A four-day course costs €625, including accommodation.

EAT YOUR WORDS

Want to know the difference between *cavallo* and *capretto*? Get behind the cuisine scene by getting to know the language. For pronunciation guidelines, see the language chapter.

Useful Phrases

I'd like to reserve a table.
Vorrei riservare un tavolo.   vo·ray ree·ser·*va*·re oon *ta*·vo·lo

I'd like the menu, please.
Vorrei il menù, per favore.   vo·ray eel me·*noo* per fa·*vo*·re

Do you have a menu in English?
Avete un menù (scritto) in inglese?   a·*ve*·te oon me·*noo* (*skree*·to) een een·*gle*·ze

What would you recommend?
Cosa mi consiglia?   ko·za mee kon·*see*·lya

I'd like a local speciality.
Vorrei una specialità di questa regione.   vo·ray *oo*·na spe·cha·lee·*ta* dee *kwe*·sta re·*jo*·ne

Please bring the bill.
Mi porta il conto, per favore?   mee *por*·ta eel *kon*·to per fa·*vo*·re

Is service included in the bill?
Il servizio è compreso nel conto?   eel ser·*vee*·tsyo e kom·*pre*·zo nel *kon*·to

I'm a vegetarian.
Sono vegetariano/a.   so·no ve·je·ta·*rya*·no/a (m/f)

I'm a vegan.
Sono vegetaliano/a.   so·no ve·je·ta·*lya*·no/a (m/f)

Food Glossary

acciughe	a·*choo*·ge	anchovies
aceto	a·*che*·to	vinegar
acqua	*a*·kwa	water
acqua minerale	*a*·kwa mee·ne·*ra*·lay	mineral water
aglio	*a*·lyo	garlic
agnello	a·*nye*·lo	lamb
alimentari	a·lee·men·*ta*·ree	food shop
animelle	a·nee·*mel*·le	sweetbreads
aragosta	a·ra·*go*·sta	lobster
arancia	a·*ran*·cha	orange
arrosto/a	a·*ro*·sto/a	roasted
asparagi	as·*pa*·ra·jee	asparagus
birra	*bee*·ra	beer
bistecca	bees·*te*·ka	steak
bollito/a	bo·*lee*·to/a	boiled
bottarga	bo·*tar*·ga	mullet roe
brioche	bree·*osh*	breakfast pastry
burrida	boo·*ree*·da	dogfish with pine nuts, parsley and garlic
burro	*boo*·ro	butter
calamari	ka·la·*ma*·ree	squid
capretto	ka·*pre*·to	kid (goat)
carciofi	kar·*cho*·fee	artichokes
carota	ka·*ro*·ta	carrot
carta di musica	*kar*·ta dee *moo*·see·ka	flat, crispy bread
cassoeula	ka·so·*we*·la	winter stew with pork
cavallo	ka·*va*·lo	horse
cavolo	*ka*·vo·lo	cabbage
ceci	*che*·chee	chickpeas
cefalo	*che*·fa·lo	grey mullet

coccoi di sautizzu	ko-*koy* dee sau-tee-*tsoo*	platter of cured meat
coniglio	ko-*nee*-lyo	rabbit
cordulas	kor-*doo*-las	tripe cooked on a skewer
cornetto	kor-*ne*-to	croissant
cotto/a	*ko*-to/a	cooked
cozze	*ko*-tse	mussels
culurgiones (or *culurzones*)	koo-loor-*jo*-nez	ravioli filled with cheese and/or potato
fagiano	fa-*ja*-no	pheasant
fagiolini	fa-jo-*lee*-nee	green beans
fegato	*fe*-ga-to	liver
finocchio	fee-*no*-kyo	fennel
formaggio	for-*ma*-jo	cheese
forno a legna	*for*-no a *len*-ya	wood-fired oven
fragole	*fra*-go-le	strawberries
frittata	free-*ta*-ta	omelette
fritto/a	*free*-to/a	fried
frutti di mare	*froo*-tee dee *ma*-re	seafood
funghi	*foon*-gee	mushrooms
gamberoni	gam-be-*ro*-nee	prawns
gelateria	je-la-te-*ree*-a	ice-cream shop
granchio	gran-kyo	crab
(alla) griglia	(a-la) *gree*-lya	grilled (broiled)
insalata	in-sa-*la*-ta	salad
latte	*la*-te	milk
lenticchie	len-*tee*-kye	lentils
limone	lee-*mo*-ne	lemon
malloreddus	ma-lo-*re*-doos	semolina dumplings
manzo	*man*-dzo	beef
mela	*me*-la	apple
melanzane	me-lan-*dza*-ne	aubergine, eggplant
melone	me-*lo*-ne	melon
merluzzo	mer-*loo*-tso	cod
miele	*mye*-le	honey
mirto	*meer*-to	myrtle berries
muggine	*moo*-jee-ne	mullet
olio	*o*-lyo	oil
olive	o-*lee*-va	olive
panadas	*pa*-na-das	savoury pie
pane	*pa*-ne	bread
panna	*pan*-na	cream
panino	pa-*nee*-no	bread roll
pasticceria	pa-stee-che-*ree*-a	pastry shop
patate	pa-*ta*-te	potatoes
pepe	*pe*-pe	pepper
peperoni	pe-pe-*ro*-nee	peppers, capsicum
pere	*pe*-ra	pears
pesca	*pe*-ska	peach
piselli	pee-*ze*-lee	peas
pizza al taglio	pee-tsa al *tal*-yo	pizza by the slice
pollo	*pol*-lo	chicken
polpo	*pol*-po	octopus
pomodori	po-mo-*do*-ree	tomatoes
porceddu	por-*che*-doo	suckling pig
prosciutto	pro-*shoo*-to	cured ham
riso	*ree*-zo	rice

ristorante	ris to *rah* nte	restaurant
rosticceria	ros tich e *ree* ya	shop selling cooked meats
rucola	*roo*·ko·la	rocket
sale	*sa*·le	salt
salsiccia	sal·*see*·cha	sausage
sebadas	se·*ba*·das	fried pastry with ricotta
sedano	*se*·da·no	celery
seppia	*se*·pya	cuttlefish
spinaci	spee·*na*·chee	spinach
spuntino	spun·*tee*·no	snack
tavola calda	*tah*·volah *kahl* dah	canteen-style eatery
tonno	*ton*·no	tuna
tramezzino	trahmet·*see*·no	sandwich
triglia	*tree*·lya	red mullet
trippa	*tree*·pa	tripe
uovo/uova	*wo*·vo/*wo*·va	egg/eggs
uva	*oo*·va	grapes
vino (*rosso/bianco*)	*vee*·no (*ros*·so/*byan*·ko)	wine (red/white)
vitello	vee·*te*·lo	veal
vongole	*von*·go·le	clams
zucchero	*tsoo*·ke·ro	sugar
zuppa (or *suppa*)	*tsoo*·pa	soup or broth

Environment

At 24,000 sq km, Sardinia is the second-largest island in the Mediterranean after Sicily. Geologically speaking it is older than mainland Italy, its granite and basalt mountains predating the Apennines and the Alps. They dominate 68% of the island in a patchwork of massifs carved up by Sardinia's four rivers, the Tirso, the Flumendosa, the Coghinas and the Mannu.

Watch the Taviani brothers' haunting film *Padre Padrone*. Its moody shots of the island's mountainous interior are deeply atmospheric.

In the east rises the Gennargentu massif, now Sardinia's main national park. It isn't particularly high – the highest peak, Punta La Marmora, is 1834m – but it is ancient and rugged. Its ridges are broken by deep canyons, rivers and a plethora of caves, while its lower valleys are forested with holm oaks and maple, rising through ranks of juniper, holly and yew trees towards the summit.

The island's forests and woodlands are among its most delightful characteristics. Standouts are the dense cork forests around Tempio Pausania and the 36-sq-km forest of the Monte Arcosu reserve southwest of Cagliari, the largest forest of holm and cork oak remaining in the Mediterranean.

Sardinia's multifarious terrains are sometimes bewildering, as dark forests give way to extensive plains 'running away into the distance' (as DH Lawrence wrote). The Campidano plain between Cagliari and Oristano is the most extensive and supplies much of the island's wheat. Another, older, type of plateau is the *giara*, a large basalt tabletop constantly whipped by the *maestrale* (northwesterly wind) and home to pony-sized horses, called *achettas* in the Sardinian dialect (*cavallini* in Italian). The *giare* of Siddi, Serri and Gesturi are particularly noteworthy.

Sardinia's 1849km coastline is one of the most pristine in the Mediterranean and offers hugely varied vistas, from the high cliffs of the east to the wide, wind-whipped dunes of the west. Numerous saltpans, marshes and lagoons also punctuate the coast in the south and west. The largest of these are Santa Gilla, west of Cagliari, and the Stagno di Cabras and the Stagno di Sale Porcus on the Sinis Peninsula, which are home to 10,000 pink flamingos. These lagoons comprise some 30,000 acres of protected wetland, nearly half of all Italy's wetlands.

FLORA & FAUNA

Cut off from the main thoroughfares of trade and commerce, Sardinia's flora and fauna (many species of which are found only here and in neighbouring Corsica) have evolved in their own idiosyncratic way. Erosion and deforestation have had some impact, and hunting remains a common pastime, but they have not had the devastating effect that they have had elsewhere in southern Italy.

Animals

Sardinia's mountains harbour a host of indigenous species, such as the swarthy *cervo sardo* (Sardinian deer), which roams the forests of Gennargentu, Monte Arcosu and Monte Sette Fratelli. In the 1960s the deer came close to extinction but they have since made a healthy recovery to some 700 animals under the watchful eye of the World Wildlife Fund (WWF).

Other large mammals include the *cinghiale sardo* (Sardinian wild boar), a smaller-than-average boar that roots around the nut groves and woodlands of lower mountain slopes. Hunting has reduced their numbers over the years, so a larger boar from mainland Italy has been imported to boost

---

LESSONS FOR INLAND DEVELOPMENT

Keep it local and keep it low-key. That is the key to revitalising Sardinia's long-neglected interior according to Simone Scalas, whose **Sardinia Hike & Bike** (www.sardiniahikeandbike.com) is one of a number of environmentally conscious operators spearheading a call to Sardinia's great un-explored wildernesses.

'You can enjoy inland Sardinia year-round as opposed to the coast, which is only really alive in the summer,' says Simone.

But any attempt to reinvigorate the interior means tackling some deeply entrenched problems. Chief among these is emigration – inland villages continue to lose their young to summer work on the coast and winter jobs in the Alpine ski resorts. The way ahead, argues Simone, lies in lessons learnt from the coastal experience.

Citing the example of the Forte Village (a huge luxury resort on the south coast near Pula), he explains: 'Ten years ago up to 90% of the people working in the Forte Village were from Pula. Then the local people started opening their own restaurants, B&Bs, even their own hotels, and now far few people are having to emigrate from the area.

'An excellent initiative is the *albergo diffuso*, which is a great way of revitalising our town's historic centres. These are hotels spread over several renovated old houses; so you might have the reception in one building, and then, 300m away, guest rooms in another building.

'Our richness is our landscape. Most Sardinians don't understand this. We still think develop-ment means building, building, building.'

---

the population. Interbreeding is creating a newer, bigger breed, so the true Sardinian boars are becoming hard to find.

On the high plateau of the Giara di Gesturi, *achettas* run wild. But even weirder are the albino donkeys of the Parco Nazionale dell'Asinara in Sardinia's northwest. The Isola Asinara is also home to 500 *mouflon* (wild sheep), some of Sardinia's oldest inhabitants. Much coveted by locals for their remarkable curved horns (traditionally used to make han-dles for Sardinian knives), the sheep were on the verge of extinction not long ago but they now scale the cliffs of the island's interior in greater and happier numbers.

Marten, wildcats, foxes and hares make up the cast of smaller mammals on the island, and along the southwestern coast's arid beaches turtles come to lay their eggs.

Sardinia's official tourist website, www.sardegn aturismo.it is an excellent source of information on the island's geography, flora and fauna.

Birds
Located on the main migration route between Europe, Asia and Africa, Sardinia is an ornithologist's paradise. Between September and March thousands of flamingos visit the island and nest in the *stagni* (lagoons) near Oristano and around Cagliari.

The flamingos are joined by a host of other birds, including herons, cranes, spoonbills, cormorants, terns, dozens of waders, ducks and more. Some 200 bird species (one-third of the total number of spe-cies in Europe) make a pit stop on the island during their spring and autumn migrations.

Reptiles thrive on the island, but there are absolutely no poisonous snakes.

Inland ducks and cranes give way to an impressive crew of raptors (again, largely migratory) – Golden and Bonelli's eagles patrol the high skies in spring and autumn, as do the black vulture, the *lammergeier* (bearded vulture) and the peregrine falcon. On the Isola di San Pietro there is a semipermanent colony of the rare Eleonora falcon, named after queen Eleonora d'Arborea, who declared the bird a protected species in 1400. The griffon vulture maintains a colony in the west of the island, along the coast between Alghero and Bosa.

Plants

To be sure of seeing the best of Sardinia's wildflowers you need to visit in spring – April tends to be the best month.

In the higher woodland country of central and northeastern Sardinia, various types of oak, especially cork oak, dominate; see the boxed text, below.

Highland flowers such as the rare peony – also known as the 'rose of Gennargentu' – add a splash of colour to barren mountain peaks, especially around Bruncu Spina and Punta La Marmora. At lower altitudes typical Mediterranean scrub, *macchia*, predominates. The term covers a wide range of plants, including gorse, juniper, heather, broom and arbutus (also known as strawberry trees). In the grassy vegetation are many flowers, including violets, periwinkle, lavender, a colourful mix of irises and many species of orchid. Perhaps the best known of the *macchia* plants is the ubiquitous *mirto* (myrtle).

Many beaches on the western and southern coasts are backed by lovely pine stands. Palm trees are quite uncommon, and most are imported. An exception is the so-called dwarf palm, the leaves of which are used to make wicker baskets.

The Greeks believed eating a certain Sardinian plant resulted in convulsions resembling laughter and death. Hence the word *sardonic*.

NATIONAL PARKS

Sardinia boasts three national parks, two regional parks and a series of mostly marine reserves that cover a meagre 4% of the island's total area.

The most extensive of the national parks is the Parco Nazionale del Golfo di Orosei e del Gennargentu, which takes up a great swath of the Nuoro province, covering parts of Le Barbagie (p200), the Supramonte (p198) and the stunning Golfo di Orosei (p207).

The Parco Nazionale dell'Arcipelago di La Maddalena (p178) encompasses all the islands of this northwestern archipelago. Isola Caprera, joined to Isola Maddalena by a narrow causeway, has its own status as a natural reserve.

The most recent of the parks is the Parco Nazionale dell'Asinara (p147), a former prison island.

Otherwise, one of the more important natural reserves is the Riserva Naturale Foresta di Monte Arcosu (p98), southwest of Cagliari, which is protected by the WWF.

Areas with some degree of protection owing to their status as marine reserves include Capo Carbonara in the southeast; the Sinis Peninsula and its offshore island, Isola Mal di Ventre; the Isola Tavolara and nearby Punta Coda Cavallo; and Isola Budelli, within the Parco Nazionale dell'Arcipelago di La Maddalena.

Walkers should equip themselves with specialist books such as *Mediterranean Wild Flowers*, by M Blamey and C Grey Wilson.

IS THE SARDINIAN CORK SCREWED?

Do your bit for the Sardinian environment and buy wine with a natural cork. Cork is big business in Sardinia, but the spread of the synthetic bottle stopper is putting the industry at risk.

According to a 2006 World Wildlife Fund report, the increased use of plastic corks could lead to the loss of up to three-quarters of the western Mediterranean's cork forests within 10 years.

The impact in Sardinia would be devastating. The island accounts for 80% of Italy's cork production and the industry is a major employer in the northern towns of Calangianus and Tempio Pausania. Each year about 120 quintals of cork bark are harvested, most of it then sold to wine bottlers.

As well as the economic aspect, there are also environmental concerns. Cork harvesting doesn't actually harm the trees – harvesters simply shave the bark off the trunk – but a lack of care might. And if the cork companies don't protect the island's cork forests (and they're unlikely to do so without a vested interest), who will?

BATTLE FOR THE COAST

Coastal development is *the* political hot potato of the moment. Former regional president Renato Soru split opinion with two measures designed to protect the coast and channel money towards the island's oft-overlooked interior.

The first, introduced in 2004, was a controversial ban on building within 2km of the coast. Dubbed the *salvacoste* (save the coast) law, it provoked a predictably hostile reaction from developers and right-wing politicians who claimed that it would result in lost income for the island.

The issue came to a head in October 2008, when a referendum was held proposing the repeal of the *salvacoste*. However, a low turn-out ensured that quorum wasn't met and the referendum failed. The law remained intact.

Equally, if not more, divisive was the introduction of a 'luxury' tax in 2006, applicable to second homes owned by nonresidents, yachts and private planes. Reactions were split on fairly predictable lines with Flavio Briatore, a Formula 1 bigwig and a well-known figure on the Costa Smeralda, leading the howls of protest. Legal suits were launched, which continue to this day.

Newly elected regional president Ugo Cappellacci has indicated he will attempt to amend the legislation introduced by Soru.

ENVIRONMENTAL ISSUES

The buzz word in Sardinia today is sustainability. Tourism, in particular, is in the spotlight as policy-makers recognise the need to protect the coast and promote models of sustainable development.

Ever since the Aga Khan established his Costa Smeralda consortium in the 1960s, Sardinian tourism has been focused on the coast. But the spread of resorts along the northeast and southern coasts has forever scarred the landscape. Efforts are now being taken to limit coastal development and channel investment inland, but they are proving divisive and controversial (see the boxed text, above).

One of the few beneficial effects of Sardinia's history of neglect is that until the 1960s there simply weren't many man-made environmental issues. The major concerns were the perennial problems of water shortages, deforestation and the inevitable effects of wind erosion caused by the *maestrale*. All these remain problematic (water management, especially, is a high-profile issue), but there are now others.

The Nuraghe Su Nuraxi is Sardinia's single Unesco World Heritage site.

Rapid industrialisation and the transition from an agricultural to a service-based economy has had profound effects. The population shift from small villages to urban conurbations was driven by the establishment in the 1960s of petrochemical and other heavy industrial plants (notably at Porto Torres, Portovesme, Sarroch, Arbatax and south of Oristano). Ultimately, this policy of creating industrial poles in deeply depressed rural regions has contributed little to the island's economy, although it has certainly created pockets of air and water pollution. The plants still operate today, but the oil crisis of the 1970s and the end of mining in the Iglesiente have doomed them to remain ugly white elephants.

Cagliari & the Sarrabus

A capital city for more than 2000 years, Cagliari wears its history with self-confidence. Grand boulevards, neo-Gothic palaces and art-nouveau cafes tell of a city used to a certain style, while overhead, the city's rocky castle provides a suitably imposing landmark.

But beyond its historical veneer and cosmopolitan appeal, Cagliari remains what it always has been – a busy, working port. And it's this that informs its gritty, down-to-earth atmosphere and vibrant buzz. Cagliari has not been prettified for the benefit of tourists and is all the more interesting for it.

Founded by the Phoenicians in the 8th century BC, the city was first developed by the Romans, who carved a vast amphitheatre out of the rocky hillside and made the area into one of the Mediterranean's main trading ports. Later, the Pisans treated Cagliari to a medieval facelift, adding impenetrable forts and transforming the city into a showcase for their territorial ambitions. The results were impressive and are still standing today.

Against this historical backdrop, Cagliari's residents enjoy their city, displaying a bonhomie far removed from the introverted reserve so common in many Sardinian towns. Restaurants and trattorias cater to locals as much as tourists, and cafes fill quickly in the early evening. A strong student population ensures life in the piazzas.

However, you don't have to travel far from the city to find yourself in a different world. The scenic hinterland of the Sarrabus is an untamed, silent wilderness and the magnificent salt-white beaches of Villasimius and the Costa Rei are all but deserted outside of the peak summer months.

HIGHLIGHTS

- Explore the medieval lanes and museums of **Il Castello** (p57), Cagliari's rocky citadel, before taking an *aperitivo* on the **Bastione San Remy** (p69)

- Feast on seafood in one of the popular eateries in Cagliari's **Marina** (p68) quarter

- Party the night away on **Poetto Beach** (p70), Cagliari's summer playground

- Work on your tan on the sandy white beaches of the **Costa Rei** (p74) and sail the lush blue waters off **Capo Carbonara** (p73)

- Don your walking boots and immerse yourself in silence on the pine-scented slopes of **Monte dei Sette Fratelli** (p75)

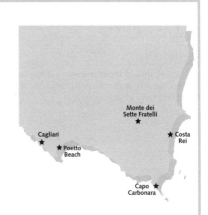

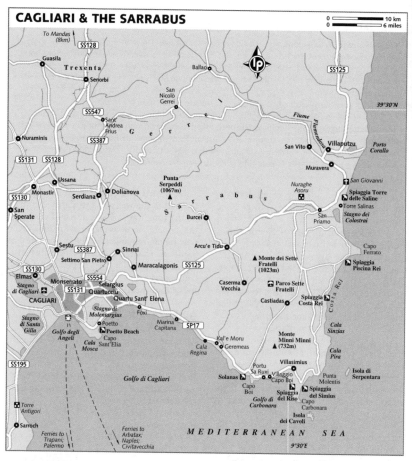

CAGLIARI & THE SARRABUS

pop 159, 310

Forget flying: the best way to arrive in Cagliari is by sea. As the ferry glides in to port the whole city spreads out before you, rising in a helter-skelter of golden-hued *palazzi*, domes and facades up to the rocky centrepiece, Il Castello. This forbidding citadel has brooded over the city since medieval times, a stern warning to uninvited guests. Down on the seafront, cars hurry past stately buildings while schoolkids cluster at pedestrian crossings and white-capped traffic police whistle at speeding scooters. This is very much a bustling Mediterranean port.

More than 2000 years of history have left their mark on Cagliari, and the city boasts archaeological remains, superb churches and several fine museums. Out to the east, Poetto Beach is the focus of summer life with its lively beachside bars and limpid blue waters.

HISTORY

The Phoenicians established themselves in the region in the 8th century BC, but it was not until the Carthaginians took control of what they called Karel or Karalis (meaning 'rocky place') around 520 BC that a town began to emerge. The Romans attached particular importance to Karalis, and Julius Caesar declared it a Roman municipality in 46 BC. For centuries it remained a prosperous port,

CAGLIARI, CAPITAL OF THE MEDITERRANEAN

Cagliari's mayor Emilio Floris has ambitious plans for his city. The centrepiece of a wide-ranging urban renewal project is a futuristic museum that he and regional President Renato Soru hope will become a new icon for the city. The Zaha Hadid–designed Museo Betile dell'Arte Nuragica e dell'Arte Contemporanea (Betile Museum of Nuraghic and Contemporary Art) will certainly make an impression if it ever gets built. With its crashing wave design and prominent seafront location, it was the subject of heated political debate at the time of writing.

The €40 million Zaha Hadid project is one of a number of ideas that City Hall is keen to implement. Dutch architect Rem Koolhaas has been asked to come up with plans for a new residential area in the Sant'Elia industrial district, and Brazilian Paulo Mendes da Rocha has been commissioned to design a new university campus. North of the city centre, construction continues on a spanking new Parco della Musica (Music Park), near the Teatro Lirico.

heading the grain trade with mainland Italy, but with the eclipse of Rome's power came more turbulent times.

Vandals operating out of North Africa stormed into the city in AD 455, only to be unseated by the Byzantine Empire in 533. Cagliari thus became capital of one of four districts, which later became the *giudicati* (provinces). By the 11th century, weakening Byzantine influence (accentuated by repeated Arab raids) led Cagliari and the other districts to become virtually autonomous.

The emerging rival sea powers of Genoa and Pisa were soon poking around. In 1258 the Pisans took the town, fortified the Castello area and replaced the local population with Pisans. A similar fate awaited them when the Catalano-Aragonese took over in 1326. The Black Death swept through in 1348, with frequent repeat outbreaks in the succeeding decades.

With Spain unified at the end of the 15th century, the Catalans were subordinated to the Spaniards. Cagliari fared better than most of the island under Spanish inertia, and in 1620 the city's university opened its doors.

The dukes of Savoy (who in 1720 became kings of Sardinia) followed the Spanish precedent in keeping Cagliari as the viceregal seat, and it endured several anxious events (such as the 1794 anti-Savoy riots). From 1799 to 1814 the royal family, forced out of Piedmont by Napoleon, spent time in Cagliari protected by the British Royal Navy.

Cagliari continued to develop slowly throughout the 19th and 20th centuries. Parts of the city walls were destroyed and the city expanded as the population grew. Heavily bombed in WWII, Cagliari was awarded a medal for bravery in 1948.

Reconstruction commenced shortly after the end of the war and was partly complete by the time Cagliari was declared capital of the semiautonomous region of Sardinia in the new Italian republic in 1949. A good deal of Sardinia's modern industry, especially petrochemicals, has since developed around the lagoons and along the coast as far as Sarroch in the southwest.

ORIENTATION

Cagliari's port and the bus and train stations are located on or near Piazza Matteotti, where you'll also find the city's tourist office. Running past the square is the broad Via Roma, part of the principal route to Poetto and Villasimius in the east, and Pula and the south coast to the west.

From Piazza Matteotti, head for La Rinascente seafront store, a useful point of reference. This marks the starting point of Largo Carlo Felice, the broad boulevard that runs up to Piazza Yenne, central Cagliari's focal square. To the east of Largo Carlo Felice is the atmospheric Marina district, where you'll find much of the city's accommodation and a plethora of eateries. On the other side of Largo Carlo Felice, the Stampace district extends up the hill to the Roman amphitheatre.

Dominating Cagliari's skyline, the Il Castello district is the old medieval centre. Accessible by elevator from just north of Piazza Yenne, this is where you'll find the city's best views and main museums. To the northeast lies the more modern Villanova quarter.

To the east, the city spreads out to the *saline* (saltpans) and Poetto Beach; in the west the housing creeps around the north shore of the immense Stagno di Santa Gilla lagoon.

INFORMATION
Bookshops
Ubik (Map p66; ☎ 070 65 02 56; Via Roma 63; ⊗ 9am-8.30pm Mon-Sat, 10am-1pm & 4.30-8.30pm Sun) Has a good selection of city and island maps.

Emergency
Police station (Map p58; Questura; ☎ 070 6 02 71; Via Amat Luigi 9)

Internet Access
Intermedia Point (Map p66; Via Eleonora d'Arborea 4; per hr €3; ⊗ 10am-1pm & 3.30-7.30pm Mon-Fri)
Lamarù (Map p66; ☎ 070 66 84 07; Via Napoli 43; per hr €3; ⊗ 9am-8pm Mon-Sat)

Laundry
Lavanderia Ghilbi (Map p66; Via Sicilia 20; per 6kg load €4; ⊗ 8am-10pm)

Medical Services
Farmacia Dr Spano (Map p66; ☎ 070 65 56 83; Via Roma 99; ⊗ 9.30am-1pm & 4.30-7.50pm Mon-Fri, 9am-1pm Sat)
Guardia Medica (☎ 070 609 52 02; Via Talete) For an emergency call-out doctor.
Ospedale Brotzu (☎ 070 53 91; Via Peretti 21) This hospital is northwest of the city centre. Take bus 1 from Via Roma if you need to make a nonemergency visit.

Money
Banco San Paolo (Map p66; Via Sassari) Has an ATM; you'll find more inside the station.
Mail Boxes Etc (☎ 070 67 37 04; Viale Trieste 65/b; ⊗ 9am-1pm Mon-Sat & 4-7.30pm Mon-Fri) An agent for Western Union.

Post
Main post office (Map p66; ☎ 070 605 41 23; Piazza del Carmine 28; ⊗ 8am-6.50pm Tue-Fri, 8am-1.15pm Sat)

Tourist Information
Tourist office (Map p66; ☎ 070 66 92 55; Piazza Matteotti; ⊗ 8.30am-1.30pm & 2-8pm) The only one in town.

Travel Agencies
CTS (Map p58; ☎ 070 48 82 60; Via Cesare Balbo 12) A branch of the national youth travel agency.
Viaggi Orrù (Map p66; ☎ 070 65 98 58; www
.viaggiorru.it; Via Baylle 111; ⊗ 9am-1pm & 4.15-7.45pm Mon-Fri, 9.30am-1pm Sat) An efficient travel agency where you can book ferries and flights and organise excursions.

DANGERS & ANNOYANCES
Cagliari is a safe town, but at night some areas are not so appealing. The steps leading up to the Bastione San Remy and the little park at the bottom of Viale Regina Margherita, for instance, attract a crowd of drunks and drug-takers. Petty theft is always a risk for tourists. Take the usual precautions, which include leaving nothing in vehicles.

SIGHTS
Most of Cagliari's sights are concentrated in four central districts: Castello, Stampace, Marina and Villanova. The obvious starting point is the hilltop Il Castello area, which boasts the city's finest museums and some blistering views. To the west, high up the hill in Stampace, Cagliari's impressive amphi-theatre is one of the few visible reminders of the city's Roman past. The cityscape and all the older buildings belong to the Pisans, but the Spaniards added the more florid district of Stampace. In the 19th century Cagliari sprawled eastwards under the Piedmontese; their legacy, Villanova, is a showcase of wide roads and imposing piazzas.

Il Castello
Built by the Pisans and Aragonese, Cagliari's medieval citadel dominates the city skyline. Precipitous white stone walls enclose what was once the fortified home of the city's ar-istocracy and religious authorities, known to locals as Su Casteddu, a term also used to describe the whole city. The walls are best ad-mired from afar – one good spot is the Roman amphitheatre across the valley to the west.

Towers & Battlements
One of only two Pisan towers still stand-ing, the **Torre dell'Elefante** (Map p66; Via Università; adult/child €4/2.50; ⊗ 9am-1pm & 3.30-7.30pm Tue-Sun Apr-Oct, 9am-4.30pm Nov-Mar) was built in 1307 as defence against the threatening Aragonese. Named after the sculpted elephant by the vicious-looking portcullis, the tower be-came something of horror show, thanks to its foul decor. The Spaniards beheaded the Marchese di Cea here and left her severed head lying around for 17 years! They also liked to adorn the portcullis with the heads of executed prisoners, strung up in cages like ghoulish fairy lights. The crenellated storey was added in 1852 and used as a prison for political detainees. Climb to the top to

CAGLIARI & THE SARRABUS

CAGLIARI

| 0 | 500 m |
| 0 | 0.3 miles |

Golfo degli Angeli

share the view that must have made them rue their captivity.

Over by the citadel's northeastern gate is the tower's twin, the 36m-high **Torre di San Pancrazio** (Map p58; Piazza Indipendenza; adult/concession €4/2.50; 9am-1pm & 3.30-7.30pm Tue-Sun Apr-Oct, 9am-4.30pm Nov-Mar). Completed in 1305, it is built on the city's highest point and commands huge views of the Golfo di Cagliari.

Inside the battlements, the old medieval city reveals itself like Pandora's box. The university, cathedral, museums and Pisan palaces are wedged into a jigsaw of narrow high-walled alleys. Once the stately residence of officials, the old town is now strung together by lines of washing, with many of the houses inviting little further inspection. However, life is returning to the area and in recent years a number of shops, bars and cafes have opened up here, ensuring a flow of students and fashionable bohemians.

You can reach the citadel from various approaches. The most impressive is the monumental stairway that ascends from busy Piazza Costituzione to **Bastione San Remy** (Map p66), formerly a strong point in the city walls and now a panoramic platform. You can also climb the **Scalette di Santa Chiara** (Map p66) from behind Piazza Yenne or, better still, take the elevator from the bottom of the Scalette.

GHETTO DEGLI EBREI

The area north of the Torre dell'Elefante, between Via Santa Croce and Via Stretta, was once Cagliari's **Ghetto degli Ebrei** (Jewish Ghetto). Under Spanish rule the entire Jewish community was expelled in 1492 and today nothing much remains except the name, applied to a restored **former barracks** (Map p66; 070 640 21 15; Via Santa Croce 18) which is used for temporary exhibitions but was closed for restoration at the time of writing. In the wake of the Jewish expulsion, the **Chiesa di Santa Croce** (Map p66; 334 178 54 33; Piazzaetta Santa Croce; guided visits 10.30am-noon Sun) was built over the ghetto's former synagogue.

This side of Il Castello is the most atmospheric and attractive. Cafes along Via Santa Croce offer grandstand views and the narrow streets appear little changed since medieval times. If you've got a moment, try to sneak a look at the beautiful vaulted vestibule of the university's **Istituto di Architettura e Disegno** (Institute of Architecture & Design; Map p66; Via Corte d'Appello 87).

CITADELLA DEI MUSEI

Cagliari's main museum complex sits at the northern end of Il Castello, where four museums have been cleverly incorporated into the remains of the old city arsenal. Ramps have also been installed, making wheelchair access possible.

Museo Archeologico Nazionale

Of the four museums, the undoubted star is the **Museo Archeologico Nazionale** (Map p58; 070 68 40 00; Piazza dell'Arsenale; adult/concession €4/2, incl Pinacoteca Nazionale €5/2.50; 9am-8pm Tue-Sun). Sardinia's premier archaeological museum, it displays artefacts spanning millennia of ancient history, including a superb collection of pint-sized nuraghic *bronzetti* (bronze figurines) on the ground floor.

In the absence of any written records, these bronzes are a vital source of information on Sardinia's mysterious nuraghic culture (approximately 1800–500 BC). In all about 400 bronzes have been discovered, many in sites of religious importance, leading scholars to conclude that they were probably used as votive offerings. Depicting tribal chiefs, warriors, hunters, mothers and animals, the figurines are stylistically crude but remarkably effective. There are even little models of the *nuraghi* (ancient stone towers) themselves.

Sensibly, the ground floor is laid out in chronological order. You move from the pre-nuraghic world of stone implements and obsidian tools, rudimentary ceramics and funny round fertility goddesses to the Bronze and Iron Ages and on to the *nuraghi*. Then come the Phoenicians and Romans, a model *tophet* (sacred Phoenician or Carthaginian burial ground for children and babies), and delicate debris such as terracotta vases, glass vessels, scarabs and jewellery from ancient Karalis (Cagliari), Sulcis, Tharros and Nora.

The 1st and 2nd floors contain more of the same but are divided by region and important sites rather than by age. Among the highlights are some Roman-era mosaics, a collection of Roman statues, busts and tombstones from Cagliari, and displays of coins.

Pinacoteca Nazionale

Above and behind the archaeological museum, the **Pinacoteca Nazionale** (Map p58; 070 68 40 00; Piazza dell'Arsenale; adult/concession €2/1, incl Museo Archeologico Nazionale €5/2.50; 9am-8pm Tue-Sun) showcases a collection of 15th- to 17th-century art. Many of the best works are *retablos* (grand altarpieces of the kind commonly found in Spain), painted by Catalan and Genoese artists for local churches.

Of those by known Sardinian painters, the four works by Pietro Cavaro, father of the so-called Stampace school and arguably Sardinia's most important artist, are outstanding. They include a moving *Deposizione* (Deposition) and portraits of St Peter, St Paul and St Augustine. Also represented are the painter's father, Lorenzo, and his son Michele. Another Sardinian artist of note was Francesco Pinna, whose *Pala di Sant'Orsola* hangs here. These images tend to show the influence of Spain and Italy rather than illuminating the Sardinian condition. However, there is a brief line-up of 19th- and early-20th-century Sardinian painters, such as Giovanni Marginotti and Giuseppe Sciuti.

Mostra di Cere Anatomiche

A kind of ghoulish Madame Tussaud's, the **Mostra di Cere Anatomiche** (Map p58; Piazza dell'Arsenale; admission €1.55; ☉ 9am-1pm & 4-7pm Tue-Sun) features a series of 23 anatomical wax models. Made by the Florentine Clemente Susini between 1802 and 1805, the bizarre but anatomically detailed models include a head with the skin peeled back to reveal its brain and inner workings, and a cutaway of a pregnant woman's torso, complete with womb and foetus.

Museo d'Arte Siamese

Cagliari's medieval heart is an unlikely place for a collection of Asian art, but that's exactly what you find at the **Museo d'Arte Siamese** (Map p58; ☎ 070 65 18 88; Piazza dell'Arsenale; adult/concession €4/2; ☉ 9am-1pm & 4-8pm Tue-Sun Jun-Sep, 9am-1pm & 3.30-7.30pm Tue-Sun Oct-May). Donated to the city by local engineer Stefano Cardu, who had spent many years in Thailand (formerly Siam), the collection is highly eclectic. Alongside Ming and Qing-era Chinese porcelain vases, you'll find silk paintings, Japanese statuettes and some truly terrifying Thai weapons.

CATTEDRALE DI SANTA MARIA & AROUND

At the district's heart, cars park in the sun-drenched **Piazza Palazzo**, once home to the city's religious authorities. Overlooking the square is the **Cattedrale di Santa Maria** (Map p66; ☎ 070 66 38 37; www.duomodicagliari.it; Piazza Palazzo 4; ☉ 8am-12.30pm & 4.30-8pm Mon-Fri, 8.30am-1pm & 4-8pm Sat & Sun),

Cagliari's impressive 13th-century cathedral. Except for the square-based bell tower, little remains of the original Gothic structure: the interior is largely baroque, the result of a radical late 17th-century makeover, and the clean Pisan-Romanesque facade is a 20th-century imitation, added between 1933 and 1938.

Inside, the once-Gothic church disappears beneath a rich icing of baroque decor. Bright frescoes adorn the ceilings, and the three chapels on either side of the aisles spill over with sculptural whirls in an effect that is both impressive and appalling. The third chapel to the right, the Cappella di San Michele, is perhaps the pinnacle of the genre. A serene St Michael, who appears (in baroque fashion) to be in the eye of a swirling storm, casts devils into hell.

Still, there are some less gaudy bits and pieces. The two intricate stone pulpits on either side of the central door were sculpted by Guglielmo da Pisa between 1158 and 1162. They originally formed a single unit which stood in Pisa's Duomo until the Pisans donated it to Cagliari in 1312. It was subsequently split into two by the meddlesome Domenico Spotorno, the architect behind the 17th-century baroque facelift, and the big stone lions that formed its base were removed to the altar where they now stand. To the right of the altar is the worn-looking *Trittico di Clemente VII*, attributed by some to the school of Flemish painter Rogier van der Weyden.

On the other side of the altar is the entrance to the **Aula Capitolare**, the crypt where many Savoy tombs are conserved. Carved out of rock, the barrel-vaulted chamber is an impressive sight with its mass of sculptural decoration and intricate carvings.

Further cathedral treasures are displayed at the **Museo del Duomo** (Map p66; ☎ 070 65 24 98; Via del Fossario 5; admission €4; ☉ 10am-1pm & 4.30-7pm), including two outstanding pieces: the *Trittico di Clemente VII*, a 15th-century work attributed to the Flemish painter Rogier van der Weyden, and the 16th-century *Retablo dei Beneficiati*, produced by the school of Pietro Cavaro.

Next door to the cathedral is the archbishop's residence, the **Palazzo Arcivescovile**, followed by the pale lime facade of the **Palazzo Viceregio** (Map p66; Palazzo Regio; ☎ 070 409 20 00; ☉ 8.30am-2pm & 3-7pm), which was once home to the Spanish and Savoy viceroys and today serves as the provincial assembly. It also stages regular exhibitions and summer music concerts.

Stampace

Stampace was Cagliari's medieval working-class district, where Sards lived huddled in the shadow of the mighty castle. In the 14th century, when the Aragonese were in charge, Sards were forbidden to enter the castle after nightfall. Those caught were thrown off the castle walls, with the benediction *stai in pace* (rest in peace), a phrase that gave rise to the name Stampace.

The focal point of the district, and indeed of central Cagliari, is Piazza Yenne. The small pedestrianised space is adorned with a **statue** (Map p66) of King Carlo Felice to mark the beginnings of the Carlo Felice Hwy (SS131), the project for which the monarch is best remembered. On summer nights, Piazza Yenne heaves as the city's young and restless come to play in its various bars and cafes. Elsewhere you'll find a number of important churches, a botanical garden, and, up the hill, Cagliari's rocky Roman amphitheatre.

CHIESA DI SANT'EFISIO

Despite its unassuming facade and modest baroque interior, the **Chiesa di Sant'Efisio** (Map p66; Via Sant'Efisio; 9am-1pm & 3.30-7.30pm Tue-Sun) is of considerable local importance. Not for any artistic or architectural reasons but rather for its ties to St Ephisius, Cagliari's patron saint. A Roman soldier who converted to Christianity and was later beheaded for refusing to recant his faith, St Ephisius is the star of the city's big 1 May festivities (see p65). An effigy of the saint, housed in the second chapel on the right, is paraded around the city on a beautifully ornate *carozza* (carriage) that is also kept here, although you'll need to ask the church warden to have a look.

Over the centuries, the saint has stood the city in good stead, saving the populace from the plague in 1652 – when the church got its marble makeover – and repelling Napoleon's fleet in 1793. You can even see French cannonballs embedded in the wall beneath a painting of St Ephisius stirring up the storm that sent the fleet packing.

At the side of the church is the entrance to the crypt where St Ephisius was supposedly held before being executed in Nora (near Pula). It's marked in stone – *Carcer Sancti Ephysii M* (Prison of the Martyr St Ephisius) – and retains the column where Ephisius was tied during his incarceration.

CRIPTA DI SANTA RESTITUTA

Just down the street is the **Cripta di Santa Restituta** (Map p66; 070 640 21 15; Via Sant'Efisio; 10am-1pm Tue-Sun), which has been in use since pre-Christian times. It's a huge, eerie, natural cavern where the echo of leaking water drip-drips. Originally a place of pagan worship, it became the home of the martyr Restituta in the 5th century and a reference point for Cagliari's early Christians. The Orthodox Christians then took it over – you can still see remnants of their frescoes – until the 13th century, when it was abandoned. In WWII it was used as an air-raid shelter, a task it wasn't up to, since many died while holed up here in February 1943. It's interesting to make out the wartime graffiti that covers the walls.

CHIESA DI SAN MICHELE

Although consecrated in 1538, the **Chiesa di San Michele** (Map p66; 070 65 86 26; Via Ospedale 2; 8am-11am & 6-9pm Mon-Sat, 7.30am-noon & 7-9pm Sun) is best known for its lavish 18th-century decor, considered the finest example of rococo in Sardinia. The spectacle starts outside with the ebullient triple-arched baroque facade and continues through the vast colonnaded atrium and on into the sumptuous interior. Before you go inside, take a minute to admire the massive four-columned pulpit in the atrium. This was built and named in honour of the Spanish emperor Carlos V, who is said to have delivered a stirring speech from it before setting off on a fruitless campaign against Arab corsairs in Tunisia. The octagonal interior is quite magnificent, with six heavily decorated chapels radiating out from the centre, topped by a grand, brightly frescoed dome. Of particular note is the sacristy, accessible from the last chapel on the left, with its vivid frescoes and intricate inlaid wood.

CHIESA DI SANT'ANNA

Stampace's largest and least interesting church is the **Chiesa di Sant'Anna** (Map p66; Piazza Santa Restituta; 7.30-10am & 5-8pm Tue-Sun). It looms out at you as if from nowhere and its imposing sand-coloured facade rises high above the little square it dominates. Largely destroyed during WWII and painstakingly rebuilt afterwards, it is basically baroque, but the Ionic columns melded into the undulating facade give it a slightly severe neoclassical edge.

ANFITEATRO ROMANO

Cagliari's most impressive Roman monument is the **Anfiteatro Romano** (Roman amphitheatre; Map p58; ☎ 070 65 29 56; Viale Sant' Ignazio; www.anfiteatroromano.it, in Italian; adult/student/child 0-6 yrs €4.30/2.80/free; 🕙 9am-1.30pm Tue-Sun & 3.30-5.30pm Sun Apr-Oct, 9.30am-1.30pm Tue-Sat & 10am-1pm Sun Nov-Mar). Dating back to the 2nd century AD, it is carved out of rock high up on the Buon Cammino hill, near the northern entrance to Il Castello. Although much of the original theatre has been cannibalised for building material over the centuries, enough has survived to pique the imagination. In its heyday, crowds of up to 10,000 people – practically the entire population of Cagliari – would gather to watch gladiators battle each other and the occasional wild animal. In summer, the amphitheatre recovers something of its vocation by hosting summer concerts – you may find it closed to visitors during concert seasons. If it is closed, don't despair, as you can get good views of it from the road outside.

ORTO BOTANICO

Just downhill from the Anfiteatro, the **Orto Botanico** (Viale Sant' Ignazio; Map p58; admission €2; 🕙 8.30am-7.30pm Mon-Sat & 8.30am-1.30pm Sun Apr-Oct, 9am-4pm Mon-Sat Nov-Mar) is one of Italy's most famous botanical gardens. Established in 1858 and extending over five hectares, the gardens contain up to 3000 species of flora, including 500 species of tropical plants and 16 types of palm tree. Specimens from as far afield as Asia, Australia, Africa and the Americas sidle up to the local carob trees and oaks. Tastefully littering the gardens are ancient ruins, an old Punic cistern, and a Roman quarry and aqueduct.

PALAZZO CIVICO

Overlooking Piazza Matteotti, the neo-Gothic **Palazzo Civico** (Map p66; ☎ 070 677 70 49; Via Roma), also known as the Municipio, is home to Cagliari's city council. Capricious, pompous and not a little overbearing, it was built between 1899 and 1913, and faithfully reconstructed after bombing in 1943. The upstairs chambers contain works by a number of Sardinian artists, including Pietro Cavaro. Admission is by prior appointment only.

Marina

Bordered by Largo Carlo Felice to the west and seafront Via Roma, the characterful Marina district is enjoyable to explore. Not so much for any specific sights, of which there are few, but for the authentic atmosphere of its dark, narrow lanes filled with artisans' shops, cafes and eateries of every description. Navigation is easy as the alleys are all based on the old Roman grid pattern.

In the heart of the district, the **Museo del Tesoro e Area Archeologica di Sant'Eulalia** (MUTSEU; Map p66; ☎ 070 66 37 24; Vico del Collegio 2; admission €4; 🕙 10am-1pm & 5-8pm Tue-Sun) displays a rich collection of religious art, as well as an archaeological area, which extends for up to 200 sq metres beneath the adjacent **Chiesa di Sant' Eulalia**. The main drawcard here is a 13m section of excavated Roman road (constructed between the 1st and 2nd centuries AD), which archaeologists think would have connected with the nearby port. Excavations are ongoing, so expect more subterranean revelations.

In the upstairs treasury you'll find all sorts of religious artefacts, ranging from exquisite priests' vestments and silverware through to medieval codices and other precious documents. Fine wooden sculptures abound, along with an Ecce Homo painting, depicting Christ front and back after his flagellation. The painting has been attributed to a 17th-century Flemish artist.

A quick uphill stroll brings you to the **Chiesa di Santo Sepolcro** (Map p66; ☎ 070 66 37 24; Piazza del Santo Sepolcro 5; 🕙 9am-1pm & 5-8pm), where the most astonishing feature is an enormous 17th-century gilded wooden altarpiece housing a figure of the Virgin Mary.

Villanova

The least attractive of Cagliari's four historic districts, Villanova extends east of Il Castello. The area was originally an artisans' quarter spilling out of the city proper, but it has long since been swamped by traffic and modern sprawl. There's not a great deal to see around here, although it's pleasant enough walking the lanes that began the original expansion – they're squashed between the eastern side of the castle and Piazza San Domenico. Backing onto the square is the Gothic **Chiostro di San Domenico** (Map p58; ☎ 070 66 28 37; Via XXIV Maggio 5) complex, one of a number of religious compounds in this formerly religious district. Admission is by request only. However, if it's churches you're after you'd be advised to carry on walking eastwards along Via San Lucifero to the Parco delle Remembranze and, beyond that, one of Sardinia's oldest churches, the Basilica di San Saturnino.

Rising above the district, a large public park covers the slopes of Monte Urpinu. On the other side of the mount, the **Stagno di Molentargius** salt marshes provide some excellent birdwatching.

East of the Centre

In the area immediately east of Villanova, you'll find two of Cagliari's most important religious sites.

BASILICA DI SAN SATURNINO & CHIESA DI SAN LUCIFERO

One of the oldest churches in Sardinia, the **Basilica di San Saturnino** (Map p58; ☎ 070 65 98 69; Piazza San Cosimo; ☺ 9am-1pm Mon-Sat) is a striking example of Paleo-Christian architecture. Based on a Greek-cross pattern, the domed basilica was built over a Roman necropolis in the 5th century, on the site where Saturninus, a much revered local martyr, was buried. According to legend, Saturninus was beheaded in 304 AD during emperor Diocletian's anti-Christian pogroms.

In the 6th century San Fulgenzio da Ruspe, a bishop in exile from Tunisia, built a monastery here. In 1098 this was reworked into the current Romanesque church by a group of Vittorini monks from Marseille. Since then the basilica has undergone various refurbishments, most notably after it was stripped in 1662 to provide building material for the Cattedrale di Santa Maria and, most recently, after it sustained severe bomb damage in WWII.

Directly across the leafy modern square is the baroque **Chiesa di San Lucifero** (Map p58; Via San Lucifero 78). Below the church is a 6th-century crypt where the tomb of the early Archbishop of Cagliari, St Lucifer, rests. In earlier times the area had been part of a Roman burial ground. It's not open to the public, but its austere 17th-century facade is worth a quick look from the outside.

EXMÀ

Housed in Cagliari's 18th-century *mattatoio* (abattoir), **Exmà** (Map p58; ☎ 070 66 63 99; Via San Lucifero 71; exhibitions €3; ☺ 10am-1pm & 5-10pm Tue-Sun Jun-Sep, 9am-1pm & 4-8pm Tue-Sun Oct-May) is a delightful cultural centre. A permanent exhibition details the restoration of the abattoir, but it's best known for its contemporary art shows

and photography exhibitions. In summer, there are frequent open-air music concerts.

SANTUARIO & BASILICA DI NOSTRA SIGNORA DI BONARIA

Dominating the Bonaria hill to the east of the city centre, the **Santuario di Nostra Signora di Bonaria** (Map p58; ☎ 070 30 17 47; Piazza Bonaria 2; donations expected; ☺ 6.30-11.45am & 4-6.45pm Mon-Sat, 6.30am-12.45pm & 4-7.45pm Sun) is a hugely popular pilgrim site. Devotees come from all over the world to pay their respects to Nostra Signora di Bonaria, a revered statue of the Virgin Mary kept in a niche behind the altar (see the boxed text, p64, for more info). The statue is said to have saved a 14th-century Spanish ship during a storm, and today mariners still pray to the Madonna for protection on the high seas. Above the altar hangs a tiny 15th-century ivory ship, whose movements are said to indicate the wind direction in the Golfo degli Angeli.

You'll find yet more model boats, as well as other ex-voto offerings and a golden crown from Carlo Emanuele I in the sanctuary's **museum** (☎ 9-11.30am & 5-6.30pm), accessible through the small cloister. There are also the mummified corpses of four plague-ridden Catalano-Aragonese nobles whose bodies were found miraculously preserved inside the church.

The sanctuary was originally part of a much bigger fortress complex built by the Catalano-Aragonese in 1323. Little remains of the original compound, apart from the truncated bell tower, which originally served as a watchtower, and the Gothic portal.

To the right of the sanctuary is the much larger **basilica**, which still acts as a landmark to returning sailors. Building began in 1704, but the money ran out and the basilica wasn't officially finished until 1926. An Allied bomb in 1943 put paid to all its marvellous decoration shortly thereafter. The building has now been meticulously repaired, thanks to a lengthy restoration that was only completed in 1998.

Northwest of the Centre
GALLERIA COMUNALE D'ARTE

If you are at all interested in modern Sardinian art, you won't want to miss the **Galleria Comunale d'Arte** (Map p58; ☎ 070 49 07 27; Viale San Vincenzo; adult/student/child 0-6yrs €6/2.60/ free; ☺ 9am-1pm & 5-8pm Wed-Mon Apr-Oct, 9am-1pm &

FRESH AIRS & GRACES

When the Catalano-Aragonese arrived to take Cagliari in 1323, it became clear it would be no easy task. So they sensibly set up camp on the fresh mountain slopes of Montixeddu, which came to be known as Bonaria (*buon'aria*, or 'good air'). In the three years of the siege, the camp became a fortress with its own church.

After ejecting the Pisans and taking the city in 1335, the Aragonese invited Mercedari monks from Barcelona to establish a monastery at the Bonaria church, where they remain to this day.

The Bonaria monks were kept well employed for centuries ransoming Christian slaves from Muslim pirates, and they are credited with saving the Genoese community of Tabarka in Tunisia and bringing them to Isola di San Pietro. But what makes this a place of international pilgrimage is a simple wooden statue of the Virgin Mary and Christ, now housed in the Santuario di Nostra Signora di Bonaria (see p63).

Legend has it that the statue was washed up after being cast overboard by Spanish seamen caught in a storm in the 14th century. Monks found the Madonna not only in perfect shape on the beach in front of their sanctuary but with a candle alight in her hand.

Over the years, Christian seamen became especially devoted to Nostra Signora di Bonaria, attributing all manner of miracles to her intervention. The Spanish conquistadors even named a future capital city (Buenos Aires in Argentina) in her honour.

3.30-7.30pm Nov-Mar) and its rich collection of works by island artists, such as Tarquinio Sinni (1891–1943). His humorous *contrasti* (contrasts), which show heavily dressed Sardinian girls standing frumpily beside glamorous, coiffed flappers, explore the social tension between traditional Sardinian ways and the perplexing freedoms of a rapidly modernising world. Another highlight is the work of Giuseppe Biasi (1885–1945), whose oils depict Sardinian life in a rich style that combines the bold brushstrokes of Gauguin with the moody atmosphere of Degas.

The gallery, housed in a neoclassical villa north of Il Castello, also displays an excellent selection of contemporary works, and the Collezione Ingrao, comprised of more than 650 works of Italian art from the mid-19th century to the late 20th century. Frequent temporary exhibitions are also held to showcase works by contemporary artists.

Outside the gallery, the colourful **Giardino da Leggere** (Garden for Reading; 9.30am-4 Mon-Sat, to 1pm Sun) is a relaxing place for a breather.

CASTELLO DI SAN MICHELE

A stout three-tower Spanish fortress, **Castello di San Michele** (Castillo de San Miguel; admission €3-10; 10am-1pm & 5-9pm Tue-Sun Apr-Oct, 10am-1pm & 3-6pm Tue-Sun Nov-Mar) stands in a commanding position northwest of the city centre. It was built in the 10th century as protection for Santa Igia, capital of the Giudicato of Cagliari, but is most famous as the luxurious residence of the 14th-century Carroz family. It is now used as an exhibition space and conference centre; admission costs vary depending on what's showing. The surrounding grounds are a peaceful green space to get away from the city.

To get there take city bus 5 from Via Roma to the foot of the hill on Via Bacu Abis. From there, a paved road runs for 800m up to the castle.

Poetto & the Sella del Diavola

An easy bus ride from the city centre, Cagliari's fabulous **Poetto Beach** is one of the longest stretches of sand in Italy. Extending 6km beyond the green Promontorio di Sant'Elia, it's an integral part of city life, particularly in summer when much of the city's youth decamps here to sunbathe by day and party by night. The long sandy strip is lined with funfairs, restaurants, bars and discos, many of which also act as *stabilmenti balneari* (private beach clubs). These offer various facilities, including showers and changing cabins, as well as renting out umbrellas and sun loungers – prices start at €15 for an umbrella and two loungers.

The southern end of the beach is the most popular, with its picturesque **Marina Piccola**, yacht club and outdoor cinema (July and August only). Looming over the marina, the Promontorio di Sant'Elia is known to everyone as the **Sella del Diavola** (Devil's Saddle).

According to local legend, the headland was the scene of an epic battle between Lucifer and the Archangel Michael. In the course of the struggle Satan was thrown off his horse and his saddle fell into the sea where it eventually petrified atop what was to become the headland. Although much of the headland is now owned by the military and closed to the public, there are several paths which offer great walking.

For Poetto you can take bus PF, PN or PQ from Piazza Matteotti.

ACTIVITIES

Not surprisingly, water sports are big at Poetto, and you can generally hire canoes at the beach clubs. From its base at Marina Piccola, the **Windsurfing Club Cagliari** (☎ 070 37 26 94; Viale Marina Piccola; www.windsurfingclubcagliari.it) offers a range of courses. A beginner's course of six one-hour lessons costs €150, while for six hours of free-style lessons you'll be looking at €200.

The **Golfo di Cagliari** is littered with the wrecks of WWII ships, making it an excellent place for divers. **Morgan Diving** (☎ 070 80 50 59; www.morgandiving.com) can arrange dives to most of these sites (€35 to €80) and is also authorised to conduct dives in the marine reserve of Villasimius. The company is based at Marina Capitana, 14km east of Cagliari, although you can make arrangements over the phone.

TOURS

Mariposas (☎ 333 590 90 24; www.mariposas.it, in Italian) can arrange anything from tours of subterranean Cagliari to city shopping trips and food and wine tastings. It can also organise tours to Nora, dives in Villasimius or a day in the Iglesiente mines.

CTM Open (☎ 348 090 92 40; adult/child 4-12 yrs/child 0-4yrs €10/5/free) runs a hop-on hop-off bus tour of Cagliari. Departures are from Piazza Yenne every half-hour between 10am and 1pm and 4pm and 7.30pm during the summer, and hourly in April, May, June and late September. English-language commentaries are provided and tickets, available onboard, are valid for the entire day.

FESTIVALS & EVENTS

Cagliari's main event is the blockbuster **Festa di Sant'Efisio** between 1 and 4 May. On the opening day thousands of Cagliaritani pour into the streets to greet the effigy of St Ephisius,

Cagliari's patron saint, as it's paraded round the streets on a bullock-drawn carriage. As the costumed procession melts away, a hard-core retinue accompanies the statue on its 40km pilgrimage to Nora. The best place to view proceedings is from the grandstand seating arranged around Piazza Matteotti and Largo Carlo Felice. Tickets for the stands (€5 to €15) are sold at **Box Office Tickets** (see p70).

Cagliari also puts on a good show for **Carnevale** in February and Easter **Holy Week**, when a hooded procession takes place between the Chiesa di Sant'Efisio and the cathedral up in Il Castello.

SLEEPING

For a busy port and capital city, Cagliari has disappointing accommodation. Most city centre hotels are in the Marina district or off busy Largo Carlo Felice. If you can't find a hotel to suit, there are a growing number of B&Bs, many of which offer excellent value for money. The association **Domus Karalitanae** (www.domus karalitanae.it) lists many B&Bs on its website.

Budget

Albergo La Perla (Map p66; ☎ 070 66 94 46; laperla1@ virgilio.it; Via Sardegna 18; s €40-45, d €50-55, tr €75-81; ⚅) Fresh from a recent refurbishment, this modest one-star hotel offers simple, airy rooms in the heart of the Marino district. Reception is in the owner's kitchen on the 1st floor, but you'll need to cart your bags up to the 2nd and 3rd floors to get to the tidy rooms, which all come with air-con, satellite TV, and en suite bathrooms. No credit cards.

Albergo Aurora (Map p66; ☎ 070 65 86 25; www.hotel cagliariaurora.it; Salita Santa Chiara 19; s €41-46, d €60-68, without bathroom s €32-37, d €48-55; ⚅) This small, welcoming hotel is just off Piazza Yenne. There's nothing flash about the ageing rooms with their pastel walls and exposed brickwork, but they're bright, spacious and honestly priced. The one big drawback is noise from the nearby bars. Air-con costs an extra €8.

our pick La Terrazza sul Porto (Map p66; ☎ 070 65 89 97; www.laterrazzasulporto.com; Largo Carlo Felice 36; per person €25-35; ⚅ 🖵) A stone's throw from the port, this is a wonderfully eccentric, gay-friendly B&B. Owner Franco has transformed his palatial top-floor flat into a welcoming haven with three guestrooms, a fully equipped kitchen and a sunny rooftop terrace. The decor is cheerfully offbeat with model cars everywhere, framed photos of planes and a

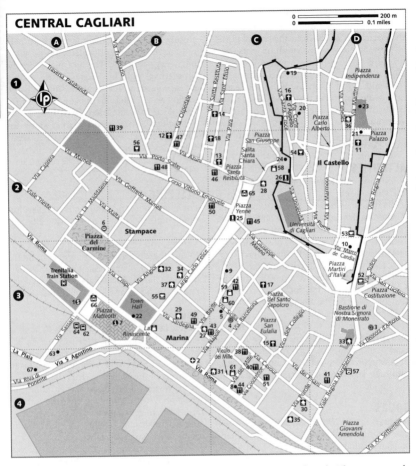

CENTRAL CAGLIARI

huge communal bathroom with a chandelier and tiny designer lav. As a further bonus, you can eat breakfast as late as you like.

B&B La Marina (Map p66; ☎ 070 67 00 65; www .la-marina.it; Via Porcile 23; s €40, d €70-75; ✕) A good-value B&B in the atmospheric Marina district. The elderly couple who run the place keep a tight ship and the four wood-beamed rooms are pristine. There are a couple of communal breakfast rooms with fridges for guest use.

Sardinia Domus (Map p66; ☎ 070 65 97 83; www .sardiniadomus.it, in Italian; Largo Carlo Felice 26; s €45-55, d €70-85, tr €108-120, q €130-144; ✕ ▢) Housed in a towering palazzo on Largo Carlo Felice, this is a slickly run B&B with exposed stone walls, lamp-lit corridors and six inviting rooms decorated with Liberty-style furnishings. Noise

can be a problem, though. The same people have a further six rooms at Cagliari Domus, a second B&B on the same floor.

Hotel A&R Bundes Jack (Map p66; ☎ /fax 070 66 79 70; www.hotelbjvittoria.it; Via Roma 75; s €48-58, d €76-88; ✕) The best budget option on the seafront, this is an old-fashioned family-run *pensione*. Run by a garrulous old boy, it has big, high-ceilinged rooms decorated with robust family furniture and sparkling Murano chandeliers. No credit cards.

Midrange
Hotel Quattro Mori (Map p66; ☎ 070 66 85 35; www .hotel4mori.it, in Italian; Via Angioi 27; s/d €75/85; P ✕) This workaday three-star hotel knows how to make a good first impression. Unfortunately,

the character of the barrel-vaulted brick lobby doesn't extend to the lookalike hospital corridors and disappointingly bland rooms. If you've got a car the €8 garage fee is cheaper than any on-street parking.

Old Caralis B&B (Map p66; ☎ 349 29 12 853; www .oldcaralis.it; Via Porcile 11; s €40-70, d €60-90; 🐼 🖳) This cosy B&B is within walking distance of the port and train station. Housed in a 19th-century palazzo, it has two guest rooms, which although not the biggest in town, are tastefully decorated with wooden furniture and comfortable beds.

Affitacamere Arcobaleno (Map p66; ☎ 070 684 83 25; www.soggiornoarcobaleno.com; Via Sardegna 38; s €60-70, d €80-90; 🐼) On a lively street packed with trattorias and restaurants, this simple guest house offers value for money in attractive brick-walled rooms. Staff are friendly and wi-fi is available.

Residenza Kastrum (Map p66; ☎ 349 522 03 15; www .karel-bedandbreakfast.it, in Italian; Via Canelles 78; s/d/tr €70/90/100, suite €90-130; 🐼) Boasting memorable views from its hilltop Castello position, this refined B&B has four rooms and a two-room suite in a tastefully refurbished apartment. It's quite a hike up from the seafront, but with plenty of bars and cafes on your doorstep you won't have trouble finding the fun.

Hotel Calamosca (☎ 070 37 16 28; www.hotelcala mosca.it; Viale Calamosca 50; s €54-60, d €84-95, tr €101-111; 🅿 🐼) About 2km out of the centre and overlooking a tiny cove, this is Cagliari's only beachfront hotel. Rooms are sunny and spacious, and for an extra €10 they come with a sea view, the same view you get from the panoramic terrace. Take bus PF or PQ from Piazza Matteotti to the football stadium and then No 11.

Top End

Hotel Regina Margherita (Map p66; ☎ 070 67 03 42; www.hotelreginamargherita.com; Viale Regina Margherita 44; s €135-148, d €180-370; 🅿 🐼 🖳) Not that you'd know it from the ghastly concrete exterior, but this is one of Cagliari's top hotels. Service is courteous and efficient, and the salmon-pink rooms provide all the corporate comforts.

T Hotel (Map p58; ☎ 070 474 00; www.thotel.it; Via dei Giudicati; r €99-410; 🐼) Adding a dash of contemporary design to Cagliari's cityscape, the T is housed in a hard-to-miss steel and glass tower. Inside, the vast, airport-style lobby features a sunken bar, slinky leather sofas and a gurgling fountain. Rooms reveal a linear, modish look with sharp, modern furniture, mosaic-tiled bathrooms and discreetly fitted mod cons.

EATING

Cagliaritani certainly enjoy eating out, and the city has an excellent selection of eateries, ranging from cheap kebab takeaways to neighbourhood trattorias and smart, top-end restaurants. There's a certain formality to life in Sardinia, so it's always best to make a reservation, especially on busy weekend evenings. Things really get going around 9.30pm, but in summer people tend to dine later.

Beware: many of the better restaurants close for at least part of August.

Restaurants

MARINA

Marina's narrow lanes are chock-full of restaurants, trattorias, bars and takeaways. Some places are obviously touristy but many are not, and the area is popular with dining locals.

Trattoria Gennargentu (Map p66; ☎ 070 67 20 21; Via Sardegna 60; meals around €20) It doesn't look much from outside, but this no-frills trattoria serves excellent food and tables fill quickly. There's a full menu of pastas and meaty mains, but the seafood is particularly good. Try the *tonno alla carlofortina*, tuna chunks served cold in a sweet tomato and onion sauce.

Il Buongustaio (Map p66; ☎ 070 66 81 24; Via Concezione 7; meals around €25; ☒ closed Mon dinner, Tue & Aug) Not only does this popular trattoria serve delicious seafood and succulent meat dishes, it also offers excellent value for money. The menu changes according to the season, but you can depend on stalwarts such as *spaghetti alla bottarga* (with dried mullet roe).

Da Lillicu (Map p66; ☎ 070 65 29 70; Via Sardegna 78; meals around €28; ☒ Mon-Sat, closed late Aug) One of Cagliari's most famous eateries, this historic trattoria has an excellent local reputation and is nearly always packed. If you can bag a table, you'll be sitting down to Sardinian seafood at its most traditional, including an ever-reliable *burrida* (catfish marinated in white-wine vinegar and served with nuts).

Ristorante Italia (Map p66; ☎ 070 65 79 87; Via Sardegna 30; meals around €30; ☒ Mon-Fri & dinner Sat, closed mid-Aug) Despite the motley bunch of sorry-looking fish in the window, this place is well regarded locally. Not for its fading decor but for the simple, well-prepared seafood. Keep it local with a crispy *fritto misto del golfo* (fried fish from the gulf of Cagliari).

Antica Hostaria (Map p66; ☎ 070 66 58 60; Via Cavour 60; meals around €40; ☒ Mon-Sat, closed Aug) Popular with local celebs, this welcoming restaurant serves classic Italian food in a warm, cosy setting. Antique furnishings and walls crowded with pictures complement the traditional menu, which features a range of meat and fish

dishes. For Sardinian surf 'n' turf start with *pennette con tonno fresco e gamberi* (pasta tubes with fresh tuna and prawns) followed by a succulent steak.

Dal Corsaro (Map p66; ☎ 070 66 43 18; Viale Regina Margherita 28; menus €50-55; ☒ Mon-Sat, closed Aug) A bastion of fine dining, this a city institution. Stiff tablecloths, silver wine buckets and elegant couples set the scene for some wonderful food. Sardinian ingredients are highlighted in creative dishes such as *raviola di cipolla e pecorino semi stagionato* (onion ravioli with mature *pecorino* cheese).

STAMPACE

Branching off Piazza Yenne, Corso Vittorio Emanuele is lined with a plethora of restaurants and bars, and is especially busy in winter. Good restaurants can also be found in the warren of adjoining streets.

our pick Monica e Ahmed (Map p66; ☎ 070 640 20 45; Corso Vittorio Emanuele 119; meals around €25; ☒ closed Sun evening) A top spot for delicious seafood at affordable prices. Monica welcomes you with a smile and then plies you with a tempting array of fishy delights. Start with a lavish antipasto of fresh cuttlefish, *ricci* (sea urchins), mussels, and lobster in vinaigrette, and follow with *spaghetti ai frutti di mare* (with mussels, clams and breadcrumbs). If you've got room left, the grilled scampi looked mighty good.

our pick L'Osteria (Map p66; ☎ 070 311 01 68; Via Azuni 56; meals around €27; ☒ closed Sun dinner) Homey decor, friendly service and authentic food – this spot-on trattoria fits the bill perfectly. Everything about the place is right, from the bare brick walls and earthenware wine jugs to the warm bread doused in olive oil, and the gorgeous food. The *fettucine con pesce spada, carciofo e menta* (pasta ribbons with swordfish, artichoke and mint) is wonderful, and the meringue served with cream and strawberries is an unpretentious, gooey delight.

Crackers (Map p66; ☎ 070 65 39 12; Corso Vittorio Emanuele 193; meals around €30; ☒ Thu-Tue, closed late Aug) A corner of Piedmont in Sardinia, Crackers specialises in northern Italian classics such as *brasato al Barolo* (meat stewed in Barolo wine) and boiled meats served with mustard. There's also a wide range of risottos, some excellent vegetable antipasti, and a thoughtful wine list.

Ristorante Quattro Mori (Map p66; ☎ 070 65 02 69; Via Angioi 93; meals around €35; ☒ Tue-Sat, closed late

Aug) Focusing on local, Sardinian fare, this is one of the city's culinary bastions. It's usually packed to the rafters with noisy, contented diners digging into super-abundant antipasti and fresh-as-you-like seafood. Reservations are essential.

La Vecchia Trattoria (Map p66; ☎ 070 65 25 15; Via Azuni 55; meals around €40; ☷ lunch Tue-Sun) Despite the try-hard decor – red-and-white checked tablecloths, rustic wood tables and fishing paraphernalia – this is a local favourite. It's located in a pretty spot and specialises in Cagliaritani cuisine, combining the flavours of *terra e mare* (land and sea). Sit inside or out on the small terrace behind the foliage.

OUT OF THE CENTRE

our pick **Il Fantasma** (Map p58; ☎ 070 65 67 49; Via San Domenico 94; pizzas €6.50; ☷ Mon-Sat) Off the beaten path, this cheerful pizzeria does the best pizza in Cagliari. It's a boisterous place with wonky tables in a low barrel-vaulted interior with a splotchy red pattern on the brick walls. Amid the chaos, the friendly waiters adroitly navigate the crowds carrying platefuls of bubbling pizza hot from the wood-fired oven. Book or expect to queue.

Ristorante Royal (Map p58; ☎ 070 34 13 13; Via Bottego 24; meals around €30; ☷ closed Sun afternoon & Mon) On a modest residential street east of the centre, this Tuscan restaurant is where Cagliaritani come to dig into succulent Florentine steak and juicy slabs of meat. There's not much fish, but there are plenty of vegetable *contorni* (side dishes) and some exemplary desserts.

POETTO

Cagliari's beach is lined with summertime bars, snack joints and restaurants, known to locals as *chioschi* (kiosks). Things get really busy here between November and March (mollusc season), when shacks serving sea urchins and mussels are set up by fishermen along the beach road. You're charged according to the number of shells left on your table.

Spinnaker (☎ 070 37 02 95; Via Marina Piccola; meals around €45; ☷ Tue-Sun May-Sep) At Marina Piccola, this is the summer outpost of Dal Corsaro. Given its seafront location, it's no surprise that the onus is on high-quality seafood, although you can also pick up pizza at the downstairs pizzeria.

Self-catering

For a delicious packed lunch go into one of the *salumerie* (delicatessens) in the Marina quarter and ask for a thick cut of *pecorino sardo* (Sardinian *pecorino* cheese) and a slice or two of smoked ham in a freshly baked *panino* (bread roll). **I Sapori dell'Isola** (Map p66; ☎ 070 65 23 62; Via Sardegna 50) is a good place to start, or pop into **Disizos** (Map p66; Via Napoli 72) for handmade pastas and delicious *seadas* (pastry desserts).

You can also pick up all sorts of edible goodies at Cagliari's historic food market, **Mercato di San Benedetto** (Map p58; Via San Francesco Cocco Ortu; ☷ Mon-Sat am).

Ice cream fans could do a lot worse than join the nightly crowds at **Isola del Gelato** (Map p66; ☎ 070 65 98 24; Piazza Yenne 35; ☷ 9am-2am Tue-Sun). This hugely popular hang-out boasts an incredible selection of ice-creamy treats, including lowfat, soy, yoghurt and *semi-freddo*, a delicious semi-frozen mousse.

DRINKING

There are some great cafes in the city centre, particularly near the seafront and up in Il Castello. Ranging from traditional wood-and-brass affairs to sharp, contemporary bars, they tend to get busy around lunchtime – many serve light meals and snacks – and then again from the early evening.

The bar scene is centred on Piazza Yenne and Corso Vittorio Emanuele, although in summer everyone moves out to Poetto.

City Centre

Antico Caffè (Map p66; ☎ 070 65 82 06; www.antico caffe1855.it; Piazza Costituzione; pasta dishes €10; ☷ 7am-2am) Cagliari's most historic cafe is unfortunately located on a busy road intersection. But that doesn't put off locals who come to lunch on salads and pastas, and to chat over leisurely coffees. There's a small outdoor terrace or you can settle inside amidst the polished wood and brass.

Caffè Svizzero (Map p66; ☎ 070 65 37 84; Largo Carlo Felice 6; ☷ Tue-Sun) At the bottom of Largo Carlo Felice, this Liberty-style place has been a stalwart of Cagliari cafe society since the early 20th century. Anything from tea to cocktails is on offer in the frescoed interior, founded by a group of Swiss almost 100 years ago.

Caffè Librarium Nostrum (Map p66; ☎ 070 65 09 43; Via Santa Croce 33; ☷ 7.30am-2am Tue-Sun) Offering some of the best views in town, this modish Castello bar has panoramic seating on top of

---

THE ALLIGATOR

Massimo Carlotto's life reads like the plot of one of his crime novels...because it *is* the plot of one of his books.

At 19, during Italy's 'years of lead', he witnessed the murder of Margherita Magello, a 25-year-old student who was stabbed 59 times. The events that followed became the novel *Il Fuggiasco* (The Fugitive). Covered in Magello's blood, Carlotto ran to fetch the police, who accused him of the killing. He was later sentenced to 18 years' imprisonment. On the advice of his lawyers, Carlotto went on the run in France and Mexico, where he was sheltered and fed by political activists for six years before he finally gave himself up. In 1993, after an international campaign, he was released with a full pardon from the president of Italy.

When in prison, Carlotto found the true-life material for the explicit crime novels he now writes. His most famous series is the Alligator, which is developed from real legal cases Carlotto claims to have heard and read up on.

The protagonist is loosely modelled on Carlotto himself; he even drives the Škoda Carlotto once drove (because many people say it is the least-stopped car in Italy). The nickname comes from the character's (and Carlotto's) favourite cocktail – seven parts calvados to three parts Drambuie, crushed ice and a slice of apple – invented by a barman in Cagliari (see Caffè Librarium Nostrum, p69), where Carlotto now lives. The cocktail's fame has since spread to bars in Rome, Milan and Naples. It's said that nobody can drink more than four.

Five of Carlotto's books have been translated into English, including *The Fugitive* (2008), *Death's Dark Abyss* (2007) and *The Goodbye Kiss* (2006). Order his books at www.massimocarlotto.it.

---

the city's medieval ramparts. If the weather's being difficult, make for the brick-lined interior and order yourself an Alligator cocktail, created in honour of the hero of Massimo Carlotto's novels (see the boxed text, above). There's occasional live music.

Caffè degli Spiriti (Map p66; Bastione San Remy; grills €17, pizza €6.50; ⏰ 9am-2am) Grab a hammock, lie back and enjoy the vibe at this stylish lounge bar on the Bastione San Remy. Inside, it's all black and brick; outside, happy drinkers sit on black leather pouffes drinking cocktails and munching pizzas under a tented canopy.

Il Merlo Parlante (Map p66; ☎ 070 65 39 81; Via Porto Scalas 69; ⏰ 7pm-3am Tue-Sun) Shoehorned into a narrow alley off Corso Vittorio Emanuele, this is the nearest thing you'll find to a student pub in Cagliari. It's a boisterous place, so expect lager on tap, rock on the stereo, and a young up-for-it international crowd.

Poetto

Emerson (☎ 070 37 51 94; Viale Poetto; ⏰ 9am-6pm winter, 8am-2am summer) Near the fourth bus stop, and one of the most popular of the seafront *chioschi*, this swank place is a bit of everything. Part cocktail lounge, part restaurant and part beach club, it dishes up everything from pasta to *aperitivi*, live music and sun loungers.

Café Oasi (☎ 070 338 08 48; Viale Poetto, 4th stop; ⏰ 9am-11pm Mon-Fri, to 2am Sat & Sun) Sitting on a low cream sofa with a regular supply of ice-cold drinks and the sea breeze in your hair is not a bad way of passing an evening. Also near the fourth bus stop, this chic seafront spot will also do you for lunch or dinner (around €35).

ENTERTAINMENT

For information on what's going on in town, ask at the tourist office or pick up a copy of the local newspaper *L'Unione Sarda*. Online, you'll find listings at www.sardegnaconcerti.com and www.boxofficesardegna.it. You can buy tickets from **Box Office Tickets** (Map p66; ☎ 070 65 74 28; www .boxofficesardegna.it; Viale Regina Margherita 43; ⏰ 10am-1pm Mon-Sat, plus 5-8pm Mon-Fri).

Concerts

Most of Cagliari's big concerts are held over the summer. Venues include the **Anfiteatro Romano** (p62), which stages a summer season of stand-up comedy, music and dance. Tickets, ranging from €10 to €70, are available from Box Office Tickets (above).

Major rock concerts by big Italian bands, and the occasional international group, are held at the open-air **Fiera Campionaria** (Viale Diaz 221) in the east of the city. Tickets generally cost from €20 – enquire at Box Office Tickets.

Theatre, Classical Music & Ballet

Cagliari has a lively theatrical scene, comprising classical music, dance, opera and drama. The season generally runs from October to May, although some places also offer a summer program.

Teatro Lirico (Teatro Comunale; Map p58; ☎ 070 408 22 30; www.teatroliricodicagliari.it; Via Sant'Alenixedda; ⏱ box office 8am-2pm Tue-Sat & 6-8pm Tue-Fri) The concert season at Cagliari's top classical music venue runs from October to May, with opera and ballet staged between April and December. The program is fairly traditional but quality is high and concerts are well attended.

Teatro Alfieri (Map p58; ☎ 070 30 22 99; Via della Pineta 29) The Alfieri hosts much of the city's classical theatre. You'll also catch the occasional Greek tragedy and contemporary drama, although performances are in Italian only. Tickets cost from €10 to €20.

Exmà (Map p58; ☎ 070 66 63 99; Via San Lucifero 71) A year-round series of small-scale concerts, mainly jazz and chamber music, are held at this cultural centre. In winter performances are held in a small, wood-beamed conference room; in summer the action moves to the outside courtyard.

SHOPPING

Cagliari is a fairly muted shopping destination. There's a refreshing absence of overtly touristy souvenir stores, although they do exist, and far fewer designer clothes boutiques than you find in most comparably sized Italian cities. That said you'll find some lovely, low-key artisans' shops tucked away in the city's nooks and crannies, particularly in the Marina district.

Durke (Map p66; ☎ 070 66 67 82; www.durke.com; Via Napoli 66) An Aladdin's cave of exquisite Sardinian sweets and pastries, this is the place to pick up a last-minute gift for your ageing sweet-toothed aunt. The pastries, all prepared according to age-old recipes, are quite special and absolutely free of preservatives and artificial additives. In fact, some of the best are made with nothing more than sugar, eggs and almonds.

Sapori di Sardegna (Map p66; ☎ 070 684 87 47; Vico dei Mille 1) Stock up on cheese, wine and pretty-packed *dolci* (sweets) at this breezy emporium just off the seafront. If you've got no room in your luggage, staff can arrange to ship orders worldwide.

Antica Enoteca Cagliaritana (Map p66; ☎ 070 66 93 86; Scalette Santa Chiara 21) Wine buffs will enjoy exploring the racks at this specialist wine shop off Piazza Yenne. Alongside labels from Sardinia and mainland Italy, you'll even find a few bottles from Australia, Chile and Argentina. You can have orders sent anywhere in the world except the USA (customs difficulties, apparently).

Loredana Mandas (Map p66; ☎ 070 66 76 48; Via Sicilia 31) For something very special, seek out this jewellery workshop. You can watch Loredana create the exquisite gold filigree for which Sardinia is so famous, and then maybe buy a piece. A pair of gold earrings will set you back anything from €160 to €1000.

If you enjoy markets, you'll like Sundays in Cagliari. On the first Sunday of the month, Cagliaritani go bargain hunting at the **Piazza del Carmine** (Map p66) antique and collectors' market. The following week the antiques move up the hill to **Piazza Carlo Alberto** (Map p66), where they also appear on the last Sunday of the month. In Il Castello, there's also a flea market every Sunday morning (except for August) on the **Bastione San Remy** (Map p66).

GETTING THERE & AWAY
Air

Cagliari's Elmas **airport** (CAG; ☎ 070 211 211; www.sogaer.it) is 6km northwest of the city centre. Flights connect with mainland Italian cities: Rome, Milan, Bergamo, Bologna, Florence, Naples, Rome, Turin and Venice, as well as Palermo in Sicily. Further afield, there are flights to and from Barcelona, Brussels, Luton, Paris and Stuttgart. In summer, there are additional charter flights.

The main airlines serving Elmas:
Air One (AP; ☎ 199 207 080; www.flyairone.it)
Alitalia (AZ; ☎ 06 22 22; www.alitalia.it)
British Airways (BA; ☎ 199 712 266; www.britishairways.com)
easyJet (U2; ☎ 899 234 589; www.easyjet.com)
Lufthansa (LH; ☎ 199 400 044; www.lufthansa.com)
Meridiana (IG; ☎ 89 29 28; www.meridiana.it)
Ryanair (FR; ☎ 899 678 910; www.ryanair.com)

Boat

Cagliari's ferry port is just off Via Roma. **Tirrenia** (Map p66; ☎ 892 123; www.tirrenia.it; Via Riva di Ponente 1; ⏱ 8.30am-12.20pm & 3.30-6.50pm Mon-Sat) is the main ferry operator, with year-round services to Civitavecchia (€48, 16½ hours),

TRENINO VERDE

If you're not in a rush, one of the best ways of exploring Sardinia's interior is on the **trenino verde** (www.treninoverde.com). A slow, narrow-gauge diesel operated by the Ferrovie della Sardegna (FdS), this runs through some of the island's most inhospitable countryside, stopping at isolated rural villages en route. There are four tourist routes: Mandas to Arbatax; Isili to Sorgono; Macomer to Bosa; and Nulvi to Palau; as well as several public-transport routes, including a metro/train link between Cagliari, Mandas and Isili.

Of the tourist routes, the twisting Mandas to Arbatax line is particularly spectacular, crossing the remote highlands of the Parco Nazionale del Golfo di Orosei e del Gennargentu.

From the metro station on Piazza Repubblica in Cagliari, a metro runs to Monserrato where you can connect with trains for Mandas. From Mandas there are two daily departures for Arbatax on the east coast.

The *trenino verde* runs between mid-June and early September.

Naples (€45, 16¼ hours), Palermo (€50, 14½ hours) and Trapani (€50, 11 hours). Book tickets at the port or at travel agencies.

See p237 for further details.

Bus

From the main bus station on Piazza Matteotti, **ARST** (Azienda Regionale Sarda Trasporti; Map p66; ☎ 800 865 042; www.arst.sardegna.it, in Italian) you can catch buses to nearby Pula (€2.50, 50 minutes, hourly) and Villasimius (€3, 1½ hours, six daily Monday to Saturday, two Sunday), as well as to Oristano (€6.50, one hour 35 minutes, two daily) and Nuoro (€14.50, 2½ hours to five hours, two daily). Tickets can be purchased from McDonald's on the square.

FMS (Map p66; ☎ 800 04 45 53; www.ferroviemer idionalisarde.it, in Italian) runs services to Iglesias (€4, one to 1½ hours, seven daily), Carbonia (€5.50, 1½ hours, seven daily), Portovesme (€5.50, two hours, one daily) and the Sulcis area. Buses leave from the main terminal at Piazza Matteotti; buy tickets from the cafe inside the station.

Also departing from Piazza Matteotti, **FdS** (Ferrovie della Sardegna; ☎ 070 34 31 12; www.ferrovie sardegna.it, in Italian) buses link with Sassari (€17, 3¼ hours, three daily), with tickets available at the bus station, and **Turmo Travel** (☎ 0789 214 87; www.gruppoturmotravel.com) runs a daily bus to Olbia (€18, 4¼ hours), for which tickets can be purchased from McDonald's.

Car & Motorcycle

The island's main dual-carriage, the SS131 Carlo Felice Hwy, links the capital with Porto Torres via Oristano and Sassari. The SS130 leads east to Iglesias.

The coast roads approaching from the east and west get highly congested in the summer holiday season.

Train

The main **Trenitalia** (Map p66; www.trenitalia.it) station is on Piazza Matteotti. Trains serve Iglesias (€3.30, one hour, 10 daily), Carbonia (€3.75, one hour, six daily), Sassari (€13.65, four hours, five daily) and Porto Torres (€14.60, 4¼ hours, two daily) via Oristano (€5.15, one to two hours, hourly). A branch line connects with Olbia (€14.60, 4¼ hours, four daily) and Golfo Aranci (€15.80, five to seven hours, five daily) via Oristano or Chilivani.

The **FdS** (☎ 070 34 31 12; www.ferroviesardegna.it, in Italian) runs a metro service from Piazza Repubblica to Monserrato, where you can connect with trains for Dolianova, Mandas and Isili.

GETTING AROUND

The centre of Cagliari is small enough to explore on foot. The walk up to Il Castello is tough, but there's an elevator at the bottom of the Scalette di Santa Chiara behind Piazza Yenne.

To/From the Airport

ARST buses run from Piazza Matteotti to Elmas airport (€2, 10 minutes, 32 daily) from 5.20am to 10.30pm. Between 9am and 10.30pm departures are every hour and half-past the hour.

A taxi costs about €25. To park at the airport you'll pay €1 for the first hour, €2.50 for two hours, and €9/18 for the first 24 hours depending on which car park you use.

Bus

CTM (Consorzio Trasporti e Mobilità; ☎ 070 209 12 10; www .ctmcagliari.it, in Italian) bus routes cover the city and surrounding area. You might use the buses to reach a handful of out-of-the-way sights, and they come in handy for the Cala Mosca and Poetto Beaches. A standard ticket costs €1 and is valid for 90 minutes; a daily ticket is €2.30.

The most useful lines:

Bus 7 Circular route from Piazza Matteotti up to Il Castello and back.

Bus 10 From Viale Trento to Piazza Garibaldi via Corso Vittorio Emanuele.

Bus 30 or 31 Along the seafront and up to the sanctuary at Bonaria.

Bus PF, PN or PQ From Piazza Matteotti to Poetto Beach.

Car & Motorcycle

Parking in the city centre means paying. On-street metered parking – within the blue lines – costs €1 per hour. Alternatively, there's a big car park next to the train station, which costs €1 per hour or €10 for 24 hours. There's no maximum stay.

Driving in the centre of Cagliari is a pain, although given the geography of the town (one big hill), you might consider renting a scooter for a day or two. **CIA Rent a Car** (Map p66; ☎ 070 65 65 03; www .ciarent.it; Via S Agostino 13; ⏰ 8.30am-1pm & 3.30-8pm daily summer, Mon-Sat winter) hires out bikes, scooters and cars from €10/30/39 daily. There's also a **Hertz** (Map p66; ☎ 070 65 10 78; Piazza Matteotti 8; www.hertz.it; ⏰ 8.30am-1pm & 3.30-7.30pm) on Piazza Matteotti and several car-rental agencies at the airport.

Taxi

There are taxi ranks at Piazza Matteotti, Piazza Repubblica and on Largo Carlo Felice. Otherwise you can call the following radio taxi firms:

Quattro Mori (☎ 070 400 101; ⏰ 24 hr)

Rossoblù (☎ 070 66 55; ⏰ 5.30-2.30am)

Taxiamico (☎ 070 826 060; ⏰ 24 hr)

THE SARRABUS

East and north of Cagliari lies the lonely Sarrabus, one of Sardinia's least-populated and least-developed areas. In its centre rises the bushy green peaks of the Monte dei Sette Fratelli, a miraculously wild hinterland

---

> **DETOUR: SERDIANA**
>
> About 20km north of Cagliari, the agricultural town of **Serdiana** is home to one of Sardinia's most celebrated wine producers, the award-winning **Cantine Argiolas** (☎ 070 74 06 06; www.cantine-argiolas.it; Via Roma 28-30; ⏰ tours 9am-1pm & 3-5pm Mon-Fri). You can visit the cantina by calling the above number and organising a guided tour.
>
> From Cagliari take the SS554 north and after about 10km follow the SS387 for Dolianova. After another 10km take the turn-off for Serdiana.

where some of the island's last remaining deer wander undisturbed.

Along the bare, hilly coast the SP17 rises and falls, providing spectacular views of the multihued sea punctuated by pretty coves like Cala Regina, Kal'e Moru and Solanas. A few kilometres short of Villasimius, a road veers south along the peninsula to Capo Carbonara, Sardinia's most southeasterly point.

CAPO CARBONARA

Although the tip of the cape remains a military zone and is off limits to visitors, the waters around Capo Carbonara are a **marine reserve** (www.ampcapocarbonara.it), accessible with an authorised diving company. The reserve includes Isola dei Cavoli, Secca dei Berni and Isola di Serpentara just off the coast from Villasimius. **Morgan Diving** (☎ 070 80 50 59; www .morgandiving.com), based at the Porto Turistico at Quartu Sant'Elena, is one licensed operator, as is **Air Sub** (☎ 070 79 20 33; www.airsub.com; Via Roma 121) in Villasimius. Both outfits lead dives to a number of local sites, including the **Secca di Santa Caterina**, a stunning underwater mountain. Reckon on €35 to 90 for a dive, depending on the location and level of difficulty.

On the western side of the peninsula is a marina and what remains of a Spanish tower, the **Fortezza Vecchia**, now used to host temporary exhibitions. South of the tower are a few sections of beach, although the main beach on this side of the peninsula is **Spiaggia del Riso**. The eastern side is dominated by the **Stagno Notteri** lagoon, often host to flamingos in winter. On its seaward side is the stunning **Spiaggia del Simius** beach with its Polynesian blue waters. The lagoon runs all the way to Villasimius.

VILLASIMIUS

pop 3320

Once a quiet fishing village surrounded by pines and *macchia* (Mediterranean scrub), Villasimius has grown into one of Sardinia's most popular southern resorts. In summer it's a lively, cheerful place, although activity all but dies out in winter.

Just off central Piazza Gramsci, the **tourist office** (☎ 070 793 02 71; www.villasimiusweb.com; Piazza Giovanni XXIII; ☺ 10am-1pm & 3.30-6.30pm Mon & Thu, 10am-1pm Tue & Wed, 10am-1pm & 4-7pm Fri) can provide information on activities in the town.

In town the main activity is browsing souvenir shops and enjoying the holiday atmosphere. The one sight of any interest is the small **Museo Archeologico** (Archaeology Museum; ☎ 070 793 02 90; Via Frau; adult/concession €3/1; ☺ 10am-12.30 & 9pm-midnight Tue-Sun mid-Jun–mid-Sep, 10am-1pm Tue-Thu, 10am-1pm & 5-7pm Fri-Sun rest of year) which has a collection of Roman and Phoenician artefacts, as well as various odds and ends recovered from a 15th-century Spanish shipwreck.

At the Porto Turistico, about 3km outside of the town centre, you can arrange boat tours (€65 per person including lunch), dives (from €36) and boat charters (€1600 to €5000 per week) with **Harry Tours** (☎ 338 377 40 51; www.harrystours.com).

The **Festa della Madonna del Naufrago**, held on the second Sunday of July, is a striking seaborne procession to a spot off the coast where a statue of the Virgin Mary lies on the seabed in honour of shipwrecked sailors.

Sleeping

Spiaggia del Riso (☎ 070 79 10 52; www.villaggio spiaggiadelriso.it; Località Campulongu; per person & tent €16, cars €4, 4-person bungalows €60-150; ☺ May-Oct; P) Set in a pine grove near the Porto Turistico, this big beachside campsite has tent pitches, bungalows, a supermarket and a children's play area. It gets hellishly crowded in midsummer, when booking is absolutely essential.

Albergo Stella d'Oro (☎ 070 79 12 55; fax 070 79 26 32; Via Vittorio Emanuele 25; s/d €50/105, half board per person €82; P) One of the few year-round hotels in town, this is a friendly, laid-back *pensione* with modest rooms and an excellent seafood restaurant (meals €25 to 30). The location is a further plus, about 50m from central Piazza Gramsci.

Stella Maris (☎ 070 79 71 00; www.stella-maris .com; Località Campulongu; half board per person €155-255;

☺ mid-Apr-Nov; P) On the road to the Porto Turistico, this is a beautiful resort hotel set in its own pine wood on a frosty white beach. Rooms are stylish, decorated with Sardinian fabrics and tasteful furniture, and the facilities are excellent.

Eating

Ristorante La Lanterna (☎ 070 79 16 59; Via Roma 62; meals around €30; ☺ closed lunch Mon) With two fish shops just down the road, it's no surprise that this cordial restaurant specialises in seafood. Speciality of the house is *spigola alla vernaccia* (sea bass cooked in Vernaccia wine), although the seafood risotto is also a classic. In summer you can dine alfresco in the small garden.

Ristorante Carbonara (☎ 070 79 12 70; Via Umberto I 60; meals around €30; ☺ Thu-Tue) About 150m down the main strip from the tourist office, this is a long-standing favourite. There's meat on the menu, but seafood stars in dishes such as *spaghetti con aragosta* (with lobster) and grilled *gamberoni* (giant prawns).

Getting There & Around

Six weekday ARST buses (two on Sundays) run to and from Cagliari (€3, 1½ hours) throughout the year. Between mid-June and mid-September there are up to seven daily services.

If you want to rent your own wheels (it's not a bad idea, as most of the beaches are a few kilometres outside of town) **Edilrent Simius** (☎ 070 792 80 37; Via Roma 77) hires out bikes (€6.50 to €10 per day), scooters (€30 to €55) and cars (€63 to €80).

COSTA REI

Stretching along Sardinia's southeastern coast, the Costa Rei boasts long strips of white sandy beach and resort-style accommodation.

From Villasimius, take the SP17 as it follows the coast north. The road actually runs a couple of hundred metres inland, but you can access the signposted beaches via the dirt tracks that branch off the main road. Crystal-clear waters and the occasional snack-cum-cocktail bar await.

About 25km out of Villasimius you hit **Cala Sinzias**, a pretty, sandy strand with two campsites. Continue for a further 6km and you come to the Costa Rei resort proper, a holiday village full of holiday villas, shops, bars, clubs and a few indifferent eateries. **Spiaggia Costa Rei** is, like the beaches to its south and north, a dazzling

---

GETTING AWAY FROM IT ALL

A world away from the urban hustle of Cagliari, Monte dei Sette Fratelli (1023m) is the highest point of the remote Sarrabus district and one of only three remaining redoubts of the *cervo sardo* (Sardinian deer). Accessible by the SS125, it offers some magnificent hiking, with routes ranging from straightforward woodland strolls to a tough 12km ascent of **Punta Sa Ceraxa** (1016m).

You can pick up a trekking map from the Caserma Forestale Campu Omu, a forestry corps station near the Burcei turn-off on the SS125. Alternatively, contact the **Coop Monte dei Sette Fratelli** (☎ 070 994 72 00 or 070 860 76 12; www.montesettefratelli.com, in Italian; via Centrale) in Castiadas, a few kilometres inland from the Costa Rei.

From Burcei, a lonely road crawls 8km up to **Punta Serpeddi** (1067m), from where you can gaze out across the whole Sarrabus to Cagliari and the sea.

---

white strand lapped by remarkably clear blue-green water.

At the resort, **Butterfly Service** (☎ 070 99 10 91; Via Colombo; www.butterflyservice.it; ☷ 9am-1pm & 4-7.30pm Mon-Sat, 10am-1pm & 4.30-7.30pm Sun) is an all-purpose agency offering everything from internet access (€8 per hour) to bike (€15), scooter (€35) and car hire (€75 per day) and excursions along the coast and up to the **Parco Sette Fratelli** (€20 to €90).

North of the resort, **Spiaggia Piscina Rei** is a continuation of the blinding white sand and turquoise water theme, with a camping ground fenced in just behin d it. A couple more beaches fill the remaining length of coast up to **Capo Ferrato**, beyond which drivable dirt trails lead north.

Accommodation at the resort is fairly bland, but the **Albaruja Hotel** (☎ 070 99 15 57; www.albaruja.it; Via Colombo; d €98-198, half board per person €65-119; ☷ mid-Apr–mid-Oct; **P**) offers comfortable, white-tiled rooms in a series of villa-style residences. By the southern entrance to the resort, **Camping Capo Ferrato** (☎ 070 99 10 12; www.campingcapoferrato.it; per person/ tent €12/10.20, 4-person bungalow €43-95; ☷ Mar-Oct) is a welcoming campsite with direct access to the beach.

The same ARST buses from Cagliari to Villasimius continue around to Costa Rei, taking about half an hour.

NURAGHE ASORU

Continuing up the coast, the Nuraghe Asoru is the best example of a *nuraghe* in south-eastern Sardinia, which is largely devoid of archaeological interest. About 5km inland of San Priamo, it stands on the northern side of the SS125. Its central *tholos* (conical-roofed) tower is in reasonable nick, but if you have already seen some of Sardinia's

important *nuraghi* this one is not likely to excite too much.

MURAVERA & TORRE SALINAS
pop 5035
On the flood plain of the Fiume Flumendosa (Flumendosa River), Muravera is not an especially interesting place and there's no great reason to stop off here. An agricultural town, it's best known for its citrus fruit, which it celebrates on the second Sunday before Easter with the **Sagra degli Agrumi** (Citrus Fair).

South of town, the lagoons and beaches of Torre Salinas are picturesquely spread out beneath a Spanish watchtower. It's a pretty, seemingly untouched area, centred on the **Stagno dei Colostrai**, home to wintering fla-mingos. On the seaward side of the lagoon, **Spiaggia Torre delle Saline** is just the first in a line of dazzling beaches and near-perfect water that continues north up the coast to the mouth of the Fiume Flumendosa.

Immersed in greenery, **Cosi in Mare…Come in Cielo** (☎ 070 99 91 23; www.torresalinas.com; Via del Mare, Località Torre Salinas; r €80-130) is a homey B&B near the Spiaggia Torre delle Saline. Decorated with antiques and paintings, it has four guestrooms, a kitchen for guest use and a wide verandah overlooking the beach.

In Muravera itself, you can get a decent bite to eat at **Ristorante Pizzeria Su Nuraxi** (☎ 070 993 09 91; Via Roma 257; pizzas from €5, meals around €28) on the busy main road. It's a relaxed, informal place that serves hale and hearty meats and good pizzas.

Three weekday ARST buses run from Cagliari to Muravera (€5.50, three hours) via Villasimius. There are also quicker inland services (€5.50, one hour 40 minutes, five Monday to Saturday, two Sunday).

Southwest Sardinia

It's the southwest's superb beaches that attract the most attention. The magnificent, untamed sands of the Costa Verde, the tropical waters of the Costa del Sud, Iglesiente's photogenic coves – these are all highlights. Yet they are not everything.

Southwest Sardinia constitutes various regions, each with its own character. Iglesias and its surrounding hills once formed the island's mining heartland, but the mines have long since closed and their ghosts now haunt the landscape. In an attempt to exorcise these melancholy memories, many of the abandoned mines have been resurrected as tourist attractions.

Offshore, the twin islands of San Pietro and Sant'Antioco charm after their own fashion: San Pietro with its animated and instantly likeable atmosphere, and Sant'Antioco with its earthy character and rich archaeological legacy. Colonised by the Phoenicians and taken over by the Romans, Sant'Antioco was a major centre in ancient times, much like the town of Nora, whose ruins impress on the south coast.

Inland, Sardinia's greatest *nuraghe* (Bronze Age stone tower), the Unesco-listed Nuraghe Su Nuraxi, sits at the heart of the voluptuous Marmilla region. One of the island's most visited sights, it takes history to new depths, dating back to the 2nd millennium BC. Nearby, the tumbledown Nuraghe Genna Maria is less obviously impressive but still important.

Away from the coast the region has largely been bypassed by development, and the tourist infrastructure is limited. However, the area's coastal charms have not escaped the developers' notice, and the southwest coast boasts a clutch of luxurious resorts rivalling anything on the Costa Smeralda.

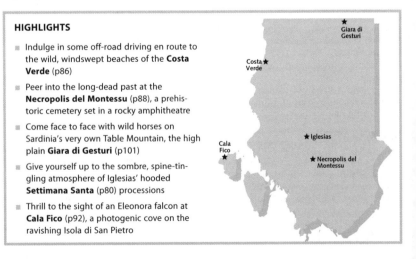

HIGHLIGHTS

- Indulge in some off-road driving en route to the wild, windswept beaches of the **Costa Verde** (p86)

- Peer into the long-dead past at the **Necropolis del Montessu** (p88), a prehistoric cemetery set in a rocky amphitheatre

- Come face to face with wild horses on Sardinia's very own Table Mountain, the high plain **Giara di Gesturi** (p101)

- Give yourself up to the sombre, spine-tingling atmosphere of Iglesias' hooded **Settimana Santa** (p80) processions

- Thrill to the sight of an Eleonora falcon at **Cala Fico** (p92), a photogenic cove on the ravishing Isola di San Pietro

★ Giara di Gesturi

Costa ★ Verde

Cala Fico ★

★ Iglesias

★ Necropolis del Montessu

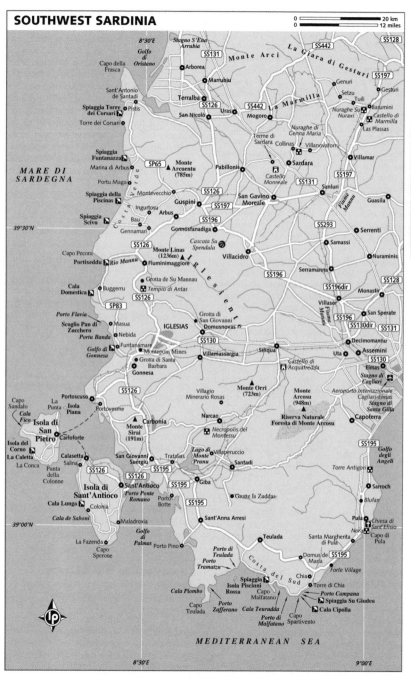

SOUTHWEST SARDINIA

0 — 20 km
0 — 12 miles

8°30'E

Golfo di Oristano

SS128

SS442

Monte Arci

La Giara di Gesturi

SS131

Stagno S'Ena Arrubia

SS197

Capo della Frasca

Arborea

Marrubiu

Genuri

Setzu
Tuili

Gesturi

Sant'Antonio de Santadi

Terralba

SS126

Uras

SS442

La Marmilla

Nuraghe Su Nuraxi

Barumini

Castello di Marmilla

Spiaggia Torre dei Corsari

Pistis

San Nicolo

Mogoro

Las Plassas

Torre dei Corsari

Terme di Sardara

Nuraghe di Genna Maria

Villamar

MARE DI SARDEGNA

Spiaggia Funtanazza

Marina di Arbus

SP65

Monte Arcuentu (785m)

Pabillonis

Collinas

Villanovaforru

Sardara

SS197

Portu Maga

Montevecchio

Costa Verde

SS126

San Gavino Moreale

Castello Monreale

Sanluri

SS131

Spiaggia della Piscinas

Ingurtosu

Guspini

SS197

Guasila

39°30'N

Spiaggia Scivu

Bau

Arbus

SS196

SS293

Serrenti

Gennamari

Gonnosfanadiga

Samassi

Nuraminis

Capo Pecora

Monte Linas (1236m)

Cascata Su Spendula

Villacidro

Portixeddu

Rio Mannu

SS126

Fluminimaggiore

Serramanna

SS128

Iglesiente

SS196

SS196dir

Cala Domestica

Buggerru

Grotta de Su Mannau

Tempio di Antas

SP83

SS126

Grotta di San Giovanni

Domusnovas

Villasor

Fiume Mannu

Monastir

SS196

San Sperate

SS130dir

SS131

Porto Flavia

Scoglio Pan di Zucchero

Masua

Nebida

IGLESIAS

SS130

Decimomannu

Uta

Assemini

SS130

Portu Banda

Funtanamare

Monteponi Mines

Villamassargia

Siliqua

Castello di Acquafredda

Elmas

Stagno di Cagliari

Golfo di Gonnesa

Grotta di Santa Barbara

Gonnesa

Villagio Minerario Rosas

Monte Orri (723m)

Monte Arcosu (948m)

Aeroporto Internazionale Cagliari-Elmas

Stagno di Santa Gilla

Capoterra

Portoscuso

La Punta

Isola Piana

SS126

Portovesme

Carbonia

Monte Sirai (191m)

Narcao

Riserva Naturale Foresta di Monte Arcosu

Capo Sandalo

Cala Fico

Isola di San Pietro

Necropoli del Montessu

SS195

Golfo degli Angeli

Isola del Corno

La Caletta

La Conca

Carloforte

Calasetta

Salina

San Giovanni Suergiu

Tratalias

Lago di Monte Pranu

Villaperuccio

Santadi

Torre Antigori

Sarroch

Punta della Colonne

SS126

SS126

SS195

Giba

Blufan

Isola di Sant'Antioco

Sant'Antioco

Porto Ponte Romano

Porto Botte

SS195

Grotte Is Zuddas

Pula

Chiesa di Sant'Efisio

Cala Lunga

Colonia

Cala de Saboni

Maladroxia

39°00'N

Golfo di Palmas

Sant'Anna Arresi

Nora

Capo di Pula

La Fazenda

Capo Sperone

Porto Pino

Teulada

Santa Margherita di Pula

Domus de Maria

SS195

Forte Village

Costa del Sud

Porto di Teulada

Porto Tramatzu

Chia

Torre di Chia

Cala Piombo

Spiaggia Isola Piscinni Rossa

Capo Malfatano

Porto Campana

Spiaggia Su Giudeu

Capo Teulada

Porto Zafferano

Cala Teuradda

Cala Cipolla

Porto di Malfatano

Capo Spartivento

MEDITERRANEAN SEA

8°30'E

9°00'E

IGLESIAS

pop 27,800

Surrounded by the undulating hills of Monte Linas and the skeletons of Sardinia's once thriving mining industry, Iglesias is an urbane and lively city. The death of mining in the 1970s hit the area hard, but Iglesias has weathered the storm with considerable spirit. Its historic centre is an appealing ensemble of lived-in piazzas, sun-bleached buildings and Aragonese-style wrought-iron balconies, and it's here that the townsfolk gather on warm summer evenings. The atmosphere is as much Spanish as Sardinian, as is the town's name, which is Spanish for 'churches'. Visit at Easter to experience a quasi-Seville experience during the extraordinary drum-beating processions.

HISTORY

Mining has been big business here since classical times. The Romans called their town Metalla, after the precious metals they mined on Monte Linas. But the Romans weren't the first to exploit the mines; when they were reopened in the 19th century, equipment belonging to the Carthaginians was discovered. Populated by slaves and immigrants, Iglesias grew, each group establishing a church. Their buildings gave the town one of its earlier names, Villa di Chiesa (Town of Churches).

Centuries later in 1257, the Pisans grabbed the Giudicato di Cagliari (Province of Cagliari) and granted Iglesias to Ugolino della Gherardesca, a Pisan captain and member of the pro-papal Ghibelline party. He had a good business head and quickly organised the town along the lines of a Tuscan *comune* (self-governing town) with its own laws and currency. He even instituted the statute of laws known as the Breve di Villa Chiesa, a revolutionary code that granted social benefits to the miners. You can still view it on request at the city's Archivio Stòrico (p80).

But Ugolino was fated to make a terrible decision when he betrayed the Ghibellines for the Milanese Guelphs. Arrested in 1288 and accused of treason, he was summarily imprisoned in the Tower of Gualandi along with two of his sons and grandsons, whom he is said to have murdered and eaten before he himself starved to death in 1289. His sons Guelfo and Lotto abandoned Villa di Chiesa and fled north. Lotto was captured and Guelfo died in

the hospital of the Knights of Jerusalem in San Leonardo de Siete Fuentes in 1295.

In 1323 the Catalano-Aragonese troops landed at Portovesme and took the town the following year, renaming it Iglesias. They had little interest in the mines and for the next 500 years the pits lay abandoned until private entrepreneurs, like Quintino Sella (after whom the main piazza is named), revived their fortunes. As the nascent centre of heavy industry in a resurgent and soon-to-be-united Italy, Iglesias once again became an important town until WWII and modern economics tolled its death knell in the 1970s.

ORIENTATION

To orientate yourself in Iglesias, start at the Piazza Quintino Sella at the southeastern corner of the historic centre. From the square, Corso Matteotti bisects the *centro storico* (historic city centre) en route to a series of small squares: Piazza La Marmora, Piazza Collegio and Piazza del Municipio.

The *centro storico* is not very big and is easily explored on foot. It's bounded by Via Roma, Via Gramsci, Via Eleonora d'Arborea and Via Campidano. The latter is still lined by the remains of the medieval walls that are now only a memory on the other streets.

The main bus stop is a short walk southwest of Piazza Quintino Sella, near the Giardini Pubblici (Public Gardens).

INFORMATION

Banco Nazionale del Lavoro (Via Roma 29) Has an ATM.

Libreria Mondadori (☎ 0781 2 37 77; Piazza La Marmora; ⊕ 9am-1pm & 5-8.15pm) A small bookshop good for maps and guides.

Main post office (Via Mercato Vecchio; ⊕ 8am-1.15pm Mon-Sat)

Tourist office (☎ 0781 25 25 39; Via Verdi 2; ⊕ 10am-1pm & 6-8pm Mon-Fri) Take these hours with a grain of salt – the official hours are not always respected.

SIGHTS

Piazza Quintino Sella & Around

Much of modern Iglesias harks back to the 19th century. This was the last big boom in the city's mining fortunes, when new laws allowed a syndicate from the Italian mainland to buy up the mines and reopen them. To herald this exciting new era, the bulk of the medieval walls were demolished and the spacious Piazza Quintino Sella was laid out in

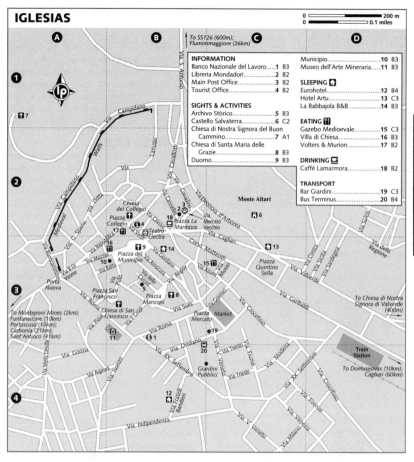

IGLESIAS

To SS126 (600m);
Fluminimaggiore (26km)

INFORMATION
Banco Nazionale del Lavoro.....**1** B3
Libreria Mondadori...................**2** B2
Main Post Office.....................**3** B2
Tourist Office..........................**4** B2

SIGHTS & ACTIVITIES
Archivo Stòrico..........................**5** B3
Castello Salvaterra....................**6** C2
Chiesa di Nostra Signora del Buon
    Cammino.............................**7** A1
Chiesa di Santa Maria delle
    Grazie.................................**8** B3
Duomo.....................................**9** B3

Municipio.................................**10** B3
Museo dell'Arte Mineraria.....**11** B3

SLEEPING 🛏
Eurohotel.................................**12** B4
Hotel Artu...............................**13** C3
La Babbajola B&B.....................**14** B3

EATING 🍴
Gazebo Medioevale.................**15** C3
Villa di Chiesa.........................**16** B3
Volters & Murion.....................**17** B2

DRINKING 🍷
Caffé Lamarmora.....................**18** B2

TRANSPORT
Bar Giardini.............................**19** C3
Bus Terminus...........................**20** B4

what had previously been a field just outside the city walls. It became the central meeting place of the town, and even today it throngs with people during the evening *passeggiata* (stroll). The statue in the centre commemorates Quintino Sella (of Sella e Mosca wine fame), Sardinian statesman and vigorous promoter of the reborn mining industry.

Just off the square, scruffy litter-strewn stairs lead up to a stout square tower. This is all that remains of **Castello Salvaterra**, Ugolino's once-mighty Pisan fortress. To get an idea of what the city looked like before the walls came down, proceed to Via Campidano, where a stretch of the 14th-century northwestern perimeter built by the Catalano-Aragonese remains defiantly in place, complete with towers.

Centro Storico

Much of the pleasure of visiting Iglesias lies in the small medieval centre. There are no great must-see sights, but the narrow, car-free lanes and suggestive piazzas are in good nick and much appreciated by locals who flock here to browse the shops and hang out in the bars. It's also in the *centro storico* that you'll find many of the churches that give the city it's name (*iglesia* is Spanish for 'church').

Dominating the eastern flank of Piazza del Municipio, the **Duomo** (Piazza del Municipio; ☾ closed for renovation) retains its lovely Pisan-flavoured facade, as does the bell tower, with its chequerboard stonework. It was begun in 1337, but Catalan architects gave it a makeover in the 16th century, which accounts for the rich internal decoration. Inside, the high-light is the gilded altarpiece which once held the relics of St Antiochus. Originally this was on the Isola di Sant'Antioco, but it was bought to Iglesias in the 17th century to protect it from pirate raids. And although the clerics were forced to return the relics to the cathedral in Sant'Antioco in the 19th century, they managed to hang on to the altar.

Across the square from the Duomo is the bishop's residence, while on the western side is the grand neoclassical **Municipio** (Town Hall). Neither of these buildings are open to the public.

From the square, Via Pullo leads to the dainty rose-red trachyte **Chiesa di San Francesco** (☎ 0781 2 42 26; Piazza San Francesco; ◷ 8am-noon & 5-8pm), a typical Catalan Gothic affair. Built over a 200-year period between 1300 and 1500, its single-nave interior is flanked by chapels squeezed in between the buttresses. Outdating it by a century or so is the nearby **Chiesa di Santa Maria delle Grazie** (☎ 0781 2 25 04; Piazza Manzoni; ◷ 7.30am-noon & 5.30-8pm), the original 13th-century facade of which is topped by a pinky baroque number, dating to the 17th and 18th centuries.

Records illustrating Iglesias' past are kept in the **Archivio Stòrico** (☎ 078 12 48 50; Via delle Carceri; ◷ 9am-1pm & 3.45-6.15pm Mon-Fri), the city's historical archive. Of particular interest is the Breve di Villa di Chiesa, the 1327 statute book of the medieval city.

Out of the Centre

Just outside the *centro storico*, on the main road into the town centre, Iglesias' main museum is the **Museo dell'Arte Mineraria** (☎ 0781 35 00 37; www.museoartemineraria.it; Via Roma 47; admission free; ◷ 7-9pm Fri-Sun Jul-Sep, 6-8pm Sat & Sun Apr-Jun, by appointment Oct-Mar). Dedicated to the town's mining heritage, it displays up to 70 extraction machines, alongside tools and a series of thought-provoking black-and-white photos. To get a real taste of the claustrophobic conditions in which the miners worked, duck down into the recreated tunnels. These were actually dug by mining students and used to train senior workers, at least until WWII, when they were used as air-raid shelters. Upstairs you'll find a collection of some 8000 carefully labelled rock and mineral specimens from Sardinia and around the world.

There are also two other churches worth seeking out. To the northwest of the cen-

tre, the white **Chiesa di Nostra Signora del Buon Cammino** is perched on a tall hill and commands lovely views over the city.

On the opposite side of town, the **Chiesa di Nostra Signora di Valverde** is another of Iglesias' historic churches. About 15 minutes' walk from Piazza Quintino Sella, it retains little of its 13th-century structure except for an elegant facade, similar to the Duomo's, with two series of blind arches in the Pisan style.

FESTIVALS & EVENTS

The week before Easter is a good time to visit Iglesias. During **Settimana Santa** (Holy Week), the town celebrates its Spanish origins and religious traditions in a series of sinister religious processions. Every night between Holy Tuesday and Good Friday, hooded members of religious brotherhoods, bearing candles and crucifixes and accompanied by a slow, deathly drum beat, bear effigies of the Virgin Mary and Christ around town.

Much cheerier is **Estate Medioevale Iglesiente** (Iglesias' Medieval Summer), a series of themed events that involve much dressing up and flag-waving. Highlights include a two-day crossbow tournament and a huge costumed procession on 13 August.

SLEEPING

Neither a big tourist town nor a major commercial centre, Iglesias is fairly short on good-value accommodation.

La Babbajola B&B (☎ 347 614 46 21; www.lababbajola.it; Via Giordano 13; per person €25-27.50) A laid-back, homey B&B in the *centro storico*. Accommodation is in a mini-apartment or one of three big double rooms, each of which features bright, bold colours and tasteful furniture. There's a kitchen and TV room for guest use, although only the apartment bedroom has an en suite bathroom.

Hotel Artu (☎ 078 12 24 92; www.hotelartuiglesias.it; Piazza Quintino Sella 15; s €46-60, d €78-90, half-board per person €60-70; P ⧆) Right in the heart of the action, this is a functional middle-of-the-road option. Beyond the awful concrete exterior, it offers comfortable modern rooms, a popular restaurant and a friendly welcome. Parking, at €3.50, is worth taking as on-street parking is difficult in Iglesias.

Eurohotel (☎ 078 12 26 43; www.eurohoteliglesias.it, in Italian; Via Fratelli Bandieri 34; s €60-80, d €80-110; P ⧆) A kitsch rendition of a Pompeian villa, the Eurohotel is difficult to miss. With its pompous porticoed entrance and curling balconies, it hardly matches the workaday buildings that surround it. Inside, there's no let-up as rooms reveal a mix of faux-gilt chairs, Murano-style chandeliers and sombre oil paintings.

EATING & DRINKING

Volters & Murion (☎ 078 13 37 88; Piazza Collegio 1; lunch/land/seafood menu €11/25/33; meals around €20; ☺ Tue-Fri) Serving everything from hamburgers and chips to pasta in spicy tomato sauce and seafood, this is a cheerful eatery near the Duomo. With the TV on in the corner and locals laughing at the bar, it's a laid-back place, as good for a meal as an evening drink.

Gazebo Medioevale (☎ 078 13 08 71; Via Musio 21; lunch set menu €13; meals around €25; ☺ Mon-Sat) Excellent value and great grilled meats. Not a bad combination, especially if you add an attractive interior – exposed brick walls lined with Sardinian masks and, for some bizarre reason, a didgeridoo – and a convenient location. Credit cards are not accepted.

Villa di Chiesa (☎ 078 12 31 24; Piazza del Municipio 8; set menu €15; meals around €25; Tue-Sun) Grab a table on Piazza del Municipio and sit down to wonderful homemade pasta at this long-standing favourite. Menu stalwarts include scrumptious *culurgiones*, which sound rude but are in fact pasta pockets stuffed with ricotta, spinach and saffron, and *sebadas* (light pastry filled with cheese and covered with honey). There's also pizza in the evenings.

Caffè Lamarmora (Piazza Lamarmora 6; ☺ 6am-1pm & 3-9.30pm) This landmark *centro storico* cafe serves deliciously strong coffee. It's not difficult to find – just look for the towering building covered in 1930s-style adverts. Confusingly, though, it shuts over lunchtime, something which doesn't make a lot of commercial sense.

GETTING THERE & AWAY
Bus

All intercity buses arrive at and leave from the Via Oristano side of the Giardini Pubblici. You can get timetable information and tickets from **Bar Giardini** (Via Oristano 8; ☺ 5.30am-2.30pm & 3.30-9pm Mon-Sat) across the road from the stops. Buses run to Cagliari (€4, one to 1½ hours, seven daily), Carbonia (€2, 45 minutes, eight daily) and Funtanamare (€1, 20 minutes, 11 daily).

Car & Motorcycle

With the exception of the dual-carriageway SS130 from Cagliari (less than an hour), road approaches to Iglesias are slow. From the south, the SS195 coastal road from Cagliari connects with the SS126 from Isola di Sant'Antioco to pass via Carbonia to Iglesias. From the north, the SS126 drops south from Oristano province to Guspini and then heads through the mountains via Arbus and Fluminimaggiore.

Train

As many as 10 daily Trenitalia trains run between Iglesias and Cagliari (€3.30, one hour).

AROUND IGLESIAS

MONTEPONI MINES

If you're at all interested in Iglesias' industrial history, you'll be fascinated by the enormous mining centre of Monteponi. Some 2km west of Iglesias, this sprawling, now abandoned, area was the black heart of the Iglesiente mining industry, one of Sardinia's most important producers of lead, zinc and silver. Extraction dates back to 1324 and continued on and off until 1992, when the entire operation transferred to Campo Pisano across the valley.

Today it's possible to visit the Galleria Villamarina, a tunnel built in 1852 to connect the mine's two principle pits. To organise a tour, you'll need to contact the **IGEA cooperative** (☎ 0781 49 13 00; www.igeaminiere.it, in Italian; adult/under 12yr €8/4.50; ☺ 8.30am-5pm Mon-Fri).

If you're without wheels, you can get a local Linea B bus from Via Oristano in Iglesias eight times a day (€0.70, 20 minutes).

GROTTA DI SANTA BARBARA

A few kilometres further along the Carbonia road are the abandoned San Giovanni lead and zinc mines. Back in the 1950s, routine excavations revealed the **Grotta di Santa Barbara** (☎ 0781 49 13 00; www.igeaminiere.it, in Italian; adult/child €12/6; ☺ 8.30am-5pm Mon-Fri), a hitherto unknown cave complex. The walls of the single enormous chamber are pock-marked with dark-brown crystals and white calcite, while stalactites and stalagmites give the impression of a ghostly underground forest. Visits are by appointment only.

SOUTHWEST SARDINIA

FUNTANAMARE

The beach that is closest to Iglesias is at Funtanamare (also spelt Fontanamare). A long strip of golden sand backed by dunes and fertile farmland, it's a hugely popular spot, although it rarely gets too crowded, if nothing else because it's so long. Strong winds make it a surfer favourite, particularly when the *maestrale* (northwest wind) is blowing.

Up to 11 daily buses run from Iglesias down to the beach (€1, 20 minutes), and there is plenty of parking if you want to drive. Another five buses head to a point known as **Plage Mesu**, further south along the same strand.

DOMUSNOVAS

About 10km east of Iglesias on the SS130 Cagliari road, the unremarkable town of Domusnovas sits at the centre of one of Sardinia's most exciting rock-climbing areas. The outlying countryside is peppered with limestone rocks, cliffs and caves, many of which are ideal for sports climbing. There are some 440 routes for both novice and experienced climbers, ranging from simple, single-pitch walls to tough 7c overhangs. Experts say climatic and rock conditions are at their best between early autumn and late spring. For more technical information, check out www.climb-europe.com/sardinia and www.sardiniaclimb.com.

Four kilometres north of Domusnovas, and signposted from the main road, the **Grotta di San Giovanni** (illuminated 9am-9pm) is well worth checking out. An 850m-long natural cave-gallery, it has only recently been closed to traffic – until 2000 you could actually drive your car straight through. If you're feeling peckish there's a bar-restaurant by the car park at the entrance.

Eight daily buses connect Iglesias and Domusnovas (€1, 15 minutes).

THE IGLESIENTE

To the north and west of Iglesias, the mountainous landscape is picturesque and strangely haunting. Wild green scrub cloaks the silent hills in a soft verdant down while abandoned houses serve as a poignant reminder of the mining communities that once thrived here. The coast is dramatic and offers superb seascapes.

All the towns in the region were connected with mining. You can visit the old galleries on guided tours run by the **IGEA cooperative** (0781 49 13 00; www.igeaminiere.it, in Italian), a locally run outfit that seeks to maintain interest in the area's history by taking vistors to places that would otherwise be abandoned. In July and August you may be able to just turn up and join a tour, but it is always advisable to book ahead as getting to these places is incredibly time-consuming.

THE COAST
Nebida

From Funtanamare, the SP83 coastal road affords spectacular views as it dips, bends and climbs its tortuous way northwards. After 5.5km you come to the small and rather drab village of Nebida, a former mining settlement sprawled along the coastal road high above the sea. The main reason to stop here is to enjoy the mesmerising views from the **Belvedere**, a panoramic viewing point accessible by a fenced-off walkway along the cliff. Dominating the seascape is the 133m-high **Scoglio Pan di Zucchero** (Sugarloaf Rock), the largest of several *faraglioni* (sea stacks) that rise out of the glassy blue waters against a majestic backdrop of sheer, rugged cliffs. Beneath, the **Laveria Lamarmora** is the shell of a building used for washing and separating minerals back in Nebida's mining days. A track winds down from the main road to the site.

About 500m further north, a side road leads down to **Portu Banda**, which has a small pebble beach.

To better explore the sea, contact **Marco Salerni** (329 792 00 93), who organises dives out of Nebida for €25 per person plus the cost of equipment hire.

Near the southern entrance to the village, the **Pan di Zucchero** (0781 4 71 14; www .hotelpandizucchero.it; Via Centrale 365; s €40-45, d €50-55) is a welcoming, family-run hotel with neat, modestly furnished rooms. It also has a restaurant which serves up healthy portions of fresh, local seafood. Right next to the hotel, a narrow lane descends steeply to a pretty sandy cove.

Local buses run between Iglesias and Masua, stopping off at Nebida (€1.50, 30 minutes, 11 daily).

Masua

A few kilometres further north, Masua is another former mining centre. Seen from above, it looks a pretty ugly prospect, but it's not entirely without interest.

Descending into town, the road leads past an abandoned mining complex to a beach that, while not Sardinia's best, is pleasant enough with its stunning close-ups of the Scoglio Pan di Zucchero.

However, the main drawcard here is the chance to visit the town's unique mining port. Until the 1920s, much of the ore mined around the Iglesiente was transported to sailing vessels that were hauled up onto the beaches. The boats then sailed down to Carloforte (on Isola di San Pietro) to transfer the load to cargo vessels. This system was done away with in 1924, when two 600m tunnels were dug into the cliffs at Masua. In the lower of the two tunnels a conveyor belt received zinc and lead ore from the underground deposits and transported it via an ingenious mobile 'arm' directly to the ships moored below. The upper tunnel was used to carry minerals to the underground deposits. Guided tours of **Porto Flavia** (☎ 0781 49 13 00; www.igeaminiere.it, in Italian; adult/child €8/4.50; ☼ 9am, 10.30am & noon Aug, rest of year by appointment only) take about one hour. To find the entrance, head down to the beach from where a road leads back uphill and then around the coast for about 2.5km.

The same road leads to a shady lookout point over the Scoglio Pan di Zucchero.

Cala Domestica

From Masua the road rises quickly in a series of tight turns as it works its way around Monte Guardianu to Buggerru. Beach-lovers should take the signposted turn-off for Cala Domestica, 5km short of Buggerru. Follow the road down to the car park at the end and you'll find yourself at a sandy beach wedged into a natural inlet between craggy cliffs. The water is a beautiful blue and sometimes curls up in decent sets of waves. A walk along the rocky path to the right of the beach brings you to a smaller, more sheltered side strand.

There's a car park, costing around €4 per day in summer (for most of the rest of the year it's free as there's nobody there). A snack bar behind the beach helps keep body and soul together.

Buggerru & Portixeddu
pop 1120

A popular resort with a small harbour and a rash of holiday apartments, Buggerru is the biggest village on this stretch of coastline. Set within the natural stone walls of a steep valley, it was established in 1860 and by the early 20th century had developed into an important mining centre with a population of 12,000. For a long time it was accessible only by sea, a fact which forced it into enterprising self-sufficiency – Buggerru had its own electricity supply before Cagliari and Sassari, as well as a hospital, a mutual benefit society and a small theatre. It wasn't all roses, though, and in 1904 Buggerru's miners downed tools and went on strike – the first ever recorded in Sardinia.

Information on the town and its environs is available at the **tourist office** (☎ 0781 5 40 93; ☼ 10am-noon & 6-8pm), situated on the SP83 coastal road.

Other than hang out on the beach, a favourite with local surfers, you can hire a boat from **Società Mormora** (☎ 328 883 33 40) down at the Porto Turistico (Tourist Harbour) and visit Buggerru's former mine, the **Galleria Henry** (☎ 0781 49 13 00; www.igeaminiere .it, in Italian; adult/child €8/4.50; ☼ 9am, 10.30am, noon, 2pm, 3.30pm, 4.30pm & 5.30pm Aug, rest of year by appointment). What makes this hour-long 1km tour a highlight are the views straight down the cliff to the sea.

The road out of Buggerru climbs high along the cliff face for a couple of kilometres before you hit the long sandy stretches of **Spiaggia Portixeddu**, one of the best beaches in the area, which extends 3km up the coast to the Rio Mannu, the river marking the end of the Iglesiente coast.

Accommodation in the area is limited, but the **Camping Ortus de Mari** (☎ /fax 0781 5 49 64; per adult/tent €8/11.50; ☼ late May–Sep) has some very basic camping facilities a little way northeast of the beach, about 1km from the Capo Pecora turn-off.

Otherwise, the pink **Hotel Golfo del Leone** (☎ 0781 5 49 52; www.golfodelleone.it; Localita Caburu de Figu; s/d €55/85, half-board per person €66.50-80) boasts sunny sea-facing rooms about 1km back from Portixeddu beach. Service is friendly, and the helpful staff can organise horse-riding excursions. The adjacent restaurant serves up decent local food for about €25 per head.

INLAND
Fluminimaggiore
pop 3050

A pretty but nauseatingly winding 26km stretch of the SS126 leads from Iglesias to Fluminimaggiore, an uninspiring town with a couple of museums and a few modest eateries. It's a disaffected place, and like Orgosolo in central Sardinia, it has vented its unhappy condition in murals around the town, many of which look back to the golden days of the mines with real nostalgia.

The town itself is of little interest, but in its environs you'll find the impressive Grotta de Su Mannau and the Roman Tempio di Antas.

Up to 10 daily buses link Iglesias with Fluminimaggiore (€2, 45 minutes). To get to the following two sites ask the driver to drop you off on the main road, from where you'll have to walk the last couple of kilometres.

GROTTA DE SU MANNAU

A few kilometres south of town, and signposted off the SS126, is the **Grotta de Su Mannau** (☎ 0781 58 04 11; www.sumannau.it; adult/concession €8/4.50; ☼ 9.30am-6pm Easter-Oct, reservations essential rest of year), the largest cave of its sort so far discovered in the Iglesiente. The standard tour takes you on a 50-minute walk through a fraction of the cave's delights, passing through several lake chambers and the Archaeological Room, so called because there is archaeological evidence that it was used as a temple for water worship. Finally you reach the Pozzo Rodriguez (Rodriguez Well), where you see an impressive 8m column, effectively a stalactite and stalagmite fused together.

More exciting tours of the cave are possible and are open to complete beginners. These tours enable you to visit dramatic chambers like the White Room or the opalescent waters of the Pensile Lake. A six- to eight-hour tour will get you to the jewel of Su Mannau, the Virgin Room, where you can see wonderful aragonites and big snow-white slopes of solidified calcium. The latter tour is the most difficult, and requires a wetsuit to pass through the various bottlenecks and siphons.

These excursions need to be organised in advance through the cave office. Costs vary according to duration and number of participants.

If you want somewhere to stay, the **Ostello Su Mannau** (☎ 347 009 53 67; www.ostellosumannau .com; r €50-70), on the unnamed road to Grotta de Su Mannau, is a tranquil three-star about 200m from the cave car park. Rooms are bright and clean and the location is idyllic, submerged in silent woods and surrounded by greenery.

TEMPIO DI ANTAS

In a lovely, woody spot 9km south of Fluminimaggiore, the sand-coloured **Tempio di Antas** (☎ 0781 58 09 90; www.startuno.it, in Italian; adult/child €3/2; ☼ 9.30am-6.30pm daily May-Oct, 9.30am-3pm Fri, Sat & Sun Nov-Apr) has stood in solitary isolation since the 3rd century AD. Built by the emperor Caracalla, it was constructed over a 6th-century BC Punic sanctuary, which itself was set over an earlier *nuraghe* settlement. In its Roman form the temple was dedicated to Sardus Pater, a local Sardinian deity worshipped by the nuraghic people as Babai and by the Punic faithful as Sid, god of warriors and hunters.

After centuries of disrepair, the temple was extensively restored between 1967 and 1976. Most impressively, the original Ionic columns were excavated and reerected. At the foot of these columns you can make out remains of the temple's Carthaginian predecessor, which the Romans cannibalised to erect their version.

Between the ticket office and the temple, a narrow trail marked as *sentiero romano* (Roman way) leads after about five minutes to what little remains of the original *nuraghe* settlement. Following the trail for 1½ hours would theoretically take you to the Grotta de Su Mannau, but we haven't tried it out.

From the main road, it's about a half-hour walk to the main site.

COSTA VERDE

One of Sardinia's great untamed coastal stretches, the Costa Verde (Green Coast) extends northwards from Capo Pecora to the small resort of Torre dei Corsari. Named after the green *macchia* (Mediterranean scrub) that covers much of its mountainous hinterland, it's an area of wild, exhilarating beauty and spectacular beaches. The best of these are only accessible by dirt track, which can be tough on hire cars but means that they are largely free of unsightly development. In fact, the Costa Verde beaches are among the wildest and most unspoilt in Sardinia.

There's no road which follows the entire length of the Costa Verde, so if you're driving northwards from Portixxedu (and you really do need to drive to get the best out of the area), you'll have to head inland along the SS126 towards Arbus and Guspini.

VILLACIDRO

pop 14,600

About 9km southeast of Arbus, a minor road leads to the Tolkienesque-sounding Gonnosfanadiga. Another 6km east on the SS196 brings you to the first of two turn-offs for Villacidro, a small agricultural town best known for its yellow saffron-based liqueur. Follow this twisting country road and about 2.5km short of Villacidro you'll see a signpost for the **Cascata Su Spendula** waterfall. All around rise imposing rock walls and a thick curtain of trees. The Italian nationalist poet Gabriele d'Annunzio, judging by his effusive verse on the subject, visited in winter!

ARBUS

pop 6780

Lounging on the slopes of Monte Linas, Arbus is home to one of Sardinia's most original museums. Up in the granite old town, just off central Piazza Mercato, the **Museo del Coltello Sardo** (☎ 070 975 92 20; www.museodelcoltello.it, in Italian; Via Roma 15; admission free; ☼ 9am-noon & 4-8pm Mon-Fri) pays homage to the ancient Sardinian art of knife-making. The museum was founded by Paolo Pusceddu, whose *s'arburesi* (knives from Arbus; see the boxed text, p134) are among the most prized of Sardinian knives. Downstairs, you can contemplate Signor Pusceddu's historic knife collection and admire some of his finest creations.

On the main road at the eastern entrance into town, **Hotel Meridiana** (☎ 070 975 82 83; www .wels.it/hotelmeridiana; Via della Repubblica 172; s €35-41, d €65-77; ℗ ☒ ☒) is a friendly place offering value for money and 26 modern, summery rooms, some with views back over town. The downstairs restaurant serves good pizza.

At the opposite end of Arbus, **Ristorante Sa Lolla** (☎ 070 975 40 04; Via Libertà 225; meals around €25; ☼ Thu-Tue) has a good local reputation. Hopefully you can ignore the gnomes on the tables, as it serves great lamb dishes and hearty bowls of steaming pasta.

ARST buses reach Arbus from Cagliari (€4.50, two hours, six Monday to Saturday, two Sunday), although it's a pretty long haul.

MONTEVECCHIO

Surrounded by wooded hills and granite peaks, the Unesco-listed **Miniere di Montevecchio** was once Sardinia's most important zinc and lead mine. A vast, now crumbling complex, it was operative until 1991 and although most people have since left, there's still a small town with a handful of inhabitants.

To visit the mines you'll have to arrange a visit with either **IGEA cooperative** (☎ 0781 49 13 00; www.igeaminiere.it, in Italian; adult/under 12yr €6/3; ☼ 8.30am-5pm Mon-Fri) or the **G. Fulgheri Cooperative** (☎ 070 934 60 00; www.coopfulgheri.it, in Italian; tours €8; ☼ 10am & 11am Sat & Sun), which also runs excursions into the heavily wooded countryside around **Monte Arcuentu** (785m), one of the last preserves of the *cervo sardo* (Sardinian deer).

From Montevecchio the SP65 twists and turns its way through the great green wilderness onwards to Torre dei Corsari. On the way there are two excellent *agriturismi* (farm-stays).

ourpick **Agriturismo Arcuentu** (☎ 070 975 81 68; Localita Monte Arcuentu; meals around €25) is 6km out of Montevecchio, just off the SP65 road. An authentic working farm, it's a great place to stop for a royal Sardinian feast. For €25 you sit down to antipasti, a choice of two pasta dishes, two mains, vegetable side dishes, fruit, dessert, coffee and an *amaro* (a bittersweet alcoholic *digestivo*). At the time of research there were no guestrooms, but according to the owner there may be five by the time you read this. Bookings are essential.

Agriturismo L'Aquila (☎ 347 822 24 26; www.aglaq uila.com; Localita Is Gennas Arbus; r per person €30, half-board per person €42-55) is a similar affair with the bonus of comfortable rustic guestrooms to sleep in. To get here take the signposted exit off the SP65 and follow the dirt track for about 2.5km.

TORRE DEI CORSARI

Marking the northernmost point of the Costa Verde, Torre dei Corsari is a small but growing resort. In itself, it's not an especially attractive place, with bland modern buildings and an ugly concrete piazza, but it does have a good beach. Stretching for about 1.5km, the broad band of golden sand is sandwiched between an emerald-green sea and a range

SOUTHWEST SARDINIA

BEACHES OF THE COSTA VERDE

From Capo Pecora head back via Portixeddu and northeast along the SS126 until you reach the turn-off for **Gennamari**, **Bau** and **Spiaggia Scivu**. If coming from the northeast, you'll see the signs on the right, 13km from Arbus. Take this narrow mountain route into the windswept, Mediterranean scrub–covered southern heights to around 450m above sea level, when the sea comes into view. Five kilometres short of the beach, Spiaggia Scivu is signposted to the left. Going straight ahead would take you to the local penitentiary, something that has helped to keep Scivu off the developers' map for many years.

You arrive at a parking area, where there's a kiosk and freshwater showers in summer only. You'll also need to bring some sort of shade (an umbrella or tent), as there are no facilities and it's very exposed. As you walk towards the beach, you find yourself atop 70m dunes from where you can view the enormous length of beach that stretches before you.

The other famous beach of the Costa Verde is the **Spiaggia della Piscinas**, some 3.7km north-east of the Spiaggia Scivu turn-off along the SS126. Take the Ingurtosu exit. This is a worthwhile exercise in its own right, as the road drops down into a valley lined with the abandoned buildings, housing and machinery of a crumbling 19th-century mining settlement.

After 9km of dirt track, you'll hit a fork. Take the left branch for Spiaggia della Piscinas, and you'll reach the beach after a further 20 minutes of off-road driving. Back from the broad strand of beach rise 30m-high dunes, known as Sardinia's desert. In summer one or two beach bars brighten the place up and offer welcome showers, umbrellas and loungers.

---

of mountainous dunes which mushroom back into green scrubland. Overlooking the southern end of the beach is the ruined watchtower from which the town takes its name. The top end of the beach is known as **Pistis** – a good long walk away or an 8km drive via **Sant'Antonio di Santadi**. There is paid parking at both ends of the beach.

Torre dei Corsari is a summer town, so arrive in winter and you'll find your eating and sleeping options severely limited.

Brezza Marina (☎ 338 367 68 86; www.brezzamarina .it; Viale della Torre; s €30-60, d €45-110) has year-round rooms and apartments dotted across town. Room size and quality varies but most are simple, white-tiled affairs with flimsy summery furniture and basic facilities. Breakfast vouchers cost €2.50.

Verdemare (☎ 070 97 72 72; www.verdemare.com; Via Colombo; r €70-158; ☺ Easter-Nov; ⛱) is a lovely place to stay. Immersed in lush gardens, it has a large terrace with distant sea views and bright, cool rooms. Air-con costs an extra €3 but you'll save yourself some money by opening the window and bedding down inside the mosquito net.

Hotel Caletta (☎ 070 97 71 33; www.lacaletta.it; d €90-148, half board per person €78-106; ☺ end Apr-Sep; P ⛱ ⛲) is a big, three-star on a rocky point overlooking the sea. Rooms have all mod-cons, there's a boomerang-shaped swimming pool, and a small disco. There's a

minimum two-week stay over the Ferragosto (15 August) period.

Self-caterers can always stock up at the **supermarket** (☎ 070 97 72 45; Piazza Stella Maris; ☺ 9am-1pm & 5-8pm) on the central square near the watchtower.

During July and August, an ARST bus runs daily from Oristano bus station to Torre dei Corsari (€4, 1½ hours).

CARBONIA & AROUND

South of Iglesias, the SS126 unfolds rapidly into flatter, less-inspiring landscapes that head straight for the south's second-largest city, Carbonia. A monument to failed Fascist ambition, the city holds little of interest for visitors today, save for a couple of modest museums and an archetypal Fascist town square. Nearby Monte Sirai offers glimpses into the island's ancient past.

To the west, Portovesme is the embarkation point for ferries to Isola di San Pietro.

CARBONIA
pop 30,300

Unless you're a real fan of Fascist architecture or intrigued by industrial history, you won't want to spend long in Carbonia. A modern town fallen on hard times, it was constructed by Mussolini between 1936 and 1938 to house workers from the nearby

Sirai-Serbariu coalfield. The town's fortunes have always been closely tied to the coal industry – its name is even a derivation of the Italian word for coal, *carbone* – and, in 1972 when mining in the area ceased, it was hit hard. The city has since trundled along in the doldrums, struggling with unemployment and managing to stay afloat thanks to small business.

Carbonia's focal point is Piazza Roma, a typically Fascist town square, dominated by the robust **Municipio** and bleak **Chiesa di San Ponziano**, the red trachyte bell tower of which is said to be a copy of Aquilea cathedral in northern Italy.

A short walk away is Carbonia's principal museum, the recently renovated **Museo Archeologico Villa Sulcis** (☎ 0781 66 50 37; Via Napoli 1; adult/child €3/2, incl Museo di Paleontologia e Speleologia & Monte Siria €5/3; ☼ 10am-8pm Wed-Sun Apr-Sep, 9am-2pm Tue-Sun Oct-Mar). Housed in the former residence of the town's mining director, it has a modest collection of archaeological finds, most of them from Monte Sirai.

Nearby, the **Museo di Paleontologia e Speleologia** (☎ 0781 69 10 06; Piazza Garibaldi; adult/child €3/2, incl Museo Archeologico Villa Sulcis & Monte Siria €5/3; ☼ 10am-8pm Wed-Sun Apr-Sep, 9am-2pm Tue-Sun Oct-Mar) is Sardinia's only dedicated speleology museum. One for the specialists, it displays fossils, minerals and all sorts of geological oddities collected from caves all over Sardinia.

Of more general interest are the ruins of the Phoenician fort at **Monte Sirai** (☎ 0781 66 50 37; adult/child incl Museo Archeologico Villa Sulcis & Monte Sirai €5/3; ☼ 10am-8pm Wed-Sun Apr-Sep, 9am-2pm Tue-Sun Oct-Mar), about 4km northwest of Carbonia on the other side of the SS126. Originally built by the Phoenicians of Sulci (modern Sant'Antioco) in 650 BC, it was taken over a century later by the Carthaginians. Although not a great deal of the fort remains, you can make out the placement of the Carthaginian acropolis and defensive tower, a necropolis and a *tophet*, a sacred Phoenician and Carthaginian burial ground for children and babies. The surrounding views are quite magnificent.

In Carbonia, buses run to/from the porticoes on Via Manno; for tickets go to Bar Balia at Viale Gramsci 4. There are services to Iglesias (€2, 45 minutes, eight daily) and Cagliari (€5.50, 1½ hours, seven daily), as well as a host of local towns.

PORTOSCUSO & PORTOVESME
pop 5350

It doesn't look good as you approach the coast. The enormous chimney stacks of a vast thermoelectric industrial complex rise above the flat landscape, offering a nightmarish landmark and presaging visions of foul, industrial sprawl. However, when you reach the coast, you'll discover that the industrial blight is actually at Portovesme, a couple of kilometres east of Portoscuso. Portoscuso itself is an attractive fishing port capped by a Spanish-era tower and surrounded by a tiny warren of agreeable lanes. Portovesme is the main ferry port for Isola di San Pietro.

You can get information at Portoscuso's helpful **tourist office** (☎ 0781 50 95 04; Via Vespucci 16; ☼ 10am-noon & 6-8.30pm Mon-Sat summer, 6-8.30pm Mon-Fri winter) near the seafront.

There's not a whole lot to do in town other than stroll the pristine streets and enjoy the laid-back atmosphere, but there's a decent sandy **beach** and you can admire sweeping views from the stout 16th-century **watchtower** (admission free; ☼ 6-8.30pm daily Jun-Sep).

Visit in early June, though, and you'll find the town a hive of activity as locals and visitors tuck into tuna dishes during the annual **Sagra del Tonno** (Tuna Festival). Portoscuso is one of the few places in Sardinia where tuna is still fished according to bloody traditional methods.

Hotel Mistral (☎ 0781 51 20 63; www.hotelmistral.191 .it; Via De Gasperi 1; s €42-54, d €60-77; ☐) is a breezy three-star with eight rooms over a popular local bar. Spacious and tastefully furnished, the lemon-tinted rooms come with modern bathrooms and satellite TV.

La Ghinghetta (☎ 078 150 81 43; laghinghetta@tiscali .it; Via Cavour 26; s €130-135, d €130-140, half board €130-175; ☼ May-Oct) skilfully combines charm, comfort and cuisine. Overlooking the beach, it has attractive, nautically themed rooms set in a series of whitewashed fishermen's houses, and a highly regarded restaurant. Specialising in seafood, set menus start at €65.

Ciccittu Pizzeria (☎ 0781 51 20 01; Via Amerigo Vespucci 6; pizzas €6, meals around €20; ☼ Wed-Mon) is a relaxed, congenial place serving a mixed menu of pizza, pastas and seafood. The local tuna features in a number of antipasti and main courses and is always worth a try.

FMS buses run to Portoscuso and neighbouring Portovesme from Iglesias (€2, 30 minutes, hourly) and Carbonia (€1.50,

35 minutes, 14 daily). You can buy your tickets from the newsagents at the top of Largo Matteotti.

Saremar (☎ 0781 50 90 65; www.saremar.it, in Italian) has up to 15 daily sailings from Portovesme to Carloforte (on Isola di San Pietro) between 5am and 9.10pm (in summer there's an additional sailing at 11.10pm). The trip takes about 30 minutes and costs €2.60 per person and €7.60 per car. Be prepared for long queues in summer.

TRATALIAS

Now a sleepy backwater, Tratalias was once the religious capital of the entire Sulcis area. When Sant'Antioco was abandoned in the 13th century, the Sulcis archdiocese was transferred to the village and the impressive **Chiesa di Santa Maria** (☎ 0781 69 70 03; admission €1; 9.30am-noon & 2.30-5.30pm Tue-Sun) was built. A curious Romanesque construction, the church presides over what little remains of the *vecchio borgo* (old town), abandoned after water from the nearby Lago di Monte Pranu started seeping into the subsoil in the 1950s. At the time of research, work was underway to convert the *vecchio borgo* into an arts and crafts centre with a museum and small hotel.

The easiest way to Tratalias is by car. The old town is 4km east off the SS195 right by the road.

NARCAO

About 15km northeast of Tratalias, this small town is worth a quick detour for its *murales* (murals), depicting life in the local mines. Its other main attraction is the annual **Narcao Blues Festival** (☎ 800 88 11 88; www.narcaoblues.it), one of Sardinia's top musical events. Held on the last weekend in July and now in its 18th year, the festival features blues, funk, soul and gospel concerts, performed by a cast of top American performers, which in previous years has included the celebrated Blind Boys of Alabama.

If you want to stay overnight in Narcao, **Agriturismo Santa Croce** (☎ 349 879 11 39; www .agriturismosantacroce.net; Localita Santa Croce; s €22-30, d €42-56), just outside the town, has modest rooms in a pink roadside bungalow, and an excellent restaurant (set menus €10 to €22; dinner by reservation only) that serves up hearty local fare, including home-reared lamb and pork.

> **DETOUR: VILLAGGIO MINERARIO ROSAS**
>
> Signposted off the main road into Narcao, the **Villaggio Minerario Rosas** is the modern reincarnation of the Rosas mine, an important source of lead, copper and zinc until it was closed in 1978. It's a striking site with its rusty minehead machinery and heavy timber structures. Strangely, though, the museum is rarely open and there's often no one around. But this shouldn't necessarily put you off as it's a beautifully remote spot, and you can still walk around the stone buildings and along silent paths into the rocky hills.

MONTESSU

One of Sardinia's largest and most important archaeological sites, the **Necropolis del Montessu** (adult/child €5/3; 9am-8pm Jun-Sep, to 6pm May, to 5pm Oct-Apr) is hidden in verdant country near Villaperuccio. Set in a rocky natural amphitheatre, the site dates back to the Ozieri period (approximately 3000 BC) and is peppered with 35 primitive tombs, known locally as *domus de janas* (literally 'fairy houses'). Many of these appear as little more than a hole in the wall, although some harbour wonderful relief carvings. Check out the **Tomba delle Spirali**, where you can clearly make out the raised relief of spirals and symbolic bulls.

From the ticket booth it's a 500m walk up to the main site. When you first arrive up the stairs from the roadway, to your immediate right is a **Tomba Santuario**, a rectangular foyer followed by three openings into a semicircular tomb area behind. Follow the trail to its right to see a cluster of tombs and then the Tomba delle Spirali.

To get to the area from Villaperuccio, take the road for Narcao and then follow the signs off to the left. It's about 2.5km.

SANTADI

Wine buffs can get to grips with the local vintage at Santadi, a busy agricultural centre a few kilometres east of Villaperuccio. The town is home to the biggest winery in the southwest, the **Cantina Santadi** (☎ 0781 95 01 27; Via Cagliari 78; www.cantinadisantadi.it; by appointment), whose reds include the highly rated Roccia Rubia and Grotta Rossa.

To get an idea of how villagers lived in the early 20th century, the **Museo Etnografico 'Sa Domu Antiga'** (☎ 078 195 59 55; Via Mazzini 37; admission €2.60; ☒ 9am-1pm & 3-5pm Tue-Sun), recreates a typical village house.

Like many rural towns, Santadi celebrates its traditions in high style. On the first Sunday of August, townspeople gather for the **Matrimonio Maureddino** (Moorish Wedding), a costumed wedding accompanied by folk dancing, eating and drinking. At the centre of events, the blushing bride and groom are transported to the main square on a *traccas* (a cart drawn by red bulls).

Five kilometres south of Santadi, the **Grotte Is Zuddas** (☎ 0781 95 57 41; www.grotteiszuddas.it, in Italian; adult/child €8/5; ☒ 9.30am-noon & 2.30-6pm Apr-Sep, noon-4pm Mon-Sat, 9.30am-noon & 2.30-6pm Sun & holidays Oct-Mar) is another of the island's spectacular cave systems. Of particular note are the helictites in the main hall. No one really knows how these weirdly shaped formations are created, although one theory suggests that wind in the cave may have acted on drops dripping off stalactites.

OFFSHORE ISLANDS

The southwest's two offshore islands, Isola di Sant'Antioco and Isola di San Pietro, display very different characters. The larger and more developed of the two, Isola Sant'Antioco, boasts little of the obvious beauty that one often associates with small Mediterranean islands, and is less pointedly touristy. Barely half an hour across the water, Isola di San Pietro presents a prettier picture with its pastel houses and bright bobbing fishing boats.

ISOLA DI SAN PIETRO

Boasting an elegant main town and some fine coastal scenery, Isola di San Pietro is a hugely popular summer destination. A mountainous trachyte island measuring about 15km long and 11km wide, it's named after St Peter who, legend has it, was marooned here during a storm on the way to Karalis (now Cagliari). The Romans had previously called it Accipitrum after the variety of falcons that nest here.

San Pietro's unique character and atmosphere come from its Genoese inhabitants,

ransomed from the Tunisian bey (governor) in 1736. Coral fishermen by profession, they had been sent to the island of Tabarka to harvest the precious commodity for the Lomellini family in Genoa. But they were abandoned to their fate and fell into miserable slavery until Carlo Emanuele III granted them refuge on San Pietro. Almost out of spite, North African pirates turned up in 1798 and made off with 1000 prisoners. It took five years for the Savoys to ransom them back. Even today the inhabitants of San Pietro speak *tabarkino*, a 16th-century version of Genoese.

Carloforte
pop 6430

The very image of Mediterranean chic, Carloforte offers a refined introduction to the island. Graceful *palazzi*, crowded cafes and palm trees line the busy waterfront while, behind, a creamy curve of stately buildings rises in a half-moon up the green hillside. There are no great sights as such, but a slow wander through the quaint, cobbled streets makes for a pleasant prelude to a seaside aperitif and a fine seafood meal at one of the town's wonderful restaurants.

INFORMATION

The helpful, multilingual **tourist office** (☎ 0781 85 40 09; www.prolococarloforte.it, in Italian; Piazza Carlo Emanuele III 19; ☒ 9.30am-12.30pm & 4.30-7.30pm Mon-Sat & Sun morning May-Sep, 10am-1pm & 5-8pm Mon-Sat & Sun morning Oct-Apr) can assist with any queries. Another useful source of information is the website www.carloforte.net, although at present it's only in Italian.

You can get money from the ATM at **Banca Intesa** (Corso Cavour 1) on the waterfront.

SIGHTS & ACTIVITIES

Uphill from the seafront, the modest **Museo Civico** (☎ 0781 85 58 80; Via Cisterna del Re; adult/child €2/1; ☒ 9am-1pm Tue & Sat, 10am-1pm & 3-6pm Wed, 3-7pm Thu & Fri, 10am-1pm Sun) is housed in a small 18th-century fort, one of the first masonry buildings to go up on the island. Of chief interest is the Tonnara Room, dedicated to the island's tradition of tuna fishing. Continuing the nautical theme, there's an assortment of boating bric-a-brac and a small collection of Mediterranean sea shells.

Aside from this one museum and the pretty distractions of the town, most of San Pietro's

TUNA IN THE EYE OF THE STORM

San Pietro islanders have fishing in the blood. For centuries the annual tuna slaughter, the *mattanza*, has been the island's biggest event. The *mattanza* is held in late May, early June, when schools of tuna stream between Isola Piana and San Pietro en route to their mating grounds. Waiting to entrap them is an elaborate system of nets that channel the tuna into a series of enclosures culminating in the *camera della morte* (chamber of death). Once enough tuna are imprisoned here, the fishermen close in and the *mattanza* begins (the word is derived from the Spanish for 'killing'). It's a bloody affair – up to eight or more fishermen at a time sink huge hooks into the thrashing tuna. Even today the *mattanza* forms the centrepiece of the big annual festival, the Girotonno. However, recent concerns about diminishing tuna stocks have placed the practice at the centre of unprecedented attention.

Driving the ever-increasing demand for bluefin tuna is Japan's insatiable appetite for sushi and sashimi (Japanese buyers snap up about 80% of the tuna caught in the Med). Tuna fishing is now a multimillion-dollar global business, and there are estimated to be around 300 tuna-fishing boats in the Mediterranean, many capable of catching up to 3000 tuna in one haul. Spotter planes have been banned by the International Commission for the Conservation of Atlantic Tunas (ICCAT), but illegal fishing remains commonplace.

Set against this context, the amount of tuna caught in Carloforte's *mattanza* is a drop in the ocean – in 2008 160 tonnes of tuna were caught against a ICCAT quota for the Med of 22,000 tonnes. But its cruelty and stark imagery – blue water turning red with blood – provides critics with a powerful visual tool in the campaign to preserve the Mediterranean tuna. Conservation groups and environmental organisations are deeply concerned about the effect industrial-scale fishing is having on the area's tuna stocks and are loudly calling for a lowering of fishing quotas. But with powerful business lobbies equally determined to oppose any such measures, it's not an issue that's going to go away any time soon.

pleasures are to be had elsewhere, either at sea or exploring the island's untamed coastline.

Operating out of a booth on the *lungomare* (seafront), **Cartur Dea** (☎ 0781 85 43 31; molo Tagliafico) is one of several outfits offering boat tours of the island. These cost €20 per person and take you round the coastal cliffs, grottoes and offshore sea stacks.

If you want to take to sea yourself, **Carloforte Sail Charter** (☎ 347 273 32 68; www.carlofortesailcharter .it, in Italian; Via Danero 52) has a fleet of sailing boats available for charter with or without a skipper – reckon on from €1500 per week. Divers can choose from several outfits including **Isla Diving** (☎ 0781 85 56 34; Viale dei Cantieri), on the main waterfront, and **Carloforte Tonnare Diving Center** (☎ 349 690 49 69; www.tonnaradive.it; Localita La Punta), which offers the chance to dive with tuna fish. Dives start at about €65.

FESTIVALS & EVENTS

Girotonno (www.girotonno.org) The island's main annual event is this four-day festival held in late May, early June. Dedicated to the tuna catch of the *mattanza* (see the boxed text, above), this festival features cooking competitions, tastings, seminars, concerts and various nautical-themed events. In 2008 it also incorporated the island's first ever **Buskers Festival**.

The musical theme continues with the **Creuza de Mà**, a three-day festival in September dedicated to cinema music. Check with the tourist office for details.

SLEEPING

Hotel California (☎ 078 185 44 70; www.hotelcalifor niacarloforte.it; Via Cavallera 15; s €32-50, d €44-90) This superfriendly family-run *pensione* is in a residential street a few blocks back from the *lungomare*. It's a modest place but its spacious, sun-filled rooms are more than adequate and its location ensures a good night's sleep.

our pick **Hotel Riviera** (☎ 0781 85 41 01; www .hotelriviera-carloforte.com, in Italian; Corso Battellieri 26; s €75-120, d €120-190, ste €250-370; ⊠) Right on the seafront, this swank, but decidedly unsnooty four-star, exudes urban chic. Its cool-tiled rooms are startlingly modern with unfussy linear furniture, white colour schemes and lavish marble-clad bathrooms. Some also have sea views and balconies, although these can cost up to €30 extra.

Hotel Hieracon (☎ 0781 85 40 28; www.hotelhi eracon.com; Corso Cavour 63; d with view €140-220, without view €90-160; 🔲) Recently restored to its art nouveau best, this seafront mansion is a fine place to stay. Period furniture and original oil paintings adorn rooms, and there's a tranquil garden where you can snooze under the palm trees. To eat at the hotel restaurant, budget for at least €30.

EATING

Tuna is the king of *tabarkina* cuisine, as the island style of cooking is known. You'll also be able to sample a fine *cuscus* (a variety of the North African couscous) alongside *zuppa di pesce* (fish soup). For those who don't eat seafood, Genoese *farinata* (a pizza-style flatbread made from chickpea flour and olives) and pesto also make a welcome appearance on many local menus.

Ristorante Pizzeria Al Castello (☎ 0781 85 62 83; Via Castello 5; pizzas €6, meals around €25; ☽ Mon-Sat) At the top of town near the Museo Civico, this restaurant is where locals come to get their pizza. It's a friendly, laid-back place with a spacious dining room and comprehensive menu. Alongside pizza, there's a full selection of pastas and mains including tuna, and it's well worth the short but steep climb to get here.

Osteria della Tonnara (☎ 078 185 57 34; Corso Battellieri 36; meals around €35; ☽ Jun-Sep) Located at the southern end of San Pietro's seafront, this small restaurant is run by the island's tuna cooperative. Not surprisingly, tuna dominates the menu, appearing in dishes such as tuna and pesto lasagne and the ubiquitous but tasty *tonno alla carlofortina* (tuna roasted and served with a tomato sauce). Booking is recommended and credit cards are not accepted.

Tonno di Corsa (☎ 0781 85 51 06; Via Marconi 47; meals around €45; ☽ Tue-Sun) This refined restaurant is the place to try tuna cooked in ways you've probably never seen before – smoked, in ragu, as tripe. Tuna tripe, known locally as *belu*, is not for everyone, but if you're tempted it's cooked in a casserole with potatoes and onions.

Da Nicolo (☎ 0781 85 40 48; Corso Cavour 32; meals around €55; ☽ Tue-Sun) A bastion of San Pietro cuisine, this island institution sits in elegant splendour on the seafront. Tables are laid out with starched formality in a glass pavilion, ready for diners who come from far and wide to try the magnificent tuna and light local couscous.

DRINKING & ENTERTAINMENT

The *lungomare* is the place where it's at. Just off the seafront, **Barone Rosso** (Via XX Settembre 26; ☽ noon-3pm & 7pm-2am Tue-Sun Mar-Oct, evening only Dec-Mar) is a popular bar with a kitsch interior, lively tunes and a few street tables. Another good option in a similar vein is **L'Oblò** (☎ 0781 85 70 40; Via Garibaldi 23; ☽ 7.30-11pm Wed-Mon mid-May–mid-Sep).

The only disco on the island, **Disco Marlin** (☎ 0781 85 01 21; ☽ 10pm-4am Sat & Sun Jul, nightly Aug) is out of Carloforte, near the *tonnara* (tuna processing plant) on the way to Punta. You'll really need a car, or a lift, to get here.

The popular La Caletta beach is also the scene of dancing fun, with summer beach parties pounding on until dawn.

GETTING THERE & AWAY

There's a **Saremar** (☎ 0781 85 40 05; www.saremar.it, in Italian; Piazza Carlo Emanuele III 29) ticket office on the *lungomare*. Regular ferries depart for Portovesme (per person/car €2.60/7.60, 30 minutes, 15 daily) and Calasetta (per person/car €2.30/6, seven daily) on the neighbouring island of Sant'Antioco.

Delcomar (☎ 0781 85 71 23; www.delcomar.it, in Italian) runs up to 14 night services to and from Calasetta. It operates a ticket booth just in front of where the ferries dock. The crossing costs €5/15 per person/car.

Between July and September, FMS buses run from Carloforte to La Punta (12 minutes, two daily), La Caletta (15 minutes, nine daily) and Capo Sandalo (18 minutes, two daily). Single/return tickets cost €1.

Around the Island

A quick 5.5km drive north of Carloforte brings you to La Punta, a desolate, windswept point with views over to the offshore islet Isola Piana. In May and June it's here that you'll witness the frenzied *mattanza*, in front of the *tonnara*. A dilapidated set of stone buildings littered with rusty anchors and smelly nets, the island's old tuna processing plant is now home to the Carloforte Tonnare Diving Center (see opposite), which as well as organising dives also runs guided tours of the old plant; contact the Diving Centre to organise a time.

Most of the island's best beaches are in the south. **Spiaggia La Bobba** looks onto two great stone *colonne* (columns) that rise out of the sea, giving the island's southernmost point its name, **Punta delle Colonne**. Continue westwards

---

CRUSADE TO SAVE THE ISLAND'S ASS

Tres cosas sunt reversas in su mundu: s' arveghe, s' ainu, e i sa femmina (There are three stubborn things in this world: sheep, donkeys and women). Sardinian proverbs tend to be cynical and to the point, evoking rural images to bludgeon home their earthy messages. Central to much of this imagery is the *asinello sardo* (Sardinian donkey), which was introduced to the island in the 3rd millennium BC from Egypt.

An affectionate and reliable worker, the diminutive *asinello* is also a regular on Sardinian menus, and with an increasing number being run over, its numbers are dwindling.

This was all the spur that Giorgio Mazzucchetti needed to jack in his work as an industrial consultant in Milan and embark on a crusade to save the loveable ass. Already enamoured with the island after numerous holidays, he bought a farm near Cala Fico on the west coast and began breeding the endangered donkeys. Starting off with 10 in 1999, he now has a healthy herd of 80.

Signore Mazzucchetti receives no official funding for his operation so is dependent on voluntary contributions and the money he raises from the occasional sale. You can help him out by visiting the **Fattoria degli Asinelli** (☎ 333 144 29 93; Localita Cala Fico; ☽ every afternoon 'until it gets dark'), near the Faro on Cala Fico, and leaving a small donation.

---

and you come to the island's most popular beach, **La Caletta** (also known as Spiaggia Spalmatore), a relatively modest arc of fine sand closed off by cliffs. Further south you can detour to view the spectacular coastline of **La Conca**.

There's some wonderful walking to be had on **Capo Sandalo**, the westernmost point of the island. From the car park near the lighthouse, a series of marked trails heads through the rocky red scrubland that carpets the cliffs. It's not exactly hard-core trekking, but you'll feel safer in a pair of walking boots.

En route to Capo Sandalo (it's only about a 20-minute drive from Carloforte), take a minute to stop off at the rocky inlet of **Cala Fico**, one of the island's most photographed spots and, along with **Isola del Corno**, home to a nesting colony of Eleonora falcons.

Accommodation is pretty thin on the ground outside of Carloforte, but the tourist office can provide a full list of B&Bs for the island.

Signposted off the road to Capo Sandalo, and at the end of a long dirt track, the salmon-pink **Hotel La Valle** (☎ 078 185 70 01; www.hotellavalle .com; Localita Commende; s €40-100, d €60-150; **P** ✖ ⚊) is a lovely rural complex in the midst of thick bush. With its tennis court, swimming pool and bright rooms, it's a wonderful place to escape the world.

If you haven't got a car, and even if you have, the ideal way to explore the island is by bike. Distances are not huge, and even if there's some hill work there's nothing too

dramatic. Between June and September you can hire bikes and scooters in Carloforte, at the **newsagents** (☎ 0781 85 41 23) at Piazza Repubblica 4. Bank on €10 for a bike per day, and from €21 to €37 for a scooter.

ISOLA DI SANT'ANTIOCO

Larger and less exuberant than Isola San Pietro, Isola di Sant'Antioco is Italy's fourth-largest island (after Sicily, Sardinia and Elba). Unlike many Mediterranean islands it's not dramatically beautiful – although it's by no means ugly – and it exudes no sense of isolation. Instead it feels very much part of Sardinia, both in character and look. The animated main town is an authentic working port, and the green, rugged interior looks like much of southern Sardinia.

In fact, since Roman times, the island has been physically linked to the Sardinian mainland by bridge – the ruins of the Roman structure lie to the right of the modern road bridge.

There are two ways of approaching the island. The simplest is to follow the SS126 south from Iglesias and Carbonia and cross the bridge to the town of Sant'Antioco. Clunkier and more romantic is the car ferry between Calasetta and Carloforte in San Pietro.

Sant'Antioco
pop 11,900

Although Isola di Sant'Antioco has been inhabited since prehistoric times, the town of Sant'Antioco was founded by the Phoenicians in the 8th century BC. Known as Sulci, it was Sardinia's industrial capital and an important port until the demise of the Roman Empire more than a millennium later. It owes its current name to St Antiochus, a Roman slave who brought Christianity to the island when exiled here in the 2nd century AD.

Evidence of the town's ancient past is not hard to find – the hilltop historic centre is riddled with Phoenician necropolises and fascinating archaeological litter.

ORIENTATION

Sant'Antioco is surprisingly big. By car, you'll approach the centre along Via Nazionale, which becomes Via Roma as it runs onto Piazza Italia. Here it changes name once again, becoming Corso Vittorio Emanuele, Sant'Antioco's main strip. From Piazza Umberto I at the end, Via Garibaldi leads down to the lively seafront stretch Lungomare Cristoforo Colombo, and Via Regina Margherita climbs to the heart of the old town.

INFORMATION

The local **tourist office** (☎ 0781 8 20 31; Piazza Repubblica 31a; ⏱ 10am-1pm & 5-9pm Mon-Fri) can help with information.

To access money, you'll find ATMs on Piazza Italia and Piazza Umberto I.

SIGHTS & ACTIVITIES

Hidden behind the modest baroque facade of the **Basilica di Sant'Antioco Martire** (☎ 078 18 30 44; Piazza Parrocchia 22; ⏱ 9am-noon & 3-6pm Mon-Sat, 10-11am & 3-6pm Sun) is a sublimely simple 5th-century church.

To the right of the altar stands a wooden effigy of St Antiochus, his dark complexion a sign of his North African origins. Refusing to recant his faith, Antiochus was shipped off by the Romans to work as a slave in the mines of the Iglesiente. But he escaped, hidden in a tar barrel, and was taken in by an underground Christian group who hid him in the church's extensive **catacombs** (admission €2.50; ⏱ 9am-noon & 3-6pm Mon-Sat, 10-11am & 3-6pm Sun).

Accessible only by guided tour, the catacombs consist of a series of burial chambers, some dating to Punic times, used by Christians between the 2nd and 7th centuries. The dead of well-to-do families went into elaborate, frescoed family niches

in the walls; a few fragments of fresco still remain. Middle-class corpses were wound up in unadorned niches, and commoners placed in ditches in the floor. A few skeletons lying *in situ* render the idea a little more colourfully.

Rising uphill from the basilica, Via Castello is named after the 19th-century Piedmontese fort, **Forte Su Pisu** (admission €2.50; ⏱ 9am-8pm Apr-Sep, 9.30am-1pm & 3-6pm Oct-Mar), which marks the highest point in town. Further down the road, and spread over the hill, are the tombs of the **necropolis** (closed to the public). Another 500m or so downhill is an 8th-century BC **tophet** (admission incl Museo Archeologico €7; ⏱ 9am-7pm Wed-Sun Apr-Sep, 9.30am-1pm & 3-6pm Oct-Mar Wed-Sun), a sanctuary where the Phoenicians and Carthaginians buried their still-born babies.

Adjacent to the *tophet*, the recently renovated **Museo Archeologico** (☎ 0781 80 05 96; www .archeotur.it, in Italian; admission €6/2; ⏱ 9am-7pm Wed-Sun Apr-Sep, 9.30am-1pm & 3-6pm Oct-Mar Wed-Sun) contains a fascinating collection of local archaeological finds, as well as a model of the town as it would have looked in the 4th century BC. Armed with a useful explanatory folder, you'll discover that the impressive pair of stone lions in the main corridor once guarded the town gates, as was customary in Phoenician towns, and that the panther mosaic at the end of the main section once adorned a Roman *triclinium* (dining room).

Back in the historic centre, you can investigate age-old living habits at the **Museo Etnografico** (Via Necropoli 24a; admission €3; ⏱ 9am-8pm Apr-Sep, 9.30am-1pm & 3-6pm Oct-Mar), with its assortment of traditional farm and household implements, and the **Villaggio Ipogeo** (admission €2.50), a series of Punic tombs that once housed the poorest of the town's poor.

To get out of town and explore the island, **Euromoto** (☎ 0781 84 09 07; Via Nazionale 57; ⏱ 9am-1pm & 4-8pm) hires out bikes and scooters for €8 and €30, as well as organising guided bike rides. These are led by volunteers, so there's no fixed rate, although you're more than welcome to leave a tip.

FESTIVALS & EVENTS

Held over four days around the second Sunday after Easter, the **Festa di Sant'Antioco** celebrates the city's patron saint with processions, traditional music, dancing, fireworks and concerts. It is one of the oldest documented saint's festivities on the island, dating to 1519.

SOUTHWEST SARDINIA

SOUTHWEST SARDINIA

SLEEPING & EATING

Hotel La Matta (☎ 0781 82 81 02; www.hotel-lamatta .com; Via Nazionale 125; s €40-75, d €70-120; ❄) Near the entrance to town, this is a small, family-run hotel with clean, cosy rooms. There's nothing particularly memorable about the decor, but the bathrooms are modern and the beds are firm. If possible ask for a room away from the main road as noise can be a nuisance.

Hotel del Corso (☎ 0781 80 02 65; www.hoteldelcorso.it; Corso Vittorio Emanuele 32; s €44-60, d €69-100; ❄) In the heart of the action, this polished three-star sits on top of the Cafè del Corso, one of the smartest and most popular drinking spots. Rooms are well-appointed, if rather characterless.

Hotel Eden (☎ 078 184 07 68; www.albergoleden.com; Piazza Parrocchia 15; s €45-50, d €65-80; ❄) A hotel with its own catacomb – now there's something to write home about. Ask the friendly owner to take you downstairs and he'll proudly point out where you can see skulls and crossbones in the dank grottoes. The hotel's homey rather than elegant, and the rooms, which can be small, are a little tired round the edges.

Various restaurants, pizzerias and snack spots are dotted about the town.

our pick **Tamarindo Blu** (☎ 0781 80 20 96; Via Azuni 28; meals around €25; ❄ Thu-Tue), which serves delicious seafood, is one of the best. Don't let the over-the-top nautical paraphernalia put you off the really very good food, served in vast portions. It's all tasty, but standout options include the mixed antipasto and grilled fish.

On the main strip, **Pizzeria Biancaneve** (☎ 0781 80 04 67; Corso Vittorio Emanuele 110; pizzas €7.50) does a roaring trade serving passers-by with pizza.

ENTERTAINMENT

The action is centred on two streets: Corso Vittorio Emanuele and, down by the sea, Lungomare Cristoforo Colombo.

Pierre (☎ 078 180 04 55; Corso Vittorio Emanuele 86; ❄ 8pm-late Wed-Mon) Wooden pews and beer on tap give this popular spot an almost authentic pub feel. It can get pretty busy on summer nights and musters up a good atmosphere.

Bar Colombo (Lungomare Cristoforo Colombo 94; ❄ Tue-Sun) One of a rash of bars and cafes on the seafront, this is where crusty fishermen come for their morning coffee, which explains why it opens for business at 4am. In summer, drinkers swell onto the outside pavement.

Also in summer, frequent free concerts are staged in Piazza Umberto I, ranging from local pop to traditional Sardinian tunes.

GETTING THERE & AWAY

Ferries connect Calasetta with Carloforte on Isola di San Pietro; see p91).

There are seven daily buses between Calasetta, Sant'Antioco (Piazza Repubblica), Carbonia (€1, 50 minutes), as well as Iglesias (€4, 1¾ hours).

Around the Island

The island's better beaches lie to the south of Sant'Antioco. About 5km south of town, **Maladroxia** is a small resort with a couple of hotels and a pleasant beach and port. You could do worse than stay at **Hotel Scala Longa** (☎ 0781 81 72 02; r €45-65, half board per person €50-65; ❄ mid-Apr–mid-Sep), a good-value one-star with seven simple rooms in a pretty villa by the port road.

Back on the main road, you pass inland before hitting a big roundabout. Head left (east) to reach Spiaggia Coa Quaddus, a wild and woolly beach about 3km short of **Capo Sperone**, the southernmost point of the island; or head right for the island's windy southwest coast. The best of beaches around here is **Cala Lunga**, where the road peters out. Before you reach the beach you'll pass the **Campeggio Tonnara** (☎ 078 180 90 58; tonnaracamping@tiscali.it; Localita Cala Saboni; per person/tent €11.30/19, 4-person bungalows €30-55; ❄ Apr-Sep), a well-equipped and wonderfully remote camping ground.

Calasetta, the island's second town, is located 10km northwest of Sant'Antioco. The town was originally founded by Ligurian families from Tabarka in 1769. There's little of great interest here, except for several beaches a few kilometres south on the northwestern coast.

To stay near the lovely **Spiaggia Le Saline** (Salina), campers can pitch their tents at the **Camping Le Saline** (☎ 0781 8 86 15; www .campinglesaline.com, in Italian; per person/tent/car €11/10/2.50, 2-person bungalow €60-90) a decent site that also boasts a pizzeria, kids' playground and tennis court.

Only a few kilometres outside Calasetta, the well-signposted **Hotel Luci del Faro** (☎ 0781 81 00 89; www.hotellucidelfaro.com; Localita Mangiabarche; s €62-140, d €92-210, half-board per person €66-128; Ⓟ ❄ 🖵 ⧉) stands in glorious solitude on an exposed plain near **Spiaggia Grande**, the island's best-known beach. Popular with cyclists, it's an excellent, family-friendly three-star with simple, sunny rooms, sweeping views and a relaxed atmosphere.

SOUTH COAST

Largely overlooked by Sardinia's publicists, the island's southern coast is quite magnificent. The central stretch, known as the Costa del Sud, is a dazzling 20km spectacle of twisting, turning road above rugged cliffs that plunge into the tantalising blue sea.

PORTO BOTTE TO PORTO DI TEULADA

Stretching 15km along Sardinia's southwestern tip, this tract of coastline is a patchwork of pine woods, lagoons and beaches. Of the beaches, the best, and busiest, is the fabulous **Spiaggia Porto Pino**, at the homonymous resort near Sant'Anna Arresi. A favourite with weekending locals, this broad swath of creamy sand is lapped by lovely, shallow waters ideal for tentative toddlers and nervous swimmers. There's ample parking and a string of cheap and cheerful pizzerias near the parking lot.

A second beach, **Spiaggia Sabbie Bianche**, just south of Porto Pino, and accessible on foot, is famous for its soft, silky dunes. However, as it's on military land, it's off limits to the public outside of July and August.

Just off the main road into Porto Pino, **Camping Sardegna** (☎ /fax 0781 96 70 13; per person/tent €6.50/10.40, 4-person bungalows €50-65; ❤ mid-May–Sep) has basic camping facilities in a pine grove on the beach. Nearby, the **Hotel Cala dei Pini** (☎ 0781 50 87; www.caladeipini.com; Localita Porto Pino; B&B per person €40-50, full-board per person per week €400-990; P ❤ ❤) is a big, modern affair, favoured by tour operators. It's not a bad option in the low season, but from June to September there's a minimum seven-night stay.

From Porto Pino you have no choice but to head inland to Sant'Anna Arresi. From here the SS195 swings south, bypassing a hilly triangle of land and Sardinia's southernmost point, Capo di Teulada. Like much of this area, the Capo is occupied by a controversial NATO base and so is usually inaccessible to the public. After 10km, branch south (away from the signs to Teulada) towards Porto di Teulada.

There are several beaches along this part of the coast, including **Cala Piombo** and **Porto Zafferano**, accessible only in July and August, and only by boat. You can pick up a boat at the small marina at **Porto di Teulada** near **Porto Tramatzu** beach.

Campers can stay at the **Portu Tramatzu Camping Comunale** (☎ 070 928 30 27; Localita Porto Tramatzu; per person/tent/car €10/9/5; ❤ week before Easter-Oct), which has modest facilities and an on-site diving centre near Porto di Teulada.

COSTA DEL SUD

One of Sardinia's most enchanting coastal drives, the Costa del Sud begins east of Porto di Teulada. The first stretch is just a prelude, passing several coves and gradually rising towards the high point of **Capo Malfatano**. As you wind your way around towards the cape, wonderful views of the coast repeatedly spring into view and just about every point is capped by a Spanish-era watchtower. Along the way, **Spiaggia Piscinni** is a great place for a dip. The sand's not amazing, but the water is an incredible colour.

Once around the bay and the next point, you could stop at **Cala Teuradda** to marvel at its vivid emerald-green water. It's a popular spot, which happens to be right by an ARST bus stop. In summer you'll find snack bars, too.

From here the road climbs inland away from the water. You can get a look at the coast here, too, if you take a narrow side road to the south at Porto Campana – it quickly turns to dust but does allow you to reach the lighthouse at **Capo Spartivento**. From here a series of beaches stretch north along the coast; watch out for signposts off the main coastal road to **Cala Cipolla**, a gorgeous spot backed by pine and juniper trees, **Spiaggia Su Giudeu** and **Porto Campana**.

At the end of this stretch you'll see another Spanish watchtower presiding over the popular summer resort of **Chia**. From the tower, you get grandstand views of the southern coast and Chia's two ravishing beaches – to the west, the long **Spiaggia Sa Colonia**; to the east, the smaller arc of **Spiaggia Su Portu**. A paradise for surfers, windsurfers and kitesurfers, these beaches play host to the annual Chia Classic surf and windsurf competition, usually held in early to mid-April.

For somewhere to stay, there's **Campeggio Torre Chia** (☎ 070 923 00 54; www.campeggiotorrechia.it; per person/tent/car €8.50/10.50/5, 4-person villas €80-120), a few hundred metres back from Spiaggia Su Portu, although it gets horribly busy in August.

Or you could try the down-to-earth **Il Gabbiano** (☎ 070 923 01 60; www.hotelilgabbiano.net; Localita Is Tramazzeddus; s €70-120, d €90-180; ❤ Easter-Oct;

(P) (X)), which has attractive, mini-bungalows dotted around a small garden.

For the ultimate view, check into the luxurious **Le Meridien Chia Laguna** (☎ 070 9 23 91; www .lemeridien-chialaguna.com; Localita Chig; s €195-1040, d €280-1040; ☽ Apr-Oct; P (X) (Ⓡ)).

From Cagliari, there are up to 10 daily ARST buses to/from Chia (€3, 1¼ hours). Then, between mid-June and mid-September, two daily buses ply the Costa del Sud, connecting Chia with Spiaggia Teulada (Porto di Teulada; €2, 35 minutes).

CHIA TO SANTA MARGHERITA DI PULA

Unless you're staying at one of the self-contained resort hotels that hog much of this part of the coast you're unlikely to glimpse much of the sea around here. Which is a crying shame because the 9km of coastline between Chia and Santa Margherita di Pula is the most beautiful on the southwest: a string of magnificent beaches lapped by crystalline waters and backed by fragrant pine woods. And it's here, in a wooded grove off the SS195, that you'll find the extraordinary **Forte Village** (☎ 070 92 15 16; www.fortevillage.com; s €290-1910, d €380-2158, half board per person €220-1110; Santa Margherita di Pula; P (X) (▢) (Ⓡ)), the godfather of all southern Sardinian resorts. Closed off to the world behind high security gates, this 250-sq km site is an unapologetic bastion of luxury with seven hotels, 10 swimming pools, shopping malls, bowling alleys, discos and up to a kilometre of beach frontage.

Fortunately, though, the area has not been completely taken over, and you can still find affordable, locally run accommodation.

Decent camping facilities are available at **Camping Flumendosa** (☎ 070 920 83 64; www.camp ingflumendosa.it; SS195km 33, Santa Margherita di Pula; per person/tent/car €8.50/8.50/2.50), about 50m or so from the beach.

ourpick **B&B Solivariu** (☎ 339 367 40 88; www.so livariu.it; SS195 km 33, Santa Margherita di Pula; per person €30-50; (X)) is an unpretentious farm B&B with three cool rooms and four colourful mini-apartments. Set amid fruit orchards – in winter you can have oranges fresh from the trees – 500m back from the beach, it offers few frills, just a genuine Sardinian welcome and hearty farm breakfasts (think *pecorino* cheese and fruit).

Opposite the camp ground is one of Santa Margherita di Pula's most reasonably priced hotels, **Hotel Mare Pineta** (☎ 070 920 83 61; www

.hotelflamingo.it; SS195km 33, Santa Margherita di Pula; half-board per person €63-115; ☽ end-May–end-Sep; P (X) (Ⓡ)), part of the more expensive Hotel Flamingo complex. It doesn't look like much from outside, but the rooms are fine and there's a vibrant tropical garden right on the edge of the beach.

ARST buses serve Santa Margherita di Pula from Cagliari (€3, one hour, nine daily).

PULA
pop 7120

Some 27km from Cagliari, Pula is a workaday, agricultural village best known for its vicinity to the Phoenician site of Nora. Apart from a small archaeological museum, there's no compelling reason to hang around, but if you do decide to stay, you'll find that village life centres on the vibrant, cafe-clad Piazza del Popolo.

Information on the immediate area is available from the **tourist office** (☎ 070 924 60 57; www .prolocopula.it, in Italian; c/o Centro Culturale Casa Frau, Piazza del Popolo; ☽ 9.30am-12.30pm & 3-6pm Mon-Fri) on the main square. You can check your email at **L'Isola del Viaggio** (☎ 070 920 83 73; Via Nora cnr Via Conte Corinaldi; per hr €4; ☽ 9am-1pm & 4.30-8pm Mon-Sat).

Sights
PULA
If you're planning to visit Nora, which you probably are if you're passing through Pula, a trip to the one-room **Museo Archeologico** (☎ 070 920 96 10; Corso Vittorio Emanuele 67; admission €2.50, incl Nora €5.50; ☽ 9am-8pm Tue-Sun May-Sep, 10am-1pm & 3-6.30pm Wed-Sun Oct-Apr) will help set the scene. Alongside ceramics found in Punic and Roman tombs, some gold and bone jewellery, and Roman glassware, there's a model of the Nora site and helpful explanations in both English and Italian.

NORA
Four kilometres south of Pula, the archaeological zone of Nora is the main sight in these parts. But before you get there, take a moment to stop off at the pint-sized **Chiesa di Sant'Efisio** (☎ 340 485 18 60; ☽ 4-7.30pm Sat, 10am-noon & 4-9.30pm Sun); you'll see it on the left as you drive towards Nora. This 12th-century Romanesque church was built on the prime beachside spot where the disgraced Roman commander Ephisius was executed for his Christian beliefs in AD 303. Despite its modest dimensions, it is the scene of great celebrations on 1 May as

pilgrims bring the effigy of St Ephisius here as part of Cagliari's Festa di Sant'Efisio (p65).

In Ephisius' day **Nora** (adult/child incl Museo Archeologico in Pula €5.50/2.50; 9am-7.30pm) was one of the most important cities on the island and the seat of Roman government, linked to Karalis (now Cagliari) in the east and Bythia in the west. However, the site was already an important trading centre long before the Romans arrived. Founded in the 11th century BC by Phoenicians from Spain, it later passed into Carthaginian hands before being taken over by the Romans in the 3rd century AD. But the town's position was exposed and by the Middle Ages it had been abandoned, the temples looted by Arab pirates and the marble columns broken.

These days only a fraction of the original site remains – much of the original city is underwater – and it's only when you reach the rocky outline of the promontory that you see any remnants of the once-great imperial city.

Upon entry, you pass a single melancholy **column** from the former temple of Tanit, the Carthaginian Venus, who was once worshipped here. Much of the glass in Pula's museum was found in this area, giving rise to theories that the whole temple may have been decorated with it. Beyond this is a small but beautifully preserved Roman **theatre** facing the sea. Towards the west are the substantial remains of the **Terme al Mare** (Baths by the Sea). Four columns (a tetrastyle) stand at the heart of what was a patrician villa; the surrounding rooms retain their mosaic floor decoration. More remnants of mosaics can be seen at a temple complex towards the tip of the promontory.

To explore the underwater ruins, contact **Conan Diving** (338 610 82 34; www.conandiving.com, in Italian; SS195 km 25), on the main SS195 between Pula and Santa Margherita di Pula.

Up to 16 local shuttle buses run between Pula and Nora.

LAGUNA DI NORA

Just before the entrance to the ancient site of Nora are the pleasant **Spiaggia di Nora** and, a little further around, the bigger **Spiaggia Su Guventeddu**. Note that you won't be permitted into the site in your bathing costume.

On the western side of the Nora promontory, you can often spy pink flamingos stalking around the Laguna di Nora. To learn more about the lagoon system and its aquatic fauna, visit the **Laguna di Nora didactic centre** (070 920 95 44; www.lagunadinora.it, in Italian; Jun-Sep), which has a small aquarium (adult/child €7/4) and runs summer excursions, including snorkelling tours (adult/child €25/12) and canoe excursions (adult/child €20/12).

Sleeping & Eating

Accommodation in Pula itself isn't up to much, but there are some lovely hotels on the road to Nora.

Nora Club Hotel (070 92 44 22; www.noraclubhotel.it; Viale Nora; s €85-130, d €125-160; P) Boasting a tranquil atmosphere and refined ambience, this polished hotel is one of Nora's few year-round options. The look is modern rustic with antique furniture and exposed wood beams married to plasma TVs and internet connections. Outside, the swimming pool shimmers in the lush garden.

Hotel Baia di Nora (070 924 55 51; www.hotelbaiadinora.com; Localita Su Guventeddu; half board per person €95-205; Apr-Oct; P) A swish four-star with all the trimmings, this is the sort of place you won't want to leave. OK, perhaps you might manage to stumble across the perfectly tended garden to the swimming pool bar, or even to the private beach.

In Pula, the cheapest option is the one-star **Quattro Mori** (070 920 91 24; Via Cagliari 10; s €30, s/d without bathroom €20/40), which has plain, fancy-free rooms above a bar near the Cagliari entrance to town.

Zio Dino (070 920 91 59; Viale Segni 14; pizzas €5, meals around €30; Mon-Sat) This difficult to miss pizzeria-cum-restaurant is a local favourite. With its name graffitied high on the wall, it serves a solid menu of pizza staples, seafood and meat dishes. The ambience leaves a little to be desired, but the food is fine and service is efficient.

Crazy Art Gelateria (Corso Vittorio Emanuele 4; gelati €2.70; 4pm-midnight Mon-Sat, noon-midnight Sun) This is the place to grab that most Italian of accessories, an ice cream. The challenge then is to look cool while licking it on Piazza del Popolo.

Getting There & Away

To get to Pula by public transport is easy – there are up to 20 daily ARST buses from Cagliari (€2, 50 minutes).

CAMPIDANO

One of Sardinia's most important agricultural zones, the Campidano is a broad, flat corridor of land extending northwest from Cagliari. The dusty yellow landscape can be a little dispiriting, especially on torrid summer days when temperatures soar and the area seems enveloped in a thick grey heat haze, but it's not totally devoid of interest.

UTA, CASTELLO DI ACQUAFREDDA & SAN SPERATE

Barely 20km northwest of Cagliari, at the eastern edge of the sprawling farm town of Uta, is one of the finest Romanesque churches in southern Sardinia. The **Chiesa di Santa Maria** (follow the brown signs for the Santuario di Santa Maria), built around 1140 by Vittorini monks from Marseille, is remarkable above all for the variegated statuary that runs around the top of its exterior.

Continuing west along the main SS131 dual carriageway, consider a quick diversion at the Siliqua crossroads, 14km west of Uta. About 5km to the south you'll see the fairy-tale image of castle ruins atop an extraordinary craggy mount. As you get closer, you come to realise that little more than the crumbling walls of the **Castello di Acquafredda** remain. The castle served as a temporary hiding place for Guelfo della Gherardesca when his father Ugolino, the reviled ruler of Iglesias, was imprisoned in Pisa and the family banished.

South of the *castello*, the **Riserva Naturale Foresta di Monte Arcosu** is a World Wildlife Fund reserve run by the **Cooperativa Il Caprifoglio** (☎ 070 96 87 14; www.ilcaprifoglio.it; admission €5; ⊙ 9am-5pm Sat & Sun) and one of the few remaining habitats of the *cervo sardo*. Covering the peak of Monte Arcosu (948m), it also harbours wild boar, martens, wildcats, weasels and plenty of birds of prey.

Some 12km northeast of Uta, San Sperate is famous for the colourful *murales* that brighten its stone walls. However, unlike those in Orgosolo, they don't represent keenly felt injustices; instead, they present a Daliesque tableau of traditional country life. Highlights include the epic *Storia di San Sperate* (Story of San Sperate) on Via Sassari. This was begun by Pinuccio Sciola (born

1942), a local sculptor who was inspired by the Mexican artist Diego Rivera.

ARST buses run to Uta from Cagliari (€1.50, 45 minutes, 10 Monday to Friday, three Sunday), although the church is about a half-hour walk from the centre. For San Sperate, buses run hourly from Cagliari (€1.50, 30 minutes). To get to Castello di Acquafredda, you'll need your own transport.

SANLURI
pop 8570

One of the biggest towns in the Medio Campidano province, Sanluri is a bustling agricultural centre. In the 14th century Queen Eleonora d'Arborea lived here for a period and it was a key member of her opposition to Catalano-Aragonese expansion. In 1409 island resistance was finally crushed at the Battle of Sanluri, paving the way for centuries of Iberian domination. Unfortunately, little remains to vouch for the town's former glory apart from Eleonora's squat, brooding castle.

Just off the main thoroughfare, Via Carlo Felice, the castle today houses the **Museo Risorgimentale Duca d'Aosta** (☎ 070 930 71 05; Via Generale Nino Villa Santa 1; adult/concession €6/4; ⊙ 4.30-9pm Tue-Mon, 10am-1pm & 4.30-9pm Sun Jul-mid Sep, 9.45-1pm & 3-7pm Sun mid-Sep–Jun) and its eclectic collection of assorted military paraphernalia. The garden displays a medieval catapult, torpedo and a couple of mortars, while inside you're treated to an extraordinary array of objects, from period furniture to military mementos from a number of modern conflicts.

A short walk away – cross Via Carlo Felice, follow Via San Rocco for a few hundred metres, and then take a left towards the Franciscan monastery at the top of the rise – is the **Museo Etnografico Cappuccino** (☎ 070 930 71 07; Via San Rocco 6; admission €3; ⊙ appointment only). This houses yet another varied collection, comprising obsidian arrowheads and Roman-era coins, farm tools, clocks and works of religious art.

Sanluri is well served by ARST bus with regular connections to/from Cagliari (€3, one hour).

SARDARA
pop 4270

Some 8km northwest of Sanluri along the SS131, Sardara is a sleepy village built around an attractive stone core. Rising in the centre of the village, the **Chiesa di San Gregorio** (Piazza San

Gregorio) makes a fetching landmark. Built between 1300 and 1325 in a mixed Romanesque Gothic style, it boasts a sombre, soaring facade and a pretty rose window.

Further uphill is the **Civico Museo Archeologico Villa Abbas** (☎ 070 938 61 83; www.coopvillabbas.sardegna .it; Piazza Liberta 7; admission €2.60, incl Chiesa di Sant'Anastasia €4.50; ⏰ 9am-1pm & 5-8pm Tue-Sun Jun-Sep, 9am-1pm & 4-7pm Oct-May), whose collection comprises finds from local archaeological sights. Among the finest pieces are two bronze statuettes found on the edge of Sardara in 1913 and dating to the 8th century BC. Outside, excavations have been carried out on the Sa Costa site that forms the museum's back yard.

You'll find more of archaeological interest a few hundred metres away at the **Area Archeologico & Chiesa di Sant'Anastasia** (☎ 070 938 61 83; www.coopvillabbas.sardegna.it; Piazza Sant'Anastasia; admission incl Civico Museo €4.50; ⏰ 9am-1pm & 5-8pm Tue-Sun Jun-Sep, 9am-1pm & 4-7pm Oct-May). The small Gothic church sits in the midst of what was once a much larger nuraghic temple complex. The focus of worship was an underground well temple, known as *Sa funtana de is dolus* (Fountain of Pain), and accessible from beneath the church (enter to your left as you face the church entrance).

A few kilometres west of the town (on the other side of the SS131) is **Santa Maria de Is Acquas**, the site of thermal baths since Roman times. About 4km to the south, a dirt road leads to the empty walls of the **Castello Monreale**, built by the governor of Arborea and used as a temporary refuge by the defeated troops of Brancaleone Doria after the Battle of Sanluri. The Catalano-Aragonese garrisoned it for a time in 1478, but thereafter it soon fell into disuse. You can see some of the colourful medieval ceramics and other material dug up in the castle in Sardara's museum.

Accommodation in Sardara is not up to much, but the town is within easy striking distance of Cagliari, and regular ARST buses connect with the capital (€4, 1¼ hours, 12 Monday to Saturday, four Sunday).

LA MARMILLA

Northeast of Sardara, the landscape takes on a livelier aspect as dusty plains give way to the undulating green hills of La Marmilla. Named after these low-lying mounds –

marmilla is derived from *mammellare*, meaning 'breast shaped' – La Marmilla is an area of bucolic scenery and quiet, rural life. It's also one of Sardinia's richest archaeological regions and it's here, in the shadow of the table-topped high plain known as La Giara di Gesturi, that you'll find the island's best-known nuraghic site, the Unesco-listed Nuraghe Su Nuraxi.

VILLANOVAFORRU & NURAGHE GENNA MARIA
pop 690

On the southern fringes of La Marmilla, Villanovaforru is a manicured, pretty little village that attracts coachloads of visitors to its archaeological sites. The village itself boasts a worthwhile museum, while a short hop to the west is the important *nuraghe* settlement of Genna Maria.

Housed in an attractive 19th-century *palazzo* in the village centre, the **Museo Archeologico** (☎ 070 930 00 50; Piazza Costituzione 4; admission €3.50, incl Nuraghe €5; ⏰ 9.30am-1pm & 3.30-7pm Tue-Sun Apr-Sep, to 6pm Oct-Mar) provides a good overview of the area's prehistoric past with finds from many local sites, including Su Nuraxi and Genna Maria. Exhibits run the gamut from nuraghic times with enormous amphorae and other pots, oil lamps, jewellery and coins.

Adjacent to the museum, the **Sala delle Mostre** (admission €1.50; ⏰ 9.30am-1pm & 3.30-7pm Tue-Sun Apr-Sep, to 6pm Oct-Mar) often hosts temporary exhibitions on local life and history.

The complex of **Nuraghe Genna Maria** (☎ 070 930 00 50; admission €2.50, incl Museo Archeologico €5; ⏰ 9.30am-1pm & 3.30-7pm Tue-Sun Apr-Sep, to 6pm Oct, Feb & Mar, 9.30am-1pm & 2.30-5pm Nov-Jan), signposted as the Parco Archeologico, is about 1km out of the village on the road to Collinas. The *nuraghe* is a tumbledown site but, archaeologically speaking, one of the most important on the island. It consists of a central tower, around which was later raised the three-cornered bastion. Much later an encircling wall was also raised to protect an Iron Age village, but little of it remains today.

To the northeast of the village, indicated off the road to Lunamatrona, the **Museo del Territorio Sa Corona Arrùbia** (☎ 070 934 10 09; www .museosacoronarrubia.it; Localita Lunamatrona; admission €6, incl chair lift €8; ⏰ 9am-1pm & 3-7pm Tue-Fri, 9am-7pm Sat & Sun) showcases the area's flora and fauna with recreations of four different natural habitats. Best of all, though, it has a *seggiovia* (chairlift), which whisks you up to a viewing point on the Giara di Siddi.

ourpick Agriturismo Su Boschettu (☎ 070 93 96 95, 3334797401; www.suboschettu.it; Localita Pranu Laccu; B&B per person €30, meals around €20-25) is a charming farm-stay nestled amid olive groves and fruit trees. Rooms are modest, but the setting is wonderfully relaxing and the food local and quite delicious.

Residence Funtana Noa (☎ 070 933 10 19; www .residencefuntananoa.it; Via Vittorio Emanuele III 66-68; s/d €42/65, half board per person €50; 🖭) offers tasteful three-star accommodation in a large, airy palazzo just down from the village centre. The style is rustic with plenty of heavy timber, antique-style furniture and brick arches.

Two ARST buses run here from Cagliari on weekdays (€4, 1½ hours). There are also services to/from Sardara (€1, 15 minutes, five Monday to Saturday) and Sanluri (€1, 15 minutes, three Monday to Saturday).

LAS PLASSAS

Zigzagging northeast from Villanovaforru, you find yourself heading in the direction of Barumini. Long before you hit this town, you will see the ruined walls of the 12th-century **Castello di Marmilla** atop a conical hill beside the hamlet of Las Plassas. The castle was part of the defensive line built on the frontier with Cagliari province by the medieval rulers of Arborea.

To get there, take the left fork (for Tuili) at the beginning of Las Plassas and you will see on your left a winding footpath to the top of this hill.

BARUMINI
pop 1380

From Las Plassas, the road leads through the voluptuous landscape to Barumini, a typical rural village of grey stone houses and quiet lanes. Guarding the crossroads at the village centre is the tiny **Chiesa di Santa Tecla**, a 17th-century church sporting a lovely, curvaceous rose window.

Nearby, the **Polo Museale Casa Zapata** (☎ 070 936 81 28; Piazza Giovanni XXIII; admission €7, incl Nuraghe Su Nuraxi €10; 🕙 10am-1.30pm & 3-7.30pm) is an attractive museum complex housed in the 16th-century residence of the Spanish Zapata family. The whitewashed villa was originally built over a 1st-millennium BC nuraghic settlement which has been skilfully incorporated into the museum's display. Here you'll also find

artefacts taken from the nearby Su Nuraxi *nuraghe*, as well as a section dedicated to the Zapata dynasty, La Marmilla's 16th-century rulers, and a small collection of agricultural tools and instruments.

A kilometre west of the village, the **Parco Sardegna in Miniatura** (☎ 070 936 10 04; www.sardegna inminiatura.it, in Italian; adult/child €12/10; 🕙 9am-5pm Mon-Sat, to 6pm Sun) is a miniature reconstruction of the whole island. One for the kids, it has a play area and plenty of picnic tables.

The nicest of Barrumi's hotels is **Albergo Sa Lolla** (☎ 070 936 84 19; www.wels.it/salolla/; Via Cavour 49 s €42-47, d €55-65, half board per person €55-60; 🅿 🖭), a tastefully refurbished farmstead with seven airy rooms and an excellent restaurant (meals €25). Breakfast costs €6. You'll need to book in July and August.

NURAGHE SU NURAXI

Sardinia's single Unesco-listed site, and the island's most famous *nuraghe,* is **Nuraghe Su Nuraxi** (adult/concession €7/5, incl Polo Museale Casa Zapata €10/8; 🕙 guided tours every 30min 9am-1pm & 2-7pm), about a kilometre west of Barumini on the road to Tuili. Note that visits are by guided tour only, usually in Italian, and that explanatory printouts are available in English. It's also worth noting that queues are the norm in summer when it can get extremely hot on the exposed site.

The focal point is the Nuraxi tower, which once had three stories and rose to a height of 20m. Dating to around 1500 BC, it originally stood in magnificent solitude, but four additional towers were later added and a connecting wall was built in 1000 BC.

The first village buildings arrived in the Iron Age, between the 8th and the 6th centuries BC, and it's these that constitute the beehive of circular interlocking buildings that tumble down the hillside. As the village grew, a more complex defensive wall was built around the core, consisting of nine towers pierced by arrow slits. Weapons in the form of massive stone balls have also been unearthed here.

In the 7th century BC the site was partly destroyed but not abandoned. In fact it grew and was still inhabited in Roman times. Elements of basic sewerage and canalisation have even been identified.

The site was rediscovered by Giovanni Lilliu (Sardinia's most famous archaeologist) in 1949, after torrential rains eroded the compact earth that had covered the *nuraghe* and made it look like just another Marmilla hillock. Excavations continued for six years and today the site is the only entirely excavated *nuraghe* in Sardinia. You can get an inkling of the work involved by seeing how many square bricks have been incorporated into the structure – these were deliberately made to stand out so they could be distinguished from the original basalt.

LA GIARA DI GESTURI

Five kilometres west of Barumini, the village of **Tuili** is one of the main gateways to La Giara di Gesturi, a high basalt plateau that looms above the surrounding country. This remarkable 45-sq-km plain, splashed with *macchia* and small cork oaks, is home to the red long-horned bulls peculiar to Sardinia, and the unique wild *cavallini* (literally 'mini horses').

The best places to find the horses, in the early morning or late afternoon, are the seasonal lakes, called *paulis* (such as Pauli Maiori). In winter the lakes usually have a shallow patina of surface water, but in the warmer months most of it evaporates. At some, such as Pauli S'Ala de Mengianu, the water trapped in underground basalt sources bubbles to the surface around the *paulis*, and that is where the horses will be slaking their thirst.

The plateau also has its own microclimate, which fosters an array of unusual flora, best seen in spring, when the ground is covered in heather and the 15 species of orchid are in bloom. It's an interesting place to go walking; paths criss-cross the plateau, and there are a few dirt tracks that make it possible to get around in a vehicle. You can see the occasional *pinedda* (thatched shepherd's hut).

You can get information from the **tourist office** (☎ 070 936 30 23; www.prolocotuili.it; Via Amsicora 3; ⊗ 9am-7pm) in Tuili, where you'll also find a number of operators offering guided excursions, including **Jara Escursioni** (⊗ 070 936 42 77, 3482924983; www.parcodellagiara.it; Via Tuveri 16). Near Barumini, **Sa Jara Manna** (☎ 070 936 81 70; www .sajaramanna.it; SS197 km 44) offers a number of tour packages either on foot (€46 for a half day in a group of 25 or under) or by 4WD (€115 for a half day). It also hires out mountain bikes (€9 for a half day). A half-day or day's excursion will include a shepherd's lunch on the plateau in one of the old *pinedda*.

Before you head up into the Giara, take time to check out the **Chiesa di San Pietro** in Tuilli, which harbours some fine works of art, including a grand *retablo* (altarpiece) made by the Maestro di Castelsardo in 1500. To visit, you'll need to ask at the tourist office.

You can also access the Giara from Setzu and, to the east, Gesturi. If you're coming from **Setzu**, turn right just north of the town. The road winds up 3km above the stark plains; at the 2km mark you'll see the Sa Domu de S'Orcu *tomba di gigante* (literally 'giant's tomb'; ancient mass grave) to the left. The asphalt peters out at the entrance to Parco della Giara, but you can follow the rough dirt track (slowly) in a normal car east to the Gesturi exit.

On the southeastern tip of the Giara, 5km up from Barumini, Gesturi is dominated by the big 17th-century **Chiesa di Santa Teresa d'Avila**, a centre of pilgrimage for the faithful, who flock here to celebrate Gesturi's greatest son, Fra Nicola 'Silenzio' (1882–1958), a Franciscan friar known for his religious devotion, wisdom and simplicity of life. His beatification in 1999 was a source of great pride to the good citizens of Gesturi, who have decorated the town with murals and grand portraits of the man they knew as Brother Silence.

Two weekday ARST buses run from Cagliari to Tuili (€4.50, 1½ hours), otherwise you'll need your own transport.

Oristano & the West

Rising from flat, coastal wetlands to remote, windswept peaks, this is an area of colourful contrasts and blinking double-takes. Popular beach resorts coexist with seemingly deserted fishing villages; pink flamingos fly into silver lagoons and deer roam in upland forests. Roman ruins and ancient *nuraghi* lay strewn about the verdant landscape.

At the heart of it all is Oristano, one of Sardinia's great medieval cities and an important market town. As the capital of the 14th-century *giudicato* (province) of Arborea, it valiantly flew the flag for Sardinian independence, and although little remains to vouch for its former glory, it's an attractive and ebullient city. A short distance to the west, the Roman city of Tharros provides a thousand photo opportunities, its sand-coloured ruins beautifully framed by the choppy blue waters of the Golfo di Oristano.

Gourmets will enjoy the area. Oristano is famous for its Vernaccia wine, and many of the market towns dotted around the Monti Ferru massif enjoy gastronomic celebrity – Seneghe for its olive oil and *bue rosso* steak; Milis for its oranges. Over on the Sinis Peninsula, residents of Cabras boast a unique diet based on the local lagoon fauna – mullet, eels, *bottarga* (mullet roe) and clams.

There are plenty of outdoor activities too. Surfers can ride waves off Capo Mannu; Bosa's Fiume Temo offers gentle canoeing, and ornithologists will enjoy spying on the region's rich birdlife. Horses have been central to life here for centuries, and riding opportunities await in the flatlands around Arborea. To see how the pros do it, Oristano's Sa Sartiglia and Sedilo's S'Ardia festivals feature reckless displays of daredevil riding.

HIGHLIGHTS

- Revel in the sweeping views from **Monti Ferru** (p112), then adjourn to **Seneghe** (p112) for a big, beefy lunch

- Give your imagination a workout at windswept **Tharros** (p110) and practise your spaghetti-western swagger at **San Salvatore** (p110)

- Throw yourself into the carnival madness of Oristano's **Sa Sartiglia** (p105) and Sedilo's **S'Ardia** (p115) festival

- Grab yourself a canoe at **Bosa** (p117) and head upstream along the Fiume Temo, Sardinia's only inland navigable river

- Bone up on ancient history at the impressive **Nuraghe Losa** (p115)

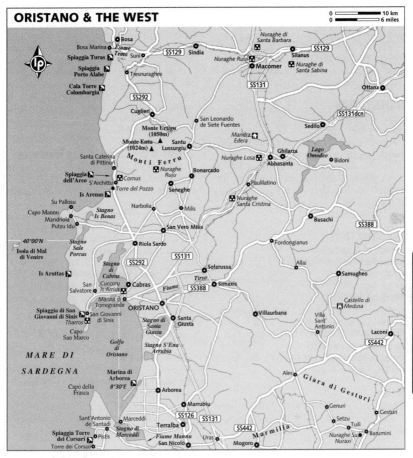

ORISTANO & THE WEST

ORISTANO

pop 32,930

With its elegant shopping streets, ornate piazzas and popular cafes, Oristano's refined and animated centre comes as a pleasant surprise after its busy and uninspiring suburbs. There's not a huge amount to see beyond some churches and an interesting archaeological museum, but it's a lovely place to hang out, and it makes a good base for the surrounding area.

HISTORY

The flat, fertile countryside around Oristano was an important nuraghic centre, but it was the Phoenicians who first put the area on the map. Arriving in the latter half of the 8th century BC, they established the city of Tharros, which later thrived under the Romans and became the de facto capital of western Sardinia.

The city was eventually abandoned in 1070 when its citizens, fed up with continuous Saracen raids, decamped to a more easily defendable inland site, Aristianis (present-day Oristano). This new city became capital of the Giudicato d'Arborea, one of Sardinia's four independent provinces, and the base of operations for Eleonora of Arborea (c 1340–1404). A heroine in the Joan of Arc mould, Eleonora organised the 14th-century war against the Spanish and wrote the Carta di Logu (Code of Laws; see p28) before dying of plague. With her death, anti-Spanish opposition crumbled and Oristano was incorporated into the rest of Aragonese-controlled Sardinia. It wasn't a good time for the city. Trade collapsed and the city suffered from plague and famine.

The construction of the Cagliari–Porto Torres Hwy in the 1820s and Mussolini's land reclamation programs gave Oristano a much-needed boost.

ORIENTATION

Oristano is not a big city and is easily covered on foot. The historic centre is a small pocket, bounded on the west by the main north–south through-road, Via Cagliari. Action is focused on busy Piazza Roma, from where pedestrianised Corso Umberto I strikes southwards towards Piazza Eleonora d'Arborea and, beyond that, Oristano's historic cathedral.

INFORMATION
Internet Access
Genius Point (Via Pietro Riccio 4; per hr €4; ☼ 8.30am-1pm & 4-8pm Mon-Fri)

Medical Services
Farmacia San Carlo (☎ 0783 7 11 23; Piazza Eleonora d'Arborea 10/11) Central pharmacy.
Guardia Medica (☎ 0783 30 33 73; Via Carducci 33) For call-out medical assistance.
Ospedale San Martino (☎ 0783 31 71; Piazza San Martino) Hospital south of the centre.

Money
There are a few banks with ATMs around Piazza Roma, including Banca Nazionale di Lavoro.

Post
Post office (☎ 0783 3 68 01; Via Mariano IV d'Arborea; ☼ 8am-6.50pm Mon-Fri, 8am-1.15pm Sat)

Tourist Information
Main tourist office (☎ 0783 3 68 31; turismo@ provincia.or.it; Piazza Eleonora d'Arborea 19; ☼ 9am-1pm & 4-6.30pm Mon-Fri) Has plenty of printed matter on the city and province.
Tourist office (☎ 0783 7 06 21; Via Ciutadella di Menorca 14; ☼ 9am-noon & 4.30-7.30pm Mon-Fri) For city information.

SIGHTS
Oristano's main sights are concentrated on the historic centre, a pretty area of stone houses, sunny piazzas and baroque streets. Little survives of the medieval walled town except for

the **Torre di Mariano II**, a 13th-century tower on Piazza Roma. Known also as the Torre di Cristoforo, this was the town's northern gate and an important part of the city's defences. The bell was added later in the 15th century.

A second tower, the **Portixedda** (☼ 10am-noon & 4-6pm Tue-Sun), just to the east off Via Giuseppe Mazzini, was also part of the city walls, most of which were pulled down in the 19th century. The tower is now used to stage temporary exhibitions.

Duomo & the Chiesa di San Francesco
Lording it over Oristano's skyline, the onion-domed bell tower of the **Duomo** (☎ 0783 7 83 99; Piazza Duomo; ☼ 7am-noon & 4-7pm Mon-Sat, 8am-1pm Sun) is one of the few remaining elements of the original 14th-century cathedral, itself a reworking of an earlier church damaged by fire in the late 12th century. The free-standing *campanile*, topped by its conspicuous maiolica-tiled dome, adds an exotic Byzantine feel to what is otherwise a typical 18th-century baroque complex.

Inside, the look is pure baroque, although the apses and Cappella del Rimedio survive from the Gothic original. It's in the latter that you'll find the 14th-century wooden sculpture *Annunziata* or *Madonna del Rimedio*, believed to have been carved by the Tuscan sculptor Nino Pisano.

Nearby, the neoclassical **Chiesa di San Francesco** (Via Sant'Antonio; admission free; ☼ 8am-noon & 5-7pm Mon-Sat, 8am-noon Sun) is worth a quick look for its famous 14th-century wooden sculpture, the *Crocifisso di Nicodemo*, considered one of Sardinia's most precious carvings.

Museo Antiquarium Arborense
Housed in a smart palazzo, Oristano's sole **museum** (☎ 0783 79 12 62; Piazzetta Corrias; adult/child €3/1; ☼ 9am-2pm & 3-8pm) boasts one of the island's major archaeological collections.

The permanent exhibition, which includes a scale model of 4th-century Tharros, is displayed on the upper floor. Things kick off with prehistoric finds from the Sinis Peninsula, including obsidian and flint spearheads and axes, bones and a smattering of jewellery. More interesting is the stash of finds from Carthaginian and Roman Tharros. Ceramics predominate, but also on show are glassware, oil lamps and amphorae, and a range of pots, plates and cups.

In a small side room off the main hall is a small collection of *retabli* (painted

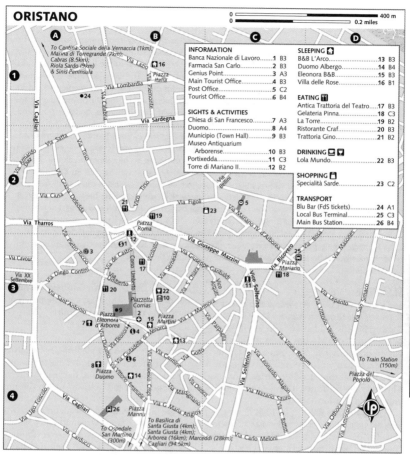

ORISTANO

INFORMATION	
Banca Nazionale di Lavoro........**1** B3	
Farmacia San Carlo....................**2** B3	
Genius Point............................**3** A3	
Main Tourist Office....................**4** B3	
Post Office..............................**5** C2	
Tourist Office..........................**6** B4	

SIGHTS & ACTIVITIES	
Chiesa di San Francesco..........**7** A3	
Duomo.................................**8** A4	
Municipio (Town Hall)............**9** B3	
Museo Antiquarium	
Arborense.........................**10** B3	
Portixedda...........................**11** C3	
Torre di Mariano II.................**12** B2	

SLEEPING	
B&B L'Arco.............................**13** B3	
Duomo Albergo.......................**14** B4	
Eleonora B&B..........................**15** B3	
Villa delle Rose.......................**16** B1	

EATING	
Antica Trattoria del Teatro.....**17** B3	
Gelateria Pinna.......................**18** C3	
La Torre..................................**19** B2	
Ristorante Craf........................**20** B3	
Trattoria Gino.........................**21** B2	

DRINKING	
Lola Mundo............................**22** B3	

SHOPPING	
Specialità Sarde......................**23** C2	

TRANSPORT	
Blu Bar (FdS tickets)................**24** A1	
Local Bus Terminal..................**25** B3	
Main Bus Station.....................**26** B4	

altar pieces) and a model of Oristano in its 13th-century prime. One series of panels, the *Retablo del Santo Cristo* (1533), by the workshop of Pietro Cavaro, depicts a group of apparently beatific saints. But take a closer look and you'll see they all sport the instruments of their gory tortures slicing through their heads, necks and hearts.

Piazza Eleonora d'Arborea & Around

Piazza Eleonora d'Arborea, Oristano's elegant outdoor drawing room, sits at the southern end of pedestrianised Corso Umberto I. An impressive, rectangular space, it comes to life on warm summer evenings when townsfolk congregate to chew the fat and children blast footballs against the glowing *palazzi*.

The city's central square since the 19th century, it's flanked by grand, self-important buildings, including the neoclassical **Municipio** (Town Hall). In the centre stands an ornate 19th-century **statue of Queen Eleonora**, raising a finger as if about to launch into a political speech. Bargain hunters should drop by on the first Saturday of the month when the piazza hosts an antique market.

FESTIVALS & EVENTS

Oristano's carnival, the **Sa Sartiglia**, is the most colourful carnival on the island. It is attended in February by hundreds of costumed participants and involves a medieval joust, horse racing and incredible acrobatic riding. See the boxed text p106.

MARDI GRAS

Sa Sartiglia is undoubtedly Sardinia's most colourful and carefully choreographed festival. Its origins are unknown and its godlike central figure, the Su Cumpoidori, smacks of pagan ritual. The jousts and costumes are undoubtedly Spanish, probably introduced to the island by the *giudici* (provincial governors), who were trained at the Court of Aragon. The word 'Sartiglia' comes from the Castilian *sortija*, meaning 'ring', and the central event of the festival is a medieval joust in which the Su Cumpoidori, the King of the Sartiglia, must pierce a star (ring) suspended overhead. The virgin brides who dress the Su Cumpoidori, along with his effeminate, godlike status and the throwing of grain, all suggest older fertility rites heralding spring.

The event is held over two days, Sunday and *martedì grasso* (Shrove Tuesday or Mardi Gras). At noon the Su Cumpoidori is 'born'. He sits on a table (the altar) and is reverently clothed and masked by the *sas massaieddas* (young virgins). From this point on he cannot touch the ground and is carried to his horse, which is almost as elaborately dressed as he. The Su Cumpoidori's white mask is framed by a stiff mantilla on top of which he wears a black top hat. In his hand he carries a sceptre decorated with violets and periwinkles with which he blesses the crowd. It is his task to start the Sartiglia, the race to the star, which he does with two other knights, his *segundu* (second) and *terzu* (third), who all try to pierce the star. The more times they strike it, the more luck they bring to the coming year. The last ritual the Su Cumpoidori performs is the Sa Remada, where he gallops along the course lying on his back. Then the games are open to acrobatic riders who perform feats that draw gasps from the crowd.

SLEEPING

B&B L'Arco (☎ 0783 7 28 49; www.arcobedandbreakfast .it; Vico Ammirato 12; d without bathroom €60) This welcoming B&B is hidden away in a quiet cul-de-sac near Piazza Martini. There are only two guestrooms, but they are spacious and tastefully decorated with exposed wood beams, terracotta tiles and dark-wood furnishings. Throughout the house, 13th-century brick arches lend a historic touch.

our pick Eleonora B&B (☎ 0783 7 04 35; www.ele onora-bed-and-breakfast.com; Piazza Eleonora d'Arborea 12; s €35, d €60-70; 🖭) Run by a charming young couple, and beautifully located on Oristano's central piazza, this characterful B&B is an excellent option. Rooms in the rambling apartment, parts of which date to medieval times, reveal a homey look with parquet floors, simple rustic furniture and the odd dash of modern colour. Wi-fi is available.

Villa delle Rose (☎ /fax 0783 31 01 01; Piazza Italia 5; s/d €50/80) Comfort trumps character at this functional three-star. On a nondescript piazza in a residential part of town, it offers pale boxlike rooms that, while almost completely featureless, do the job nicely enough. For €85 you can get a room with a small kitchenette.

Duomo Albergo (☎ 0783 77 80 61; www.hotelduomo .net; Via Vittorio Emanuele II 34; s €70-80, d €108-130; 🖭 🖵) Inside and out, Oristano's top hotel is a refined, elegantly understated four-star. Outside the simple facade is a model of discretion, while inside, guestrooms reveal a quiet, cool decor with white colour schemes, light fabrics and unobtrusive furniture.

EATING

Eating in Oristano is a pleasure, especially if you like fish. There's a good range of reasonably priced restaurants, and the nearby Stagno di Cabras lagoon and Golfo di Oristano ensure a steady supply of fresh seafood. Local staples include mullet *(muggine)*, sometimes known as *pesce di Oristano* (Oristano fish), which often appears on menus as *mrecca* (boiled, wrapped in pond grass and then dried and salted). Grilled eel is popular, as are *patelle*, limpetlike dark clams.

Gelateria Pinna (☎ 0783 7 00 32; Piazza Mariano 38; 🕙 Mon-Sat) A short walk east of the town centre, this unassuming *gelateria* is popular with locals – always a good sign. Alongside all your favourite flavours are some lesser-known concoctions including a wine ice cream.

La Torre (☎ 0783 30 14 94; Piazza Roma 52; pizzas €6.50, meals around €25; 🕙 Tue-Sun) This place doesn't look like much from outside; in fact, it's not so amazing inside either. No matter, it serves the best pizza in town. If you're off pizza but just want to enjoy the hectic weekend atmosphere, there's a full menu of pastas and grilled main courses.

Trattoria Gino (☎ 0783 7 14 28; Via Tirso 13; meals around €27; 🕙 Mon-Sat) An old-school neighbourhood trattoria, this place has been serving tasty, no-nonsense food since the 1930s. The menu covers most bases, but it's the seafood that really stands out. Start with an *antipasto di mare*, a mixed seafood platter, before diving into chargrilled *seppia* (cuttlefish).

Ristorante Craf (☎ 0783 7 06 69; Via de Castro 34; meals around €35; ☺ Mon-Sat) A city stalwart, Craf is housed in a former 17th-century granary with brick vaulted dining rooms and folksy clutter. The onus is on hearty country fare such as *panne frattau* (Sardinian bread soup), pastas with legumes, and grilled meat, including *asinello* (donkey).

Antica Trattoria del Teatro (☎ 0783 7 16 72; Via Parpaglia 11; meals around €40; ☺ Mon-Sat) This refined and intimate *centro storico* restaurant is a good place to push the boat out and try something different. Something like *panada di anguille*, a kind of rustic eel pie, served with grated *casizolu* cheese. There's also a vast choice of cheese and a comprehensive beer selection.

DRINKING

The historic centre is full of bars and cafes. One of the most popular is **Lola Mundo** (Piazzetta Corrias 14; ☺ Mon-Sat), a good-looking bar set on a pretty cobbled piazza. With its square-side seating and relaxed jazz tunes, it's a good spot to hang out over an aperitif.

SHOPPING

Specialità Sarde (☎ 0783 7 27 25; Via Figoli 41; ☺ Mon-Sat) Stock up on Sardinian gourmet specialities at this gourmet gift shop. As well as wine and cheese, you'll find all sorts of tempting preserves in pretty jars.

Cantina Sociale della Vernaccia (☎ 0783 3 31 55; Via Oristano 149, Rimedio) Oristano is famous for its fortified white Vernaccia wine, and this is the place to buy it. Most of Oristano's local producers bring their grapes here to be crushed, so you can be assured of genuine quality.

GETTING THERE & AWAY
Bus

From the main bus station on Via Cagliari ARST buses leave for a number of destinations including Santa Giusta (€1, 15 minutes, half-hourly) and Cagliari (€6.50, two hours, two daily).

For northern towns, FdS runs buses from outside the **Blu Bar** (Via Lombardia 30; ☺ 6am-10pm Mon-Sat), where you buy tickets. Destinations include Sassari (€7.50, two hours, three daily) and Nuoro (€7.50, 2½ hours, six daily).

Car & Motorcycle

Oristano is just off the SS131 highway, which connects Cagliari with Sassari and Porto Torres. Branch highways head off to the northeast for Nuoro and Olbia.

Train

The main Trenitalia train station is in Piazza Ungheria, east of the town centre. Up to 12 daily trains, sometimes involving a change en route, run between Oristano and Cagliari (€5.65, one to two hours). Only a handful make the run to Sassari (€9.65, 2½ hours, four daily). For Olbia there are only two through trains (€10.95, 2¾ hours); otherwise you have to change at Ozieri-Chilivani or Macomer.

GETTING AROUND
Bus

The town centre is easily covered on foot, although you will probably want to use buses to get in from the train station. The *rossa* (red) and *verde* (green) lines stop at the station and terminate in Piazza Mariano.

The *azzurra* (blue) buses run from various stops along Via Cagliari (including the main terminal) to Marina di Torregrande (€0.70 if bought at a *tabacchi* or at the Via Cagliari bus station, or €1.10 if bought on the bus, 15 minutes).

Car & Motorcycle

Parking is not too bad if you leave your car a little out of the centre. In the centre, pay-and-display parking (per hour €0.60; 8.30am–1pm and 4–7.30pm Monday to Saturday) is available within the blue lines.

Taxi

You'll find that taxis tend to congregate at the train station and around Piazza Roma. To phone for one, call ☎ 0783 7 02 80 or ☎ 0783 7 43 28.

AROUND ORISTANO

Oristano's main beach is at the small resort of **Marina di Torregrande**, 7km west of the city. Behind a long, sandy strip, the village presents a familiar seaside scene with

ORISTANO & THE WEST

suntanned locals parading down a palm-flanked *lungomare* (promenade) and dodgy music emanating from bars. Out of season it's a different story and you'll find the holiday homes shuttered and most of the restaurants closed.

The one and only building of any historical note is the stout 16th-century Aragonese watchtower, after which the resort is named. Once you've seen that, there's not much to do except don your swimmers and head to the beach. You can hire sun loungers and umbrellas on the beach – reckon on about €16.50 per day. **Eolo** (☎ 329 613 64 61; www.eolowindsurf.com, in Italian; Lungomare Eleonora d'Arborea) organises sailing and windsurfing courses, as well as renting out equipment (windsurfs from €13 per hour).

At the southern end of town, **Spinnaker** (☎ 0783 2 20 74; www.spinnakervacanze.com, in Italian; Marina di Torregrande; per person/car €20/4, bungalows from €42; ❄ 🐕) is a large, shady campsite with 100 tent pitches, bungalows and its own private beach. **Torre Grande** (☎ 0783 2 22 28; campeggiotorregrande@libero.it; Via Stella Maris 8; per person/tent €6/9.50; ❄ May-Sep) is a more modest campsite a few hundred metres back from the beach.

The resort's top restaurant is **Da Giovanni** (☎ 0783 2 20 51; Via Colombo 8; meals around €40, tourist menu €23; ❄ Tue-Sun) whose nondescript setting on the main road out of town belies an excellent reputation. The seafood is particularly good in dishes like *ravioli di pesce in salsa di gamberi* (fish ravioli in prawn sauce) and *muggine locale* (local mullet).

Of the seafront eateries, the **Maestrale** (☎ 0783 2 21 21; Lungomare Torregrande; pizzas €8, meals around €35; ❄ Tue-Sun) is a good bet for a laid-back pizza or a plate of seafood pasta.

The beach strip is lined with summertime bars. A few kilometres inland on the road to Cabras, **BNN Fashion Club** (☎ 338 235 75 40; SP 94, km 1.8) is a popular bar-cum-disco serving Italian tunes, house and international pop.

From Oristano, city buses on the *azzurra* line run from various stops along Via Cagliari (including the main terminal) to Marina di Torregrande (€0.70 or €1.10 if bought on bus, 20 minutes).

SOUTH OF ORISTANO

South of Oristano, flat plains extend in a patchwork of wide, open fields interspersed with canals, lagoons and the odd pocket of pine wood. It's a featureless, and sometimes strange, landscape dotted with sleepy villages and agricultural towns. It wasn't always like this, though. Until Mussolini launched an ambitious drainage and reclamation program in 1919, the area was largely covered with malarial swampland and thick cork forests.

SANTA GIUSTA
pop 4750

A bustling agricultural village, Santa Giusta lies on the shores of the Stagno di Santa Giusta, Sardinia's third-largest lagoon. Once the Punic town of Othoca, it is best known for its extraordinary basilica, one of the first, and finest, examples of Pisan-Romanesque architecture in Sardinia.

Built between 1135 and 1145, the **Basilica di Santa Giusta** (☎ 0783 35 92 05; ❄ free guided tours 9am-1pm & 2-6pm Mon-Fri) rises like a galleon aground in the lagoon. Up close it is long and low, with blind arcades, a typically Tuscan central portal, and a severe Lombard facade. Inside, three naves are separated by marble and granite columns looted from the Roman towns of Tharros and Othoca. Topping the whole austere ensemble is a fine wood-beamed ceiling.

For four days around 14 May, the basilica takes centre stage during celebrations of the town's annual **Festa di Santa Giusta**.

Six kilometres to the south of town, the **Stagno S'Ena Arrubia** is a paradise for birdwatchers. Flamingos, herons, coots and ospreys are regularly sighted.

If you want to hang around, there's a well-equipped campsite, **Camping S'Ena Arrubia** (☎ 0783 80 90 11; www.campeggio-sardegna.com; Strada 29; per person/tent/car €13/5/3) on the southwest side of the lagoon (follow the signs from the main Santa Giusta–Arborea road).

Buses from Oristano's main bus station leave half-hourly to Santa Giusta (€1, 15 minutes).

ARBOREA
pop 3975

Founded by Mussolini in 1928, Arborea bears all the hallmarks of its Fascist inception – severe grid-patterned streets, an immaculate central piazza and an array of fantastical architectural styles.

The immediate focus is **Piazza Maria Ausiliatrice**, a beautifully tended square that wouldn't look out of place in a Swiss

ORISTANO & THE WEST

Alpine village. Overlooking it is the clocked facade of the Tyrolean-style **Chiesa del Cristo Redentore** (☩ mass 7.30am, 9am & 7pm). Over the road, the art nouveau **Municipio** houses the town's **archaeological museum** (☎ 0783 8 03 31; Viale Omodeo; admission free; ☩ 10am-1pm Mon-Fri) with its small collection of locally found artefacts.

If you want to stop over, the **Hotel Gallo Blanco** (☎ 0783 80 02 41; www.locandagallobianca.it; Piazza Maria Ausiliatrice 10; s/d €28/52, without bathroom €26/48) is an old-fashioned hotel with eight modest rooms and a decent restaurant (meals around €30).

Marina di Arborea

Hidden behind a thick pine wood 2km north-west of Arborea, Marina di Arborea sits at the head of a long, sandy beach. It is little more than a seafront hotel and a car park, although it is being increasingly swamped by the **Horse Country Resort** (☎ 0783 80 51 73; www.horse country.it; Strada a Mare 24; half board per person €71-128; P X ⬚), a vast complex of 1000 beds, two swimming pools and excellent sporting facilities. The resort is the biggest equestrian centre in Sardinia and one of the most important in Italy, with a stable of Arabian, Andalucian and Sardinian horses. Staff can arrange horse-riding lessons as well as day trips to Marceddi, Tharros and the Costa Verde.

MARCEDDI

Looking over the mouth of the **Stagno di Marceddi**, this tiny fishing village is the embodiment of a backwater. For much of the year the only signs of modern life are a few battered cars and the ragged electricity lines flapping over dirt roads. The lagoon, which separates the Arborea plains from the Costa Verde, is an important wildlife habitat, harbouring flamingos, cormorants and herons.

If you decide to linger, you can get an excellent fish lunch at **Da Lucio** (☎ 0783 86 71 30; Via Sardus Pater 34; meals around €35; ☩ lunch Fri-Wed Sep-Jun, lunch & dinner daily Jul & Aug) down on the waterfront. If that's shut, grab a *panino* at the **bar** (Via Sardus Pater 46; ☩ 8am-9pm) down the road.

SINIS PENINSULA

Spearing down into the Golfo di Oristano, the Sinis Peninsula feels like a world apart. Its limpid lagoons – the Stagno di Cabras, Stagno Sale Porcus and Stagno Is Benas – and snow-white beaches lend it an almost tropical air, while the low-lying green countryside appears uncontaminated by human activity. In fact, the area has been inhabited since the 5th century BC. *Nuraghi* litter the landscape and the compelling Punic-Roman site of Tharros stands testament to the area's former importance.

Although summer is the obvious time to visit, winter (October to March) is not without its appeal, as the shallow waters fill with flocks of migrating birds. The queen of the show is the gorgeous pink flamingo.

Sports fans will enjoy great surfing, wind-surfing and some fine diving.

CABRAS

pop 8700

Sprawled on the southern shore of the Stagno di Cabras, Cabras is an important fishing town and centre of the island's mullet fishing – the local *bottarga* is much sought-after and well worth trying. The town is not an especially sightly place, but you'll eat well and the archaeology museum is worth a quick once-over.

Sights

The town's one site of interest is the **Museo Civico** (☎ 0783 29 06 36; www.penisoladelsinis.it, in Italian; Via Tharros 121; admission €2, incl Tharros €5; ☩ 9am-1pm & 4-8pm Jun-Sep, 9am-1pm & 3-7pm Oct-May), located at the southern end of town. The museum houses finds from the prehistoric site of **Cuccuru Is Arrius**, 3km to the southwest, and Tharros. Of particular interest is a series of obsidian and flint tools said to date back to the neolithic cultures of Bonu Ighinu and Ozieri.

Festivals & Events

On the first Sunday of September, the **Festa di San Salvatore**, several hundred young fellows clothed in white mantles set off on the **Corsa degli Scalzi** (Barefoot Race) – an 8km dash to the sanctuary of San Salvatore. They bear with them a figure of the Saviour to commemorate an episode in 1506, when townspeople raced to San Salvatore to collect the figure and save it from Moorish sea raiders. They race back to Oristano, in a similar fashion the following day.

Sleeping & Eating

Sa Pedrera (☎ 0783 37 00 40; www.sapedrera.it; Strada Provincial Cabras; d €66-140, q €120-252, half board per person €50-91; P 🕃) About 7.5km out of town, on the main road down to San Giovanni di Sinis, this relaxed three-star has cool, unfussy rooms looking onto a lush green garden. Liberal use of exposed stonework, plus a large fireplace, lend an authentic rustic feel.

Il Caminetto (☎ 0783 39 11 39; Via Cesare Battisti 8; meals around €35; 🕃 Tue-Sun) One of the best-known restaurants in the area, this busy spot attracts hungry customers from far and wide. The main allure is the fishy menu, featuring Cabras classics *muggine affumicato* (smoked mullet) and *aguidda incasada* (eel with Sardinian pecorino cheese).

L'Oliveto (☎ 0783 39 26 16; Via Tirso 23; meals €30-35; 🕃 Wed-Mon) Tucked away in an olive grove near the northern edge of town, this is a popular, laid-back restaurant-cum-pizzeria. Seafood rules the roost, but you can also get decent pizza and filling meat dishes.

Getting There & Away

ARST buses run every 20 minutes or so from Oristano (€1, 15 minutes).

SAN SALVATORE

Used as a spaghetti-western film set during the 1960s, San Salvatore is a weird place. The village is centred on a dusty town square, around which rows of minuscule terraced houses, known as *cumbessias*, stand as if on silent parade. For much of the year these simple shacks are deserted, as is the rest of the village, but in late August they are opened to house pilgrims for the Feast of San Salvatore. This nine-day-long celebration is focused on the 16th-century **Chiesa di San Salvatore** (🕃 9.30am-1pm & 3.30-6pm Mon-Sat & Sun morning) in the centre of the village square.

Under the church, there is a stone *ipogeo* (underground vault) dating to the nuraghic period. The original sanctuary was associated with a water cult, and you can still see a well in the main chamber. It was later converted into a Roman-era church, and the dark stone walls bear traces of 4th-century graffiti and faded frescoes.

Just beyond the turn-off for the village (blink and you've missed it) are a couple of excellent-value *agriturismi* (farm-stays). Signposted off to the right, the **Agriturismo Su Pranu** (☎ 0783 39 25 61; www.supranu.com; Localita

San Salvatore; B&B per person €32-40, half board per person €50-60; 🕃) is a genuine working farm with six bright guestrooms and a superb restaurant. The menu depends on what's available on the day, but vegetables and fruit are home-grown and the meat, including *porceddu*, is cooked to perfection on a big outdoor barbecue.

Over the road, **Agriturismo Sinis** (☎ 0783 39 25 61; www.agriturismoilsinis.it; Localita San Salvatore; B&B per person €32-40, half board per person €50-60; 🕃) is run by the same family and has a further six bedrooms.

SAN GIOVANNI DI SINIS

At the southern tip of the Sinis Peninsula, about 5km beyond San Salvatore, the road passes through the small settlement of San Giovanni di Sinis. By the roadside car park you'll see the sandstone **Chiesa di San Giovanni di Sinis** (🕃 9am-7pm Jun-Sep, to 5pm Oct-May), one of the two oldest churches in Sardinia (Cagliari's Basilica di San Saturnino is older – see p63). It owes its current form to an 11th-century makeover, although elements of the 6th-century Byzantine original remain, including the characteristic red dome. Inside, the bare walls lend a sombre and surprisingly spiritual atmosphere.

THARROS

From San Giovanni in Sinis, the road continues past a strip of pizzerias, bars and cafes up to **Tharros** (☎ 0783 39 73 06; admission incl Museo Civico in Cabras €5; 🕃 9am-7pm Jun-Sep, to 5pm Oct-May), the once mighty port founded by the Phoenicians in the 8th century BC. Set magnificently against the blue sea, these ancient ruins count among southern Sardinia's most thrilling sights. Try to visit early in the morning or just before sunset, when the site is at its quietest and most atmospheric.

History

Capo Marco, the southernmost point of the Sinis Peninsula, was already home to a thriving nuraghic culture when the Phoenicians established a base here in about 730 BC. Tharros thrived and was eventually absorbed into the Carthaginian empire. But, as an important naval base in a strategic position, it was always vulnerable and when the Romans attacked the Carthaginians, it fell to the rampant legionnaires.

It remained a key naval town, but once the main road from Cagliari to Porto Torres was completed it was effectively sidelined.

Nevertheless, it got a thorough overhaul in the 2nd and 3rd centuries AD. Increasingly aggressive raids from the Vandals and later from the North African Saracens led to its abandonment in 1070. Much of the ancient city was subsequently stripped to build the new capital at Oristano.

Sights & Activities

As you approach the site it is impossible to see even a glimmer of the ruins until you reach the hilltop ticket office. From here follow a brief stretch of *cardo* (the main street in a Roman settlement) until you reach, on your left, the *castellum aquae*, the city's main water reserve. Two lines of pillars can be made out within the square structure. From here the **Cardo Massimo**, the city's main throughfare, leads up to a bare rise topped by a Carthaginian acropolis and a *tophet*, a sacred burial ground used to bury children. Also up here are traces of the original nuraghic settlement.

From the bottom of the Cardo Massimo, the **Decumano** runs down to the sea passing the remains of a **Punic temple** and, beyond that, the Roman-era **Tempio Tetrastilo**, marked by its two solitary columns. These are, in fact, reconstructions, although the Corinthian capital balanced on the top of one is authentic.

Nearby is a set of **thermal baths** and, to the north, the remains of a **palaeo-Christian baptistry**. At the southernmost point of the settlement is another set of baths, dating to the 3rd century AD.

For a free bird's-eye view of the site, head up to the late-16th-century **Torre di San Giovanni watchtower** (admission €3; 9am-7pm Jun-Sep, to 5pm Oct-May), which is occasionally used for exhibitions. From here you can look down on the ruins, as well as the golden **Spiaggia di San Giovanni di Sinis**, a popular beach, which extends on both sides of the tower. There is nothing to stop you wandering down the dirt tracks to Capo San Marco and the lighthouse.

Getting There & Away

In July and August, there are five daily ARST buses for San Giovanni di Sinis from Oristano (€1.50, 35 minutes). Parking near the site costs €2 for two hours, €4 per day.

BEACHES

The beaches on the Sinis Peninsula are well worth tracking down. One of the best is **Is Aruttas**, whose white quartz sand was for years

---

GETTING AWAY FROM IT ALL

A few kilometres out of Tharros, and signposted off the main road, the Parco Comunale Oasi di Seu is a veritable Eden of Mediterranean flora. Once you've navigated the 3km dirt track to the entrance, you enter a silent world of sandy paths and undisturbed nature. Herby smells fill the air, rising off fragrant masses of *macchia* (scrub), rosemary, dwarf palms, pine trees and spinneret.

---

carted off to be used in aquariums and on beaches on the Costa Smeralda. However, it's now illegal to take any. The beach is signposted and is 5km west off the main road leading north from San Salvatore.

Within walking distance of the beach, **Camping Is Aruttas** (0783 39 11 08; www.camp ingisaruttas.it; Localita Marina Aruttas; per person/tent/car €14/free/3.50; mid-May-Sep) has modest camping facilities set amidst olive trees and Mediterranean shrubbery.

At the north of the peninsula, the popular surfing beach of **Putzu Idu** is backed by a motley set of holiday homes, beach bars, and surfing outlets. One such, the **Capo Mannu Kite School** (347 007 70 35; www.capomannukiteschool.it) runs kitesurfing lessons for all levels.

Next door to the **Scuba Café** (Lungomare Putzu Idu; 9am-10pm winter, 7am-2am summer), one of the very few places that remains open in winter, is **9511 Diving** (349 291 37 65; www.9511.it), a small outfit also open year-round whose PADI-qualified instructors lead dives (from €50 including equipment hire), snorkelling trips (€25 per person) and excursions to the eloquently named **Isola di Mal di Ventre** (Stomach Ache Island), 10km off the coast.

There are various operators offering tours to the island. Another is **Mare Mania** (347 191 94 80; www.mare-mania.it, in Italian; 8am-1pm 3-8pm summer only), which operates out of a kiosk on the main road into the village. Half-day/day tours cost €19/22, or €46 with lunch thrown in.

On the right as you approach Putzu Idu, you'll see the **Stagno Sale Porcus**, a wide, flat lagoon that hosts flamingos in winter and is baked to a shimmering white crust in summer. Horse riding around the lagoon can be arranged through **Orte e Corru Ranch** (0783 52 81 00; Localita Oasi di Sale Porcus).

Two weekday ARST buses run to Putzu Idu from Oristano (€2, 55 minutes). In July and August, there are an additional four services.

RIOLA SARDO
pop 2140

The single main reason to stop off at this otherwise drab town is to stay at the wonderful **Hotel Lucrezia** (☎ 0783 41 20 78; www .hotellucrezia.it; Via Roma 14/a, Riola Sardo; s €75-90, d €120-150; ✗ ⬛). Housed in an ancient *cortile* (courtyard house), it has rooms surrounding an inner courtyard complete with wisteria-draped pergola, fig and citrus trees. The decor is unapologetically rustic, with high 18th-century antique beds and mighty wooden furniture. Free bikes are provided, and the welcoming staff regularly organise cooking, painting and wine-tasting courses.

MONTI FERRU

Rising to a height of 1050m (Monte Urtigu), the volcanic Monti Ferru massif is a beautiful and largely uncontaminated area of ancient forests, natural springs and small market towns. Seneghe produces some of Sardinia's best olive oil, and the island's finest beef, and Milis is famous for its sweet succulent oranges. But more than the towns, it's the glorious verdant countryside that is the main draw. Lonely roads snake over rocky peaks covered in a green down of cork, chestnut, oak and yew trees while falcons and buzzards float on warm air currents overhead. Mouflon and Sardinian deer are slowly being introduced back to their forest habitats after coming close to extinction.

MILIS
pop 1660

A one-time Roman military outpost (its name is a derivation of the Latin word *miles*, meaning soldier), Milis is a small and prosperous village, surrounded by the orange orchards that have brought it wealth.

The manicured village centre is dominated by the 18th-century **Palazzo Boyl**, a fine example of Piedmontese neo-classicism. In the late 19th and early 20th centuries, it became something of a literary meeting place, and Gabriele D'Annunzio, Grazia Deledda and Honoré de Balzac all spent time here. Now, the *palazzo* houses Milis' small **museum** (☎ 0783 5 16 65; Piazza Martiri; admission free; ✆ by appointment only) dedicated to traditional costumes and jewellery.

There are also a couple of churches worth a passing glance. Opposite Palazzo Boyl, the 14th-century **Chiesa di San Sebastiano** features an impressive rose window in its Gothic-Catalan facade, and near the eastern entrance to town, the Tuscan-Romanesque **Chiesa di San Paolo** harbours some interesting paintings by 16th-century Catalan artists.

In early November, Milis holds the **Rassegna del Vino Novello** (Festival of Young Wine), a chance for Sardinia's wine producers to show off their best products. You can do the rounds sampling the wines and grazing the food stalls that line the streets.

SENEGHE
pop 1915

Seneghe is an essential stop on any gastronomic tour of central Sardinia. A dark stone village with little obvious appeal, it is famous for its extra-virgin olive oil, a one-time winner of the prestigious Premio Nazionale Ercole Olivario award (the Oscars of the Italian olive-oil industry). Beef is another speciality. Russet-red *bue rosso* cows are bred only here and in Modica in Sicily, and gourmets consider the meat to be among the finest in Italy.

The village also provides food for the soul, hosting an annual poetry festival in late August or early September. The Settembre dei Poeti is a four-day celebration of local and international poetry with readings, Q&A sessions and a poetry slam competition – a thoroughly entertaining, dramatic performance in which adversaries improvise rhyming responses to each other, much like a freestyle rap battle.

You can stock up on olive oil at the **Oleificio Sociale Cooperativo di Seneghe** (☎ 0785 5 46 65; www .oleificiodiseneghe.com; Corso Umberto I; ✆ 9am-12.30pm & 5-7.30pm Mon-Fri) on the Bonarcado road into town. You'll pay around €6 for 0.5L; €37.50 for 5L.

To feast on the local beef, head for the **Osteria Al Bue Rosso** (☎ 0783 5 43 84; Piazzale Montiferru 3/4; meals €30-35; ✆ lunch & dinner Fri & Sat, dinner by reservation Sun & Tue-Thu), an unprepossessing restaurant in a 1920s dairy by the exit to Narbolia. Here you can try a number of beefy dishes,

ORISTANO & THE WEST

HIKE THE IRON MOUNTAIN

The best way of exploring Monti Ferru is to ditch the car and walk. This scenic route leads up to the summit of Monte Entu, at 1024m one of the highest peaks in western Sardinia. It's not especially demanding, although you should allow about four hours.

You'll need a car to get to the start, which is by the Nuraghe Ruju, outside of Seneghe. From Seneghe, head towards Bonarcado and after a few hundred metres follow the sign for S'iscala. Leave your car at the Nuraghe Ruju and join the path a few metres down from the car park, in the wood to the left of the stone wall. Heading upwards you'll arrive at an opening, marked by a holm-oak tree, where you should go left. Carry on past the wooden gate until you reach a second metal gate. Go through it and continue until you reach a fork in the trail. Head left for some marvellous views of the coast, as far as Alghero on a clear day. From here you can continue onwards to the foot of the volcanic cone that marks the summit of Monte Entu.

---

including *insalata di bue rosso* (beef salad) and delicious grilled *filetto* (filet steak). The organically produced house wine is pretty good too. Management can advise on B&Bs in the area.

BONARCADO
pop 1645

About 5km northeast of Seneghe, the sleepy village of Bonarcado is home to one of Sardinia's most unlikely pilgrimage sites. According to an edict issued by Pope Pius VII in 1821, anyone who confesses at the tiny **Santuario della Madonna di Bonacattu** between 14 and 28 September will receive full plenary indulgence. Constructed in the 7th century, and modified some 800 years later, the sanctuary is little more than a chapel with a dome on top. There are no official opening hours, but you'll usually find it open.

A short walk away, the modest Romanesque **Chiesa di Santa Maria**, once part of a medieval monastery, stands in the centre of a sombre grey square.

SANTU LUSSURGIU
pop 2560 / elev 503m

On the eastern slopes of Monti Ferru, Santu Lussurgiu lies inside an ancient volcanic crater. The main point of interest is the small *centro storico*, a tight-knit huddle of stone houses banked up around a natural amphitheatre. Further information is available from the small **tourist office** (☎ 0783 55 10 34; Via Santa Maria 40; ⊙ 9.30-11am Mon-Fri summer, 9.30am-1pm Mon-Fri winter) just off the main through road.

Santu Lussurgiu has long been known for its crafts and is still today a production centre for ironwork, woodwork and leatherwork. Investigate the town's rural traditions

at the **Museo della Tecnologia Contadina** (Museum of Rural Technology; ☎ 0783 55 06 17; Via Deodato Meloni), which has a comprehensive collection of rural tools, utensils and machines. The museum was closed for renovation at the time of research but is due to be reopened.

Santu Lussurgiu boasts two excellent hotels, both in the *centro storico*. Housed in a beautifully restored 17th-century palazzo, the **our pick** **Antica Dimora del Gruccione** (☎ 0783 55 20 35; www.anticadimora.com, in Italian; Via Michele Obinu 31; per person/half board €38/60; ❎) oozes character with its double-flanked staircase, creaking floorboards and stone arches. Rooms are spread over various sites in the historic centre, but the best are on the 1st floor of the main mansion.

Sas Benas (☎ 0783 55 08 70; www.sasbenas.it; Via Cambosu; s €40-60, d €70-100, half board per person €55-80) is a similar set-up with elegant rustic rooms in four different houses. It also runs a renowned restaurant (tasting menu €30) specialising in delicious, local fare, so expect plenty of *bue rosso* beef, *casitzolu* cheese and Santa Lussurgiu sausages.

SAN LEONARDO DE SIETE FUENTES

From Santu Lussurgiu, the road to Cuglieri twists steeply up the eastern flank of Monti Ferru. Before you've got far, a minor road heads off right (towards Macomer) for San Leonardo de Siete Fuentes, a tiny woodland hamlet famous for its gurgling spring waters. Its grandiose name is a reference to the seven fountains (*siete fuentes*) through which the water gushes.

In the village centre, a path leads up to the charming 12th-century **Chiesa di San Leonardo**, a Romanesque church that once belonged to the Knights of St John of Jerusalem. Beyond this, trails continue uphill, through the oak and elm woods. It's pretty easygoing walking, ideal for parents with little 'uns.

CUGLIERI
pop 3005 / elev 483m

Perched high on the western face of Monti Ferru, the farming village of Cuglieri makes an excellent lunch stop. You'll build a growling appetite by climbing up to the town's landmark **Basilica di Santa Maria della Neve**, a hulking church whose silvery dome is visible for miles around. The views down to the sea are quite something.

You might also want to stock up on olive oil at the **Azienda Agricola Peddio** (☎ 0785 36 92 54; Corso Umberto 95; ☻ 8.30am-1pm & 3-8pm Mon-Fri) on the main road through the village. A litre of oil costs between €6 and €7.50.

And now for lunch. Hidden among the grey stone houses of the *centro storico* is the **our pick** **Albergo Desogos** (☎ /fax 0785 3 96 60; Via Cugia 6; s/d €18/36, meals €15-20), a modest hotel and fine restaurant. There is a menu, but if you're not sure what to order you'll be perfectly safe in the hands of the maternal owner who will happily ply you with a lip-smacking array of cured hams, marinated vegetables and tangy cheeses. And that's just for the antipasto. If you've got room, the pastas and meat courses are similarly huge.

There are five ARST buses between Cuglieri and Oristano (€3, one hour) between Monday and Saturday. In July and August, there are an additional two buses on Sunday.

SANTA CATERINA DI PITTINURI & AROUND

The northern Oristano coast features some superb beaches around the popular resort of **Santa Caterina di Pittinuri**. The town's beach, capped by white cliffs, is fairly small but its shallow, protected waters are ideal for small kids.

A few kilometres to the south, the **Spiaggia dell'Arco** at **S'Archittu** features a dramatic stone arch which rises 6m above the emerald green waters. Inland from S'Archittu, and accessible by a signposted dirt track off the SS292, are the scanty remains of the Punic-Roman town of **Cornus**, scene of a historic battle in 215 BC. The isolated site is open to free exploration.

About 3km south of **Torre del Pozzo** (also known as Torre Su Putzu), tracks lead off the main road to **Is Arenas** beach, which at 6km is one of the longest in the area.

Campers are well catered to in this neck of the woods. There are three camp-sites on the seaward side of the SS292, including **Camping Is Arena** (☎ 0783 5 22 84; www .campingisarenas.it; per person/tent/car €10/13/free), immersed in pine trees near the homonymous beach. For something more upmarket, **Hotel La Baja** (☎ 0785 38 91 49; www.hotellabaja.it; Via Scirocco 20, Santa Caterina di Pittinuri; s €55-105, d €90-160; ☻ May-Sep; P ✗ ☎) offers sunny four-star rooms, a panoramic swimming pool and wonderful sea views from its solitary headland location.

From Oristano, ARST buses run to Santa Caterina (€2, 40 minutes, five Monday to Saturday, plus two on Sunday in July and August) and S'Archittu (€2, 40 minutes, five daily Monday to Saturday, plus two on Sunday in July and August). They will stop on request at the camping grounds.

LAGO OMODEO CIRCUIT

Surrounded by the green hills of the Barigadu, Lago Omodeo is Sardinia's largest man-made lake. Some 22km long and up to 3km wide, it was created between 1919 and 1924 to supply water and electricity to the agricultural lands around Oristano and Arborea. The countryside around it is sparsely populated and rich in archaeological interest with two of central Sardinia's most important nuraghic sites.

SANTA CRISTINA & PAULILATINO

The main feature of the nuraghic complex of Santa Cristina is the central well temple, one of the most important and best preserved in Sardinia. The worship of water was a fundamental part of nuraghic religious practice, and there are reckoned to be about 40 sacred wells spread across the island.

Just off the SS131, the **Nuraghe Santa Cristina** (☎ 0785 5 54 38; admission incl Museo Archeologico-Etnografico in Paulilatino €5; ☻ 8.30am-9.30pm May-Sep, to 9pm Oct-Apr) sits on the high Abasanta plateau a few kilometres south of Paulilatino. Before you get to the remains you'll pass the **Chiesa di Santa Cristina**, an early Christian church dedicated to Santa Cristina. The church and the terraced

THE ARDENT GUARD

On 6 and 7 July Sedilo hosts Oristano's most exciting festival, **S'Ardia**, when nearly 50,000 people pack themselves into the tiny village to see Sardinia's most reckless and dangerous horse race.

It celebrates the Roman Emperor Constantine, who defeated the vastly superior forces of Maxentius at Rome's Ponte Milvio in AD 312. Since then, however, the festival has received a Christian gloss. Tales say Constantine received a vision before the battle, in which he saw a cross inscribed with the words 'In Hoc Signo Vinces' ('in this sign you will conquer'). He took the sign as the insignia for his forces, and the following year he passed an edict granting the Christians religious freedom. So, locally, although not officially, he was promoted to St Constantine (Santu Antine in the local dialect).

The race circles his sanctuary and the stone cross bearing his insignia. One man – the Prima Pandela (First Flag) – is chosen to bear Constantine's yellow-brocade standard. He selects two of the best horsemen to ride with him, and they choose three cohorts each. These men will be the Prima Pandela's guard and, armed with huge sticks, they will strive to prevent the hundred other horsemen from passing him. To be chosen as the Prima Pandela is the highest honour of the village. Only a man who has proven his courage and horsemanship and substantiated his faith can carry the flag.

On 6 July the procession prays in front of the stone cross and the riders are blessed by the parish priest. In theory the priest should start the race, but in practice it is the Prima Pandela who chooses his moment and flies off at a gallop down the hill. The other horsemen are after him in seconds, aiming to pass him before he reaches the victory arch. Hundreds of riflemen shoot off blanks, exciting the horses. The stampede towards the narrow entrance of the victory arch is the most dangerous moment, as any mistake would mean running into the stone columns at top speed. In 2002 one rider died. If all goes well, the Prima Pandela passes through the arch and races on to circle the sanctuary, to deafening cheers from the crowd.

muristenes (pilgrims' huts) that surround it are opened for only nine days a year – for the feast days of Santa Cristina, around the second Sunday in May, and San Raffaele Arcangelo, on the fourth Sunday in October.

From the church, follow a path east for 100m to the nuraghic village, set in a peaceful olive grove. Inhabited up to the early Middle Ages, the village is focused on the extraordinary *tempio a pozzo* (well temple), which dates to the late Bronze Age (11th to 9th century BC).

To get to the well, you go through a finely cut keyhole entrance and down a flight of 24 superbly preserved steps. From the bottom you can gaze up at the perfectly constructed *tholos* (conical ceiling), through which light enters the dark well shaft. Every 18 years, one month and two days, the full moon shines directly through the aperture into the well. Otherwise you can catch the yearly equinoxes on 21 March and 23 September, when the sun lights up the stairway down to the well.

Continuing 5km up the SS131 brings you to **Paulilatino**, an agricultural town whose grey stone houses lend it a somewhat severe demeanour. Finds from the Santa Cristina site are displayed in the **Museo Archeologico-Etnografico** (☎ 0785 5 54 38; Via Nazionale 127; admission incl Santa Cristina €5; ☼ 9am-1pm & 4.30-7.30pm Tue-Sun May-Sep, 9am-1pm & 3-5.30pm Tue-Sun Oct-Apr) alongside farm and domestic implements from tougher rural days.

NURAGHE LOSA & AROUND

A few kilometres north of Paulilatino and just off the SS131, the **Nuraghe Losa** (☎ 0785 5 23 02; www.nuraghelosa.net, in Italian; adult/child €3.50/2; ☼ 9am-1hr before sunset) is one of Sardinia's most impressive *nuraghi*.

The site's centrepiece is a stout three-sided keep, around which three circular towers are set, two joined by a wall, and one standing independently. The central tower has lost its top floor but still rises to a height of almost 13m. Archaeologists have dated it to the Middle Bronze Age, about 1500 BC.

Entrance is by way of one of the side towers, which is connected to the main keep by an internal corridor. Passages lead left and right off the corridor to two towers, one fully enclosed, the other open.

If you want to stay in the vicinity, there's an excellent country hotel within easy driving distance. The welcoming, kid-friendly **Mandra Edera** (☎ 320 151 51 70; www.mandraedera .it, in Italian; r per person €49-59, ste €59-69, half-board per person €69-89; ⌚ end Apr-1st week Oct; P 🐕 🏊) is a lovely ranch-style hotel set amidst towering oak trees and fruit orchards. Rooms are in bungalows laid out on neat lawns and there's a smart restaurant (meals around €23). The big draw, however, is the stables. Riding lessons cost €7.50 for kids, €15 for adults, and riding excursions start at €20 per hour. Note that there's a minimum two-night stay. To get here, exit the SS131 at the Abbasanta turn-off 2km north of Nuraghe Losa, double back over the bridge, and follow the road until you see the signpost off to the right.

FORDONGIANUS

Southwest of Lago Omodeo, almost at the confluence of the Tirso and Mannu Rivers, sits the spa town of Fordongianus, most easily reached along the SS388 from Oristano.

The spa waters around here were known to Ptolemy, and the Romans established a health spa here, naming it Forum Traiani. Their 1st century AD baths, the **Terme Romane** (☎ 0783 6 01 57; www.forumtraiani.it, in Italian; admission incl Casa Aragonese €4; ⌚ 9.30am-1pm & 3.30-8pm Tue-Sun Jul-Aug, to 7pm Sep, to 6.30pm Apr-Jun, 9.30am-1pm & 2.30-5.30pm Nov-Mar, 9am-1pm & 3-6pm Oct), are still in operation today. In the centre of the complex you'll see a rectangular pool that was once surrounded by a portico,

some of which still stands today (although only one side).

The red trachyte stone of which everything is built lends the village a rosy glow. As red as the rest is the lovely late-16th-century **Casa Aragonese** (admission incl Terme Romane €4; ⌚ same hr as above), a typical aristocratic Catalan house. The strange statues outside, also in the ubiquitous trachyte, are the result of an annual sculpture competition held here.

Seven weekday buses connect with Oristano (€2, 40 minutes).

NORTH OF ORISTANO

North of the beautiful Monti Ferru region the land flattens out towards Macomer, a workaday agricultural centre and important transport hub. To the northwest, Bosa is quite different, a pretty medieval town topped by a formidable hilltop castle.

MACOMER
pop 10,835

You probably won't want to hang around too long in Macomer. It's not an unpleasant place, but unless you're passing through, there's really no great reason to stop off here.

If you do have some time to kill, there's the modest **Museo Etnografico** (☎ 0785 7 04 75; Corso Umberto 225; admission €3; ⌚ 10am-12.30pm & 4-8pm Mon-Fri, Sat am), which houses a motley collection of home furnishings and utensils. If it's shut ask over the road at **Esedra Escursioni**

ANTONIO GRAMSCI

A giant of 20th-century political thought, Antonio Gramsci (1891–1937) was one of the founding fathers of Italian communism. Born to a poor family in Ales, he later moved to Ghilarza and then on to Cagliari and Turin.

It was in Turin that his political thoughts came to fruition. A vociferous advocate of trade unionism – at the time Turin was at the forefront of Italian industrialisation – he joined the Socialist Party in 1913 and six years later cofounded the Marxist newspaper *L'Ordine Nuovo*. Internal rifts within the Socialist Party led to division and, in 1921, Gramsci and a group of fellow activists broke away to form the Italian Communist Party. Much influenced by events in Russia – he visited Moscow in 1922 and married a Russian violinist – Gramsci was arrested by the Fascist police in 1926 and sentenced to 25 years in prison. He died in 1937 at the age of 46.

Of Gramsci's ideas, the best known is his theory of hegemony, which holds that to challenge the cultural homogenisation through which the ruling classes maintain control it's necessary for the working class to arm themselves with alternative cultural and aspirational beliefs.

In **Ghilarza** you can visit the **Gramsci House** (☎ 0785 54 1 64; www.casagramscighilarza.org; Corso Umberto I 36; admission free; ⌚ 10am-1pm & 4-7pm Fri-Sun winter, 10am-1pm & 4.30-7.30pm Wed-Mon summer) where the great man lived between 1898 and 1914.

(☎ 0785 74 30 44; www.esedraescursioni.it; Corso Umberto 206), where you can also arrange excursions and trips on the *trenino verde* (see p72 for further details).

Those with a car can visit the 15m-high **Nuraghe di Santa Barbara**, off the SS131 about 2km north of Macomer, or, near the town hospital, the dilapidated **Nuraghe Ruiu**. A third *nuraghe*, the **Nuraghe di Santa Sabina** is south of Silanus, 15km east of Macomer, positioned next to a sweet Byzantine chapel.

For a bite to eat, **Ristorante Su Talleri** (☎ 0785 7 16 99; Corso Umberto I 228; pizza €6, meals €25-30; ☉ Mon-Sat) offers all the ambience of a 1980s roller-disco but does pretty good food, including takeaway pizza.

Macomer is a major rail hub. Trenitalia trains connect with Oristano (€3.30, 45 minutes, nine daily), Cagliari (€8.75, 1¾ hours, 10 daily) and Sassari (€6.35, 1¾ hours, four daily). A handful of buses head eastwards to Nuoro (€4, 1¼ hours, four daily).

The train and bus stations are at the western edge of town along Corso Umberto.

BOSA
pop 8045

Bosa is one of Sardinia's most attractive towns. Seen from a distance, its rainbow townscape resembles a vibrant Paul Klee canvas, with pastel houses stacked on a steep hillside, tapering up to a stark, grey castle. In front, moored fishing boats bob on a glassy river and palm trees line the elegant riverfront.

Lying on the banks of the Fiume Temo (River Temo), Sardinia's only navigable inland waterway, Bosa was established by the Phoenicians and thrived under the Romans. During the early Middle Ages it suffered repeat raids by Arab pirates, but in the early 12th century the Malaspina family (a branch of the Tuscan clan of the same name) moved in and built their huge castle. In the 19th century, the Savoys established lucrative tanneries here, but these have since fallen by the wayside.

Orientation

Most of Bosa lies on the north bank of the Fiume Temo. The main strip, Corso Vittorio Emanuele, is one block north of the riverfront and leads down to the two central piazzas: Piazza Costituzione and Piazza IV Novembre. West of here, the modern town is laid out in a simple grid pattern.

DETOUR: BIDONI

DETOUR: BIDONI

On the eastern side of Lago Omodeo, the hamlet of Bidoni hides one of Sardinia's strangest museums. The creepy **Museo S'Omo 'e sa Majarza** (The Witch's House; ☎ 0783 69 0 44; Via Monte 9; adult/concession €3/2; ☉ on request), signposted as the Museo del Territorio, is dedicated to witches and local folklore and features the reconstruction of a 16th-century witch's cave. Visits are by guided tour only.

Bidoni is signposted from Ghilarza, the main town on the western side of Lago Omodeo.

South of the river, Via Nazionale runs 3km west to Bosa Marina, the town's seaside satellite.

Information

Banco di Sardegna (Piazza IV Novembre) Has an ATM.
Farmacia Passino (☎ 0785 37 60 47; Corso Vittorio Emanuele 51) Central pharmacy.
Post office (Via Pischedda; ☉ 8am-6.50pm Mon-Fri, 8am-1.15pm Sat) In the modern town.
Tourist office (☎ 0785 37 61 07; www.infobosa.it, in Italian; Via Alberto Azuni 5; ☉ 10am-1pm Thu-Sat) If it's shut, as it usually is, staff at the Casa Deriu museum are very helpful.
Web Copy (☎ 0785 37 20 49; Via Vincenzo Gioberti 12; per hr €4; ☉ 9am-1pm & 4.30-8 Mon-Sat) For internet.

Sights

Commanding huge panoramic views, the hilltop **Castello Malaspina** (☎ 333 544 56 75; admission €2.50; ☉ 10am-1pm & 4-7pm Jul, 10am-1pm & 4-7pm Aug, 10am-1pm & 3.30-6pm Apr-Jun, Sep & Oct) was built in 1112 by the Tuscan Malaspina family. Little remains of the original structure except for the skeleton – the imposing walls and a series of tough brick towers – and, inside, a humble 4th-century chapel, the **Chiesa di Nostra Signora di Regnos Altos**. This houses an extraordinary 14th-century fresco cycle depicting saints ranging from a giant St Christopher through a party of Franciscans to St Lawrence in the middle of his martyrdom on the grill.

You can get to the castle by any route up through the maze of lanes in Sa Costa, the medieval old town. You're bound to get lost at some point, but unless you're in a rush, it's quite enjoyable just meandering through the

ORISTANO & THE WEST

BOSA

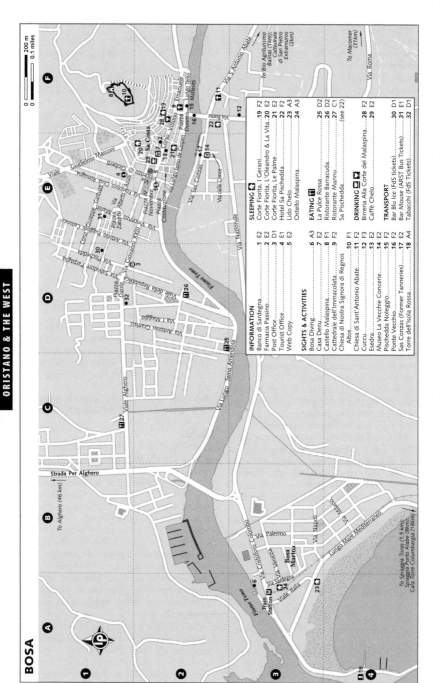

		0 200 m
		0 0.1 miles

INFORMATION

Banco di Sardegna	1	E2
Farmacia Passino	2	E2
Post Office	3	D1
Tourist Office	4	E1
Web Copy	5	E2

SIGHTS & ACTIVITIES

Bosa Diving	6	A3
Casa Deriu	7	E2
Castello Malaspina	8	F1
Cattedrale dell'Immacolata	9	F2
Chiesa di Nostra Signora di Regnos		
Altos	10	F1
Chiesa di Sant'Antonio Abate	11	F2
Cuccu	12	F3
Esedra	13	E2
Museo La Vecchie Concerie	14	E2
Pischedda Noleggio	15	F2
Ponte Vecchio	16	F2
Sas Conzas (Former Tanneries)	17	E2
Torre dell'Isola Rossa	18	A4

SLEEPING

Corte Fiorita, I Gerani	19	F2
Corte Fiorita, L'Oleandro & La Vita	20	E2
Corte Fiorita, Le Palme	21	E2
Hotel Sa Pischedda	22	F2
Lido Chelo	23	A3
Ostello Malaspina	24	A3

EATING

La Pulce Rossa	25	D2
Ristorante Barracuda	26	D2
Ristorante Mannu	27	C1
Sa Pischedda	(see 22)	

DRINKING

Birreria Alla Corte del Malaspina	28	F2
Caffè Chelo	29	E2

TRANSPORT

Bar Blu Ice (FdS tickets)	30	D1
Bar Mouse (ARST Bus Tickets)	31	E1
Tabacchi (FdS Tickets)	32	D1

lanes. If you want to visit between November and April, it's best to phone ahead.

At the bottom of the hill, near **Ponte Vecchio**, the **Cattedrale dell'Immacolata** (Piazza Duomo; ☻ 10am-noon & 4-7pm) is a rare if not overly riveting example of rococo (officially called Piedmontese baroque). From here the main boulevard, **Corso Vittorio Emanuele**, leads west past smart 17th-century houses whose wrought-iron balconies set an elegant tone.

Along the way, **Casa Deriu** (☎ 0785 37 70 43; Corso Vittorio Emanuele 59; adult/concession €4.50/2; ☻ 10.30am-1pm & 8.30-11pm Tue-Sun Jul & Aug, 11am-1pm & 5.30-8.30pm Tue-Sun Jun, 10am-1pm & 4-6pm Tue Sun rest of yr) houses the town's museum. Each of the three floors has a different theme related to the city and its past: the 1st floor features a display on the old tanning business and typical products from the surrounding region; the 2nd floor has been decorated as a typical 19th-century interior; and the top floor is dedicated to Melkiorre Melis (1889–1982), one of Sardinia's most important modern artists.

Over the river, the former 19th-century tanneries line up along the southern bank in an area known as **Sas Conzas**. To get an idea of what this area must have been like when the tanneries were in full swing – and many were still in business until after WWII – the **Museo La Vecchie Concerie** (☎ 329 414 49 21; Via delle Conce 13; admission €2; ☻ 11am-1pm & 6-11pm) has a small collection of photos and old tools. Panels (in English and Italian) explain the whole smelly business.

A short walk from here, over Via Roma, is the little **Chiesa di Sant'Antonio Abate**, usually closed to the public but the focus of a town festival dedicated to the saint on 16 and 17 January and again at Carnevale. Two kilometres further upstream is the 11th-century **Cattedrale di San Pietro Extramuros** (☎ 0785 37 32 86; admission €1; ☻ 10am-1pm & 4-7.30pm Tue-Sun Jul & Aug, 10am-1pm & 3.30-6pm Tue-Sun Apr-Jun, Sep & Oct), with its Gothic facade and largely Romanesque interior.

Activities

The river, the hills, the sea down the road – Bosa has much to offer outdoor enthusiasts. If you want to join an organised tour, **Esedra** (☎ 0785 37 42 58; www.esedrasardegna.it; Corso Vittorio Emanuele 64; ☻ 9.30am-1pm & 4.30-8pm Mon-Sat, 10.30am-1pm Sun) offers a wide range of packages, including river cruises, birdwatching excursions, boat tours, and trips on the *trenino*

verde. Prices depend on the activity and size of the group but are usually between €25 and €35 per person. Esedra operates out of a shop on the main strip where you can pick up ISOLA certified craftwork.

You can hire bikes and scooters at **Cuccu** (☎ 0785 37 54 16; Via Roma 5), a mechanic's on the southern side of the river – €8 per day for a bike and €40 for a scooter. On the other side of the river, **Pischedda Noleggio** (☎ 339 489 01 05; Lungo Temo Matteotti) can set you up with bikes (per day €10), canoes (€25 for half a day) and *gommone* (dinghies, €35 for half day).

Bosa is also an important wine centre, renowned for its dessert wine, Malvasia. To tour local producers ask at the tourist office for information on the local wine route, the Strada della Malvasia.

Festivals & Events

Bosa's **Carnevale** kicks off with a burning pyre outside the Chiesa di Sant'Antonio Abate and follows with days of parades. The last day, *martedi grasso*, is the most intriguing. In the morning townsfolk dress in black to lament the passing of Carnevale, while in the evening groups of boisterous locals dress in white to hunt the *giolzi*, a manifestation of the carnival that is said to hide in people's groins. To find it locals hold lanterns up to each other's nether regions shouting 'Giolzi! Giolzi! Ciappadu! Ciappadu!' [*Giolzi! Giolzi! Gotcha! Gotcha!*].

For four days around the first Sunday of August, Bosa celebrates the **Festa di Santa Maria del Mare**. Fishermen form a colourful procession of boats to accompany a figure of the Virgin Mary along the river from Bosa Marina to the cathedral.

In the second week of September, streets in the old town are bedecked with huge palm fronds, flowers and *altarittos* (votive altars) for the **Festa di Nostra Signora di Regnos Altos**.

Sleeping

Bio Agriturismo Bainas (☎ 339 209 0 967, 0785 37 31 29; agriturbainas@tiscali.it; Via San Pietro; B&B per person €30-35, half board per person €47-53) Surrounded by fields of artichokes, and olive and orange trees, this modest *agriturismo* is about 1km outside of town. There are few frills, but the four guestrooms in the dark ochre farmstead are modern and tastefully decorated. Outside, there's a verandah with blissful views. In

ORISTANO & THE WEST

August, there's a minimum stay of a week; in July and the rest of the year, three days.

Hotel Sa Pischedda (☎ 0785 37 30 65; www.hotel sapischedda.it; Via Roma 8; s €40-80, d €60-105; P ✕) A hotel since the 19th century, this three-star on the southern side of the river is full of character. Rooms are surprisingly straight-forward although many retain individual touches – some have frescoed ceilings, others are split-level or offer river views (for which you pay an extra €5). The hotel restaurant is highly regarded.

ourpick Corte Fiorita (☎ 0785 37 70 58; www .albergo-diffuso.it; Via Lungo Temo de Gasperi 45; s €45-90, d €65-115; ✕ 🖳) A so-called *albergo diffuso*, Corte Fiorita has beautiful, spacious rooms in four refurbished *palazzi* across town; one on the riverfront and three in the historic centre. No two rooms are exactly the same, but the overall look is rustic-chic with plenty of exposed stonework, wooden beams and vaulted ceilings. Reception is at Le Palme, from where the owner will ferry you up to your room in an electric buggy – a good way of seeing the *centro storico*.

Eating

La Pulce Rossa (☎ 0785 37 56 57; Via Lungo Temo Amendola 1; pizzas €6, meals around €25) Located down in the modern town, this friendly family-run restaurant serves up filling working-man's fare at decidedly untouristy prices. For a real gut-buster make sure you try the house speciality, *pennette Pulce Rossa*, a rich con-coction of pasta tubes, giant prawns, cream and saffron.

Ristorante Barracuda (☎ 0785 37 45 10; Viale della Repubblica; meals around €28) This big, bustling res-taurant is on a residential street 10 minutes' walk from the centre. The atmosphere is laid-back and the food is similarly unpretentious with the emphasis on hearty, home-cooked pastas and simple seafood dishes.

Ristorante Mannu (☎ 0785 37 53 06; Viale Alghero 28; meals around €30) Despite its unenticing lo-cation – next to a busy petrol station – this restaurant serves fine island food. A novel dish to try is the *agliata di razze*, an unusual combination of fish rays served in a sweet garlic sauce. If you want to stick to safer ter-rain, the homemade *panadinas* (like ravioli) are a reliable bet.

Sa Pischedda (☎ 0785 37 30 65; Via Roma 8; meals around €30; ☽ Wed-Mon, daily summer) At the hotel of the same name, this is one of Bosa's best

restaurants. Specialising in fish, both fresh-water and saltwater, it has tables laid out on a romantic riverside verandah and in a styl-ish back garden. The menu features classics like mullet *bottarga* (salted roe) and *fregola alla arselle* (rice-shaped pasta with clams and cherry tomatoes).

Drinking

A good people-watching spot, **Caffè Chelo** (☎ 0785 37 30 92; Corso Vittorio Emanuele 71; ☽ 8am-10pm, later in summer) is an original Liberty-style cafe with street-side tables overlooking Piazza Costituzione.

For a more publike atmosphere, get down to **Birreria Alla Corte del Malaspina** (Corso Vittorio Emanuele 39; ☽ 8pm-2am Mon-Sat), a cosy drinking den on the central strip.

Getting There & Away
BUS
All buses terminate at Piazza Zanetti. There are FdS services to/from Alghero (€3–4.50, 55 minutes, four daily) and Macomer (€2.50, 50 minutes, nine daily). ARST buses serve Sassari (€5.50, 2¼ hours, two daily) and Oristano (€5.50, two hours, four daily Monday to Saturday). Buy FdS tickets at the tabacchi on Viale Alghero or **Bar Blu Ice** (Via Azuni 19); get ARST tickets at **Bar Mouse** (Piazza Zanetti).

CAR & MOTORCYCLE
Bosa is connected to Macomer by the SS129bis, and to Alghero by the scenic coastal road, the SP105. In central Bosa it is generally easy to find street-side parking in the modern town, west of the centre.

Getting Around
Up to 20 daily FdS buses run from central Bosa (Piazza Zanetti) to Bosa Marina (€1, 10 minutes).

BOSA MARINA & THE COAST
At the mouth of the Fiume Temo, about 3km from Bosa proper, Bosa Marina is a busy summer resort set on a wide, kilo-metre-long beach. Overlooking the beach, the Catalano-Aragonese **Torre dell'Isola Rossa** (admission €2.50; ☽ 11am-1pm & 2.30-6.30pm Sat & Sun Apr-Jun, 10.30am-7.30pm daily Jul-Aug) is used to host temporary exhibitions.

Bosa Diving (☎ 335 818 97 48; www.bosadiving.it, in Italian; Via Cristoforo Colombo 2) offers dives (from

€35) and snorkelling excursions (€25), as well as hiring out canoes (from €7) and dinghies (from €25). It also runs biweekly tours to beaches on the Capo Marargiu (€18 per person), just north of Bosa Marina.

If you have your own transport, you can search out a number of other beaches. Stretching south are the **Spiaggia Turas**, **Spiaggia Porto Alabe** and **Cala Torre Columbargia**. The first two are respectively a 1.5km and 8km drive from Bosa Marina and can get busy in high season. The last is reached via the town of Tresnuraghes and involves some dusty trail driving. It's about an 18km drive from Bosa Marina.

For a different take on the area, the **trenino verde** (www.treninoverde.com) runs, slowly, between Bosa Marina, Tresnuraghes and Macomer. Every Saturday in July and August it leaves Macomer at 9.30am and arrives at Bosa Marina at 11.17am (the return journey is by FdS bus).

From Bosa Marina there's a Saturday and Sunday return service to Tresnuraghes (45 minutes), where you can connect with an FdS bus for Macomer. Fares are: Macomer to Bosa Marina (single/return €9.50/13); Bosa Marina to Tresnuraghes (single/return €8/11).

In Bosa Marina, there's cheap accommodation at the HI-affiliated **Ostello Malaspina** (☎ 0785 37 50 09, 346 236 38 44; www.valevacanze.com; Via Sardegna 2; dm/d €16/40; ☺ year-round; 🕸), not far from the beach. Staff can arrange boat trips, canoe and dinghy hire, and there's an evening meal available for €10. Air-con costs €5 on top of room rates.

For a real treat, **Lido Chelo** (☎ 0785 37 38 04; www.lidochelo.it; Lungo Mare Mediterraneo; 2-bed apt €70-190; 🕸 P) has modern apartments right on the beach. The management also runs the adjacent ice-cream cafe, with a more formal restaurant upstairs. Note that there's a two-day minimum stay.

ORISTANO & THE WEST

Sassari & the Northwest

Boasting a varied and at times dazzling coastline, the island's second-largest city, and a remote national park, Sardinia's northwestern corner covers most bases. Yet the advent of mass tourism – and much of the coastline is given over to tourism – has done little to dull the character of this proud and self-confident region.

The main gateway and most celebrated destination, Alghero, is a case in point. Beautiful and defiantly self-contained, it's distinctly Spanish in atmosphere, a result of centuries of Catalan rule. Similarly, Sassari's cosmopolitan outlook can be attributed to its past as a Genoese city. History has left its mark on Sardinia's northwest, not only in bricks and mortar but also in spirit, and the area seems less Sardinian than other parts, less rural and less reserved.

For many visitors this area is all about the coast, about the perfect white and blues of the Spiaggia della Pelosa, the cliffs of Alghero's Riviera del Corallo, or the delicious coves of the Parco Nazionale dell'Asinara. But head inland and you'll discover a different world.

The fertile lands of the Logudoro, once the granary of the Roman Empire, are silent and strangely alluring. Architectural and archaeological gems litter the sun-bleached countryside: a string of Pisan-Romanesque churches stands testimony to past glories, while tumbledown ruins tell of prehistoric times. Highlights include the Nuraghe Santu Antine, itself littered with the enormous building blocks of other long-gone *nuraghi* (stone towers), the weird ziggurat of Monte d'Accoddi – the only example in the Mediterranean – and the necropoli at Anghelu Ruiu.

HIGHLIGHTS

- Spy on albino donkeys and birds of prey on the **Parco Nazionale dell'Asinara** (p147); eye up the beach life on the **Spiaggia della Pelosa** (p147)

- Weave through the medieval lanes and robust ramparts of Sardinia's Catalan enclave, **Alghero** (p148)

- See how prehistoric cavemen lived in the Grotta di San Michele in **Ozieri** (p131), then check out their tools in the town's Museo Archeologico

- Dive into the Mediterranean's largest underwater lake and explore the fairy-tale **Grotta di Nettuno** (p161) on the windswept and rugged **Capo Caccia** (p161) headland

- Clock the views over to Corsica from Castelsardo's impregnable hilltop **castello** (p136)

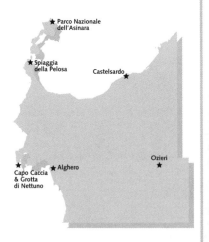

★ Parco Nazionale dell'Asinara

★ Spiaggia della Pelosa

Castelsardo ★

Ozieri ★

★ Alghero
Capo Caccia & Grotta di Nettuno ★

SASSARI & THE NORTHWEST

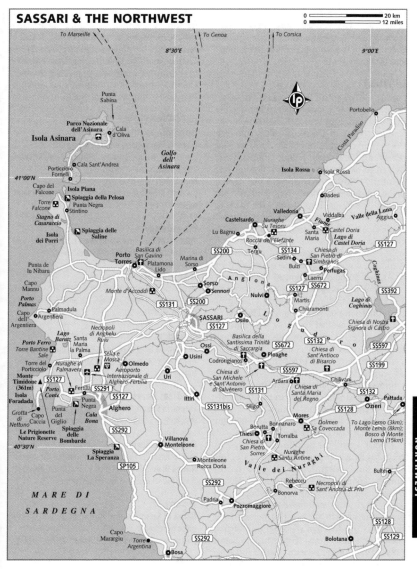

0 — 20 km
0 — 12 miles

To Marseille

To Genoa

To Corsica

8°30'E

9°00'E

Punta Sabina

Portobello

Parco Nazionale dell'Asinara

Cala d'Oliva

Isola Asinara

Golfo dell' Asinara

Costa Paradiso

Porticciolo Fornelli

Cala Sant'Andrea

Isola Rossa

Isola Rossa

41°00'N

Capo del Falcone

Isola Piana

Badesi

Torre Falcone

Spiaggia della Pelosa

Punta Negra
Stintino

Valledoria

Viddalba

Valle della Luna

Aggius

Stagno di Casaraccio

Castelsardo

Nuraghe Su Tesoru

Fiume

Santa
Maria

Castel Doria

Lago di Castel Doria

SS127

Isola dei Porri

Spiaggia delle Saline

Lu Bagnu

Roccia dell'Elefante

Tergu

Chiesa di San Pietro di Simbranos

SS127

Punta de lu Nibaru

Basilica di San Gavino

Porto Torres

Platamona Lido

Marina di Sorso

SS200

Sedini

SS134

Bulzi

Simbranos

Perfugas

Capo Mannu

Monte d'Accoddi

Sorso

A n g l o n a

Laerru

SS127

SS672

SS392

Porto Palmas

Sennori

Nulvi

Martis

Coghinas

Capo dell'Argentiera

Palmadula

Argentiera

SS131

SS200

SASSARI

Osilo

Chiaramonti

L   o

Lago di Coghinas

Chiesa di Nostra Signora di Castro

SS127

Lago Baratz

Santa Maria la Palma

Necropoli di Anghelu Ruju

Basilica della Santissima Trinità di Saccargia

g u

SS132

d o r o

SS597

Porto Ferro

Torre Bantine Sale

Ossi

SS672

Chiesa di Sant'Antioco di Bisarcio

Monte Timidone (361m)

Torre del Porticciolo

Nuraghe di Palmavera

Sella e Mosca

Olmedo

Usini

Codrongianos

Ploaghe

SS597

SS199

Chilivani

Isola Foradada

SS127

Fertilia

SS291

Aeroporto Internazionale di Alghero-Fertilia

Uri

Chiesa di San Michele e Sant'Antonio di Salvènero

Ardara

Chiesa di Santa Maria del Regno

SS132

Grotta di Nettuno

Capo Caccia

Punta del Giglio

Punta Negra

SS127

Alghero

Ittiri

SS131

Siligo

SS128

Pattada

Ozieri

Cala Bona

Mores

Dolmen Sa Coveccada

To Lago Lerno (3km); Monte Lerno (8km); Bosco di Monte Lerno (15km)

Le Prigionette Nature Reserve

Spiaggia delle Bombarde

SS292

Villanova Monteleone

Bonnanaro

Thiesi

Borutta

Torralba

Nuraghe Santu Antine

Chiesa di San Pietro Sorres

V a l l e   d e i   N u r a g h i

Bultei

Spiaggia La Speranza

SP105

Monteleone Rocca Doria

M A R E   D I   S A R D E G N A

SS292

Rebeccu

Bonorva

Necropoli di Sant'Andrea di Priu

40°30'N

Padria

Pozzomaggiore

SS128

Capo Marargiu

Torre Argentina

SS292

Bosa

Bolotana

SS129

SASSARI

pop 121,700

Sardinia's second city is proud and cultured, a vibrant university town with a medieval heart and a modern outlook. Like many Italian towns it hides its charms behind an outer shell of drab apartment blocks and confusing, traffic-choked roads. But once through to the inner sanctum it opens up, revealing a grand centre of wide boulevards, impressive piazzas, and stately *palazzi*. In the evocative and run-down *centro storico* (historic centre) medieval alleyways hum with Dickensian activity as residents run about their daily business amid grimy facades and hidden churches.

Tourism has yet to make a big impact on Sassari, and what you see is absolutely the real thing. The city might be a bit ragged round the edges but the atmosphere is unpretentious and totally genuine.

HISTORY
Sassari (Tatari in the local dialect) owes its medieval rise to prominence to the decline of its coastal counterparts. As the ancient Roman colony of Turris Libisonis (modern Porto Torres) succumbed to malaria and repeated pirate raids, people gradually retreated to Sassari. Porto Torres (and at one point the town of Ardara) remained capital of the Giudicato di Torres (or Logudoro), but Sassari's increasing importance led it to break away from the province and, with support from Genoa, declare itself an autonomous city state in 1294.

But the Sassaresi soon tired of Genoese meddling and in 1321 called on the Crown of Aragon to help rid them of the northern Italians. The Catalano-Aragonese arrived in 1323, but Sassari soon discovered it had leapt from the frying pan into the fire. The first of many revolts against the city's new masters came two years later. It took another century for the Iberians to fully control Sassari.

For a time the city prospered, but waves of plague and the growing menace from Ottoman Turkey sidelined Sardinia, leaving Sassari to slide into decline in the 16th century. A century later the founding of the city's university, Sardinia's first, was a rare highlight in this otherwise grim period.

It wasn't until the middle of the 19th century that Sassari began to take off again, following the modernisation of Porto Torres and the laying of the Carlo Felice highway between the port, Sassari and Cagliari. Since 1945 the city has maintained a slow pace of economic growth. It has also been an industrious producer of national politicians, including former presidents Antonio Segni (1891–1972) and Francesco Cossiga (b 1928), the charismatic communist leader Enrico Berlinguer (1922–84), and Beppe Pisanu, interior minister in Silvio Berlusconi's second government (2001–06).

ORIENTATION
Sassari's centre is not the easiest place to navigate. The most obvious focus is Piazza Italia, the city's biggest square, and the starting point of busy Via Roma. In the grid-pattern streets flanking Via Roma, you'll find the archaeological museum, some hotels and a fistful of restaurants. Northwest of Piazza Italia, Piazza Castello and Piazza Azuni mark the entrance to the historic centre, the main strip of which, Corso Vittorio Emanuele II, runs down to Piazza San Antonio, near the train station.

INFORMATION
Bookshops
Libreria Messaggeri e Sarde (Map p128; Piazza Castello 11) Best for Sardinian literature (mainly in Italian). Upstairs has maps and guides.
Mondadori (Map p128; ☎ 079 201 20 98; Largo Cavallotti 17) Has an excellent choice of maps and a small selection of English-language books.

Emergency
Police station (Questura; off Map p125; ☎ 079 249 50 00; Via Ariosto 3) The main police headquarters.

Internet Access
Net Gate Internet (Map p128; ☎ 079 23 78 94; Piazza Universita 4; per hr €3; 🕑 9am-1.15pm & 3.30-7.30pm Mon-Fri, 9am-1pm Sat)

Laundry
Lavalandia (Map p128; Corso Vittorio Emanuele II; 6kg wash €4; 🕑 9am-9pm) One of Sardinia's few self-service laundrettes.

Medical Services
Farmacia Simon (Map p128; ☎ 079 23 11 44; Piazza Castello 5; 🕑 8pm-9.10am) Pharmacy that does the night shift.
Guardia Medica (Map p128; ☎ 079 206 22 22; Via Maurizio Zanfarino 23) For nonemergency medical assistance.
Nuovo Ospedale Civile (Map p125; ☎ 079 206 10 00; Via De Nicola) Hospital south of the centre.

Money
Banca di Sassari (Map p128; Piazza Castello 8) Western Union representative.
Banca Intesa (Map p128; Piazza Italia 23) Has an ATM.

Post
Post office (Map p128; Via Brigata di Sassari 13; 🕑 8am-6.50pm Mon-Fri, to 1.15pm Sat)

Tourist Information
Tourist office (Map p128; ☎ 079 23 17 77; aastss@ tiscali.it; Via Roma 62; 🕑 9am-1.30pm & 4-6pm Mon-Thu, 9am-1.30pm Fri) Has information on Sassari and the surrounding area.

<segment? no>

SASSARI

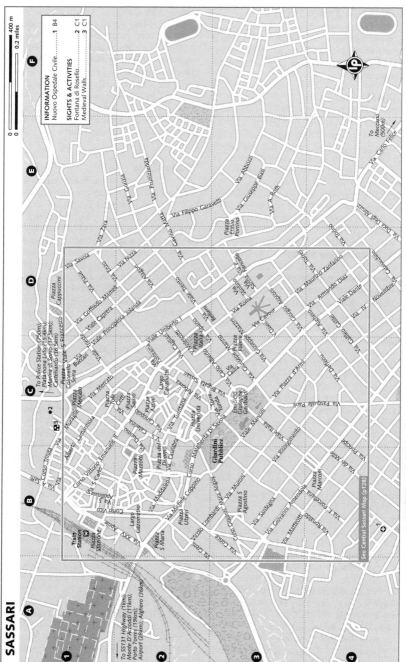

400 m
0.2 miles

INFORMATION
Nuovo Ospedale Civile..........1 B4

SIGHTS & ACTIVITIES
Fontana di Rosello................2 C1
Medieval Walls.....................3 C1

To Meccano (500m)

To Police Station (750m);
Platamona Lido (15.4km);
Marine di Sorso (17.5km);
Castelsardo (36.5km)

To SS131 Highway (1km);
Monte D'Accoddi (11km);
Porto Torres (19km);
Airport (28km); Alghero (36km)

See Central Sassari Map (p128)

SASSARI & THE
NORTHWEST

DANGERS & ANNOYANCES

There are no reasons for special concern in Sassari, although you should take the usual common-sense precautions in the centre, especially in the less salubrious streets around the station.

SIGHTS

Sassari's small medieval centre is not in great nick, but it retains enough of its 13th-century character to reward a leisurely look. Unlike many Italian towns, Sassari did not simply expand beyond its historic walls; instead, it regenerated itself over the centuries by eliminating the old to make way for the new. Fortunately, some jewels survived the revamps, and Sassari's two grand churches – the Duomo and Chiesa di Santa Maria di Betlem – are impressive.

Museo Nazionale Sanna

In a grand Palladian villa on Via Roma, **Museo Nazionale Sanna** (Map p128; ☎ 079 27 22 03; Via Roma 64; admission €3.10; ✆ 9am-8pm Tue-Sun) houses a comprehensive archaeological collection, a small painting gallery and an ethnographical section dedicated to Sardinian folk art. The archaeological section is the real draw.

Exhibits are displayed in seven chronologically ordered rooms, starting with the Sala Preistorica, which showcases the island's very earliest Stone Age and neolithic finds. In this and the next room you'll find an array of fossils, pottery fragments and finds from the 3rd-century BC temple of Monte d'Accoddi (p131).

Beyond these two rooms, the museum opens up in a series of displays dedicated to megalithic tombs and *domus de janas* (literally 'fairy houses'; tombs cut into rock). The highlight is the sophisticated bronze-ware, including axe heads and similar tools, weapons, bracelets, votive boats and *bronzetti* (bronze figurines depicting humans and animals).

Room X is dedicated to Phoenician and Carthaginian objects. Some exquisite pottery is mixed in with gold jewellery and masks. Rooms XI and XII contain Roman finds, mostly ceramics and oil burners but also some statuary and a sprinkling of coins, jewellery and household objects. Off to one side lies a stash of heavy Roman anchors.

The museum's *pinacoteca* (picture gallery) displays works from the collection of Giovanni Sanna, a mining engineer whose family built the museum and after whom it is named. The works are mostly ponderous 18th-century paintings, although the fine 14th-century Pisan triptych *Madonna con Bambino* (1473), by Bartolomeo Vivarini, is worth seeking out.

There is also a small collection of Sardinian folk art in the separate ethnographic section (currently closed for refurbishment) with an eclectic array of carpets, saddlebags, embroidered clothes and curious terracotta hot-water bottles.

Piazza Italia

Sassari's largest piazza, Piazza Italia, is one of Sardinia's most impressive public spaces. Covering about a hectare, it is surrounded by imposing 19th-century buildings, including the neoclassical **Palazzo della Provincia** (Map p128), seat of the provincial government. Opposite, the red neo-Gothic **Palazzo Giordano** (Map p128) provides a palatial home for the Banca San Paolo. Presiding over everything, the statue of King Vittorio Emanuele II was unveiled in 1899 to much pomp and costumed celebration, in anticipation of the grand folk celebration that would become the city's main festival, the Cavalcata Sarda. The piazza also marks the starting point for Sassari's other big jamboree, I Candelieri (see opposite).

Museo della Brigata Sassari

Sassari is home to one of Italy's most revered army regiments. The Sassari Brigade was established in 1915 and during WWI established a reputation for bravery in the face of appalling conditions. You can glean something of the suffering they endured in the tiny **Museo della Brigata Sassari** (Map p128; Piazza Castello; admission free; ✆ 8.30am-4pm Mon-Thu, to noon Sat) in the regiment's city-centre barracks. Uniforms, photos, documents and other memorabilia testify to the ferocious bravery of the Sardinian soldiers, who were thrown into battle against the Austrians in northern Italy. There are old guns and grenades on show, and a re-creation of a wartime trench. Most touching, however, are the proud poses of the men in the old black-and-white photographs.

Corso Vittorio Emanuele II & Around

The main strip in the historic centre, Corso Vittorio Emanuele II follows the path of the original Roman road from Porto Torres to Cagliari. Little has survived to suggest its

13th-century heyday (it was at the time the top address in town), but if you look above the shop windows, you'll find a few faint signs of past grandeur among the chipped and scarred stonework.

A case in point is **Casa Farris** (Map p128; Corso Vittorio Emanuele II 25), whose high Gothic windows have withstood centuries of neglect. A few metres on, on the other side of the road, **Casa di Re Enzo** (Map p128; Corso Vittorio Emanuele II 42) provides a remarkable 15th-century Catalan Gothic setting for an undies shop. Wander inside for a closer look at the vibrant frescoes and frilly knickers.

Opposite, the **Teatro Civico** (Map p128) was a 19th-century addition, built to a Liberty style in 1826, and modelled on Turin's Teatro Carignano.

North of Corso Vittorio Emanuele II, **Piazza Tola** was medieval Sassari's main market, and you'll still find a market here on weekday mornings. It is also where condemned heretics were burned in front of spectators on the balcony of the 16th-century **Palazzo d'Usini** (Map p128), now the city public library.

From the piazza, take Via Alberto Lamarmora and Via Rosello for Piazza Mercato, a busy and unsightly traffic junction outside the city walls. Here, in a sunken patch of grass, you'll find the Renaissance **Fontana di Rosello** (Map p125; 9am-1pm & 5.30-8.30pm Tue-Sat, 5.30-8.30pm Sun May-Sep, 9am-1pm & 4-7pm Tue-Sat, 9am-1pm Sun Oct-Apr), Sassari's most famous fountain. A monumental marble box ringed by eight lion-head spouts and topped by two fine marble arches, it was for a long time the focus of city life.

A short walk away, down Corso Trinita, you can admire the only substantial remnant of the city's **medieval walls** (Map p125).

Duomo di San Nicola & Around

Sassari's baroque **Duomo** (Map p128; Piazza Duomo; 8.30am-noon & 4-7.30pm) rises like an exotic beast over the otherwise sober streets of the medieval centre. What hits you first is the 18th-century baroque facade, a giddy free-for-all of sculptural joie de vivre, with statues, reliefs, friezes and busts. It's all just a front, though, because inside the cathedral reverts to its true Gothic character. The facade covers a 15th-century Catalan Gothic body, which was itself built over an earlier Romanesque church. Nothing remains of this except for the 13th-century *campanile* (bell tower). Of

note inside are the frescoes in the left transept and the Gothic fresco in the first chapel on the right. In the neighbouring chapel, check out the fine painting of the *Martirio dei SS Cosma e Damiano* (Martyrdom of Saints Cosimo and Damien).

The narrow streets around here are full of life. At some point you'll almost certainly arrive in Piazza Mazzotti, locally dubbed Piazza di Demolizione (Demolition Piazza) and arguably one of Sardinia's ugliest squares. It was once a warren of old streets like the rest of the quarter, but hard-to-control prostitution plagued its narrow lanes, so the authorities decided to knock it all down and create a car park instead.

Chiesa di Santa Maria di Betlem

With its distinctive dome and proud Romanesque facade, the **Chiesa di Santa Maria di Betlem** (Map p128; Piazza di Santa Maria; 7.15am-noon & 5-8pm) reveals a curious blend of architectural styles. The exterior betrays Gothic and even vaguely Oriental admixtures. Inside, the Catalan Gothic vaulting has been preserved, but much baroque silliness has crept in to obscure the original lines of the building. Lining each aisle in the chapels stands some of the giant 'candles' that the city guilds parade about town for the 14 August festivities.

FESTIVALS & EVENTS

Cavalcata Sarda (Sardinian Riding Festival) One of Sardinia's most high-profile festivals is held in Sassari on the second-last Sunday of May. Thousands of people converge on the city to participate in costumed processions, to sing and dance, and watch fearless horse-riders exhibit their acrobatic skills.

I Candelieri A second big festival, held every 14 August. Teams wearing medieval costume and representing various 16th-century guilds bear nine wooden columns (the 'candlesticks') through the town. The celebrations have their origins in 13th-century Pisan worship of the Madonna of the Assumption.

SLEEPING

Accommodation in Sassari is limited to a handful of business-oriented hotels and a clutch of B&Bs. Rates are generally cheaper at weekends and over the summer when everyone deserts the city for the sea.

Casa Chiara (Map p128; 079 200 50 52, 333 695 71 18; www.casachiara.net; Vicolo Bertolinis 7; s/d €30/60;) In the buzzing uni area, this is a laid-back B&B with a breezy, homey atmosphere. Resembling

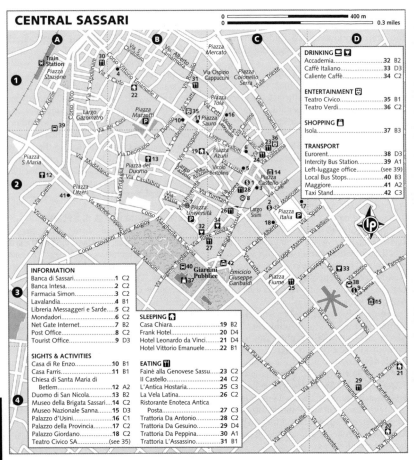

a well-kept student flat, it's got three colourful bedrooms, a dining room and a cheerfully cluttered kitchen.

Frank Hotel (Map p128; ☎ 079 27 64 56; www.frank hotel.com; Via Armando Diaz 20; s €45-50, d €65-75; P ⊠) Good for a quick stopover, the pea-green Frank is a reliable choice. There's nothing memorable about the tired white rooms, or indeed about much of the hotel, but you're not paying a lot, and it's near the centre. The free parking is a real bonus in a town where space is at such a valuable commodity.

Hotel Vittorio Emanuele (Map p128; ☎ 079 23 55 38; www.hotelvittorioemanuele.ss.it, in Italian; Corso Vittorio Emanuele II 100-102; s €50-65, d €70-89; ⊠ ▣) Housed in a renovated medieval *palazzo*, this slick three-star provides corporate comfort at rea-

sonable rates. Rooms are spacious and bright with a sterile colour scheme. Gourmets will appreciate wine tastings in the stone-clad cellar and refined food at the restaurant.

Hotel Leonardo da Vinci (Map p128; ☎ 079 28 07 44; www.leonardodavincihotel.it; Via Roma 79; s €55-80, d €75-110; P ⊠ ▣) This popular business hotel is within comfortable walking distance of the centre's sights and restaurants. Staff are polite and efficient, and the rather bland rooms are comfortable enough. There's free wi-fi and on-site parking for €8.

EATING

Eating in Sassari is a real pleasure. Eateries range from cheap student cafes to smart, refined restaurants, and standards are universally high. A local curiosity is *fainè*, a cross between a crêpe and a pizza with a base made from chickpea flour.

Fainè alla Genovese Sassu (Map p128; Via Usai 17; meals €3.50-6; ✔ Mon-Sat) A no-frills spot for a cheap fill-up, this is Sassari's original purveyor of *fainè*. There's nothing else on the menu, but with a wide range of toppings you should find something to suit your tastes.

Trattoria L'Assassino (Map p128; ☎ 079 23 50 41; Via Ospizio Cappuccini 1/a; set lunch €8-12; ✔ Mon-Sat) A model trattoria in a tiny back alley, L'Assassino is popular with local workmen who come here to lunch on simple pastas and chunks of roast meat. You can also order a selection of eight starters for €18 (minimum two people).

Trattoria Da Peppina (Map p128; ☎ 079 23 61 46; Vicolo Pigozzi 1; meals around €20; ✔ Mon-Sat) No-frills doesn't really cover it. This spit and sawdust trattoria wouldn't know a frill if it fell over one, but it knows how to cook meat. The menu is a masterpiece of plain speaking, listing its dishes as beef, pork, horse.

Trattoria Da Antonio (Map p128; ☎ 079 23 42 97; Via Arborea 2/b; meals around €25; ✔ Tue-Sun) Affectionately known as *Lu Panzone* (the Big Belly), this boisterous, unpretentious trattoria does a great line in homespun, no-nonsense food. Chow down on local salami, followed by that old Italian chestnut, pasta *e ceci* (pasta and chickpeas).

our pick **Trattoria Da Gesuino** (Map p128; ☎ 079 27 33 92; Via Torres 17G; meals around €30; ✔ Mon-Sat) Halfway between an earthy neighbourhood trattoria and an upmarket restaurant, Da Gesuino hits exactly the right tone. It's relaxed, but service is efficient, the interior is inviting and the food is excellent. The menu covers all the usual bases with pasta, risottos, fresh fish and grilled meats. A standout choice is the *risotto con scampi e verdura* (risotto with scampi and vegetables).

Ristorante Enoteca Antica Posta (Map p128; ☎ 079 200 61 21; Via Torre Tonda 26; meals around €30; ✔ Mon-Sat) Traditional cuisine is given a modern makeover at this designer wine-bar-cum-restaurant. Typical of the approach is *tortellacci verdi al formaggio di fossa con funghi porcini e timo selvattico* (pockets of green pasta stuffed with cheese and served with porcini mushrooms and wild thyme). There's also a decent wine list of Italian and Sardinian labels.

La Vela Latina (Map p128; ☎ 079 23 37 37; Largo Sisini 8; meals around €30; ✔ Mon-Sat) Vegetarians please note – this much-loved *centro storico* restaurant is not for you. But if you're a carnivore

with a yen for culinary adventure you'll find plenty of hard-core meat dishes, including *trippa* (tripe), *cervella* (brain) and *lingua di vitello* (ox tongue).

Il Castello (Map p128; ☎ 079 23 20 41; Piazza Cavallino de Honestis 6; meals around €35; ✔ Thu-Tue Oct-May, daily Jun-Sep) A favourite with the theatre crowd, this formal restaurant has tables laid out in a glass pavilion overlooking Piazza Castello. The menu is seasonal, but you'll always find a tempting selection of seafood and meaty main courses.

L'Antica Hostaria (Map p128; ☎ 079 20 00 60; Via Giuseppe Mazzini 27; meals around €45; ✔ Mon-Sat) Hidden behind a discreet exterior, L'Antica Hostaria is one of Sassari's top restaurants. In intimate surroundings you are treated to inventive cuisine rooted in local tradition, such as fricassee of lamb with white beans and red peppers. Desserts are similarly impressive, and there's a more than adequate wine list.

DRINKING

With its big student population and busy business community, Sassari has a vibrant cafe culture. You'll find a number of popular spots on Via Roman and further south on Via Torre Tonda, a lively student strip. Many places stay open late and some offer occasional live music.

Caffè Italiano (Map p128; Via Roma 38/40; ✔ Mon-Sat) One of the best places on Via Roma is this big, bustling bar with pavement tables and a stylish interior. Business folk like to lunch here, and young locals come most afternoons to chat over an aperitif.

Accademia (Map p128; Via Torre Tonda 11; ✔ Mon-Sat) In the university district, this place has tables in an attractive wrought-iron pavilion. It gets very busy at lunchtime and on Friday and Saturday nights, when it stays open until 2am. If you're lucky you might also catch a gig here.

Along the same road, the **Caliente Caffè** (Map p128; Via Torre Tonda 1/b) is a cool wine bar with outdoor tables beneath a stretch of 13th-century city wall.

ENTERTAINMENT
Nightclubs

Sassari's clubbing scene is not a patch on Alghero's, but if you want to dance late, jump in a taxi and head out to **Meccano** (off Map p125; ☎ 079 27 04 05; Via Carlo Felice 33; ✔ 11pm-late Thu-Sat), a mainstream disco on the eastern edge of town.

Theatre

The town's theatres don't tend to move into gear until September or October, after the sting has gone out of the summer heat. For show information check the local newspaper *La Nuova Sardegna* or contact the theatres directly.

Sassari's main theatre is the **Teatro Civico** (Map p128; ☎ 079 23 21 82; Corso Vittorio Emanuele II 39), which stages plays and classical musical concerts. Nearby, **Teatro Verdi** (Map p128; ☎ 079 23 94 79; Via Politeama) doubles as a cinema when it's not hosting dance performances or opera, usually between October and January.

SHOPPING

Isola (Map p128; ☎ 079 23 01 01; ☽ 9.30am-1pm & 5-8pm Mon-Fri & Sat morning) Located in the town's green Giardini Pubblici, this is the place to find the best in Sardinian craftwork, including nice ceramic ware, traditional rugs and some extremely impressive wrought-iron work.

GETTING THERE & AWAY

Air

Sassari shares Alghero's **Fertilia airport** (off Map p125; ☎ 079 93 52 82; www.algheroairport.it), about 28km west of the city centre. For information on flights, see p157.

Bus

Sassari's **bus station** (Map p128) is on Via XXV Aprile near the train station. You can buy tickets at the station, where there's also a small left-luggage office (€1.50 per bag).

ARST (☎ 800 865 042; www.arst.sardegna.it, in Italian) buses serve Oristano (€9.50, 2¼ hours, seven daily), Porto Torres (€1.50, 35 minutes, hourly) and Castelsardo (€2.50, one hour, 11 Monday to Saturday).

FdS (☎ 800 460 220; www.ferroviesardegna.it, in Italian) buses run to Alghero (€3, one hour, hourly) and other destinations in the locale.

For Olbia port, **Turmo Travel** (☎ 0789 214 87; www.gruppoturmotravel.com) has two daily buses (€6.50, 1½ hours).

Car & Motorcycle

Sassari is located on the SS131 highway linking Porto Torres to Cagliari. From Alghero, take the road north towards Porto Torres and then the SS291 east to Sassari. You take the same route from Fertilia airport.

A host of car-hire outlets are based at Fertilia airport. In Sassari itself, you can pick up wheels at **Eurorent** (Map p128; ☎ 079 23 23 35; www.rent.it; Via Roma 56) and **Maggiore** (Map p128; ☎ 079 23 55 07; Piazza Santa Maria 6).

Train

The main train station (Map p128) is just beyond the western end of the old town on Piazza Stazione. Direct trains run to Cagliari (€13.75, 4¼ hours, four daily), Oristano (€8.75, 2½ hours, five daily) and Olbia (€6.35, one hour 50 minutes, four daily).

There are also 11 daily FdS trains running between Sassari and Alghero (€2.20, 35 minutes).

Once a week, between the end of June and early September, the **trenino verde** (www.treninoverde.com) departs from Sassari for the slow panoramic ride to Tempio Pausania (€12.50, two hours 35 minutes).

GETTING AROUND

To/From the Airport

Up to five daily ARST buses run from the main bus depot on Via XXV Aprile to Fertilia airport (€3.50, 30 minutes). A further three depart from the stop on Via Turati.

For the Aeroporto Olbia Costa Smeralda you'll need to catch the train/bus to Olbia and then the city bus to the airport.

Bus

ATP (☎ 079 263 80 00; www.aptsassari.it, in Italian) orange buses run along most city routes, although you're unlikely to need one in the small city centre. In summer, they also run to beaches north of Sassari from the terminus on Via Eugenio Tavolara. Tickets cost €0.80 on city routes and €1.10 for the Buddi Buddi beach line.

Car & Motorcycle

Parking is generally a nightmare. Within blue lines, hourly rates cost up to €2 for the first two hours and €1 for each hour thereafter. Get tickets from traffic wardens or newsagents.

Taxi

You can catch a taxi from ranks on Emiciclo Giuseppe Garibaldi (Map p128) or along Viale Italia and Via Matteotti. To phone for one call **Taxi Sassari** (☎ 079 25 39 39).

SASSARI & THE
NORTHWEST

AROUND SASSARI

The most scenic route from Sassari to the coast is the SS200, lined with umbrella pines standing sentry as it passes through the twin market towns of **Sennori** and **Sorso**. These towns are famous for their wine and together produce the sweet Moscato di Sorso-Sennori. A good place to try some is the well-known restaurant **Da Vito** (☎ 079 36 02 45; Via Napoli 14; meals around €40) in Sennori, which serves delicious seasonal food.

At weekends, the Sassaresi abandon the city for the long sandy beaches at **Platamona Lido**. This is a cheerful and, on summer weekends, crowded spot known optimistically as the Sassari Riviera.

Regular summer buses run from Sassari up to a point just east of Platamona and then the length of coast as far as Marina di Sorso. Take the Buddi Buddi bus (line MP) from Via Eugenio Tavolara.

Midway between Sassari and Porto Torres, 11km along the SS131, you'll find a signpost for the temple of **Monte d'Accoddi** (admission €3.10; ⊙ 9am-8pm Apr-Sep, to 4.30pm Oct-Mar), built in the 3rd millennium BC. Nowhere else in the Mediterranean has such a structure been unearthed – the closest comparable buildings are the fabled ziggurats of the Euphrates and Tigris River valleys in the Middle East. Excavations have revealed there was a Neolithic village here as early as 4500 BC. The temple went through several phases and appears to have been abandoned around 1800 BC. Soon after, the first *nuraghe* began to be raised.

Unfortunately, you don't actually see anything like the Mayan temple you might be imagining. Instead you can just make out a rectangular-based structure (30m by 38m), tapering to a platform and preceded by a long ramp. On either side of the ramp are a menhir and a stone altar believed to be for sacrifices.

THE LOGUDORO & MONTE ACUTO

Extending south and east of Sassari, this fertile area has been inhabited since nuraghic times and is rich in archaeological interest. It was an important granary for the Roman Empire and still today the landscape is a patchwork of rugged slopes and golden wheat fields – the name Logudoro means 'place of gold'. As the medieval Giudicato del Logudoro, it enjoyed a medieval heyday, and it's to this period that many of the area's impressive churches date. In the heart of the region is the *comune* of Monte Acuto, a collection of village communities sharing a common mountain heritage. You'll find www.monteacuto.it (in Italian) a useful website.

It's not an immediately alluring area, but if you've got a car, you'll find it rewards a little exploration.

OZIERI
pop 11,100

A prosperous agricultural town, Ozieri sits in a natural hollow, its 19th-century centre sloping upwards from a striking central piazza. The surrounding hills were once home to a number of thriving Neolithic settlements and the town has lent its name to a period in prehistory – the Ozieri (or San Michele) culture, which spanned the millennium between 3500 and 2700 BC.

You can investigate the town's rich archaeological legacy at the wonderful **Museo Archeologico** (☎ 079 785 10 52; Piazza Micca; admission €3.50, incl Grotta di San Michele €5; ⊙ 9am-1pm & 4-7pm Tue-Sat, 9.30am-12.30pm Sun), one of Sardinia's best small museums. Housed in the Convento di Clarisse, an 18th-century convent, it has a small but rich collection, including a couple of copper ingots (nuraghic settlements were trading copper as far back as the neolithic age), some surprisingly modern-looking tools, and a selection of fine ceramic fragments found in the **Grotta di San Michele** (☎ 079 785 10 52; admission €3.50, incl Museo Archeologico €5; ⊙ 9am-1pm Fri & Sat, 9.30am-12.30pm Sun), itself well worth a visit. The *grotta,* signposted from the top of town, was used as a habitation as well as a tomb and place of cult worship.

Not far from the museum, Ozieri's bombastic **Cattedrale dell'Immacolata** (Piazza Duomo) harbours an important work of art, the *Deposizione di Cristo dalla Croce* (Deposition of Christ from the Cross), by the enigmatic Maestro di Ozieri.

During December Ozieri hosts one of the island's major poetry competitions, the **Premio di Ozieri**. It started in 1956, inspired by the *gare poetiche* (poetry wars) that took place

---

THE CHURCHES OF THE LOGUDORO

The **Basilica della Santissima Trinità di Saccargia** (Comune di Codrongianus; admission €1.50; ☷ 9am-8pm Jun-Aug, to 6.30pm Sep, to 6pm May, to 5.30pm Oct, to 5pm Apr, to 4.30pm Mar) lies in the centre of a fertile valley, just 15km southeast of Sassari along the SS597 Olbia road. You can't miss its stripy limestone and basalt *campanile* (bell tower), which dominates the horizon as you approach. Legend has it that it was built by the Giudice Constantino di Mariano in 1116, after he and his wife camped the night here and received a revelation that they were to have their first longed-for child. The delighted Giudice built the church and a neighbouring monastery, which the pope gave to the Camaldolite monks. Little remains of the monastery, although the dramatically simple church with its blind basalt walls is still in use.

A further 3km down the road you'll see the abandoned **Chiesa di San Michele e Sant'Antonio di Salvènero** at the road junction to Ploaghe, but continue to Ardara, 10km further on. It was once the capital of the Giudicato di Torres, and a quick turn to the left as you enter the town will bring you face to face with the brooding mass of the **Chiesa di Santa Maria del Regno**, made of greying basalt. One of its oddest features is the squat bell tower, finished in a rough-and-ready manner after the church was completed and not at all typical of the style.

Further east along the SS597 you'll see a turn-off for the majestically ruined 11th- to 12th-century **Chiesa di Sant'Antioco di Bisarcio** (☎ 079 78 02 57; admission €1.50; ☷ 9am-4pm Sat & Sun, other days on request), 2km north of the highway. The bell tower was decapitated by a burst of lightning, and much of the facade's decoration has been lost, but the uniquely French-inspired porch and interior convey the impression of its one-time grandeur.

From here continue along the SS597 and see the tiny **Chiesa di Nostra Signora di Castro** on the banks of the Lago di Coghinas, or head north along the winding SS132 to **Chiesa di San Pietro di Simbranos** (or delle Immagini) at Bulzi and the **Chiesa di San Giorgio** at Perfugas.

If you're planning this tour, the hotel **Funtanarena** (☎ 079 43 50 48; www.funtanarena.it; Via S'Istradoneddu 8/10; s €63-70, d €94-105; ☐) is a convenient, and delightful, place to stay. In the small village of Codrongianos, 14km from Sassari, it's housed in a refurbished manor house surrounded by fragrant fruit trees and olive groves. The nine country-style rooms are furnished with framed prints of flowers, wrought-iron beds and parquet floors.

---

informally at local festivals, and now showcases the work of Italian and Sardinian poets.

Accommodation in Ozieri is thin on the ground, which is a shame, but if you decide to stop over you'll find decent, slightly fading rooms at **Hotel Il Mastino** (☎ 079 78 70 41; fax 079 78 70 59; Via Vittorio Veneto 13; s/d €45/66), a characterless no-nonsense affair round the corner from the central Piazza Garibaldi. For a bite to eat, **Ristorante Pizzeria L'Opera** (☎ 079 78 70 26; Piazza Garibaldi; meal €30) serves pizzas and excellent lamb chops in a strange concert-hall setting.

By public transport the easiest way to get to Ozieri is by ARST bus from Sassari (€4, one hour, five Monday to Saturday). These drop you off near Piazza Garibaldi.

NURAGHE SANTU ANTINE & AROUND

Heading west from Ozieri, you pass through **Mores**, to the south of which lies the majestic **Dolmen Sa Coveccada**, said to be the largest dolmen (a megalithic chambered tomb) in the Mediterranean. Dating to the end of the 3rd

millennium BC, the rectangular construction consists of three massive stone slabs, roofed by a fourth, weighing around 18 tonnes. As it stands, it reaches a height of 2.7m, is 5m long and 2.5m wide. To find it, take the exit just before you enter Mores from the east and follow the road for a further 10km or so.

From Mores follow the road for **Torralba**, an unremarkable village at the head of the Valle dei Nuraghi (Valley of the Nuraghi). The land around here is scattered with prehistoric *nuraghi*, but pride of place goes to the **Nuraghe Santu Antine** (☎ 079 84 72 96; www.nuraghesantuantine.it; admission €3; ☷ 9am-sunset), 4km south of the village. One of the largest nuraghic sites in Sardinia, it is focused on a central tower, now standing at 17.5m but which originally rose to a height of 25m. Around this, walls link three bastions and enclose a triangular compound. Its oldest parts date to around 1600 BC, but much of it was built over successive centuries.

You enter the compound from the southern side and can walk through the three towers, connected by rough parabolic archways. The entrance to the main tower is separate. Inside, four openings lead into the chamber from an internal hall. Stairs lead up from the hall to the next floor, where a similar but smaller pattern is reproduced. Apart from tiny vents there is no light, and the presence of the dark stone is overwhelming. You ascend another set of steps to reach the floor of what was the final, third chamber, now open to the elements.

Back in Torralba, the **Museo Archeologico** (☎ 079 84 72 96; Via Carlo Felice 143; admission incl Nuraghe Santu Antine €3; ✆ 9am-8pm Apr-Oct, to 5pm Nov-Mar) has a scale model of the *nuraghe* and a modest collection of finds lifted from the site.

On weekdays there are up to nine buses from Sassari to Torralba (€2.50, 1½ hours). To get to the *nuraghe* from there you'll have to walk (about 4km).

Borutta

On the map it's a fairly straightforward drive up to the village of Borutta, but in practice it can be confusing – signs point you in the right direction and then abandon you to your navigational instincts. It's worth persevering though, as Borutta boasts a fine example of Romanesque architecture, the **Chiesa di San Pietro Sorres** (☎ 334 853 77 51; admission €2.50; ✆ guided visits 8.30am-noon & 3.30-6.30pm Mon-Sat, 9.30-10.30am & 3.30-6.30pm Sun).

The original 12th-century Pisan church and adjacent abbey had long been abandoned when a community of Benedictine monks moved in in 1955. They soon got busy, rebuilding the abbey and scrubbing the church into shape. The white-and-grey banded facade has three levels of blind arches and is decorated with some lovely elaborate stonework. Of note inside is an intriguing stone Gothic pulpit set on four legs.

Necropoli di Sant'Andrea di Priu & Around

About 7km east of Bonorva, a ridge-top farming town just off the main SS131, the **Necropoli di Sant'Andrea di Priu** (☎ 348 564 26 11; admission €3.50; ✆ 10am-1pm & 3-5.30pm, to 7.30pm summer) lies in the thick of lush, verdant countryside. An isolated site, accessible by a narrow potholed road, it is made up of around 20 small grottoes carved into the trachyte and dating as far back as 4000 BC. The **Tomba del Capo**, accessible only with a guide, is by far the most interesting. In the early Christian period three of the main rooms were transformed into a place of worship, and partly restored frescoes from the 5th century survive in two of them. Most striking is the fresco of a woman in the *aula* (hall) where the faithful heard Mass.

On the road back up to Bonorva, it's worth taking an hour or so to stop off at **Rebeccu**, a windswept and largely abandoned medieval hamlet carved into calcareous rock. The village, signposted off to the left, is the unlikely setting for a film festival in mid-August.

Getting around this area without your own transport is well-nigh impossible, although a few ARST buses run from Sassari to Bonorva (€4, 70 minutes, five on weekdays).

THE NORTH COAST

Extending 70km from Sardinia's northwestern tip round to Castelsardo, this stretch of coast encompasses the sublime and the distinctly unsightly. The industrial sprawl around Porto Torres, the north coast's busiest port, is far from inviting, but you don't have to go far to find some superb beaches. A few kilometres to the west, the Spiaggia della Pelosa is one of Sardinia's most famous beachside haunts.

PORTO TORRES
pop 22,100

Not one of Sardinia's most alluring towns, Porto Torres is a busy working port surrounded by a fuming petrochemical plant.

DETOUR: MONTE LERNO

About 5km east of Pattada, **Lago Lerno** presents a bucolic picture. Although an artificial lake – it was created in 1984 by damming the Rio Mannu – it fits perfectly into the surrounding scenery with grassy slopes gently rising from the still waters and rocky **Monte Lerno** (1094m) looming in the near distance. Nearby, deer, mouflon and wild horses roam in the **Bosco di Monte Lerno** (Monte Lerno Wood). To get to the wood, exit Pattada and follow for Oschiri. After about 11km, turn right and continue over the Rio Mannu into the northwest reaches of the forest.

SARDINIA'S CUTTING EDGE

Of all the fine knives made in Sardinia, the most prized is *sa pattadesa* (the Pattada knife), and these days they are only made by a handful of artisans. The classic Pattada knife, first made in the mid-19th century, is the *resolza*, with its so-called myrtle-leaf-shaped blade that folds into a horn handle. Only the finest knives have their blades protected in such a way. To a Sardinian a *sa pattadesa* is the ultimate in Sardinian craftsmanship, more impressive than any valuable piece of jewellery.

Most of the best craftsmen only work to order and take at least two days to fashion such a knife, folding and tempering the steel for strength and sharpness. The handle is then carved from a single piece of mouflon horn. If you're looking at a handle that is two parts screwed together, you're not looking at a quality piece. A good knife will cost at least €10 a centimetre.

In the past such knives were made all over the island, but now only a few towns follow the traditional methods. **Pattada** is the most famous, although quality knives are also made in Arbus, Santu Lussurgiu and Tempio Pausania. The classic *s'arburesa* (from Arbus) has a fat, rounded blade and is used for skinning animals, while the *lametta* of Tempio Pausania is a rectangular job good for stripping the bark from cork oaks. Of the *pattadesa* knives the best known is the *fogarizzu*. The best *s'arburesa* to look for is the *pusceddu*.

Note that it is illegal in Italy to carry a blade longer than 4cm.

There's no compelling reason to hang around, but if you find yourself passing through – and you might, especially if heading to or from Corsica – there are a couple of worthwhile sights, most notably the Basilica di San Gavino, one of Sardinia's most important Romanesque churches.

Porto Torres had its heyday under the Romans, who founded it as their main port on Sardinia's north coast. It remained one of the island's key ports until the Middle Ages and was capital of the Giudicato di Torres.

Orientation

The port is north of the town centre, at the western end of the seafront road, Via Mare. From nearby Piazza Colombo and adjacent Piazza XX Settembre, the main strip, Corso Vittorio Emanuele, leads south through town.

Information

Banca Nazionale del Lavoro (Corso Vittorio Emanuele 20) One of several banks with ATMs along the main drag.
Post office (Via Ponte Romano; ⏰ 8am-1.15pm Mon-Fri) Three blocks right of Corso Vittorio Emanuele.
Tourist office (☎ 079 51 50 00; Piazza Garibaldi 17; ⏰ 8am-2pm) A couple of streets back from the port just off the *corso*.

Sights & Activities

BASILICA DI SAN GAVINO

The limestone **Basilica di San Gavino** (☎ 347 400 12 88; crypt €1.50, guided tour €2.50; ⏰ 9am-1pm & 3-7pm Mon-Sat May-Sep, 11am-1pm & 3-7pm Sun, to 6pm Oct-Apr)

is Sardinia's largest Romanesque church. Built between 1030 and 1080, it is notable for the apses on either end – there is no facade – and its two dozen marble columns, pilfered by the Pisan builders from the nearby Roman site. Underneath the main church, a crypt is lined with religious statuary and various stone tombs.

The church is built over an ancient pagan burial ground and takes its name from one of the great Sardinian saints, the Roman soldier Gavino, who commanded the garrison at Torres in Diocletian's reign. Ordered to put to death two Christian priests, Protus and Januarius, he was converted by them and he himself shared their martyrdom. All three were beheaded on 25 October 304. Evidence for these events is scanty, but the legend of the *martiri turritani* (martyrs of Torres) flourishes.

To get here follow Corso Vittorio Emanuele south from the port for about 1km. The basilica is one block west of the street.

PARCO ARCHEOLOGICO & ANTIQUARIUM

Most of Roman Turris Libisonis lies beneath the modern port, but some vestiges have been uncovered. Known collectively as the 'archaeological park', it is made up of the remains of public baths, an overgrown Roman bridge and the so-called Palazzo del Re Barbaro. The latter is the centrepiece and constitutes the main public bathing complex of the Roman city. Parts of the town's main roads, some *tabernae* (shops) and some good floor mosaics can also be seen on the site, which is entered via the **Antiquarium** (🕑 closed for restoration). Almost all the items in this museum were found in Roman Turris, and they include a range of ceramics, busts, oil lamps and glassware. The site is near the train station, about a five-minute walk from the centre.

BOAT TRIPS
Operating out of a kiosk on the seafront, **Le Ginestre** (☎ 079 51 34 93; 🕑 10am–noon & 6-8pm) is one of several outfits offering excursions to the Parco Nazionale dell'Asinara (p147). A day trip, including a tour of the island on a dinky train, costs €41.50 per adult and €26.50 for four- to 10-year-olds.

Sleeping & Eating
Hotel Elisa (☎ 079 51 32 60; www.hotelelisaportotorres .com; Via Mare 2; s €40-50, d €68-73; 🍴) Convenient and comfortable, this straightforward three-star is only a block back from the port and a stone's throw from Corso Vittorio Emanuele. Rooms are functional and modern with dark parquet and an aquamarine colour scheme.

Crossing's Café (Corso Vittorio Emanuele 53; 🕑 Fri-Wed) A lively pub on the main strip, this place is good for a *panino* or a street-side beer.

Cristallo (☎ 079 51 49 09; Piazza XX Settembre 11; meals €35-40; 🕑 Tue-Sun) Above a popular *pasticceria* (pastry shop)/bar on street level, this modern restaurant serves great seafood and a selection of favourites, including several tasty lamb concoctions.

Getting There & Away
Tirrenia (☎ 89 21 23; www.tirrenia.it), **Grandi Navi Veloci** (☎ 010 209 45 91; www.gnv.it) and **Moby Lines** (☎ 199 30 30 40; www.mobylines.it) all run ferries between Porto Torres and Genoa. Tirrenia and GNV ferries sail year-round, while Moby operates between mid-May and September. Fares for the 11-hour crossing cost between €86 and €105.

SNCM (☎ France 0825 88 80 88; www.sncm.fr) and **CMN La Méridionale** (☎ France 0810 20 13 20; www.cmn .fr) together operate ferries to/from Marseille (€78, 15 to 17 hours) via Corsica. Note, however, that in July and August some of these ferries sail from Toulon instead. You can purchase tickets at **Agenzia Paglietti** (☎ 079 51 44 77; fax 079 51 40 63; Corso Vittorio Emanuele 19). For more details on ferry routes see p237.

Most buses leave from Piazza Colombo, virtually at the port. There are services to Sassari

(€1.50, 30 to 40 minutes, six daily), Alghero (€2.50, one hour, six daily Monday to Friday, five daily Saturday and Sunday) and Stintino (€2.50, 45 minutes, four Monday to Saturday, two Sunday). Get tickets at **Bar Acciaro** (Corso Vittorio Emanuele 38) or news-stands.

Trains run to Sassari (€1.55, 20 minutes, four daily), Cagliari (€16.05, 4½ hours, two daily) and Olbia (€8.35, 2¼ hours, one daily).

EAST OF PORTO TORRES
East of Porto Torres, the SP 81 and its continuation the SS200 follow the coast as it gradually rises up to Castelsardo. For much of the way the road is flanked by pine woods, behind which you'll find various isolated beaches. Inland, the flat-topped tablelands of the Anglona, a struggling farm district, lie sandwiched between the Gallura to the east, Logudoro to the south and the small Romangia district to the west.

Castelsardo
pop 5700
An attractive and popular day-trip destination, Castelsardo huddles around the high cone of a promontory jutting into the Mediterranean. Towering over everything is a dramatic *centro storico*, a hilltop ensemble of dark alleyways and medieval buildings seemingly melded onto the grey rock peak.

The town was originally designed as a defensive fort by a 12th-century Genoese family. Named Castel Genoese, it was the subject of much fighting and in 1326 fell to the Spanish, who changed its name to Castel Aragonese. It became Castel Sardo (Sardinian Castle) in 1767 under the Piedmontese. By then this outpost, once an independent *citta demaniali* (royal city), had lost its defensive raison d'être. Now the fortress is a museum, and locals linger as reluctant custodians.

ORIENTATION
Buses pull up in Piazza Pianedda, where the coast road (undergoing several name changes as it passes through town) meets Via Nazionale, the main street that winds up to the top of the old town. You can drive all the way to the end of this road, but parking is often impossible.

INFORMATION
Tourist office (☎ 079 47 15 06; Piazzetta del Popolo; 🕑 10am-12.30pm & 5-7.30pm) Note that these hours

are flexible and the office is often closed. An alternative, and more reliable, source of information is the *comune*'s website: www.comune.castelsardo.ss.it.

SIGHTS

The most interesting part of town is the hilltop historic centre, lorded over by the medieval **Castello**, around which the original town was established. Built by the Doria family and home to Eleonora d'Arborea for a period, it commands superb views over the Golfo di Asinara to Corsica. It also houses a museum, the **Museo dell'Intreccio** (☎ 079 47 13 80; Via Marconi; admission €2; ☿ 9.30am-1pm & 3-5.30pm Tue-Sun Nov-Mar, to 6.30pm Tue-Sun Mar, to 7.30pm daily Apr, to 8.30pm daily May, to 9pm daily Sep, 9am-midnight daily Jul & Aug), dedicated to the basket-weaving for which the town is famous.

Just below the castle is the **Chiesa di Santa Maria**, largely a 16th-century structure, famous for its 13th-century crucifix, known as the *Critu Nieddu* (Black Christ).

A town landmark, the slender bell tower of the **Cattedrale di Sant'Antonio Abate** is topped by a brightly tiled cupola. In a setting worthy of a Grimm brothers' fairy tale, the church almost appears suspended in mid-air atop the craggy cliffs. Inside, the main altar is dominated by the *Madonna con gli Angeli*, a painting by the mysterious Maestro di Castelsardo. More of his works can be seen in the **crypts** (admission €2; ☿ 10.30am-1pm & 6.30pm-midnight) below the church. A series of small rooms chiselled out of the living rock, these are what remain of the Romanesque church that once stood here. The crypt exit takes you past neat lawns that separate you from the Spanish-era seaward battlements.

A couple of fairly small **beaches** flank the promontory.

FESTIVALS & EVENTS

On the Monday of Holy Week, the people of Castelsardo celebrate a series of Masses and processions as part of **Lunissanti**, ending with a solemn evening torchlight parade through the old town to the Chiesa di Santa Maria.

SLEEPING

It's definitely worth staying the night in Castelsardo, especially as there are a number of excellent-value B&Bs.

ourpick **B&B Sa Domo de Minnanna** (☎ 079 47 10 49, 349 367 61 05; Via Mezzu Tappa; per person €25-35) This is a charming, homey B&B in a tiny

cul-de-sac just below the *centro storico*. It's all very down to earth with old family photos and a simple kitchen, but the exposed stone walls and old-fashioned furniture lend a lovely authentic touch.

Casa Doria (☎ 349 355 78 82; www.casadoria.it; Via Garibaldi 10; r €55-80; ☒) One of a number of B&Bs in the medieval centre, this has all the trappings of a rustic guest house: period furniture, wrought-iron bedsteads, wooden ceilings. There are three rooms, each simply decorated, and a 3rd-floor breakfast room with fantastic views.

Hotel Riviera (☎ 079 47 01 43; www.hotelriviera .net; Lungomare Anglona 1; d €78-168, half board per person €57-99; ☒ ☒) Overlooking the town's bay at the western entrance to town, this is a glossy and formal three-star with comfortable modern rooms and a highly rated restaurant, Ristorante Fofo.

A few kilometres west of Castelsardo, just outside the average beach resort of Lu Bagnu, is one of the island's few youth hostels. The **Ostello Golfo dell'Asinara** (☎ 079 47 40 31; ostello.asinara@tiscalinet.it; Via Sardegna 1; dm/q/d per person €13/15/18; ☿ Easter & mid-Jun–mid-Sep) has no-fuss accommodation in a range of rooms including doubles and four-bed family rooms. There's a large verandah, a games room and evening meals (€10) are available. You can also hire bikes and canoes here.

EATING

Il Piccolo Borgo (☎ 079 47 05 16; Via Seminario 4; plates €10; ☿ Tue-Sun) A handy place for a light lunch, this small *centro storico* bar serves various snacks including a delicious platter of cured hams, olives and cheeses.

ourpick **La Trattoria** (☎ 079 47 06 61; Via Nazionale 20; meals around €25; ☿ closed Mon Oct-May) Delicious food, friendly service and value for money. La Trattoria has kept it simple and does it very well. The food is classic Sardinian with plenty of juicy meats, earthy vegetables, and some wonderful pastas, including *pasta mazzafrissa*, made with ewe's milk; the atmosphere is warm and cheerfully hectic.

La Guardiola (☎ 079 47 07 55; Piazza Bastione 4; lunchtime set menus €18/22, meals around €35; ☿ closed Mon Oct-May) Dine on quality seafood while admiring wonderful views from La Guardiola's panoramic pavilion at the top of the old

(Continued on page 145)

Outdoors

Keep your cool in the pristine waters of the Golfo di Orosei (p207)

DALLAS STRIBLEY

Long renowned for its silky beaches and flash resorts, Sardinia is one of the Mediterranean's great outdoor playgrounds. The island's rugged, unspoilt hinterland and its dramatic coastline provide a magnificent arena for a whole host of activities.

Studded with canyons, caves and cliffs, the Gennargentu national park is a mecca for outdoor enthusiasts. Hikers can take on Italy's toughest trek, the aptly named *selvaggio blu* (savage blue), and explore vertical chasms and prehistoric villages. Daredevil bikers can get their fix on insane mountain paths, while rock climbers can go vertical on slabs of limestone.

Hiking to the prehistoric village of Tiscali (p211) ANDREW PEA

Cycling and climbing are hot in Sardinia right now. Both are being promoted as part of an island-wide drive to encourage sustainable tourism, and facilities are improving all the time. There are a growing number of companies offering bike tours. That said, cyclists will have to earn their rewards in Sardinia. The hilly landscape makes for some pretty tough pedal work.

Climbing can be tackled all across the island but the main areas are the Golfo di Orosei and the Ogliastra, where stark limestone spikes boast some thrilling ascents. To the southwest, Domusnovas is the island's top winter climbing destination.

Offshore, the action goes beyond posing for the paparazzi. Windsurfers and kitesurfers flock to the northern coast to pit themselves against fierce local winds, and surfers ride 5m waves off the Sinis Peninsula. Divers will be spoilt for choice with underwater caves off Alghero, shipwrecks in the Golfo di Cagliari and underwater ruins at Nora.

Sardinia's deep-rooted horse culture expresses itself in various riding opportunities, many in the flatlands around Oristano. This area also provides some fantastic birdwatching.

WALKING

Sardinia's ancient and varied landscape offers spectacular walking. Hundreds of kilometres of trails criss-cross the island, ranging from simple coastal strolls to tough mountain treks. However, many of the longer routes are not marked and can be tricky to navigate solo. If in doubt, consider hiring a guide from a local hiking cooperative.

The most popular walking area is the rugged Parco Nazionale del Golfo di Orosei e del Gennargentu, which encompasses Sardinia's highest point, Punta La Marmora (1834m), the limestone Supramonte massif and the dramatic arc of the Golfo di Orosei.

Dorgali and Oliena make excellent bases for hikers, both towns being within striking distance of prehistoric Tiscali (p211), and the spectacular gorge of Gola Su Gorruppu (p210).

Trails on the Golfo di Orosei lead to beautiful coves and fabulous beaches, such as Cala

SELVAGGIO BLU – THE ULTIMATE CHALLENGE

Reckoned by many as the toughest trek in Italy, Sardinia's seven-day *selvaggio blu* (savage blue) is not for the amateur ambler. Stretching 45km along the Golfo di Orosei's imperious coastline, it's a far cry from the well-marked trails that criss-cross the rest of the island. Traversing wooded ravines, chasms, gorges, cliffs and caves, it's not well signposted (a deliberate decision to keep it natural) and there's no water en route. Furthermore, it involves rock climbs of up to grade 4+ and abseils of up to 45m. On the plus side, it boasts some of Italy's most spectacular and unspoilt coastal scenery.

For information on the *selvaggio blu*, Italian speakers can consult www.selvaggioblu.it, a comprehensive website with descriptions of each day's walk, advice on what to take and when to go (namely in spring or autumn).

Gonone, Cala Luna and Cala Goloritze (see the boxed text, p213). To really get to grips with the coast, the Selvaggio Blu trek (see left) runs for 45km between Baunei and Cala Gonone.

Further north, there's great walking on Monte Limbara (1359m; p187), near Tempio Pausania, and through Gallura's weird rocky landscape. Good spots include Capo Testa and Isola Caprera (p180) in the Arcipelago di La Maddalena. The Capo Caccia headland (p161) also offers good rambling along the coast.

Less dramatic perhaps, but no less intriguing, is the unexplored countryside around Monti Ferru (p112), and La Giara di Gesturi (p101), a huge plateau.

The best time for walking is late spring (between April and June), when the flowers are out in full force and the landscape retains a rich green flush. September to October is another good time.

CYCLING

Cycling is a superb way of escaping the crowds and exploring Sardinia's empty wilderness. The roads are well maintained and relatively free of traffic – you can go hours without seeing another soul – and the landscape is sensational. But it's pretty tough-going and you'll need to be fit.

For those more into scenery than endurance records, the west coast is the place to be. Although not exactly easy, the two-day 108km circular ride from Alghero to Bosa (see the boxed text, p159) boasts some great sea views over the Riviera del Corallo and Capo Caccia.

Leave your car at home and discover the natural beauty of Sardinia on two wheels

ANDREW PEACOCK

For more of the same, try the coast between Iglesias and the Sinis Peninsula. The coastal road twists and turns past the old mining town of Buggerru before sweeping inland to Arbus and the Costa Verde (p84), one of Sardinia's great untamed coastal stretches. Long dirt tracks lead down to superb, unspoilt beaches.

Ambitious cyclists should head for the Gennargentu, where tarmacked roads cling to rugged mountainsides, swoop down steep valleys and meander through dense forests. Mountain bikers will relish the freedom of the stony mountain trails.

The best time for cycling is between March and June and then September and November. Tourist offices can sometimes provide cycling information, otherwise **Sardinia Hike and Bike** (☎ 070 924 32 329; www.sardiniahikeandbike.com) has an excellent website with free downloadable maps and detailed route itineraries. Another good operator is **Ichnusa Bike** (www.ichnusabike.it), who organises guided rides throughout the island.

Coastal rock climbing

PHILIP & KAREN SMITH

CLIMBING

Rock climbers have long appreciated Sardinia's vertiginous coastline and rocky interior.

The most popular and best-known destination is Cala Gonone (p211), whose sheer limestone faces set some severe challenges. There's a huge variety of climbs in the surrounding countryside, covering a range of styles – slabs, steep walls, overhangs, single-pitch and easier multipitches.

Inland, the claustrophobic rock walls of the Supramonte (p198) provide some exhilarating multipitch climbing with ascents of up to 600m. Down the coast, and accessible by boat from Cala Gonone, Cala Goloritze is home to the famous Aguglia tower, a 165m spike with accessible multipitch routes.

Currently one of the hottest year-round venues is the Ogliastra province, with attention centred on Ulassai (p217) and Jerzu (p217). Here climbers of all levels can pit themselves against a series of imposing limestone towers, known locally as *tacchi* (heels), and 45 routes on the Bruncu Pranedda canyon.

Over on the other side of the island, the unexceptional town of Domusnovas (p82) is a renowned winter climbing centre, at its best between late autumn and early spring. There are some 440 routes in the outlying countryside covering everything from easy single-pitch walls to demanding overhangs and tough slabs.

For a good introduction to Sardinian climbing check out www.climb-europe.com/sardinia .htm and www.sardiniaclimb.com.

DIVING

With its crystal-clear waters, spectacular grottoes, granite coastlines and some of the longest, cleanest beaches in the Mediterranean, Sardinia is a diver's paradise. There are plenty of schools offering courses and guided dives for all levels, as well as equipment hire for experienced divers.

Sardinia's offshore islands are popular locations. You can explore gorges full of colourful fish, shellfish and coral in the waters off the Isola di San Pietro (p89) and an underwater labyrinth off Isola Caprera in the Arcipelago di La Maddalena (p180). The Isola Tavolara

GET THE INSIDE TRACK – DIVING

A passionate PADI-qualified diver, Giulia Fonnesu is an expert on diving in Sardinia.

Where are your favourite sites? Alghero is a magical place for diving – it's really rich in fish, coral, beautiful sea fans and amazing caves. When you go into the Nereo Cave, the largest underwater grotto in Europe, it's like going into a majestic cathedral.

The Secca del Papa at the Isola Tavolara is like an enchanted garden. It always makes me think of a luxurious condominium populated by marine creatures! The Isola dell'Asinara is another good spot – I've never seen corvinas bigger than those there. At Carloforte, you'll find lobsters, corvinas, sea breams, and a spectacular seabed.

I also really like the relics in the Golfo di Cagliari, even if they can sometimes be very demanding, and the Arcipelago di Maddalena.

Where's the best place for beginners to learn? Anywhere. It's up to the instructor to make the dives safe and descend to a depth suitable for the divers.

Where are the hardest dives? I'd say in the Golfo di Cagliari because the relic dives go pretty deep. The Alghero caves are not for beginners either. You need specific licences and specialisations: deep, wrecks, enriched air, or cave certification. Even the Secca del Papa can be demanding under certain current conditions. Some divers don't like the so-called 'jump into the blue' which involves a passage through the deepest blue without sight of the seabed or the *secca*. This can cause disorientation and panic leading to breathing problems. But these are all dives that you can prepare for by getting the correct training, which can last between two and seven days.

Have you noticed a change in the underwater conditions over the years? Yes, there's a lot more mucilage than before, particularly in the north. Octopuses are becoming much rarer, and the groupers are becoming less shy – they're used to us divers now and are getting really big.

A diver discovers Sardinia's underwater kingdom at Capo Caccia (p161)

ROBERTO RINALDI / SIME/4CORNERS IMAGES

(p169) boasts one of the island's most beautiful dives, the Secca del Papa, a marine Eden rich in kaleidoscopic flora and fauna.

Underwater caves are a recurring feature of Sardinian diving. King of them all is the Nereo Cave (p151; off Alghero), the largest underwater grotto in the Mediterranean. Here you can see Alghero's famous frilly red coral flourishing in sun-streaked waters. Over on the Golfo di Orosei, Oyster Cave is alive with live oysters, prawns and mussels.

But there's more to Sardinia's extensive marine underworld than caves, coral and seafood. In the Golfo di Cagliari (p55)

> ## RESPONSIBLE DIVING
>
> Please consider the following tips when diving:
>
> - Take great care in underwater caves. Spend as little time within them as possible as your air bubbles may be caught within the roof and thereby leave organisms high and dry. Take turns to inspect the interior of a small cave.
> - Resist the temptation to collect or buy corals or shells or to loot marine archaeological sites (mainly shipwrecks).
> - Ensure that you take home all your rubbish and any litter you may find as well. Plastics in particular are a serious threat to marine life.
> - Do not feed fish.
> - Minimise your disturbance of marine animals.

experts can explore the wreck of the *Romagna*, a steamship built in 1899 and sunk in 1943. Away to the west, much of the ancient town of Nora (p96) lies underwater, its remains providing an exciting and atmospheric archaeological dive.

Another popular location is Villasimius (p74), where the best-known dive is the Secca di Santa Caterina, an underwater mountain pitted by deep canyons and red-coral caves.

WINDSURFING, KITESURFING & SURFING

Sardinia's windswept waters provide some of the best surfing in the Med. Top international competitors regularly stop by for championship events such as the Kitesurf World Cup, off the beaches between Vignola and Santa Teresa di Gallura, and the Chia Classic windsurfing event in the southwest.

The island's windsurf capital is Porto Pollo (p178) on the northeast coast. Beginners can experiment in safe, sheltered waters while experts enjoy the high winds that whistle through the channel between Sardinia and Corsica. You'll find a number of schools here and at the nearby Isola dei Gabbiani offering all sorts of water sports, including sailing and kitesurfing.

Other windsurfing hotspots include the beautiful Spiaggia della Pelosa (p147) on the northwestern coast, the beach at Funtanamare (p82), near Iglesias, and Cagliari's huge Poetto Beach (p64).

Committed surfers prefer the huge rolling waves of the west coast, in particular the Sinis Peninsula, where waves can reach 5m around the wild Capo Mannu. A favourite beach is Putzu Idu at San Giovanni di Sinis (p111). Kitesurfing is also popular here, with various schools catering to newbies and hardened veterans. Another prime spot on the west coast is the isolated Spiaggia della Piscinas (see the boxed text, p86), one of Europe's longest beaches.

An excellent website for booking windsurfing holidays in Sardinia is www.planetwindsurf.com.

Beginners and veteran sailors alike can experience the joys of sailing in Sardinia

DALLAS STRIBLEY

SAILING

Sailing in Sardinia doesn't have to mean designer togs and a sparkling 150m mega-yacht moored in Porto Cervo, although it's certainly that as well. The sport is taken seriously and there's a full calendar of regattas, culminating in the World Championships held in Cagliari in September. Throughout the summer, thousands of yachts take to the waters off the Costa Smeralda and the more choppy Straits of Bonifacio between Sardinia and Corsica.

For some idyllic summer sailing you can pick up a boat in Carloforte and tootle around the Isola di San Pietro (p89), or charter the gorgeous Dovesesto (p212) for a long weekend on the Golfo di Orosei. For lessons, the Sporting Club Sardinia in Porto Pollo (p178) offers a range of courses, as does the Club della Vela at Porto Conte (p160) near Alghero.

Waterskis, jet skis, motorised dinghies and other water-sports paraphernalia are a feature of all the bigger and more popular beach resorts.

The main sailing portal for the island is www.sailingsardinia.it (in Italian), which has some excellent links to individual charter companies.

HORSE RIDING

Riding horses is a popular activity on the island, and is a wonderfully liberating way of exploring the Sardinian countryside. The displays of equestrian ability that are the highlight of so many traditional local festivals attest to the islanders' deep-rooted affinity with horses.

You'll find excellent equestrian centres all over the island, but especially around Oristano and Cagliari. The leading riding centre is the Horse Country Resort near Arborea (p109)

which offers all sorts of equestrian packages. Still in the province of Oristano, but some way to the northeast, the Mandra Edera (p116) is a lovely place for a ride.

Over on the east coast, the Cooperativa Goloritzè (p217) can arrange rides around the highland Altopiano del Golgo plain.

As a rough guide, an hours' riding generally costs about €15.

CAVING, CANOEING & BIRDWATCHING

From its base in Gavoi, **Barbagia No Limits** (☎ 0784 52 90 16; www.barbagianolimits.it) is one of a number of outfits offering canyoning and caving excursions in the Gennargentu. For something less dramatic, they also hire out canoes on the picturesque Lago di Gusana. Another reliable adventure sports outfit is **Atlantikà** (www.atlantika.it), which has bases in Dorgali and Cala Gonone.

On a different track, birdwatchers will have a high time of it in Sardinia. The wetlands around Oristano and the lagoons of the Sinis Peninsula are an important habitat and staging post for migratory birds. Further down the coast, the Isola di San Pietro (p89) is celebrated for its Eleonora falcons.

Other ornithological hotspots include the Stagno di Molentargius marshes near Cagliari (p63) and the coast between Alghero and Bosa. In Bosa, **Esedra** (☎ 0785 37 42 58; www .esedrasardegna.it) can organise birdwatching excursions.

Hire a kayak and get up close to a shipwreck off the coast of Porto San Paolo (p169)

CUBOIMAGES SRL / ALAMY

(Continued from page 136)

town. The lunch menus – pasta, main course and side dish – are a good way of saving a bob or two.

Cormorano (☎ 079 47 06 28; Via Colombo 5; meals up to €55; ⏱ closed Tue Oct-May) Just round the corner from Piazza Pianedda, this is another good option for high-end seafood. There's a creative edge to many of the dishes, which include an excellent *linguine con sarde* (thin pasta with sardines) and grilled fish served with crayfish and prawns.

SHOPPING

You can't fail to notice the handicrafts shopping emporia in Castelsardo. As you wander through the old town you'll still see women settled on their doorsteps, creating intricate baskets and other objects of all shapes and sizes.

GETTING THERE & AWAY

ARST and other buses stop just off Piazza Pianedda. They run each way between Sassari (€2.50, one hour, 10 Monday to Saturday, four Sunday), Santa Teresa di Gallura (€5.50, 1½ hours, three daily) and Lu Bagnu (€1, five minutes, six Monday to Saturday, four Sunday). Buy tickets from the nameless *edicola* (news-stand) on the square.

Around Castelsardo

With your own vehicle you could comfortably take in the following places in a one-day circuit from Castelsardo. If you're relying on public transport it becomes substantially more difficult.

TERGU

Barely 10km south of Castelsardo lies a fine Romanesque church, the **Nostra Signora di Tergu**. The church is set in a pleasant garden, partly made up of the few visible remains of a monastery which once housed up to 100 Benedictine monks. Built in the 12th century of dark wine-red trachyte and white limestone, the facade is a particularly pretty arrangement of arches, columns, geometric patterns and a simple rose window.

SEDINI

From Castelsardo, the SS134 Sedini road leads to one of the area's most loveable landmarks, the **Roccia dell'Elefante** (Elephant Rock), a bizarre trachyte rock by the junction with the SS200. Its uncanny resemblance to an elephant has been the source of local interest for millennia, as witnessed by the presence of some *domus de janas* in the hollow interior.

Eleven kilometres south of the elephant is Sedini, a small, sleepy town with a well-known *domus de janas*. Gouged out of a huge calcareous rock by the town's main throughroad, Via Nazionale, the prehistoric tomb was lived in by farmers in the Middle Ages, and used as a prison until the 19th century. It now houses a small **museum** (⏱ 349 844 04 36; http://web.tiscali.it/sedini; admission €2; ⏱ 10am-1pm & 3-8pm May-Sep, rest of year on request) displaying traditional farming and household implements.

ARST buses run from Castelsardo (€1.50, 25 minutes, three daily).

NURAGHE SU TESORU & VALLEDORIA

Backtracking to the Roccia dell'Elefante, you can pick up the SS200 towards Valledoria. Just beyond the elephantine rock, you'll see the Nuraghe Su Tesoru on the left-hand side of the road. One of the last *nuraghi* to be built, it's best admired from the comfort of your own car as stopping on the main road is not very convenient.

Seven kilometres on and you arrive at the sprawling town of Valledoria, fronted by beaches that stretch more than 10km east to the small fishing village of Isola Rossa. There are several camping grounds in the area, including **Camping La Foce** (☎ 079 58 21 09; www.foce .it; Via Ampurias 1, Valledoria; 2-person tent & car €18-35, d bungalows €35-90; **P** 🐕), which has great facilities and backs onto a lagoon.

A couple of ARST buses running from Castelsardo stop in Valledoria (€1, 25 minutes), although if you can't convince the bus driver to stop at the camping ground turn-off, you'll have to hitch or walk.

WEST OF PORTO TORRES

West of Porto Torres, the flat land has a desolate feel, especially when the *maestrale* (northwesterly wind) blows in, whipping the *macchia* (Mediterranean scrub) and bleak rocks. But follow the road to the northwestern tip and you'll find laid-back Stintino, approached via its shimmering *saline* (saltpans), and the fabulous Spiaggia della Pelosa, one of Sardinia's most celebrated beaches.

Stintino

pop 1240

Until not very long ago Stintino was a remote and forgotten fishing village. But in recent years tourism has replaced tuna as its main source of income, and it's now a sunny little resort, wedged tidily between two ports – one full of bobbing blue fishing boats (Porto Mannu), the other given over to yachts (Porto Minori). Its pastel-painted houses add charm, while its location near the much-feted Spiaggia della Pelosa and Isola Asinara make it a useful summer base.

Many of Stintino's residents are descended from the 45 families who established the village in 1885. They settled here after being forcibly removed from Isola Asinara to make way for a new prison and quarantine station. The villagers turned to the sea for their livelihood and developed a reputation for tuna fishing, culminating in the annual *mattanza* (slaughter).

Your best bet for information is the private **Agenzia La Nassa** (☎ 079 52 00 60; www.escursioniasinara .it; Via Tonnara 35; ☺ 8.30am-1pm & 5-8pm daily Mar-Oct, rest of year by appointment), which can advise on local accommodation and excursions. It also has internet (€4 per hour), and car and bike hire (bikes per day €10, cars from €60).

Online, www.infostintino.it is a useful resource.

SIGHTS

Stintino's tuna-fishing heritage is documented at the **Museo della Tonnara** (☎ 079 52 00 81; Porto Mannu; adult/child €2/1; ☺ 6-11.30pm daily Jun–mid-Sep) at Porto Mannu. The museum's six rooms are ordered as the six chambers of the *tonnara* (the net in which the fish are caught), and filled with documents, seafaring memorabilia, photos and film, all recalling this centuries-old trade. The *tonnara* here was shut down in 1974, although locals attempted to revive it briefly in the late 1990s for scientific purposes. The *mattanza* still takes place in Carloforte and Portoscuso, in the south, as well as a couple of spots in Sicily. For more on the tuna hunt, see the boxed text, p90.

Just south of Stintino a signpost left directs you to the abandoned *tonnara* and the **Spiaggia delle Saline**, once the site of a busy saltworks, now a beautiful white beach. The marshes extend inland to form the **Stagno di Casaraccio**, a big lagoon where you might just see flamingos at rest.

ACTIVITIES

Stintino is the main gateway to the Parco Nazionale dell'Asinara, and during summer a regular fleet of ferries operates out of Porto Mannu; see opposite for details.

Windsurfers and divers are well catered to in these parts with various operators hiring out equipment and organising lessons/dives. You'll find most of these at Spiaggia della Pelosa (opposite).

In late August you can also catch Stintino's **regatta**, a race of 'Latin' sailing boats, the triangular sails of which fill the narrow causeway between Stintino and the Isola Asinara.

SLEEPING

Most of the big resort hotels are up the coast at Capo del Falcone (opposite), but there are some pleasant low-key choices in Stintino.

Hotel Geranio Rosso (☎ 079 52 32 92; fax 079 52 32 93; Via XXI Aprile 4; s €40-70, d €60-110, half board per person €60-80; ☒) This modest, year-round hotel has simple rooms with chandeliers and floral fabrics, and a decent downstairs pizzeria. It's also well located right in the centre of town.

Albergo Silvestrino (☎ 079 52 34 73; www.silvestrino .it, in Italian; Via XXI Aprile 4; s €45-75, d €70-130, half board per person €50-95; ☒) Difficult to miss at the sea end of the main street, this is a smart three-star. Rooms are summery with cool tiled floors and functional, unfussy furniture, and the restaurant, the best in Stintino, serves scrumptious seafood (meals €35 to €40).

EATING

You can eat at both the hotels mentioned earlier – pizza at Hotel Geranio and top-end seafood at Silvestrino. Stintino restaurants tend to specialise in seafood, which can be pricey.

Lu Fanali (☎ 079 52 30 54; Lungomare Cristoforo Colombo 89; pizzas €7) A good spot for a cheap and cheerful pizza down on the seafront, Lu Fanali is a friendly, unbuttoned kinda place with a wide terrace and a solid selection of pizzas, pasta and ice cream.

Skipper (☎ 079 52 34 60; Lungomare Cristoforo Colombo 57; lunchtime menu €12; ☺ 6am-11pm Tue-Sun) A longstanding favourite, this casual bar is a jack of all trades. You can sit down on the sea-view terrace and order anything from coffee and cocktails to seafood pastas, lasagne, hamburgers, salads and *panini*. It's all good and none of it is expensive.

Ristorante Da Antonio (☎ 079 52 30 77; Via Marco Polo 16; meals around €40; ☒ closed Thu Oct-Apr) Setting its sights higher than most, this elegant restaurant dishes up classic fish dishes with some style. Menu stalwarts include *polpo marinato* (marinated octopus) and an abundant *fritto misto* (mixed fry). On the flip side, the service can be very slow.

GETTING THERE & AWAY

Between June and mid-September, there are three daily buses between Stintino and Alghero's Fertilia airport (€7, 50 minutes).

ARST runs four weekday buses (two on Sundays) to Stintino from Porto Torres (€2.50, 45 minutes) and Sassari (€4, one hour 10 minutes). Services are increased between June and September.

Capo del Falcone

Holiday complexes, residences and holiday homes fill in the gaps between Stintino and Capo del Falcone. The main draw here is the **Spiaggia della Pelosa**, a dreamy image of near beach-perfection: a salt-white strip of sand lapped by shallow, turquoise waters and fronted by strange, almost lunar, licks of land. A craggy islet capped by a Catalano-Aragonese watchtower completes the picture. In high summer you will, of course, have to share the scene with tens of thousands of fellow admirers, but visit in the low season and you'll find the crowds far more manageable.

Two kilometres north of Stintino, just before Pelosa beach, you'll find the **Asinara Diving Centre** (☎ 079 52 70 00; www.asinaradivingcenter.it; Porto dell'Ancora) at the Ancora hotel. It offers a range of dives around Capo del Falcone and the Asinara park, including night and enriched-air dives. Further north, on the Spiaggia della Pelosa, the **Windsurfing Centre Stintino** (☎ 079 52 70 06; www.windsurfingcenter.it) rents out windsurfers (€15 per hour) and canoes (from €8 per hour), as well as offering windsurfing lessons (€30 per lesson) and courses (€155).

There's no shortage of accommodation around here, although most places are mid-to top-end resort hotels. One of the best is the gorgeously sited **La Pelosetta Residence Hotel** (☎ 079 52 71 88; www.lapelosetta.it; half board per person €60-115, 4-bed apt per week €322-1190; ☒ May-Sep). Its classy seafront restaurant (meals €40) virtually sits on the Spiaggia della Pelosa. There's

a mix of rooms (available on a daily basis), and self-catering apartments (rented out by the week), all with uninterrupted sea views. Note that half board is obligatory.

Year-round ARST buses run to the beach from Stintino (€1, five minutes, four Monday to Saturday, three Sunday). In summer bus services are considerably increased.

To park within the blue lines by the side of the road you'll be looking at around €5 for half a day.

Parco Nazionale dell'Asinara

Sardinia's second-largest offshore island (the largest is Isola Sant'Antioco), Isola dell'Asinara (Donkey Island) is named after the island's most famous resident – its unique *asino bianco* (albino donkey). There are estimated to be about 120 examples on the island, along with 80 other animal species, including mouflon (silky-haired wild sheep) and Pellegrine falcons.

Ironically, though, until it was designated a national park in 1997, the island was home one of Italy's most notorious maximum-security prisons. Now closed, the prison was built, along with a quarantine station for cholera victims, in 1885.

Tours of the island are only possible with licensed operators, setting out from Stintino or Porto Torres (see p135).

From May through to late October, **Linea Parco** (☎ 079 52 31 18; Porto Mannu; ☒ ticket office 9.30am-12.30pm & 4-7pm) sells tours from a kiosk near the ferry port. There are a number of options available, but the standard tour costs €36 per person (excluding lunch) and departs at 9am.

Agenzia La Nassa (☎ 079 52 00 60; www.escursioniasinara.it; Via Tonnara 35; ☒ 8.30am-1pm & 5-8pm daily Mar-Oct, rest of year by appointment) also has a number of packages, ranging from €16.50 to €52 per person. The cheapest, available between June and September, covers your ferry passage only, leaving you free to walk or cycle within designated areas on the island. The more expensive options provide 4WD or bus transport.

Although much of the island is off limits to visitors, including the beach of **Cala Sant'Andrea** (a breeding ground for turtles), most tours provide a good overview. Swimming breaks are usually programmed for **Cala d'Oliva** or **Punta Sabina** beaches, both in the north of the island.

Note that many tours do not include lunch so either take a picnic or head to Cala D'Oliva where there's a restaurant.

ALGHERO

pop 40,600

For many people a trip to Sardinia means a trip to Alghero, the main resort in the northwest and an easy flight from many European cities. Although largely given over to tourism, the town has managed to avoid many of its worst excesses, and it retains a proud and independent-minded spirit. It has long been an important fishing port, and still today fishing provides a vital contribution to the local economy. In gastronomic terms, Alghero's lobster is one of the island's great treats.

The main focus is the picturesque historic centre, one of the best preserved in Sardinia. Enclosed by robust, honey-coloured seawalls, this is a tightly knit enclave of shady cobbled lanes, Spanish Gothic *palazzi* and cafe-lined squares. Below, yachts crowd the marina and long, sandy beaches curve away to the north. Hanging over everything is a palpable Spanish atmosphere, a hangover of the city's past as a Catalan colony. Even today, more than three centuries after the Iberians left, the Catalan tongue is still spoken and street signs and menus are often in both languages.

HISTORY

A modern city by Sardinian standards, L'Alguerium (named after algae that washed up on the coast) started life as an 11th-century fishing village. Thanks to its strategic position, it was jealously guarded by its Genoese founders who, despite a brief Pisan interregnum in the 1280s, managed to retain control until the mid-14th century.

Alghero forcibly resisted the Catalano-Aragonese invasion of Sardinia in 1323, but after 30 years of struggle it finally fell to the Spanish invaders in 1353. Catalan colonists were encouraged to settle here, and after a revolt in 1372 the remaining Sardinians were expelled and relocated inland. From then on Alghero became resolutely Catalan and called itself Alguer.

The settlement remained a principal port of call in Sardinia for its Catalano-Aragonese and subsequently Spanish masters. Raised to the status of city in 1501, it experienced a frisson of excitement when the Holy Roman Emperor (and king of Spain) Charles V arrived in 1541 to lead a campaign against North African corsairs. Unhappily, the discovery of the Americas was bad news for Alghero, whose importance as a trading port quickly ebbed.

In 1720 the town passed to the House of Savoy. By the 1920s the population was scarcely more than 10,000. Heavy bomb damage suffered in 1943 and the onset of tourism in the late 1960s led to frenetic building, the result being the modern new town that mushrooms out of the historic centre.

ORIENTATION

Alghero's historic centre is on a small promontory jutting into the sea, with the new town stretching out behind it and along the coast to the north. Several of the classier hotels and some lively summer bars spread out along the coastal road south, while Alghero's beaches stretch to the north, backed by residential blocks, hotels and a camping ground. Intercity buses arrive in Via Catalogna, just outside the historic centre. The train station is about 1km north, on Via Don Minzoni.

INFORMATION

Bookshops

Il Labirinto (Map p152; ☎ 079 98 04 96; Via Carlo Alberto 119) A small store with a good range of books (mostly in Italian) on all things Sardinian. Also a small selection of English books.

Libreria Ex Libris (Map p152; Via Carlo Alberto 2) Has a nice selection of art books, maps, guidebooks and some English novels.

Emergency

Police station (Map p152; ☎ 079 972 00 00; Piazza della Mercede 4)

Internet Access

Bar Miramare (Map p152; ☎ 079 973 10 27; Via Gramsci 2; per hr €5; ☷ 8.30am-1pm & 4.30pm-2am)

Poco Loco (Map p152; Via Gramsci 8; per hr €5; ☷ 7pm-1am) A concert venue with three computers and a bowling alley.

Medical Services

Farmacia Bulla (Map p152; ☎ 079 95 21 15; Via Garibaldi 13)

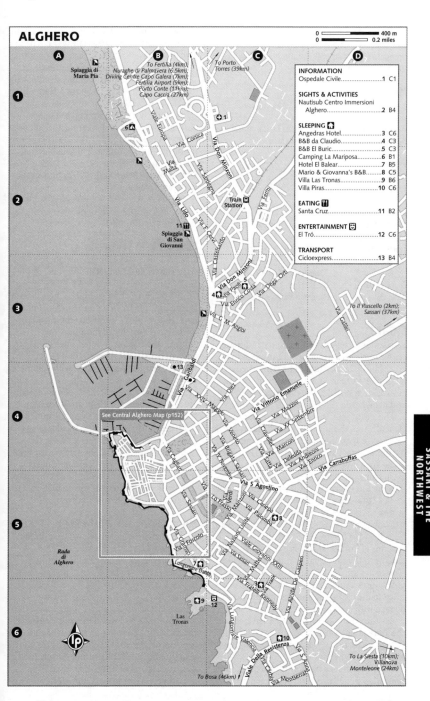

ALGHERO

| 0 | 400 m |
| 0 | 0.2 miles |

INFORMATION
Ospedale Civile.......................**1** C1

SIGHTS & ACTIVITIES
Nautisub Centro Immersioni
  Alghero..............................**2** B4

SLEEPING
Angedras Hotel.....................**3** C6
B&B da Claudio.....................**4** C3
B&B El Buric.........................**5** C3
Camping La Mariposa.............**6** B1
Hotel El Balear......................**7** B5
Mario & Giovanna's B&B........**8** C5
Villa Las Tronas.....................**9** B6
Villa Piras...........................**10** C6

EATING
Santa Cruz..........................**11** B2

ENTERTAINMENT
El Tró.................................**12** C6

TRANSPORT
Cicloexpress........................**13** B4

Spiaggia di
Maria Pia

To Fertilia (4km);
Nuraghe di Palmavera (6.5km);
Diving Centre Capo Galera (7km);
Fertilia Airport (9km);
Porto Conte (11km);
Capo Caccia (27km)

To Porto
Torres (39km)

Viale Europa

Via Corsica

Via Sardegna

Via Don Minzon

Via Malta

Via Lido

Via F. Ferret

Via C. Castellardo

Via Paoli

Via Fermi

Train
Station

Spiaggia
di San
Giovanni

Via Don Minzoni

Via Enrico Costa

Via Pegli Orti

Via C. M. Angioj

Via Callea

To Il Ruscello (2km);
Sassari (37km)

Via Garibaldi

Via Diez

Via XXIV Maggio

Via Veneto

Via Vittorio Emanuele

Via Mazzini

Via Cavallera

Via XX Settembre

Via Marconi

Via IV Novembre

Via Brigata Sassari

Via Satta

Via Deledda

Via Andreoni

Via Enrico

Via Carrabuffas

Via Caboto

Via Sassari

Via S Agostino

La Frasca

Via Marconi

Via Canepa

Via Palomba

Via Nazario Sauro

Via G. Foscolo

Via Gramsci

Viale Giovanni XXIII

Via Sassari

Via Alghero

Via Fratelli Kennedy

Via Alcide De Gasperi

Via Monserrato

Via Alghero

Via Chiara

Via Nuraj

Lungomare Dante

Lungomare Valencia

Viale Della Resistenza

Las
Tronas

Rada
di
Alghero

See Central Alghero Map (p152)

To La Siesta (10km);
Villanova
Monteleone (24km)

To Bosa (46km)

See Central Alghero Map (p152)

SASSARI & THE NORTHWEST

Farmacia Cabras (Map p152; ☎ 079 97 92 60; Lungomare Dante 20) English-speaking service.

Ospedale Civile (Map p149; ☎ 079 99 62 00; Via Don Minzoni) The main hospital.

Money

You'll find banks with ATMs all over the old town.

Banca Carige (Map p152; Via Sassari 13) Has an ATM.

Banca di Sassari (Map p152; Via La Marmora)

Post

Main post office (Map p152; Via Carducci 35; ☒ 8am-6.50pm Mon-Fri, to 1.15pm Sat)

Tourist Information

Airport tourist office (off Map p149; ☎ 079 93 51 50; ☒ 8.30am-1pm & 3.30-10pm)

Tourist office (Map p152; ☎ 079 97 90 54; www .comune.alghero.ss.it, in Italian; Piazza Porta Terra 9; ☒ 8am-8pm Mon-Sat, 10am-1pm Sun Apr-Oct, 8am-8pm Mon-Sat Nov-Mar) The best tourist office in Sardinia with helpful English-speaking staff and tons of practical information.

SIGHTS

A leisurely stroll around Alghero's animated *centro storico* is a good way of tuning in to the city's laid-back rhythms. The dark, medieval lanes come to life in the early evening when crowds swell the alleyways to parade their tans and browse the shop windows.

The entire city centre was originally enclosed, but in the 19th century the land-ward walls were torn down and partially replaced by the **Giardini Pubblici** (Map p152), a green space that now effectively separates the old town from the new.

Near the Giardini, the 14th-century **Torre Porta a Terra** (Map p152; ☎ 079 973 40 45; Piazza Porta Terra; adult/child €2.50/1.50; ☒ 9am-1pm & 6pm-11pm Mon-Sat Jul & Aug, 9.30am-1pm & 4.30-8pm Mon-Sat mid-May–Jun & Sep, 10am-1pm & 5-7pm Mon-Sat Oct-Mar) is all that remains of Porta a Terra, one of the two main gates into the medieval city. A stumpy 23m-high tower known originally as Porta Reial, it now houses a small multimedia museum dedicated to the city's past and, on the 2nd floor, a terrace with sweeping, 360-degree views.

To the south, another impressive tower, the **Torre di San Giovanni** (Map p152; ☎ 339 468 77 54; Largo San Francesco; ☒ depends on exhibition) hosts temporary art exhibitions.

Guarding the sea by busy Piazza Sulis, **Torre Sulis** (Map p152) closes off the defensive line

of towers to the south of the old town. To the north the **Bastione della Maddalena** (Map p152), with its eponymous tower, forms the only remnant of the city's former land battlements.

Just west of the bastion, and overlooking the crowded marina, is **Porta a Mare** (Map p152), the second of Alghero's medieval gateways. Steps by the gate lead up to the portside bastions, which stretch around to **Torre della Polveriera** (Map p152) at the northernmost tip of the *centro storico*. The Mediterranean crashes up against the seaward walls of the **Bastioni Marco Polo** (Map p152) and **Bastioni Cristoforo Colombo**, the city's western wall. Along these seaward bulwarks are some inviting restaurants and bars where you can camera-snap the sunset over a cocktail.

Cattedrale di Santa Maria

Overlooking Piazza Duomo, Alghero's over-sized **Cattedrale di Santa Maria** (Map p152; ☎ 079 97 92 22; Piazza Duomo; ☒ 7am-noon & 5-7.30pm) appears out of place with its pompous neoclassical facade and fat Doric columns. An unfortunate 19th-century addition, the facade was the last in a long line of modifications that the hybrid cathedral has endured since it was built on Catalan Gothic lines in the 16th century. Inside it's largely Renaissance, with some late-baroque baubles added in the 18th century. Free guided tours (in Italian) of the cathedral are available between 10am and 1pm Monday to Friday between February and September.

Of greater interest is the Catalan **campanile** (Map p152; adult/child €2/free; ☒ 7-9.30pm Tue, Thu & Sat Jul-Aug, 5-8pm Tue, Thu & Sat Sep, on request rest of year) around the back in Via Principe Umberto. A fine example of Catalan-Gothic architecture, this is the tall octagonal tower that you see towering over Alghero's rooftops.

Museo Diocesano d'Arte Sacra

In the former Oratorio del Rosario, the **Museo Diocesano d'Arte Sacra** (Map p152; ☎ 079 973 30 41; www.algheromuseo.it; Piazza Duomo; adult/concession €3/2; ☒ 10am-12.30pm Thu-Tue year-round & 5-8pm Apr, May, late Sep & Oct, 6-9pm Jun & early Sep, 6.30-9.30pm Jul & Aug) houses the cathedral's collection of religious artefacts, including silverware, statuary, paintings and wood carving. A ghoulish touch is the reliquary of what is claimed to be one of the *innocenti* (newborn babies slaughtered by Herod in his search for the Christ child). The tiny skull is chilling, but apparently it appealed to Alghero artist

Francesco Pinna, who received it from a Roman cardinal in the 16th century.

Piazza Civica

Just inside Porta a Mare (Sea Gate) at the northeastern tip of the *centro storico*, Piazza Civica is Alghero's showcase square. In a former life it was the administrative heart of the medieval city, but where Spanish aristocrats once met to debate affairs of empire, tourists now converge to browse jewellery displays in elegant shop windows, eat ice cream and drink at the city's grandest cafe. Caffè Costantino occupies the ground floor of the Gothic **Palazzo d'Albis** (Map p152), where the Spanish emperor Charles V stayed in 1541.

Chiesa di San Francesco

In contrast to the self-aggrandising cathedral, the **Chiesa di San Francesco** (Map p152; ☎ 079 97 92 58; Via Carlo Alberto; 🕙 7.30am-noon & 5-8.30pm) is a model of architectural harmony. Hidden behind an austere stone facade, it was originally built to a Catalan-Gothic design in the 14th-century but was later given a successful Renaissance facelift after it partially collapsed in 1593. Of note is the 18th-century polychrome marble altar and a strange 17th-century wooden sculpture of a haggard Christ tied to a column.

Through the sacristy you can enter the beautiful 14th-century cloisters, the 22 columns of which connect a series of round arches. The buttery sandstone used in the arcades and columns lends it special warmth and makes it a wonderful setting for summer concerts.

Chiesa di San Michele

Further along Via Carlo Alberto, the *carrer major* (main street) of the medieval town, the **Chiesa di San Michele** (Map p152; ☎ 079 97 92 34; 🕙 30 mins before Mass at 7pm Mon-Sat, 9am & 7pm Sun) is best known for its maiolica dome, typical of churches in Valencia, another former Catalan territory. The present tiles were laid in the 1960s, but this doesn't detract from its beauty.

Just before you reach the church you cross Via Gilbert Ferret. The intersection is known as the *quatre cantonades* (four sides), and for centuries labourers would gather here in the hope of finding work.

ACTIVITIES

From the port you can take a boat trip along the impressive northern coast to Capo Caccia (p161) and the grandiose Grotta di Nettuno (p161) cave complex. There are a number of operators offering day tours with fishing and swimming stops (prices range from about €40 to €100 per person), but if you just want to go to the caves and back it makes sense to use the **Navisarda ferry** (Map p152; ☎ 079 95 06 03; adult/child return €14/7, not incl cave entrance fee), which departs hourly between 9am and 5pm from June to September, and four times daily the rest of the year.

You can organise dives with a handful of outlets in Alghero, including **Nautisub Centro Immersioni Alghero** (Map p149; ☎ 079 95 24 33; www .nautisub.com; Via Garibaldi 45), which offers diving (from €38), snorkelling (€25) and kit hire (€25 for air tank, regulator, jacket and lead belt), as well as a number of boat tours. A few miles from Alghero, signposted off the main road to Capo Caccia, the **Diving Centre Capo Galera** (off Map p149; ☎ 079 94 21 10; www.capo galera.com; Localita Capo Galera) operates out of a big white villa on a panoramic promontory. Dives and courses are available for all levels, but more advanced swimmers will enjoy some superlative cave diving, including exploration of the Nereo Cave, the biggest underwater grotto in the Mediterranean. Dives start at €20 and full kit hire costs €18. The centre also offers accommodation (doubles €65 to €100, six-person rooms €110 to €180) and serves up splendid barbecue dinners.

If you prefer your fun on terra firma, Alghero's beaches extend along Via Garibaldi, north of the port. **Spiaggia di San Giovanni** (Map p149) and the adjacent **Spiaggia di Maria Pia** (Map p149) are long and sandy although they're not the best in the area. Nicer by far are Spiaggia Bombarde and Spiaggia del Lazzaretto, both located beyond the airport at Fertilia, and both accessible by local bus (see p158). In Alghero you can hire umbrellas and sun loungers at the beach for about €8 per day, as well as windsurfers (€10) and canoes (€10). Bus line AO covers the length of the beachfront.

Horse riding is available in various centres in the vicinity; the tourist office has a list. As a rough guide rides cost from €15 to €20 per hour.

COURSES

Brush up on your Italian with a course at **Stroll & Speak** (Map p152; ☎ 339 489 93 14; www .strollandspeak.com; Via Cavour 4; 🕙 9am-1pm & 2.30-8pm Mon-Sat), an established language school in the

SASSARI & THE
NORTHWEST

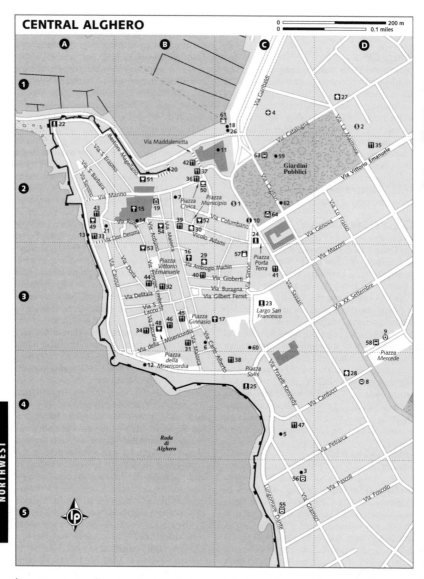

historic centre. Bank on €200 (10 hours), €285 (15 hours) or €360 (20 hours) of individual lessons in a week.

TOURS

Parents can pacify fractious kids with a **horse-and-cart tour** (Map p152; ☎ 079 97 69 27; adult/2-10yr €5/3.50; ☯ 10am-11pm Jul & Aug, to 8.30pm Apr-Jun, Sep & Oct) of the old town. Tickets for the 25-minute trot are available from the start point on the port side of Bastione della Maddalena.

The **Trenino Catalano** (Map p152; adult/under 8yr €5/3; ☯ 10am-1pm & 4.30-11pm Jul & Aug, 10am-1pm & 3.30-9pm Apr-Jun & Sep) is a miniature train that chugs around the centre. Departures are half-hourly from the port; buy tickets on board.

For information on boat tours see the Activities section on p151.

FESTIVALS & EVENTS

Alghero has a full calendar of festivals and events, although spring and summer are the best times to catch an event.

February

Sagra del Bogamari Alghero locals pay homage to the humble sea urchin by eating mountain-loads of the spiky molluscs. Runs from the end of January into February.

Carnevale On *martedì grasso* (Shrove Tuesday) an effigy of a French soldier (the *pupazzo*) is burned at the stake amid much merry-making.

March/April

Easter Holy Week Figures of Christ and the Virgin Mary are borne through town in enactments of the *Misteri* (Passion of Christ) and *Incontru* (Meeting of the Virgin with Christ).

July/August

Estate Musicale Internazionale di Alghero (International Summer of Music) Throughout July and August, classical music concerts are staged at the Chiesa di San Francesco and other outdoor settings.

Ferragosto (Feast of the Assumption) Alghero puts on a show on 15 August with fireworks, boat races and music.

SLEEPING

Accommodation in Alghero is largely geared to the summer season and many places close over winter, typically between November and February. Reservations are a good idea year-round but become essential in July and August. The tourist office has full accommodation lists, available online at www.comune .alghero.ss.it/alghero_turismo/dormire.htm.

Budget

There are very few hotels catering to independent budget travellers so your best bet is to go for a B&B or self-catering apartment, of which there are plenty across town. For a full list click the 'Bed & Breakfast' link at the web address given earlier.

Camping La Mariposa (off Map p149; ☎ 079 95 03 60; www.lamariposa.it; Via Lido 22; per person/tent/car €11/13/4, 4-person bungalows €47-78; ⏱ Apr-Oct; 🖳) About 2km north of the centre, this camping ground is on the beach, set amid pine and eucalyptus trees. This, and the excellent facilities, including a windsurfing school and diving centre, make it a popular choice.

B&B da Claudio (Map p149; ☎ 079 98 42 36; http://web .tiscali.it/b_and_b_da_claudio; Via Don Minzoni 7; s €22-32, d €44-64) This welcoming, value-for-money B&B is in a modern apartment near the seafront. There's nothing fancy about the facilities, but the three bedrooms, two of which share a bathroom, are homey and clean, and the beach location is convenient.

Mario & Giovanna's B&B (Map p149; ☎ 339 890 35 63; www.marioandgiovanna.com; Via Canepa 51; d/tr/q €55/65/70, apt per person €50-70) Cheerfully cluttered with ornaments, paintings and Giovanna's lovingly tended collection of English porcelain, this B&B has three sunny rooms and a small courtyard garden. Located in the blander modern part of town, it's about a 15-minute stroll to the historic centre. Mario also has self-catering apartments to rent.

Also recommended:

Mamajuana (Map p152; ☎ 339 136 97 91; www .mamajuana.it; Vicolo Adami 12; s €40-60, d €60-90) Location rather than luxury is the key at this cramped *centro storico* B&B.

B&B El Buric (Map p149; ☎ 079 989 20 19; www .alghero-sardegna.com; Via Enrico Costa 26; r €60-80; P) A summery B&B in a 6th-floor flat near the beach.

Midrange

Villa Piras (Map p149; ☎ 079 97 83 69; www.villapiras.it; Viale della Resistenza 10; s €55-77, d €75-100; ☒) A rare year-round hotel, Villa Paris is about 15 minutes southwest of the *centro storico*. Rooms are simple, spacious affairs with plain, unfussy furniture and bare cream walls. In summer breakfast is served on the small outdoor terrace. Air-con costs an extra €7.

Hotel San Francesco (Map p152; ☎ 079 98 03 30; www .sanfrancescohotel.com; Via Ambrogio Machin 2; s €45-70, d €70-105; ☒) You'll need to book early to get a room at Alghero's only *centro storico* hotel. Housed in an ex-convent – the monks still live on the 3rd floor – the rooms are straightforward but comfortable with white walls, pine furniture and brown tiled floors. If available, ask for a room overlooking the medieval cloisters.

our pick Angedras Hotel (Map p149; ☎ 079 973 50 34; www.angedras.it; Via Frank 2; s €53-68, d €75-110; ☒ 🖳) A model of whitewashed Mediterranean style, the Angedras has cool, airy rooms with big French doors opening on to sunny patios. The chic terrace, where breakfast is served in summer, is a cool place for iced drinks on hot summer evenings. Guests get 10% discount at the restaurant of the same name on Bastioni Marco Polo (see opposite).

Hotel El Balear (Map p149; ☎ 079 97 52 29; www .hotelelbalear.it; Lungomare Dante 32; s €58-79, d €86-130, half board per person €68-88; 🕑 Mar-Oct; ☒) A seafront location inevitably leads to higher rates and this boxy three-star is no exception. There's a bustling, lived-in feel about the whole place, and rooms, while comfortable enough, are small. Still, staff are friendly and the sea views make up for the minor shortcomings.

Hotel La Margherita (Map p152; ☎ 079 97 90 06; www.hotellamargherita.it; Via Sassari 70; s €60-80, d €80-115, with view extra €15; P ☒) La Margherita has seen better days, but behind the slightly tired air there's a wonderfully endearing hotel. Spangly chandeliers (with energy-saving bulbs) hang down from high ceilings, antiques pepper the airy, spacious rooms, and breakfast is served on a terrace with a wonderful panorama. Parking costs €7.

Top End

Hotel Catalunya (Map p152; ☎ 079 95 31 72; www.hotel catalunya.it; Via Catalogna 20; s €90-138, d €120-196; P ☒) Towering over the Giardini Pubblici, this big business hotel has all the facilities and little character. Uniformed staff welcome guests to the smart tiled lobby and lead up to white rooms decorated with bold blue furniture.

Villa Las Tronas (Map p149; ☎ 079 98 18 18; www .hotelvillalastronas.it; Via Lungomare Valencia 1; s €120-230, d €170-398; P ☒ 🖳 🖳) A 19th-century art nouveau palace once used as a holiday home by Italian royalty, this ravishing hotel is set in its own lush gardens on a private promontory. The rooms are pure fin de siècle with acres of brocade, elegant antiques and moody oil paintings. A beauty centre, complete with indoor pool, hammam-massage facility and gymnasium, adds to the decadence.

EATING

Seafood rules in Alghero, a fishing town famous for its sardines and rock lobsters. However, lobster doesn't come cheap so always get it weighed before you order it – on the menu its price is usually listed as per gram.

Budget

Gelateria Arcobaleno (Map p152; Piazza Civica 34) Ice cream is a pleasure almost everywhere in Alghero, but according to the UK's *Sunday Times* this tiny hole in the wall serves 'the best ice cream in town'. To find out for yourself, join the queue and get stuck into a delicious tub of hazelnut and *stracciatella*.

Il Ghiotto (Map p152; ☎ 079 97 48 20; Piazza Civica 23; meals €10-15; 🕑 Tue-Sun) One of the few places in Alghero where you can sit down and fill up for as little as €10. At lunchtime the curtain comes up on a tantalising spread of *panini*, pastas, salads and main courses. There's seating in a dining area behind the main hall or outside on a busy wooden terrace.

Spaghetteria Al Solito Posto (Map p152; ☎ 328 913 37 45; Piazza della Misericordia; meals €15-20; ⏰ Fri-Wed) Not the place for a lingering dinner, this small barrel-vaulted place is one of the most popular eateries in town. The atmosphere is TV-on-in-the-corner and the menu is limited (pasta with a range of sauces), but the food is good and the bustling vibe is fun. Booking is recommended.

For takeaway pizza, **Pata Pizza** (Map p152; ☎ 079 97 51 77; Via Maiorca 89) is a central option.

Many of Alghero's stylish cafes also serve decent food menus, including Diva Caffè and Caffè Latino (see p156).

Midrange

Nettuno (Map p152; ☎ 079 97 97 74; Via Maddalenetta 4; pizzas €7, meals around €35; ⏰ Thu-Tue) Don your best boating togs for a meal at this boisterous pizzeria/restaurant overlooking the marina. The menu is heavily slanted towards seafood with stalwarts such as *spaghetti alle vongole* (with clams) and *zuppa di pesce* (fish soup).

Angedras Restaurant (Map p152; ☎ 079 973 50 78; www.angedrasrestaurant.it; Bastioni Marco Polo 41; lunch menu €16, meals around €35; ⏰ Wed-Mon) Dining on Alghero's honey-coloured stone ramparts is a memorable experience. This is one of the better restaurants on the walls, serving a largely traditional menu, including the king of all Sardinian meat dishes, *porceddu* (roast suckling pig).

Osteria Machiavello (Map p152; ☎ 079 98 06 28; Bastioni Marco Polo 57; land/sea menus €16/18, meals around €35; ⏰ Wed-Mon) With tables on the city walls, this is a panoramic spot for a memorable dinner. The menu covers most tastes with grilled meats, including horse, and a number of classic fish dishes. Try the *zuppa di cozze e vongole* (mussel and clam soup).

Trattoria Maristella (Map p152; ☎ 079 97 81 72; Via Fratelli Kennedy 9; meals around €27) Visitors and locals flock to this bustling little trattoria for reliable seafood – the *insalata di mare* (seafood salad) is excellent – and Sardinian specialities such as *culurgiones* (ravioli stuffed with potato, pecorino cheese and mint). All at very honest prices.

Osteria Taverna Paradiso (Map p152; ☎ 079 97 80 07; Via Principe Umberto 29; meals around €30; ⏰ Tue-Sun) Cheese is king at this convivial, unpretentious trattoria. Owner and 'Cheese Master' Pasquale Nocella adores the stuff and takes great delight in introducing it to his guests in its many myriad forms – a cheese platter costs €16.

If cheese isn't your thing, there are excellent grilled meats and hearty pastas.

Il Refettorio (Map p152; ☎ 079 973 11 26; Vicolo Adami 47; meals around €30; ⏰ closed Tue in winter) A wine bar that does food or a restaurant where you can drink? Either way, Il Refettorio is a good-looking place with tables outdoors under a low stone arch and inside, in a vaulted interior. Aperitif hour attracts a well-dressed, fashionable crowd.

Santa Cruz (Map p149; Via Lido 2; pizza €6.50-8, meals around €30; ⏰ Tue-Sun) This brash Spanish joint is good for pizza, paella (€15) and grilled meats. More than the food, though, it's the beachside location that's the real draw. Occasional beach parties add to the already upbeat atmosphere.

La Cueva (Map p152; ☎ 079 97 91 83; Via Gioberti 4; meals €30-35; ⏰ Wed-Mon) A bright hole-in-the-wall arrangement, this is a good place to tuck into *paella valenciana* (traditional Spanish paella; €18), one of Alghero's culinary legacies from its days as a Catalan colony. There's also an ample choice of pastas and grilled meats.

Borgo Antico (Map p152; ☎ 079 98 26 49; Via Zaccaria 12; meals around €35; ⏰ closed Sun dinner) Housed in an ex-convent, this is a formal restaurant with outdoor seating on an atmospheric piazza. It's known for its excellent seafood which appears in dishes like *spaghetti all'aragosta* (lobster spaghetti; €38 for two people) and *triglie al cartoccio* (red mullet roasted in tin foil).

Top End

Al Tuguri (Map p152; ☎ 079 97 67 72; www.altuguri.it; Via Maiorca 113; tasting menus veg/sea/land/€36/40/40; ⏰ Mon-Sat) Serious vegetarian food is something of a novelty in Sardinia, and this is the place to find it. A discreet restaurant decorated in traditional rustic style, it serves a dedicated vegetarian menu alongside more traditional seafood and meat dishes. Booking is advisable.

Il Pavone (Map p152; ☎ 079 97 95 84; www.ristorante ilpavone.com; Piazza Sulis 3/4; meals around €45; ⏰ closed Sun lunch) The granddaddy of Alghero dining, Il Pavone can still cut it. Defiantly retro in look – its interior is a cheerful ensemble of period furniture, antiques and heavy paintings – it serves a mix of innovative Sardinian fare and old-fashioned classics.

Andreini (Map p152; ☎ 079 98 20 98; www.ristorante andreini.it; Via Ardoino 45; meals around €55; ⏰ Tue-Sun) In recent years this elegant restaurant has become a point of reference for creative, modern cuisine in Alghero. Tables are set beneath a huge fig tree where you can dine on beautifully presented food, served in adventurous combinations of fruit, fresh fish, meat and herbs.

Self-Catering

You can stock up on picnic supplies at Alghero's fresh produce **market** (Map p152; entrance Via Sassari 23; ☻ 6.30am-1.30pm & 4.30-8.30pm Mon-Sat) between Via Sassari and Via Cagliari. Otherwise, there's a **Euro Spin supermarket** (Map p152; Via La Marmora 28; ☻ 8.30am-9.30pm Mon-Sat, 9am-1.30pm & 5-9pm Sun) near the Giardini Pubblici.

DRINKING

There's no shortage of drinking options in Alghero. Popular areas include the beaches, the city ramparts, and the seafront south of the historic centre. In summer many places stay open late, typically to around 2am.

Baraonda (Map p152; ☎ 079 97 59 22; Piazza della Misericordia; ☻ 10am-2am) Burgundy walls and black-and-white jazz photos set the tone at this moody wine bar. In summer sit out on the piazza and watch the world parade by.

Diva Caffè (Map p152; ☎ 079 98 23 06; Piazza Municipio 1; cocktails €7; ☻ 10am-midnight Mon-Sat) A favourite lunch venue (pastas €6) for passing tourists, the Diva shows her true colours at night when the suntanned sophisticates drop by for a cocktail on the square. It stays open late on Fridays and Saturdays in summer.

Caffè Latino (Map p152; ☎ 079 97 65 41; Bastioni Magellano 10; cocktails from €4.80; ☻ 9am-11pm Wed-Mon, to 2am daily in summer) Up on the ramparts overlooking the port, this chic bar is a summer classic. Kick back on the grey rattan chairs, order from the ample menu, and listen to the breeze rattle the masts of the boats below you.

Caffè Costantino (Map p152; ☎ 079 97 61 54; Piazza Civica 31; ☻ 7.30am-midnight Thu-Tue) On Alghero's showpiece piazza, this is the classiest cafe in town. It's also one of the busiest, attracting a constant stream of tourists to its tables on the edge of the square. There's a full food menu alongside the drinks list, although if you just want to eat you'll get better value for money almost everywhere else.

Buena Vista (Map p152; Bastioni Marco Polo 47; cocktails €6.50-8; ☻ 3.30pm-3am) Fabulous mojitos, fresh fruit cocktails, stunning sea sunsets – what more could you want of a seafront bar? Upbeat tunes and a cavernous interior

add to the vibe at this popular bar on the western walls.

Other options include the following:

Jamaica Inn (Map p152; Via Principe Umberto 57; cocktails €6; ☻ Tue-Sun) A cheerful pub good for wine, beer and bar snacks (€6), including bruschetta.

Mill Inn (Map p152; Via Maiorca 37; ☻ Thu-Tue) A cosy drinking den beneath stone vaults. Occasional live music.

ENTERTAINMENT

As the bars begin to quieten from around 1am, the action shifts to the waterfront south of the old city. In summer you'll find crowds here until about 4am.

Live Music

Poco Loco (Map p152; ☎ 079 973 10 34; Via Gramsci 8; ☻ 7pm-1am) A popular all-purpose venue with internet, beer on tap, pizza, live music and an upstairs bowling alley (closed on Mondays). Concerts cater to most tastes, although jazz and blues headline more than most.

L'Arca (Map p152; ☎ 079 97 79 72; Lungomare Dante 6; ☻ 8am-2am) A rocking bar on the southern *lungomare* (seafront promenade). Inside, DJs conduct the mayhem between Thursdays and Saturdays, while outside, drinkers add to the festive atmosphere on the crowded seafront.

Nightclubs

Alghero's nightlife attracts punters from all over northern Sardinia. The scene is at its hottest in summer, but you can usually catch some action on winter weekends. The biggest clubs tend to be out of town, making transport a problem unless you can bag a lift or have around €35 for a taxi. Clubs open late, usually around midnight, and admission costs around €15, which might or might not include a drink.

El Trò (Map p149; ☎ 079 973 30 00; Via Lungomare Valencia 3; ☻ 9pm-late Tue-Sun) A disco pub on the rocks, El Trò becomes a steamy mosh pit on hot summer weekends as hyped up holidaymakers dance til dawn on the seafront dance floor.

Il Ruscello (off Map p149; ☎ 339 235 07 55; www .ruscellodisco.com, in Italian; SS Alghero-Olmedeo; ☻ nightly Jul & Aug, Fri & Sat Jun & Sep, Sat rest of year) One of Alghero's historic clubs, Il Ruscello attracts top Sardinian DJs and a clued-up crowd who dance long and hard to commercial, house and revival. The club is about 2km northeast of Alghero on the road to Olmedo.

BLOOD-RED GOLD

Since ancient times the red coral of the Mediterranean has beguiled and bewitched people. Many believed it to be the petrified blood of the Medusa, attributing to it aphrodisiac and other secret qualities, and fashioning amulets out of it.

Alghero's coast south of Capo Caccia is justifiably called the Riviera del Corallo (Coral Riviera). The coral fished here is of the highest quality and glows a dark orangey-red. The strong currents around the headland mean the little coral polyps have to work super hard to build their small coral trees, making them short and very dense to withstand the drag of the sea. Technically speaking, this is great news for Alghero's jewellers, as it means the coral trees have few air pockets – the sign of top-quality coral.

The coral is a precious commodity and its fishing is tightly regulated – in fact, coral fishing has been halted in the past two years. It's difficult work, requiring sophisticated equipment and decompression chambers, as the coral is fished at a depth of 135m. It's then sold to Alghero's jewellers in chunks, prices varying according to colour, quality and size.

Agostino Marogna has been working in the business for years and now owns the finest coral shop in Alghero. Their signature necklaces composed of big, round coral beads often take years to create. To make one smooth red ball results in nearly 60% wastage. As there is only a certain amount of coral for sale each year, they often have to put these necklaces aside until the new season, when they have to hunt for exactly the same shade and quality of coral. Such necklaces can cost as much as €30,000. Most items in the shop go for less, though, with prices starting at around €100. You'll find **Marogna** (Map p152; ☎ 079 98 48 14; Piazza Civica 34) at Palazzo d'Albis.

La Siesta (off Map p149; ☎ 079 98 01 37; www .lasiestadisco.net, in Italian; Localita Scala Piccada; ☾ from 1am nightly Jul & Aug, Sat Jun) About 10km out of town, this is another big, open-air affair with four dance floors, mainstream tunes and a regular program of live music. For big nights, there is sometimes a shuttle bus (€1.50) from Alghero town centre.

SHOPPING

Browsing the elegant shop windows along Via Carlo Alberto, the main shopping strip, is part and parcel of a trip to Alghero. Throughout the historic centre, the streets are lined with shops selling foodie souvenirs, designer threads and jewellery made from Alghero's famous coral (see the boxed text, above).

Enodolciaria (Map p152; ☎ 079 97 97 41; Via Simon 24) This is an Aladdin's cave of edible treats. Shelves groan under the weight of bottles of island wine, olive oil, pretty packets of pasta, jars of vegetables and tins of local tuna.

GETTING THERE & AWAY

Air

Alghero's **Fertilia airport** (AHO; ☎ 079 93 52 82; www.algheroairport.it) is about 9km northwest of Alghero. It's served by a number of low-cost carriers, including Ryanair and Air One, with connections to mainland Italy,

and destinations across Europe, including Barcelona, Birmingham, Dublin, Frankfurt, Liverpool and London.

For more flight information, see p233.

Bus

Intercity buses stop at and leave from Via Catalogna, by the Giardini Pubblici. Buy tickets at the booth (Map p152) in the gardens.

Up to 11 daily buses (15 on weekdays) run to/from Sassari (€2.50 to €3, one hour). ARST also runs buses to Porto Torres (€2.50, one hour, eight daily Monday to Friday, five daily Saturday and Sunday) and Bosa (€4.50, one hour 35 minutes, two daily). These Bosa buses travel inland via Villanova Monteleone, but there's also a daily bus that follows the scenic coastal route (€3, one hour 10 minutes).

There are no direct links with Olbia. Instead you have to travel to Sassari, from where you can pick up the Turmo Travel link (see p130).

Car & Motorcycle

From Sassari, the easiest route is via the SS291, which connects with the SP19 into Alghero. Approaching from Bosa, there are two routes: one along the inland SS292 and the other, one of Sardinia's great coastal drives, along the SP105 (see the boxed text, opposite).

Train
The train station (Map p149) is 1.5km north of the old town on Via Don Minzoni. Up to 11 FdS trains a day run to/from Sassari (€2.20, 35 minutes).

GETTING AROUND
Your own feet will be enough to get you around the old town and most other places, but you may want to jump on a bus to get to the beaches.

To/From the Airport
Up to 11 daily FdS buses (€0.70, 20 minutes) connect the airport with Piazza Mercede in the town centre. Two daily **Logudoro Tours** (☎ 079 28 17 28) buses run to Cagliari (€20, 3½ hours), Oristano (€15, 2½ hours) and Macomer (€10, 1½ hours). To/from Nuoro, **Redentours** (☎ 0784 3 14 58; www.redentours.com) has three daily buses (€20, 2¼ hours) for which bookings are required.

A taxi to the airport costs around €25.

Bus
Line AO runs from Via Cagliari (via the Giardini Pubblici) to the beaches. Urban buses also operate to Fertilia as well as several places beyond. You can pick up these buses at stops around the Giardini Pubblici. Tickets (€0.70) are available at florists **Floridea** (Map p152; Via Cagliari 4) in the park and most *tabacchi* (tobacconists).

Car & Motorcycle
Although summer can get hectic, it is generally possible to find parking not too far from the old centre. In the streets around the Giardini Pubblici, on-street parking between the blue lines costs €0.70 for the first hour, €1 for the second and €1.50 for the third. Get tickets from parking attendants, meters or *tabacchi*.

Local and international car-hire companies have booths at Fertilia airport. **Avis** (Map p152; ☎ 079 93 50 64; Piazza Sulis 9) also has a handy office in town.

Operating out of a hut on the seaward side of Via Garibaldi, **Cicloexpress** (Map p149; ☎ 079 98 69 50; www.cicloexpress.com; Via Garibaldi) hires out cars (€65 per day), scooters (€55) and bikes (€8).

Taxi
There's a **taxi rank** (Map p152) on Via Vittorio Emanuele near the tourist office. Otherwise you can call for one by phoning 079 989 20 28.

RIVIERA DEL CORALLO

Heading northwards from Alghero the coastal road sweeps scenically round to the west, passing through Fertilia, a low-key resort, and Porto Conte, a broad bay sprinkled with hotels and discreet villas. The end of the road, quite literally, is Capo Caccia, a rocky headland famous for its thrilling cave complex, the Grotta di Nettuno. Along the way there are a couple of great beaches and some interesting archaeological sites. Inland, the landscape flattens out and you'll find one of the island's top wine producers as well as a number of hospitable and peaceful *agriturismi* (farm-stay accommodation).

FERTILIA
Sandy, pine-backed beaches fringe the coast round to Fertilia, about 4km northwest of Alghero. A rather soulless little town with ruler-straight streets and robust rationalist *palazzi*, its atmosphere comes as something of a surprise to visitors after Alghero's medieval hustle. It was built by Mussolini, who intended it to be the centre of a grand agricultural reclamation project, and who brought in farmers from northeastern Italy. Later postwar refugees arrived from Friuli-Venezia Giulia, bringing with them an allegiance to the lion of St Mark, symbol of Venice, which adorns the statue at the waterfront.

There's not a great deal to see or do once you've pottered around the seafront, but there are a couple of excellent beaches nearby. A few kilometres west of town, the **Spiaggia delle Bombarde** is a local favourite, set amid greenery and well equipped with umbrellas, sun loungers and a kids' play area. If it's too crowded, and it does get extremely busy in summer, you could try the next beach along, the **Spiaggia del Lazzaretto**. Both beaches are signposted off the main road, but if you don't have your own car, the Capo Caccia bus from Alghero passes nearby.

MARE E MONTE

One of Sardinia's great scenic roads unfurls along the coast south of Alghero to Bosa, 46km away. The corniche dips and curves through the coastal cliffs, offering sensational panoramas and taking in the best of *il mare* (the sea) and *il monte* (the mountains). It can be done as either a full-day road trip or a two-day 108km cycling tour (detailed in the following paragraphs). It's best to travel south via the inland road (SS292) through Villanova Monteleone and return via the coastal corniche to enjoy the spectacular views of the Riviera dei Corallo and Capo Caccia.

For the cyclist, day one (62km) is the hardest, a classic up-and-over day gaining ground to 600m. The road winds up into the hills, revealing views across the water to Capo Caccia, before dipping over a ridge into deep woods that take you out of sight of the coast. After 23km you reach **Villanova Monteleone** (567m), perched like a natural balcony on the slopes of the Colle di Santa Maria. The centre of town is just off the main route and every morning except Sunday you'll find a produce market here (follow the signs to *mercato*).

On the high road beyond Villanova you will enjoy some great coastal views as the road bobs and weaves through shady woods. The final 5km climb is far outweighed by the sizzling 10km descent to Bosa.

The return journey via the corniche road takes you along a truly spectacular stretch of deserted coastline (bring sandwiches and water). There's only one significant climb of 6.2km to 350m, but the effort is offset by the commanding views. The brilliant white cliffs of Capo Caccia (after 16km) can often be seen on the northern horizon. Other than the jangle of goats' bells from the rugged, high slopes or a bird of prey winging on the thermals, there's little to disturb you.

There are two swimming spots along the way: a path to the beach after about 5.4km (look for cars parked by the roadside) just south of Torre Argentina, and **Spiaggia La Speranza** at 35.4km. Here you can lunch on fresh seafood at **Ristorante La Speranza** (☎ 079 91 70 10; meals around €35; ⊙ closed Wed winter) before the final 10.8km run into Alghero.

Sleeping & Eating

Hostal de l'Alguer (☎ /fax 079 93 20 39; www.alghero hostel.com; Via Parenzo 79; dm €18, per person in s/d/tr/q €30/25/22/20, meal €9.50; P 🖳) One of Sardinia's very few Hostelling International hostels, this place is clean, welcoming and characterless. You won't want to hang around much, as rooms are in a series of prefab bungalows in a dusty compound, but if you're going to be on the beach all day, it's not a bad call.

Hotel Punta Negra (☎ 079 93 02 22; www .hotelpuntanegra.it; Strada Fertilia-Porto Conte; s €110-250, d €140-320; ⊙ Apr-Nov; P 🍴 🏊) If you're looking for a relaxed beachside retreat, this big, rambling four-star will do very nicely, thank you very much. Set in a pine grove, it sports a white, airy Mediterranean look and offers an impressive array of facilities: private beach, tennis court, pool, rooms with sea views. You'll find it about 1km west of town.

Acquario (☎ 079 93 02 39; Via Pola 34; meals around €35; ⊙ Tue-Sun, daily summer) This is a popular eatery in the centre of town, on the waterfront near the central belltower. The onus is on classic local food so expect abundant seafood pastas, fresh fish, and *seaddas* (fried pastry puffs filled with ricotta) for dessert.

Getting There & Away

From Alghero, take local bus AF for Fertilia (€0.70, 15 minutes); it runs hourly between 7am and 9.40pm.

NORTH OF FERTILIA

About 7km north of Alghero, just to the left (west) of the road to Porto Torres, lie scattered the ancient burial chambers of the **Necropoli di Anghelu Ruiu** (admission €3, with guided tour €5, with audioguide €6, incl Necropoli di Palmavera €5, with guided tour €8, with audioguide €10; ⊙ 9am-7pm May-Oct, to 6pm Apr, 9.30am-4pm Mar, 10am-2pm Nov-Feb). The 38 tombs carved into the rock, known as *domus de janas*, date from between 2700 BC and 3300 BC. Most of the sculptural decor has been stripped off and removed to museums, but in some of the chambers you can make out lightly sculpted bull's horns, perhaps the symbol of a funeral deity.

Continue north up the road, and after a further 2km or so you come to the 650-hectare estate of Sardinia's top wine producer, **Sella e Mosca** (☎ 079 99 77 00; www.sellaemosca.com). Here you can join a free guided tour of the estate's lovingly tended **museum** (⊙ 5.30pm Mon-Sat end May-Oct, by request rest of the year) and learn how the company grew to become the island's best-known vintner. The museum also has a small archaeological section dedicated to the Necropoli di Anghelu Ruiu. Afterwards, sample some of the wines at the beautiful **enoteca** (wine shop; ☺ 8.30am-1pm & 3-6.30pm Mon-Sat year-round, plus 8.30am-8pm Sun mid-Jun–end Sep).

With your wine you'll want food and fortunately there are a number of delicious eating stops dotted around the countryside.

Agriturismo Barbagia (☎ 079 93 51 41; www.agriturismobarbagia.it; Localita Fighera, Podere 26; meals around €30) A wonderful *agriturismo* offering simple accommodation (rooms €30 to €40) and abundant farmhouse food. Kids will enjoy the swings while mum and dad enjoy their meal on the shaded terrace overlooking the lawn.

Agriturismo Sa Mandra (☎ 079 99 91 50; www.aziendasamandra.it; Localita Fighera, Podere 21; meals around €35) Feast like royalty at this beautiful *agriturismo* 2km north of the airport. The daily menu is fixed, but you're not exactly short of choice with antipasti of cured ham, salami, herbed cheese, and marinated vegetables. Then there's pasta followed by a choice of roast lamb or suckling pig. Book early and come hungry.

Da Bruno (☎ 079 93 00 98; www.hotelfertilia.it; Strada Santa Maria la Palma; fixed menu €30, meals around €45; ☺ daily summer) In the Hotel Fertilia, a couple of kilometres north of Fertilia, Da Bruno is a rustic-style restaurant serving great seafood and seasonal meats, including boar, lamb and pork. Rooms are available at the **hotel** (s €70-80; d €85-110, half board per person €72.50-110) year-round.

From Alghero, there are two daily buses which pass by the turn-off for Sella e Mosca (€1.50, 25 minutes).

NURAGHE DI PALMAVERA

Back on the coast, a few kilometres west of Fertilia on the road to Porto Conte, is the **Nuraghe di Palmavera** (admission €3, with guided tour €5, with audioguide €6, incl Necropoli di Anghelu Ruiu €5, with guided tour €8, with audioguide €10; ☺ 9am-7pm May-Oct, to 6pm Apr, 9.30am-4pm Mar, 10am-2pm Nov-Feb), a 3500-year-old *nuraghe* village. At its centre stands a limestone tower and an elliptical building with a secondary sandstone tower that was added later. The ruins of smaller towers and bastion walls surround the central edifice, and beyond the walls are the packed remnants of circular dwellings, of which there may have been about 50 originally.

The circular **Capanna delle Riunioni** (Meeting Hut) is the subject of considerable speculation. Its foundation wall is lined by a low stone bench, perhaps for a council of elders, and encloses a pedestal topped by a model *nuraghe*. One theory suggests there was actually a cult to the *nuraghi* themselves.

You'll need your own transport to get here. The AF local bus (€0.70, 15 to 20 minutes) from Alghero passes through here but returns via an inland route, which will leave you stranded.

PORTO CONTE

Known more poetically as the Baia delle Ninfe (Bay of Nymphs), Porto Conte is a lovely unspoilt bay, its blue waters home to an armada of bobbing yachts and its green shores thick with mimosa and eucalyptus trees. The main focus is Spiaggia Mugoni, a hugely popular beach which arcs round the bay's northeastern flank. With its fine white sand and protected waters, it makes an excellent venue for beginners to try their hand at water sports. The **Club della Vela** (☎ 338 148 95 83; www.clubdellavelaalghero.it) offers windsurfing, canoeing, kayaking and sailing courses, as well as renting out boats.

Just west of Ponte Conte, and signposted off the main road, **Le Prigionette Nature Reserve** (☎ 079 94 90 60; admission free; ☺ 8am-4pm Mon-Fri, to 5pm Sat & Sun) sits at the base of Mount Timidone (361m). Encompassing some 12 sq km, and nicknamed the Arca di Noé (Noah's Ark) because of the variety of animals introduced here since the 1970s, it has well-marked forest paths and tracks, suitable for walkers and cyclists. You're unlikely to spot many animals, but the park is home to deer, unique white donkeys from the Isola Asinara, Giara horses and wild boar. Griffon vultures and falcons fly its skies. There's no admission charge, but you'll need to show ID to get in.

Right at the southern tip of the bay, near where the road peters out next to a Catalano-Aragonese tower and lighthouse, you'll find the **Hotel El Faro** (079 94 20 30; www.elfarohotel.it; Porto Conte; s €160-420, d €232-920; P ☒ ☐ ☒), a gorgeous, manicured complex with two pools, a private jetty and coolly stylish rooms.

Regular FdS buses run between Porto Conte and Alghero (€1, 30 minutes, up to 10 daily between June and September, six daily in the rest of the year).

GETTING AWAY FROM IT ALL

About 11km north of Lago Baratz, the tiny inlet of Argentiera is dominated by the ghostly ruins of its silver mine, once the most important on the island. *Argento* (silver) was first extracted here by the Romans and continued right up to the 1960s when the mine was finally abandoned. The dark brick mine buildings, now held together by wooden scaffolding, rise in an untidy jumble from a small grey-sand beach. You can't actually go into them, but they make for a stark and melancholy sight.

If you fancy overnighting, the **Hostel Argentiera** (☎ 07953 02 19; www.hostelargentiera.it; d per person €30-35) is a brand-new hostel with beds in sunny doubles, and an on-site restaurant. A few metres back from the beach, the **Bar Il Veliero** (☎ 079 53 03 61; Via Carbonia 1; panini €3.50) sells snacks, pastas and main courses.

Argentiera is at the end of the SP18, signposted from Palmadula.

CAPO CACCIA

The road running down the eastern flank of the nature reserve skirts the waters of Porto Conte on its way to Capo Caccia, a dramatic cape jutting out high above the Mediterranean. White cliffs sheer up from impossibly blue waters affording wonderful seascapes; just before the road ends, there's a signposted viewing point from where from you get a dramatic view of the cape and the wave-buffeted offshore island, Isola Foradada.

A few hundred metres further on brings you to a car park at the entrance to the **Escala del Cabirol**, a vertiginous 656-step staircase that descends 110m of sheer cliff to the **Grotta di Nettuno** (☎ 079 94 65 40; adult/child €10/5; ☺ guided tours 9am-7pm Apr-Sep, to 5pm Oct, to 4pm Jan, Mar, Nov & Dec), an underground fairyland of stalactites and stalagmites. Note that if you're going to walk the steps, and it's a pretty exhilarating experience, it takes about 15 minutes to get down them. Tours of the caves, which depart on the hour, last around 45 minutes and take you through narrow walkways flanked by forests of curiously shaped stalactites and stalagmites, nicknamed the organ, the church dome (or warrior's head) and so on. At its furthest point the cave extends back for a kilometre, but a lot is not open to the public, including several freshwater lakes deep inside grotto. In bad weather the grotto is closed.

If you don't fancy the staircase, you can visit the cave via boat trips from Alghero (see p151).

To get to the cape by public transport from Alghero, an FdS bus departs from Via Catalogna (€3.50 return, 50 minutes) daily at 9.15am and returns at midday. It runs right to the cape and stops in the car park, where you'll find the staircase down to the grotto. From June to September, there are two extra daily runs, departing at 3.10pm and 5.10pm and returning at 4.05pm and 6.05pm.

Alternatively, the 27km makes for a scenic and relatively easy-going bike ride.

NORTH OF CAPO CACCIA

The road north of Porto Conte leads through the flat, green land known as the Nurra. As you head north, the first turn-off takes you to the coast at **Torre del Porticciolo**, a tiny natural harbour, backed by a small arc of beach and overlooked by a watchtower on the northern promontory. High cliffs mount guard on the southern side, and you can explore adjacent coves along narrow walking trails.

Six kilometres to the north, and hidden behind thick tracts of pine woods, is one of the island's longest stretches of wild sandy beach, **Porto Ferro**. To get there, take the Porto Ferro turn-off and, before reaching the end of the road (which is where the bus from Alghero stops), take a right (follow the Bar Porto Ferro signs). Buses run from Alghero (€1.50, 35 to 65 minutes depending on route and traffic) twice daily and three times in high summer.

From Porto Ferro a series of back roads lead 6km inland to **Lago Baratz**, Sardinia's only natural lake. Surrounded by low hills, the lake attracts some bird life, although the winged fellows tend to hang about the less accessible northern side. Paths circle the lake's marshy banks and there's a 3km dirt track connecting with the northern tip of Porto Ferro beach.

South of the lake, the workaday village of Santa Maria la Palma is home to the **Cantina Sociale di Santa Maria la Palma** (☎ 079 99 90 08; www.santamarialapalma.it; ☺ 8am-1pm & 2.30-6.30pm Mon-Fri, 8am-1pm Sun, longer hours in summer), the area's second winery after the grand Sella e

Mosca spread. You can mosey around the *enoteca* and fill up with wine straight from the barrel.

There are a couple of accommodation options along this section of coast, including the shady **Porticciolo Villagio Camping** (☎ 079 91 90 07; www.torredelporticciolo.it; per person/tent/car €14/14/free, 2-person bungalows €56-126; P ⊠), a big, professionally run campsite a few steps back from the beach.

ourpick **Agriturismo Porticciolo** (☎ 079 91 80 00; www.agriturismoporticciolo.it; Localita Porticciolo; B&B per person €30-45, 4-person apt per week €600-1000; P ⊠) This welcoming place is a 24-hectare working farm with 100 pigs, along with pleasant accommodation inside small apartments. The restaurant, housed in a grand barn with a heavy timber ceiling and huge fireplace, serves delicious homemade food that should satisfy your stomach's demands.

Olbia & the Gallura

Home to Sardinia's most celebrated stretch of coast, the Costa Smeralda, Gallura provides many of the island's classic images: limpid azure waters lapping onto pearly white beaches; weird, wind-whipped licks of rock tapering into transparent seas; and aging celebrities wooing bikini-clad beauties on their 100m yachts.

Ever since the international jet set discovered Sardinia in the 1960s, Gallura's fantastical coastline has been the island's international calling card. The Costa Smeralda has become one of the Med's most feted resorts, a gilded enclave of luxury hotels, secluded beaches and exclusive marinas. To the north, the Parco Nazionale dell'Arcipelago di La Maddalena boasts some of the island's most memorable seascapes, and windsurfers flock to the windswept waters of the Strait of Bonifacio, the strait that divides Sardinia from Corsica.

For many visitors, Gallura's ravishing beaches and tropical waters are Sardinia. But while they are undeniably beautiful, they represent just a fraction of Gallura's true character. Until the 1960s and the advent of tourism, Gallura was a wild and remote region without so much as a paved road. Farmers and shepherds eked out a meagre existence on the tough and begrudging land. To a modern tourist paying €10 for a can of coke in Porto Cervo, this might seem little more than local folklore, but head inland and it becomes all the more believable. The tough granite landscape, the lonesome valleys and swaths of cork forest – these have all shaped the area's rural and inward-looking character.

And it's inland Gallura that surprises. From the wooded heights of Monte Limbara to Arzachena's archaeological sights and the bucolic setting of Lago di Liscia, there is no end of alternatives to beach-bumming on the coast.

HIGHLIGHTS

- Don your sea legs and island-hop around the **Parco Nazionale dell'Arcipelago di La Maddalena** (p178)

- Take to the slopes of **Monte Limbara** (p187) and explore the endless cork forests around **Tempio Pausania** (p185)

- Feel the wind in your hair as you windsurf the wild waters off **Porto Pollo** (p178)

- Swap the glamour of the coast for the haunting silence of **Lago di Liscia** (p176) and the nearby **Li Licci** (p176) *agriturismo*

- Clamber the weirdly sculptured boulders of **Capo Testa** (p185)

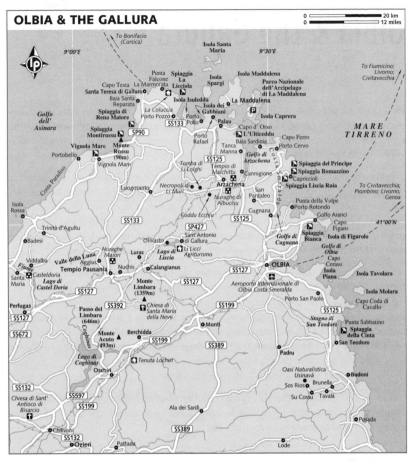

OLBIA & THE GALLURA

OLBIA

pop 50,200

The main gateway to the Costa Smeralda, Olbia is a busy and unsightly transport hub. Industrial sprawl covers much of the low-lying bay, and thunderous roads run right into the heart of the city. It's not an easy place to warm to, but nor is it as bad as it might immediately seem. There's a small, well-kept *centro storico* (historic city centre), which is home to a number of excellent restaurants and lively piazzas, and the main pedestrianised strip is a fun place to hang out and enjoy a meal or a drink on warm summer evenings.

HISTORY

Archaeological evidence has revealed the existence of human settlement in Sardinia's northeast in the mid-neolithic period (about 4000 BC), but Olbia was almost certainly founded by the Carthaginians in the 4th or 5th century BC. Certainly Carthaginians had been present in the area since the mid-6th-century BC as proved by their participation in the Battle of Mare Sardo (a naval battle between Greek colonists from Corsica and a combined Etruscan and Carthaginian fleet in 538 BC, considered by some to be the first ever naval battle in Western waters).

Under the Romans, Olbia became an important military and commercial port – a dozen or so relics of Roman vessels were unearthed in the 1990s. Known as Civita, it went on to become the capital of the Giudicato di Gallura, one of the four independent kingdoms that encompassed Sardinia in the 12th and 13th centuries. But when the Catalano-Aragonese took control, decline set in. Not until the arrival of the highways and railway in the 19th century did the town show signs of life again. The surrounding area was slowly drained and turned over to agriculture and some light industry, and the port was cranked back into operation. Now as a working industrial centre and joint capital of the recently formed Olbia-Tempio province, Olbia is thriving.

ORIENTATION

Ferries arrive at the Stazione Marittima, Olbia's modern ferry terminal at the end of a 1km causeway called the Banchina Isola Bianca. Heading inland from the terminal, the causeway meets Viale Principe Umberto, which leads left to connect with Corso Umberto, the town's main thoroughfare. Largely closed to traffic, this strip leads from the waterfront to the train station, about 1km away. En route it passes the central interlocking squares of Piazza Margherita and Piazza Matteotti. The web of narrow streets to either side of Corso Umberto constitute what might be called the 'old town', although nothing much dates to more than a century ago. The bulk of the hotels, restaurants and bars are crowded into this small area.

INFORMATION

Banca di Sassari (Corso Umberto 3) Has an ATM.
Guardia Medica (☎ 0789 55 24 41; Via Canova) For nonemergency, call-out medical assistance.
Inter Smeraldo (☎ 0789 2 53 66; www.intersmeraldo .com; Via Porto Romano 8/b; per hr €5; ☽ 9.45am-1.15pm & 4-8.30pm Mon-Sat) A busy internet cafe with 10 terminals.
Ospedale Viale Aldo Moro (☎ 0789 55 22 00; Viale Aldo Moro) Olbia's hospital is just north of the centre.
Post office (Via Aquedotto 5; ☽ 8am-6.50pm Mon-Fri, to 1.15pm Sat)
Tourist office (☎ 0789 55 77 32; www.olbiaturismo .it; Via Alessandro Nanni 18; ☽ 8am-2pm & 3-6pm Mon-Thu, 8am-2pm Fri) The website is good; the office is better for glossy brochures than practical information.
Unicredit Banca (Corso Umberto 165) Another ATM.
Unimare (☎ 070 2 35 24; www.unimare.it; Via Principe Umberto 1; ☽ 8.30am-12.30pm & 3.30-7.30pm Mon-Fri, 8.30am-12.30pm Sat) A central travel agent where you can book ferries and flights.

SIGHTS

You won't need long to do the sights in Olbia for the simple reason that there aren't many. Or rather, there's one: the Romanesque **Chiesa di San Simplicio** (Via San Simplicio; ☽ 7.30am-1pm & 3.30-6pm). Considered to be Gallura's most important medieval monument, this granite church was built in the late 11th and early 12th centuries on what was then the edge of town. It is a curious mix of Tuscan and Lombard styles with little overt decoration other than a couple of 13th-century frescoes depicting medieval bishops.

Another granite church worth a brief look is the **Chiesa di San Paolo** (Via Cagliari) with its pretty Valencian-style tiled dome (added after WWII).

To the south of Corso Umberto, the tightly packed warren of streets that represents the original fishing village has a certain charm, particularly in the evening when the cafes and trattorias fill with groups of hungry locals. A stroll along the *corso*, culminating in a drink on Piazza Margherita, is an agreeable way to spend the evening.

FESTIVALS & EVENTS

During July and August, outdoor concerts are staged in the city centre as part of the **L'Estate Olbiese**, a cultural festival that includes concerts, performances, readings and cabarets.

SLEEPING

Hotel Cavour (☎ 0789 20 40 33; www.cavourhotel.it; Via Cavour 22; s €50-65, d €75-90; P ☒) Guests are met with a warm smile at this inviting hotel in Olbia's old town. Rooms are white affairs with unfussy furniture, pastel fabrics and double-glazed windows, which do a pretty good job of keeping noise out.

Hotel Terranova (☎ 0789 2 23 95; www.hotelte rranova.it; Via Garibaldi 3; s €63-85, d €86-130; P ☒) On a narrow lane in the heart of the old town, this is a friendly, family-run three-star with small, cosy rooms and invaluable parking (€7). It's within walking distance of the action but if you haven't the energy to go out, the hotel restaurant, Ristorante Da Gesuino (meals €35 to €40), is known for its wonderful seafood.

B&B Lu Aldareddu (☎ 0789 6 85 79; www .lualdareddu.com; Localita Monte Plebi; r €70-100; ☒) This lovely rustic B&B is housed in an 18th-century farmhouse on the tree-covered slopes of Monte Plebi, a low-lying hill about 10km

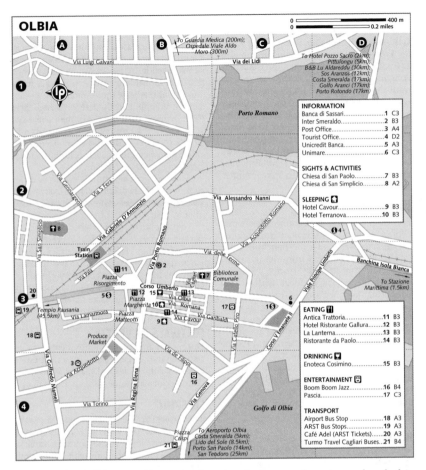

north of Olbia (off the main SS125 towards Arzachena). There are four rooms decorated in breezy farmhouse style. From here you are within reasonable cycling distance of the Costa Smeralda's finest beaches.

Hotel Pozzo Sacro (☎ 0789 5 78 55; www.hotelpo zzosacro.com; Localita Pozzo Sacro, Strada Panoramica Olbia; r €120-230; P ⊠ □ ⍟) You'll need your own wheels to get to this tasteful four-star complex 2km east of Olbia. Once there, you'll find it's got pretty much all you need – elegant rooms in terraced stone villas, a restaurant, pool and fine views of the bay of Olbia.

EATING

Gallurese cooking has its quirks, including *suppa cuata*, a casserole made of layers of bread, cheese and meat ragu drenched in broth and baked to a crispy crust. Look out for some fine Vermentino white wines, too.

ourpick **Antica Trattoria** (☎ 0789 2 40 53; Via Pala 4; fixed menus €15/19.80/25, meals around €23; ⍟ Mon-Sat) The sight of the antipasto buffet here tells you all you need to know. Trays of marinated anchovies, vegetables in olive oil, creamy potato salad, and a whole lot more, sit there just waiting to be eaten. There's also excellent pizza, pastas and fail-safe meat dishes. It's very popular with locals and outsiders alike, and can get very busy.

La Lanterna (☎ 0789 2 30 82; Via Olbia 13; pizzas €8, meals around €30; ⍟ Thu-Tue winter, daily summer) The Lanterna distinguishes itself with its cosy subterranean setting and beautifully fresh food. Start off with sweet and sour sardines and move on to fresh fish of the day served with potatoes and cherry tomatoes. The meals are as simple as it gets, and really quite delicious.

Ristorante da Paolo (☎ 0789 2 16 75; enter via Via Garibaldi 18 or Via Cavour 22; meals around €30; ❤ Mon-Sun) With its exposed stone walls and timber ceilings, this cheerful restaurant is an atmospheric spot for some hearty Sardinian food. Carnivores can choose from a selection of full-on meat dishes, including an unusual *cinghiale in agrodolce* (sweet and sour boar), while for vegetarians there's *risotto ai funghi* (mushroom risotto).

Hotel Ristorante Gallura (☎ 0789 2 46 48; fax 0789 2 46 29; Corso Umberto 145; meals around €55; ❤ Tue-Sun) On Olbia's pedestrianised main strip, this is one of the best restaurants in town, indeed in the whole of northern Sardinia. Waiters breeze through the cluttered dining room bearing intriguing platters of exotic food including pasta with cuttlefish ink and wild oysters, and roast goat perfumed with myrtle. Reservations are essential. Upstairs, there are six modest guestrooms (single €50 to €65, double €75 to €85), although unlike the restaurant, these are no great shakes.

DRINKING & ENTERTAINMENT
Piazza Margherita is the hub of cafe life. **Enoteca Cosimino** (☎ 0789 21 00 13; Piazza Margherita 3) is a popular venue for a leisurely drink. By day it's a cafe, serving coffee and *cornettos* (Italian croissants), but in the evening it morphs into an elegant wine bar with cocktails (€7.50) and *vino* on the menu.

At the weekend, night owls can head to **Boom Boom Jazz** (Via de Filippi; ❤ Thu-Sun Oct-May), one of Olbia's historic clubs, for some disco-driven fun, or to the central **Pascia** (☎ 338 594 55 90; Via Catello Piro; ❤ 10.30pm-late Fri-Sun) for a dressier, more lounge scene.

GETTING THERE & AWAY
Air
Olbia's **Aeroporto Olbia Costa Smeralda** (OLB; ☎ 0789 56 34 44; www.geasar.it) is about 5km southeast of the centre. At the time of research, more than 50 airlines were operating flights into the airport, including Alitalia, Austrian Airlines, Iberia, Lufthansa, Meridiana and the low-cost operators Air Berlin, easyJet, Ryanair and TUIfly. Destinations served

include most mainland Italian airports as well as London, Manchester, Paris, Madrid, Barcelona, Hamburg, Amsterdam, Vienna and Prague. For more information on flights and airlines, see p233.

The airport is not big but services are excellent. There's a left-luggage office (€5 per bag per day) and some good shopping. The airport website is also a useful source of information about Sardinia.

Boat
Olbia's ferry terminal, Stazione Marittima, is on Isola Bianca, an island connected to the town centre by the 1km causeway, Banchina Isola Bianca. All the major ferry companies have counters here, including the following:

Grandi Navi Veloci (☎ 010 209 45 91; www.gnv.it) To/from Genoa.

Moby Lines (☎ 199 30 30 40; www.mobylines.it) To/from Civitavecchia, Genoa, Livorno and Piombino.

Tirrenia (☎ 892 123; www.tirrenia.it) To/from Civitavecchia and Genoa.

SNAV (☎ 081 428 55 55; www.snav.it) To/from Civitavecchia.

You can book tickets at any travel agent in town, or directly at the port.

For timetable information and fare details see p237.

Bus
Azienda Regionale Sarda Trasporti (ARST; ☎ 800 865 042; www.arst.sardegna.it, in Italian) buses run from Olbia to destinations across the island. Get tickets from **Café Adel** (Corso Vittorio Veneto 2; ❤ 5am-10pm), just over the road from the main bus stops. Destinations include Arzachena (€2, 45 minutes, 11 daily), Golfo Aranci (€1.50, 25 minutes, six daily from mid-June to mid-September) and Porto Cervo (€3, 1½ hours, one Monday to Saturday). Further afield you can get to Nuoro (€7.50, 2½ hours, five daily), Santa Teresa di Gallura (€4.50, 1½ hours, five daily) and Sassari (€6.50, 1½ hours, one daily Monday to Saturday) via Tempio Pausania (€3).

Turmo Travel (☎ 0789 2 14 87; www.gruppoturmotravel.com) runs a weekday bus from Cagliari (€18, 4½ hours), arriving in Piazza Crispi. Another daily bus runs from the port to Sassari (€6.50, 1½ hours). Get tickets at the Stazione Marittima or on the bus.

Car & Motorcycle

Car hire is available at the airport, where all the big international outfits are represented, and at the Stazione Marittima ferry terminal. Bank on about €50 per day for a Fiat Punto.

Train

The station is off Corso Umberto. One train a day runs directly to Cagliari (€14.60, four hours). Otherwise you change at Chilivani (€4.60, 70 minutes, eight daily) and sometimes Macomer as well. Up to three trains run to Sassari (€6.35, one hour 50 minutes) and up to six to Golfo Aranci (€2, 25 minutes).

GETTING AROUND

You are unlikely to need local buses, except for getting to the airport and the Stazione Marittima. Buy tickets at tobacconists and some bars.

To/From the Airport

Local bus 2 (€0.80 or €1.30 if ticket is bought on board) runs half-hourly between 7.30am and 8pm from the airport to Via Goffredo Mameli in the centre. A **taxi** (☎ 0789 6 91 50) costs €15.

Several buses for destinations around the island depart from the airport, including a service for Nuoro run by **Deplano** (☎ 0784 29 50 30; www.deplanobus.it), which operates five times a day from June to September. Tickets cost €10 and journey time is two hours.

Bus

Local buses are run by **ASPO** (☎ 0789 55 38 56; www.aspo.it). Bus 9 (€0.80 or €1.30 if ticket is bought on board) runs every half-hour between Stazione Marittima and the town centre (Via San Simplicio).

Car & Motorcycle

Driving in Olbia is no fun thanks to a confusing one-way system and almost permanent roadworks. The main strip, Corso Umberto, is closed to traffic between Piazza Margherita and Via Goffredi Mameli. Metered parking (€0.60 per hour) is available around Olbia. Near the station is a good place to look.

Taxi

You can sometimes find taxis on Corso Umberto near Piazza Margherita. Otherwise call ☎ 0789 6 91 50 or ☎ 0789 2 27 18.

AROUND OLBIA

Olbia's main beach is the busy **Lido del Sole** (catch bus 5), about 6km east of the airport off the main southbound road, the SS125. It's fine for a swim, but far preferable is the swath of white sand at **Pittulongu** or **Sos Aranzos** to the north of town.

GOLFO ARANCI
pop 2330

Located on the northern tip of the Golfo di Olbia, 18km northeast of Olbia, Golfo Aranci is an important summer transport hub. Most people pass through the town without a second glance, and while it's not an especially beautiful place, it's not unpleasant and is worth considering as a cheap (or rather less expensive) alternative to the Costa Smeralda, a few kilometres up the coast. There are three sandy white beaches in town – **Spiaggia Primo**, **Secondo** and the best of the three, **Terzo** (translated as First Beach, Second and Third), and with your own transport you can easily get to others. It's also well equipped for families, with a number of public parks and well-maintained playgrounds.

Rising up behind the port are the craggy heights of **Capo Figaro** (340m), now a minor nature reserve. Trails criss-cross the *macchia* (Mediterranean scrub), leading up to an abandoned lighthouse on the summit, known as *il vecchio semaforo* (old traffic light). It was from here that Guglielmo Marconi sent the first radio signal to the Italian mainland in 1928.

For information on trekking and other activities, head to the helpful **tourist office** (☎ 346 757 94 73; Via Liberta; www.visitgolfoaranci.it; ⏰ 9am-1pm & 4-8pm) near the port. Staff can suggest local guides and tell you about the snorkelling and spear-gun fishing off the **Isola di Figarolo**, a small islet coquettishly poised off the coast. There are plenty of diving outfits operating out of the port. For a truly memorable experience, the **Bottlenose Diving Research Institute** (☎ 0789 183 11 97; www .thebdri.com; Via Diaz 4) runs daylong cruises in search of the bottlenose dolphins that inhabit these waters. There's no guarantee that you'll see one, but there have been 930 sightings since 1999, so the odds aren't bad. Budget for adult/child €150/110 for the five-to seven-hour expedition.

Sleeping & Eating

La Lampara (☎ 0789 61 51 40; www.lalamparahotel.com; Via Magellano; d €70-140, tr €85-155; ☾ Mar-Oct ☒) La Lampara is a delightful family-run hotel just off the main street. Its 10 summery rooms are a blaze of blue and white with cool tiled floors and simple, no-frills furniture.

Hotel Gabbiano Azzurro (☎ 0789 4 69 29; www.hotelgabbianoazzurro.com; Via dei Gabbiani; half board per person €83-168; ☾ Easter-end Oct; P ☒ ☒) Overlooking the beautiful aquamarine waters of Spiaggia Terzo, the Gabbiano Azzurro is a big, anonymous hotel that caters to coachloads of foreign tourists. But that shouldn't necessarily put you off, as the facilities, including two pools, are excellent and the beachside location is a winner.

Seafood features heavily in the restaurants lined up on and around Via della Liberta. Down by the port, **Ristorante Miramare** (☎ 0789 4 60 85; Piazzetta del Porto 2; meals €25-30) is a typical portside restaurant with a fishy menu and bustling atmosphere.

Getting There & Away

Between June and September six daily ARST buses link Golfo Aranci with Olbia (€1.50, 25 minutes). Trains (€2.20, 25 minutes) also cover the same route, running five times daily year-round.

Tirrenia (☎ 892 123; www.tirrenia.it) and **Sardinia Ferries** (☎ 199 400 500; www.sardiniaferries.com) operate ferries to Golfo Aranci between March and October. For details, see the boxed text, p240.

SOUTH COAST

The busy coast south of Olbia is peppered with resorts that heave with tourists in summer and all but shut down in winter. Typical of the type is Porto San Paolo, the main embarkation point for Isola Tavolara, and 11km further south, San Teodoro, an increasingly trendy destination with young Italians.

PORTO SAN PAOLO & ISOLA TAVOLARA

The small but lively resort of Porto San Paolo lies 14km south of Olbia along the SS125. Unless you've booked a holiday apartment here, the one real reason to stop off is to catch a boat for the Isola Tavolara.

At Easter time, and from mid-July to September, **boat excursions** depart from the port. Outward-bound boats leave on the hour between 10am and 1pm, and return trips set off at 12.30pm, 4.30pm and 5.30pm. The return trip (25 minutes each way) costs €12.50 per person, but longer cruises taking in the smaller Isola Molara and Piana will set you back €25 a head.

The Isola used to be known as the Island of Hermes, perhaps because you need wings to reach the plateau (565m), which is inhabited only by sea birds and falcons, as well as a few nimble-footed wild goats. The few people who live here reside on the western side on the **Spalmatore di Terra**, where the boats land.

Aside from snacking at a couple of beachside eateries, there is nothing much to do but splash about in the translucent water of the **Spiaggia Spalmatore**, and admire the incredible views of Tavolara's heights and mainland Sardinia. You could wander down to the little cemetery to see the graves of Tavolara's kings (the title was bestowed by Carlo Alberto in 1848 after a successful goat-hunting trip), each marked with a crown. The present 'king', Tonino Bertoeoni, runs one of the island's two restaurants, **Ristorante da Tonino** (☎ 0789 5 85 70; Via Tavolara 14; meals €30-35), whose sunny terrace is a fine spot for pizza and fresh seafood.

Tavolara's rocky coves present some wonderful diving opportunities around the underwater mountain of Secca del Papa. You can arrange dives with **Centro Sub Tavolara** (☎ 0789 4 03 60; www.centrosubtavolara.com; Via Molara 4/a). Reckon on €45 for a single dive.

Since 1991 the island has hosted a summer **cinema festival**, usually in mid- to late July. Special boats ferry ticket-holders from Porto San Paolo out to the island in the evening for screenings at 9.30pm. For details log on to www.cinematavolara.it (in Italian).

Back on the mainland, there's not much to hold you in San Paolo, but you can get a tasty, wood-fired pizza at **Cala di Junco** (☎ 0789 4 02 60; Via Nenni 8/10; meals around €30; ☾ Wed-Mon) before heading off.

SAN TEODORO

pop 3920

One of the most popular resorts on this stretch of coast, San Teodoro is an attractive town of model piazzas and pretty, pastel-coloured houses. In recent years it has become a trendy hang-out, its vibrant after-hours scene providing a more accessible alternative to the mega-bucks atmosphere up on the Costa Smeralda. Daytime action is centred on the town's beaches, where you'll find operators offering all sorts of water sports and boat excursions. Inland, there's plenty of scope for trekking, mountain biking and horse riding.

The efficient **tourist office** (☎ 0784 86 57 67; www.santeodoroturismo.com, in Italian; Piazza Mediterraneo 1; ☉ 9am-1pm & 4pm-midnight Jun-Sep, 9am-1pm & 3-6pm Oct-May) can provide information on local operators and tour guides. Another useful website is www.visitsanteodoro.com (in Italian).

San Teodoro's beach, **Cala d'Ambra**, is about half a kilometre downhill from the centre. To the north extends the even more impressive **Spiaggia La Cinta**, a broad band of open sand sandwiched between the transparent topaz sea and the **Stagno San Teodoro**, a large lagoon home to lots of bird life. La Cinta is a popular sports beach and a good place to try your hand at kitesurfing. **Wetdreams** (☎ 0784 85 20 15; www.wetdreams.it; Via Sardegna), a surf shop on the beach, offers three-hour introductory sessions for €160.

Sleeping & Eating

There's no shortage of accommodation in San Teodoro, although most hotels are three-star and above, and many close over winter. You can find a list on www.visitsanteodoro.com and the tourist office website.

Camping San Teodoro (☎ 0784 86 57 77; www.campingsanteodoro.com; Via del Tirreno; per person/tent/car €10.10/10.50/free, 4-person bungalow €64-106; ☉ May-mid-Oct) About 800m from the town centre, this popular campsite is set in a huge tree-

filled plot right on the southern end of La Cinta beach.

Hotel L'Esagono (☎ 0784 86 57 83; www.hotelesagono.com; Via Cala d'Ambra; half board per person €50-119; ☉ end Mar-Oct) Down on the beachfront, this is a smart complex with fine facilities and a beautifully tended palm-fringed garden. Rooms, housed in low villas nestled in the greenery, are bright and sunny with locally embroidered bedspreads that display a refreshing lack of chintz.

La Taverna degli Artisti (☎ 0784 86 60 60; Via del Tirreno 17; pizzas €6, meals around €30) Great food and service are on the menu here. Seafood predominates – try the *spaghetti alla bottarga* (mullet roe). There's also pizza to take away.

Drinking & Entertainment

San Teodoro really comes into its own after dark. There are plenty of bars and several clubs within easy striking distance. In town, the **Bhudda del Mar** (☎ 0784 86 52 52; Piazza Gallura) is a favourite with the young drinking crowd who revel in the cool beer and laid-back atmosphere, and it also serves dinner. The most central club is **L'Ambra Night** (☎ 0784 866 64 03; Via Cala d'Ambra; ☉ 10.30pm-late), down by the beach, opposite Hotel L'Esagono. A smart disco with an outdoor dance floor, it rocks to a mainly commercial beat. Just south of town, off the exit road from the SS125, the **Luna Glam Club** (☎ 338 978 97 76; www.lalunadisco.com; Localita Stirritoggiu; ☉ 10.30pm-late) pulls in a glossy 30-plus crowd. To fit in, and get past the eagle-eyed bouncers, you'll need to dress the part.

Getting There & Away

ARST buses make the run up the coast to Olbia (€2.50, 40 minutes, six daily, up to nine on weekdays) and inland to Nuoro (€6.50, one hour 50 minutes, five daily). Deplano buses also run to/from Olbia airport

---

DETOUR: OASI NATURALISTICA USINAVA

Some 14km inland from Budoni, a village 10km south of San Teodoro, the **Oasi Naturalistica Usinava** (☎ 328 648 60 63; www.usinava.it) is a fabulous place to escape the summer crowds. Covering 11.46 sq km of land, and encompassing forests, jaw-toothed conical peaks, water torrents and *macchia* (Mediterranean scrub), it's home to an array of Sardinian fauna including mouflon, wild boar, coots, grouse and hares. To overnight in the oasis, book a berth in one of the three *pinettos* (typical stone huts with thatched roofs) that have been set up to take guests. A night in one of these four-bed huts will cost €18.

To get to the oasis from Budoni, follow the road for Brunella, Talava, Su Cossu and Sos Rios. About 1.5km beyond Sos Rios you'll find the station of the Forestry guard.

THE CHANGING FACE OF THE COSTA

Long a byword for upmarket luxury, the Costa Smeralda is living strange times. Recent summers have seen signs of cracks appearing in the gilded cage in which the coast's tanned habitués like to lock themselves. In 2007 Italian rocker Zucchero was bombarded with bottles at an outdoor concert and then, in August 2008, legendary Lothario and Costa regular Flavio Briatore was pelted with sand as he and a group of friends tried to land dinghies on the crowded beach of Capriccioli.

What's going on? Were these incidents symptomatic of a wider malaise? Newspaper reports presented the episode as a kind of communal spleen-venting against the ostentation and arrogance of the rich. Italian holidaymakers, already feeling the effects of a stuttering economy and angered by price hikes for beach umbrellas and sun loungers, were in no mood to make way for a party of wealthy celebs. But one episode doesn't make a revolution, and the Costa hasn't suddenly become a hotbed of revolutionary fervour. It is changing, though, and could well be changing more.

In 2003 the US property tycoon Tom Barrack bought control of the Costa Smeralda Consortium (the local landowner) for a reported €290 million. A year later he submitted plans to the Comune of Arzachena for a far-reaching facelift of Porto Cervo, including the construction of 12 new piazzas, underground car parks, a seafront promenade, new parks and pathways.

As of yet, there's little sign of these developments, but there's no denying that the Costa has changed since its inception in the early 1960s. The brainchild of flamboyant millionaire, Karim Aga Khan (born 1937), the Costa was established in 1962 by a group of international investors which bought the 55km stretch of coastline and quickly transformed it into a haven of luxury.

At the outset, the new landowners laid down strict building regulations. The introduction of non-native plants was prohibited, all electricity cables and water conduits had to be laid underground, no street advertising was allowed and buildings had to be in keeping with the surroundings. But these constrictions failed to deter the developers, and by the late 1980s some 2500 villas had been built in the area. Since then construction has slowed, coming to a halt in 2004 with the introduction of regional legislation banning building within 2km of the coast. How this controversial, and much disputed, law will affect Barrack's long-term plans remains to be seen.

(€3.50, 30 minutes, five daily) and Nuoro (€10, 1¼ hours, five daily).

COSTA SMERALDA

Back in 1961 the Aga Khan and some pals bought a strip of beautiful Sardinian coast from struggling farmers and created the Costa Smeralda. Almost half a century later and the Emerald Coast is *the* summer destination for aspiring models, Russian oligarchs, aging aristocrats and balding media moguls. Starting at Porto Rotondo on the Golfo di Cugnana, about 17km north of Olbia, it stretches for 55km northwards up to the Golfo di Arzachena. The 'capital' is the yachtie haven of Porto Cervo, although Porto Rotondo attracts its fair share of paparazzi attention as base of Silvio Berlusconi's island operations.

PORTO CERVO

A curious, artificial vision of Mediterranean beauty, Porto Cervo is a surreal sight. Its pseudo-Moroccan architecture – part of a grand plan to incorporate the best of Greek, North African, Spanish and Italian architecture in a utopian beachside village – and perfectly manicured streets are strangely sterile and almost totally lacking in character. For apart from the magnificent coastal scenery that surrounds it, there's nothing remotely Sardinian about Porto Cervo. Instead, it resembles exactly what it is: a purpose-built leisure centre for the super-rich.

Sights & Activities

As nearly everyone in Porto Cervo has a boat (it has the best marine facilities on the island), most of the action takes place elsewhere during the day, in the paradisal inlets and on the silky beaches. Things begin to heat up in the early evening when the playboys and girls come out to browse the boutiques and pose in the piazzas.

The place to be seen is the **Piazzetta**, a small square at the centre of a web of discreet shopping alleys. From the Piazzetta, stairs lead down to the **Sottoportico della Piazzetta**, where you can tempt fate in a string of fancy boutiques. Above it all stands Michele Busiri Vici's **Chiesa di Stella Maris** (☎ 0789 9 20 01; Piazza Stella Maris), an odd white building which hosts classical-music concerts in the summer. Unsurprisingly, it's also done rather well in the donations department, receiving El Greco's impressive *Mater Dolorosa* as a Dutch aristocrat's bequest.

For a more modern take on art, the recently opened **Louise Alexander Gallery** (Via del Porto Vecchio 1; www.louise-alexander.com; ☙ May-Sep) stages temporary exhibitions showcasing works by contemporary artists. It also sells modern art, so if you're in the market for an Andy Warhol drop them a line.

Sleeping & Eating

Hotel Le Ginestre (☎ 0789 9 20 30; www.leginestrehotel .com; Localita Porto Cervo; half board per person €115-250; ☙ May-Sep; P ✗ ⊛ ⍟) This lovely hotel complex is 1km south of Porto Cervo. In typical Costa style it has rooms in low-lying ochre buildings interwoven with perfect lawns and manicured plants. Uniformed staff provide impeccable service and the facilities furnish all the requisite comforts.

Il Peperone (☎ 0789 90 70 49; cnr Via Cerbiatta & Via Sa Conca, meals around €35; ☙ Easter-Oct) One of the more affordable options in Porto Cervo, this is a laid-back pizzeria-cum-restaurant on the main road into town. There's nothing spectacular about the food but it's decent enough and there are some lovely homemade desserts.

Drinking & Entertainment

Porto Cervo's nightlife is a strictly summer-only scene. People-watching is one of the few affordable options, although the moment you sit down at a bar you'll be looking at around €10 for a coke. Strangely, for such a swish resort, one of the favourite drinking hang-outs is an English-style pub, the nautically themed **Lord Nelson Pub** (Porto Cervo Marina; ☙ 5pm-late).

To get in on the real action, however, you'll need to dress to the nines and head a couple of kilometres south of town. Here, by the side of the road, you'll find two of the area's top clubs: **Sopravento** (☎ 0789 9 47 17; Localita Sottovento; ☙ 10.30pm-6am Jun–mid-Sep) and, across the road, the even more exclusive **Sottovento** (☎ 0789 9 24 43; Localita Sottovento; ☙ midnight-6am Apr-Sep), a VIP hang-out frequented by international high rollers. Getting in to either of these places is

no party and depends entirely on the whim of the stony-faced bouncers.

The biggest disco in these parts is the aptly named **Billionaire** (☎ 0789 9 41 92; www.billionaireclub .it; Localita Alto Pevero; ☙ 8pm-4am Jul-Sep), where camera crews interview miniskirted celebs on the dance floor. A loud, brash place, it's almost impossible to get into unless you know someone or book dinner at the swank restaurant. Not surprisingly, prices are exorbitant.

Getting There & Away

ARST has up to five bus connections between Porto Cervo and Olbia (€3, 1½ hours).

Between June and September, **Sun Lines** (☎ 348 260 98 81) buses run from Olbia airport to the Costa Smeralda, stopping at Porto Cervo and various other points along the coast.

BAIA SARDINIA

From Porto Cervo the coast road swings north and west 7km to Baia Sardinia, just outside the Costa Smeralda but for all intents and purposes a Costa resort like its more famous neighbours. The main attraction is the beach, **Cala Battistoni**, a hugely popular strip of sand lapped by remarkable blue waters. If you can't find any room on the sand but still fancy a swim, the nearby **Aquadream** (☎ 0789 9 95 11; Localita la Crucitta; adult/concession €18/12; ☙ 10.30am-7pm mid-Jun–mid-Sep) water park is a possible alternative, especially if you've got kids.

Sleeping & Eating

The resort is aimed at the family market, with plenty of complexes overlooking the bay. Prices are hardly bargain basement, but they're a lot more reasonable than Porto Cervo.

Hotel La Rocca (☎ 0789 93 31 31; www.hotellarocca .it; Localita Pulicino; half board per person €85-170; ☙ May-Oct; P ✗ ⊛ ⍟) A postcard ensemble of pastel pink villas, green lawns and flower-lined walkways, La Rocca is a plush four-star retreat with cool, summery rooms and excellent facilities. The pool has a natural rocky fountain, and there's a free shuttle bus to Baia Sardinia and Porto Cervo.

Le Querce (☎ 0789 9 92 48; www.lequerce.com; Localita Cala Bitta; 2-person cottages €70-157; ☙ Apr-Oct) Escape the hordes at this tranquil haven overlooking the bay. Set in a beautiful landscaped garden are four stone *stazzi* (traditional houses), which have been converted into delightful self-catering cottages. Inside, the rustic decor incorporates giant red boulders which protrude up into tiled floors. No children under 12.

News Café (☎ 0789 9 94 84; Piazza Centrale; ⏰ 8am-2am) In the seafront arcade, this central cafe is a popular meeting point and good for a quick *panino* at lunchtime.

L'Approdo (☎ 0789 9 90 60; pizzas from €5, meals around €30; ⏰ noon-midnight) Right on the beach, this is an excellent spot to tuck into classic Sardinian seafood. Start with spaghetti *alle arselle* (with clams) before tackling a plate of grilled calamari. If seafood doesn't do it for you there's a good range of pizzas.

Entertainment

Phi Beach (☎ 0789 95 50 12; www.phibeach.it; Forte Capellini) One of the coast's hottest venues, this is a great place to hang out and watch the sunset. By day it's a regular bathing club with sun loungers and umbrellas to hire, but as the sun goes down it transforms into a cool lounge bar and restaurant. All the while DJs spin chilled sounds in the background.

Ritual (☎ 337 81 69 34; Localita La Crucitta; ⏰ 11pm-5am) Just out of town on the road for Porto Cervo, this club is an old favourite. Even if you're not going to dance it's worth a look for the sexy cavernous interior gouged out of the rockside. Admission will cost between €15 and €40 depending on the event.

Getting There & Away

From Olbia, the Sun Lines bus service to Porto Cervo continues on for 15 minutes to Baia Sardinia (see opposite).

SOUTH OF PORTO CERVO

Despite all its superficial fluff, the Costa Smeralda is quite stunning: the Gallura's bizarre granite mountains plunging into emerald waters in a series of dramatic fjordlike inlets.

Travelling south, one of the best beaches is **Spiaggia del Principe** (or Portu Li Coggi), apparently the Aga Khan's favourite, a magnificent crescent of white sand bound by unspoilt green *macchia* and Caribbean blue waters. To find it, follow the signs for Hotel Romazzino, but before reaching the hotel turn right at Via degli Asfodeli. Park your car at the barrier and then walk for the last half a kilometre or so. Nearby, the easier-to-find **Spiaggia Romazzino** is named after the rosemary bushes which grow in such abundance.

Next along is **Capriccioli**, another splendid beach with crystalline waters and a pleasant setting. Beyond that keep your eyes peeled for a turn-off to **Spiaggia Liscia Ruia**, shortly before reaching the grand Moorish fantasy that is the Hotel Cala di Volpe.

You finally reach the end of the Costa at the Golfo di Cugnana. The drive is nicely finished off by a spectacular view of **Porto Rotondo**, a second marina developed in 1963 following the success of Porto Cervo. Resembling an upmarket harbourside suburb of Sydney or San Francisco, Porto Rotondo is where Italian PM Silvio Berlusconi maintains his main Sardinian residence, the pharaonic Villa Certosa.

Sleeping

Villaggio Camping La Cugnana (☎ 0789 3 31 84; www .campingcugnana.it; Localita Cugnana; per person/tent/car €17.50/free/4.50, 2-person bungalows per week €255-595; ⏰ May-Sep) One of the very few budget options on the Costa, this slick seaside camping ground is on the main road just north of Porto Rotondo. It boasts a supermarket, swimming pool and a free shuttle bus to whisk you away to some of the better Costa Smeralda beaches.

our pick La Villa Giulia (☎ 0789 9 86 29, 3485111269; www.lavillagiulia.it; Monticanaglia; d €65-89; ⏰ Apr-Nov) At the top of a tough dirt track, this wonderful B&B has six rooms in a rustic stone villa. The rooms, with their homey furnishings and jolly-tiled bathrooms, are fairly modest, but the lovely natural surroundings, warm welcome and spectacular rates make this a real winner. There's also the possibility of renting the villa's basement as a single apartment with two bedrooms and a kitchen. The villa is about 2km inland from Spiaggia Liscia Ruia and signposted off the main coastal road.

Hotel Capriccioli (☎ 0789 9 60 04; www.hotelcapri ccioli.it; Localita Capriccioli; half board per person €98-167; ⏰ Apr-Sep; P ⏰ ⏰) In an area dominated by luxury hotel chains, it's a real pleasure to find a welcoming family-run place like the Hotel Capriccioli. Right on the Capriccioli beach, it offers bright rooms furnished in typical Sardinian style with wrought-iron beds and classical island fabrics.

SAN PANTALEO

Although only about 16km from Porto Cervo, the rural village of San Pantaleo provides a welcome dose of authenticity after the sterile resorts on the coast. And with some great accommodation, it's worth considering as a base for exploring the area.

The village sits high up behind the coast, surrounded by gap-toothed peaks. Each of the pointy summits has a name, a typical conceit in San Pantaleo, which has become something of an artists' haven. It is also one of the few Sardinian villages set around a picturesque piazza, a sturdy little church at one end. In summer you'll often find a bustling market here, and in spring the blossoms make it picture-perfect.

Browsing the shops is a favourite pastime here. You can admire a collection of ethnic and eastern antiques at the **L'Antiquaire de San Pantaleo** (☎ 335 38 12 14; Via Caprera 10; ☼ by appointment), and enjoy works by local artists at the small gallery **Arte in Piazza** (☎ 338 165 45 21; Piazza Vittorio Emanuele).

After that, take a pew at chic little **Caffè Nina** (Piazza Vittorio Emanuele 3; cheese platter €10; ☼ 7am-2am end Mar-Oct) and enjoy a glass of Vermentino with some *pecorino* and olives.

Between 27 July and 30 July San Pantaleo holds its annual knees-up, a weekend of general jollity with traditional Sardinian dancing.

ourpick Hotel Arathena (☎ 0789 6 54 51; www.arathena.it; Via Pompei; d €120-276; ☼ Mar-Oct; P ✗ ☐ ☲) This gorgeous hotel is the town's finest. Knotted, gnarled wood beams and ochre-tinted stone walls set the tone, while rooms are furnished with terracotta tiles, wood and natural fabrics. Outside, an infinity pool shimmers against a sublime backdrop of green peaks.

Near the entrance to the village is the **Hotel Sant'Andrea** (☎ 0789 6 52 98; www.giagonigroup.com, in Italian; Via Zara 43; s €67-106, d €110-180, half board per person €85-130; ☼ Apr-Oct; P ✗ ☲), which has tasteful, cosy rooms. You can be sure of an excellent homemade breakfast here, as the same family manages the highly regarded **Ristorante Giagoni** (☎ 0789 6 52 05; Via Zara 36/44; meals around €60; ☼ Tue-Sun Apr-Oct), the menu of which features meat classics such as *porceddu* and a daily selection of fresh fish. Bookings are recommended.

Another more informal choice is the **Agriturismo Ca' La Somara** (0789 9 89 69; www.calasomara.it; r €37-68, half board per person €57-88; P ☲), 1km along the road to Arzachena. A relaxed, ramshackle farm, it offers 12 simple guest

rooms and a cosy country dining room. Credit cards are not accepted.

ARST runs five daily buses to San Pantaleo from Olbia (€1.50, 35 minutes) and Arzachena (€1, 20 minutes).

ARZACHENA & AROUND

Arzachena sits well behind the front lines of coastal tourism and serves as a springboard to some inland treasures: a series of mysterious *nuraghi* (stone towers) ruins and two *tombe di giganti* (literally 'giants' tombs'; ancient mass graves).

ARZACHENA
pop 12,100

Were it not for its position a few kilometres inland from the Costa Smeralda, Arzachena would be overlooked as just another workaday town with a mildly interesting historical centre. Which is pretty much what it is. But with the Mediterranean's most exclusive resorts an easy drive away, it has gone from being a humble shepherds' village in the 1960s to something of a tourist centre, and in summer its population virtually doubles.

Most people use it as a base for exploring the Costa, but if you want to hang around, action is focused on **Piazza del Risorgimento**, a small piazza with a couple of cafes, and a stone church, the **Chiesa di Santa Maria delle Neve**. A short stroll away is the bizarre **Mont'Incappiddatu**, a mushroom-shaped granite rock at the end of Via Limbara. Archaeologists believe the overarching rock may have been used as a shelter for Neolithic tribespeople as long ago as 3500 BC.

Sleeping & Eating
To get to these two accommodation options, turn right (if exiting Arzachena) just after the Galmarket supermarket at the northern edge of town.

ourpick B&B Lu Pastruccialeddu (☎ 0789 8 17 77; www.pastruccialeddu.com, in Italian; Localita Lu Pastruccialeddu; s €50-100, d €70-120; P) Housed in a typical stone-built farmstead, this is a smashing *agriturismo* (farm-stay accommodation) with seven simple rooms in a lovely, tranquil spot. It's run by the ultrahospitable Caterina Ruzittu, who grew up here and who prepares the sumptuous breakfasts – a vast spread of biscuits, yoghurt, freshly baked cakes, salami, cheese and cereals.

Agriturismo Rena (☎ 0789 8 25 32; www.agriturismorena.it; Localita Rena; half board per person €90-120; ☒ Mar-Oct; **P**) It's half board only at this hilltop *agriturismo*, but that's no great sacrifice as the farmhouse food is a delight – cheese, honey, meat and wine are all home produced. Rooms vary, but the overall look is rural with heavy wooden furniture and thick beams holding up 100-year-old ceilings. The restaurant (meals €25 to €30) is open to non-residents by reservation.

Trattoria La Vecchia Arzachena (☎ 0789 8 31 05; Corso Garibaldi; meals around €25; ☒ Mon-Sat) This old-school trattoria is a good option for hearty, no-nonsense Italian food. The cheerful, laid-back atmosphere goes well with tasty *tagliatelle* and classic *scaloppine* (breaded veal).

Il Fungo (☎ 0789 8 33 40; Via Lamarmora 21; pizzas from €5, meals around €30; ☒ daily summer, closed Wed winter) Wood-fired pizza and cracking seafood are the hallmarks of this popular eatery. Locals come here to grab a takeaway and chat with the *pizzaiola* (pizza-maker) while out-of-towners sit down to huge helpings of fresh fish and grilled meat.

Getting There & Away

Arzachena has good bus connections. ARST services run to/from Olbia (€2, 45 minutes, nine daily), Santa Teresa di Gallura (€2.50, one hour, five daily) and Palau (€1, 25 minutes, five daily). Regular buses also link with the Costa Smeralda resorts, namely Porto Cervo and Baia Sardinia.

Between mid-June and mid-September you can pick up the **trenino verde** (☎ 0789 8 12 08; www.treninoverde.com, in Italian) to Tempio Pausania (€9.50, 70 minutes, two daily).

AROUND ARZACHENA

What makes Arzachena interesting is the countryside around it. Dozens of *nuraghi* and *tombe di giganti* litter the verdant landscape.

The nearest *nuraghe* to town, and certainly the easiest to find, is the Nuraghe di Albucciu, on the main Olbia road, about 3km south of Arzachena. This, along with the Tempio di Malchittu and Coddu Ecchju, is managed by the **Lithos** (☎ 0789 8 15 37) cooperative, which runs guided tours of the sites and offers a series of ticket combinations: €3 for a single site, €5 for two and €7.50 to €10 for all three. Guided tours, available in English by prior

arrangement, cost €7.50 for a single site, €10 for all three.

One of Gallura's finest prehistoric relics, the **Nuraghe di Albucciu** (admission €3; ☒ 9am-7pm) is unusual for several reasons, not least for its flat granite roof instead of the usual *tholos* (conical shape) and its warren of what appear to be emergency escape routes.

Accessible via a 2km track from the Nuraghe di Albucciu ticket office, the **Tempio di Malchittu** (admission €3; ☒ 9am-7pm) dates back to 1500 BC. It is one of a few temples of its kind in Sardinia, but the experts can only guess at its original purpose. It appears it had a timber roof and was closed with a wooden door, as was Nuraghe di Albucciu. From this relatively high point you have views over the surrounding territory.

Taking the Arzachena–Luogosanto road south, you can follow signs to **Coddu Ecchju** (admission €3; ☒ 9am-7pm), one of the most important *tombe di giganti* in Sardinia. The most visible part of it is the oval-shaped central stele (standing stone). Both slabs of granite, one balanced on top of the other, show an engraved frame that apparently symbolises a door to the hereafter, closed to the living. On either side of the stele stand further tall slabs of granite that form a kind of semicircular guard of honour around the tomb.

From the *tombe di giganti* return to the Arzachena–Luogosanto road and turn left (west) for Luogosanto. After about 3km turn right (signposted) for Li Muri and Li Lolghi, both managed by the local cooperative **Anemos** (☎ 340 820 97 49; www.anemos-arzachena.it, in Italian). Follow for a further 2km (partly on a dirt trail) until you reach a junction. The left fork leads 2km uphill along another dirt track to the necropolis of **Li Muri** (admission €3, incl Li Lolghi €5; ☒ 9am-7pm daily Easter-Oct, by appointment rest of year), a curious site made up of four interlocking megalithic burial grounds, possibly dating to 3500 BC. Archaeologists believe that VIPs were buried in the rectangular stone tombs. At the rim of each circle was a menhir or betyl, an erect stone upon which a divinity may have been represented.

Back down at the junction, the right fork (asphalt) takes you to the entrance to **Li Lolghi** (admission €3, incl Li Lolghi €5; ☒ 9am-7pm daily Easter-Oct, by appointment rest of year), another *tomba di gigante*, similar to that of Coddu Ecchju. The central east-facing stele, part of which was snapped off and later restored, dominates

OLBIA & THE GALLURA

the surrounding countryside from its hill-top location.

LAGO DI LISCIA & AROUND

From Arzachena, the SP427 heads inland into the undeveloped and utterly transfixing heart of Gallura. The road bobs and weaves through lush green fields and wood-crested hills as it twists its way up to the agricultural town of **Sant'Antonio di Gallura** en route to Lago di Liscia, one of Sardinia's unspoilt secrets. An 8km-long artificial lake, the main source of water for Gallura's east coast, it is set beautifully amid granite-scarred hills and woods of billowing cork and oak trees. The best place to admire it is a picnic spot at a tiny nature reserve, signposted as *olivastri millenari*, above the southern shores. The **olivastri** (☎ 079 64 72 81; admission €2, with guided tour €2.50; ☯ 9am-sunset daily Mar-Dec) are a group of wild olive trees that have been growing for thousands of years. Scientists from the University of Sassari have calculated that the biggest, measuring 20m in circumference and reaching a height of 14.5m, is about 3800 years old. Certainly, it's quite a specimen, its gnarled and twisted trunk writhing upwards like something out of *Lord of the Rings*. To get to the site from Sant'Antonio di Gallura follow the road for Luras and Tempio Pausania, then take the turning marked *olivastri millenari*. After a further 10km or so, there's a short, steep dirt track up to the left – the *olivastri* are at the top.

our pick **Li Licci** (☎ 079 66 51 14; www.lilicci.com; Localita Stazzo La Gruci; B&B per person €50, half board per person €65-75; ☯ Easter-Nov) To really appreciate the empty silence that lies so heavily over this area, book a night or two at Li Licci, one of the region's best *agriturismi*. Set deep within an oak wood – its name means 'oak trees' in the local dialect – it's a picture-postcard stone farmhouse with simple rooms and a highly regarded restaurant (meals €30 to €35 for nonresidents; booking preferred). The cordial English owner, Jane Ridd, will happily organise excursions for you and advise on the walking, horse riding and rock climbing opportunities in the area, as well as proudly pointing out her 200-year-old olive tree.

CANNIGIONE

Some 5km northeast of Arzachena, Cannigione sits on the western side of the Golfo di Arzachena, the largest *ria* (inlet) along this coast. Originally a fishing village

established in 1800 to supply the Maddalena islands with food, it grew bigger when coal and cattle ships began to dock at its harbour in the 1900s and is now a prosperous, and reasonably priced, tourist town.

The helpful Ascor **tourist office** (☎ 0789 8 85 10; Via Nazionale 47; ☯ 9.30am-12.30pm & 5.30-8pm Mon-Sat year-round, plus 9.30am-12.30pm Sun in summer) has bags of information on Cannigione and the surrounding area.

Down at the port, there are various operators offering excursions to the Arcipelago di La Maddalena, including **Consorzio del Golfo** (☎ 0789 8 84 18; www.consorziodelgolfo.it). Bank on €35 to €40 per person. Diving, snorkelling and boat hire are available from **Anthias** (☎ 0789 8 63 11; www.anthiasdiving.com; Tanca Manna), on the seafront between Cannigione and Palau. Dives start at €45, while snorkelling excursions cost €50/25 per adult/child. Boat hire comes in at a whacking €750 for half a day, although that also gets you lunch and a skipper. You'll find the best beaches north of Cannigione at **Tanca Manna** and **L'Ulticeddu**.

Sleeping

Hotel del Porto (☎ 0789 8 80 11; www.hoteldelporto.com, in Italian; Via Nazionale 94; d €90-206, half board per person €57-120; ☯ May-Sep; ✖ ⬚) This is a good central choice for bright and breezy accommodation. Rooms, many of which overlook the marina, are simply decorated with traditional Sardinian fabrics and polished tiles. The downstairs restaurant (meals €30 to €35) is a further plus.

Li Capanni (☎ 0789 8 60 41; www.licapanni.com; Via Lungomare; s €138-158, d €170-230; ℗ ✖ ⬚) Owned by musician Peter Gabriel, this tranquil retreat is on the coast between Cannigione and Palau. Rooms are in six stone cottages laid out in a peaceful garden and linked by winding paths that lead to a restaurant. Another path meanders downhill to a private beach, where you can snorkel and go kayaking.

Getting There & Away

Regular **ARST** (☎ 0789 2 11 97) buses make the run to Arzachena (€1, 10 minutes, four Monday to Saturday), Baia Sardinia (€1, 30 minutes, three Monday to Saturday), Palau (€1, 20 minutes, two Monday to Saturday) and Olbia (€2.50, one hour, four Monday to Saturday).

PALAU

pop 3930

The main gateway to the Arcipelago di La Maddalena, Palau is a well-to-do and over-developed summer resort, its lively streets lined with surf shops, boutiques, bars and restaurants. It's also something of a minor transport hub with direct ferry connections to Genoa. Out of town, the stunning coast is famous for its bizarre weather-beaten rocks, like the Roccia dell'Orso, 6km east of Palau. If you have a car it's worth a drive up here for the fabulous views.

Information

The multilingual staff at the **tourist office** (☎ 0789 70 70 25; www.palau.it; Palazzo Fresi; 9am-1pm & 4.30-7.30pm daily May-Oct, 9am-1pm Mon-Sat Nov-Apr) can provide information about the surrounding area, including the Arcipelago di La Maddalena. Check your email at **Bar Frizzante** (Via Capo d'Orso 20; per hr €6.50; 7.30am-1am Mon-Sat).

Sights & Activities

Palau is a beach resort pure and simple, and its only sight is a wind-whipped fort, **Fortezza di Monte Altura** (closed at the time of writing) 3km west of town. It was built to help defend the north coast and Arcipelago di La Maddalena from invasion – something it was never called on to do.

Other than that the main activities in Palau are the boat excursions around the Maddalena islands. Down at the port, **Petagus** (☎ 0789 70 86 81; www.petag.it) is one of several outfits offering such tours. Trips, which cost €35 per person and include lunch, take in several stops and give you time to swim on well-known beaches.

Sleeping & Eating

Camping Acapulco (☎ 0789 70 94 97; www.camping acapulco.com; per person incl tent & car €17.50, 4-person bungalows €260-540; Apr-Sep) An excellent camping ground 500m west of town right on the edge of a good beach. Alongside tent pitches, there are also neat white bungalows with terracotta roofs and red doors, available with or without a kitchenette.

Hotel La Roccia (☎ 0789 70 95 28; www.hotellaroc cia.com; Via dei Mille 15; s €48-84, d €78-130; Easter-Oct; P) A very friendly three-star, La Roccia offers bright, spacious rooms and excellent value for money. The blue-and-white boating decor lends a Mediterranean feel and the balconies provide some fantastic views.

San Giorgio (☎ 0789 70 80 07; Largo La Maddalena 8; pizzas €7, meals around €30; closed Mon winter) One of the most popular eateries in town – booking is a good idea – this pizzeria-cum-restaurant dishes up reliable pizzas and large helpings of pasta and fresh fish. Of the pastas, the spaghetti *allo scoglio* (with mixed seafood) is an excellent bet, as is the grilled fish.

La Gritta (☎ 0789 70 80 45; Località Porto Faro; meals €70-80; Thu-Tue Mar-Oct) One for a special occasion, La Gritta is a memorable place to dine. Floor-to-ceiling windows allow you to take in the wondrous coastal scenery while the superbly presented seafood combines modern techniques with classic Italian ingredients. Cheese buffs will enjoy a selection of up to 20 different cheeses, while everyone will appreciate the classic Sardinian desserts.

Getting There & Away

BOAT

Car ferries to Isola Maddalena are operated by three companies: **Enermar** (☎ 899 20 00 01; www.enermar.it), **Saremar** (☎ 892 123; www.saremar .it), and **Delcomar** (☎ 0789 73 90 88; www.delcomar .it). Delcomar runs four night crossings between 12.30am and 4.30am. The other two have crossings every 15 minutes between 6.15am and 7.30pm and then hourly until 11.45pm. The 20-minute crossing costs €5 per passenger, €13 for a small car.

Enermar also runs a summer service to Genoa (€70.50, 11 hours, five weekly) from June to September.

BUS

There are ARST buses connecting Palau with Olbia (€2.50, 1¼ hours, eight daily), Santa Teresa di Gallura (€2, one hour, five daily) and Arzachena (€1, 25 minutes, five daily).

Between mid-June and mid-September, **Nicos-Caramelli** (☎ 0789 67 06 13) buses run frequently to nearby destinations like Isola dei Gabbiani (€1.50, 40 minutes), Porto Pollo (€1.50, 35 minutes), Capo d'Orso (€1, 20 minutes), Baia Sardinia (€4, 35 minutes) and Porto Cervo (€4, 50 minutes).

In the same summer period, Turmo Travel buses connect Palau with Olbia airport (€5, 50 minutes, six daily).

OLBIA & THE GALLURA

All buses leave from the port, and you can purchase tickets on board or at **Stefy's Bar** (Via Razzoli 12), right at the top of town.

TRAIN

The *trenino verde* runs from Palau port to Tempio Pausania (€11, 1¾ hours, two daily) from 25 June to 5 September. It's a slow ride along a narrow-gauge line through some great countryside.

PORTO POLLO & ISOLA DEI GABBIANI

Seven kilometres west of Palau, windsurfers converge on Porto Pollo (also known as Portu Puddu) for what are considered some of the best conditions on the island. You can also try kitesurfing, canoeing, diving and sailing.

Along the beachfront there are various outfits hiring out kit and offering lessons. You'll find **Paolo Silvestri** (☎ 0789 70 50 18; www.silvestri.it, in Italian) on the Isola dei Gabbiani, just across the causeway that separates Porto Pollo from the next bay, Porto Liscia. He offers windsurfing, kitesurfing and diving packages, ranging in price from €35 for a single windsurf lesson to €45 for a guided dive and €195 for a four-lesson kitesurfing course. The **Sporting Club Sardinia** (☎ 0789 70 40 01; www.portopollo.it) offers more or less the same, as well as sailing courses for various levels. A block of five two-hour beginners' lessons costs €145. Kit hire is around €18 per hour for a windsurf.

On Isola dei Gabbiani, there's a convenient camping ground, **Camping Isola dei Gabbiani** (☎ 0789 70 40 19; www.isoladeigabbiani.it; per person/tent €10/22, 2-person bungalows €40-90), which also offers caravan and bungalow accommodation. Those with campervans can stay at the car park at the end of the road, by the beach.

Buses on the Palau–Santa Teresa di Gallura route stop off at the signposted road junction, from where you have to walk about 2km.

PARCO NAZIONALE DELL'ARCIPELAGO DI LA MADDALENA

One of Sardinia's most revered beauty spots, the **Arcipelago di La Maddalena** provides some spectacular, windswept seascapes. A national park since 1996 – the **Parco Nazionale dell'Arcipelago di La Maddalena** (www.lamaddalen

apark.it) – it consists of seven main islands and 40 islets, as well as several small islands to the south. The seven principal islands are the high points of a valley, now underwater, that once joined Sardinia and Corsica. When the two split into separate islands, waters filled the strait now called the Bocche di Bonifacio. Over the centuries the prevailing wind, the *maestrale* (northwesterly wind), has helped to mould the granite into the bizarre natural sculptures that festoon the archipelago.

The area is an important natural habitat, and although national-park status has imposed protection, the area's ecosystem remains fragile. For a number of years proposals have been on the table to create a joint Italian-French marine park, the Parco Marino Internazionale delle Bocche di Bonifacio (www.bocchedibonifacio.org, in Italian), but as of yet nothing has been formalised.

Nelson and Napoleon knew the strait well, as did that old warhorse Giuseppe Garibaldi, who bought Isola Caprera for his retirement. The US Navy has also been a historic presence, but in January 2008 it withdrew from the area after a controversial 35-year sojourn. Up to 60 other islets, chips of granite, are sprinkled about, the best of which are Isola Spargi, Isola Santa Maria, Isola Budelli and Isola Razzoli.

ISOLA MADDALENA

pop 11,500

Just over the water from Palau, the pink-granite island of Maddalena lies at the heart of the archipelago. As you approach by ferry, it looks hot, dry and stony, its terracotta houses and apartments blurring into a severe rocky background. But once you dock, you'll be taken by the urbane character of the place, its cobbled piazzas and infectious holiday atmosphere. But changes are afoot. In the wake of the US naval withdrawal, Maddalena is hosting the 2009 G8 summit. An €800 million financial package has been agreed, of which €300 million has been earmarked for the revamping of Maddalena's former military bases.

Until the end of the 17th century the island's small population lived mainly in the interior, farming a meagre living out of the poor soil. But when the Baron des Geneys arrived with the Sardo-Piedmontese navy in 1767 to establish a naval base they gladly

PARCO NAZIONALE DELL'ARCIPELAGO DI LA MADDALENA

gave up their hilltops and relocated to the growing village around Cala Gavetta, now La Maddalena's main port.

Information

The **tourist office** (☎ 0789 73 63 21; www.lamaddalena.com; Cala Gavetta; ☺ 9am-1pm Mon-Sat), to the right of the port as you face seawards, has limited information on the archipelago. The **Banco di Sassari** (Via XX Settembre 34) is one of several banks with ATMs in the town centre. Check your email at **MaxCard** (☎ 0789 73 10 81; Largo Matteotti 10; per hr €4.80; ☺ 9.30am-12.30pm & 5-8pm Mon-Sat).

Sights

Strolling around the lively centre of La Maddalena, the island's main town, is the main activity here, perhaps stopping for a coffee along Via Vittorio Emanuele or a cold beer in Piazza Garibaldi, hub of the evening *passeggiata* (stroll).

Other than that you could pass half an hour or so inspecting the religious bits and bobs in the **Museo Diocesano** (☎ 0789 73 74 00; Via Baron Manno; admission €2; ☺ 10am-12.30pm & 3.30-8pm Tue-Sun May-Sep, 10am-noon, 3-7pm Tue-Sun Oct-Apr), at the back of the modern Chiesa di Santa Maria Maddalena.

A 20km panoramic road circles the island, allowing easy access to several good beaches such as **Giardinelli**, **Monti della Rena**, **Lo Strangolato** and **Cala Spalmatore**. About a kilometre out of town, on the road to Cala Spalmatore, is the **Museo Archeologico Navale** (☎ 0789 79 06 33;

OLBIA & THE GALLURA

Localita Mongiardino; admission €4; by appointment 9.30am-12.30pm & 3.30-6.30pm), which exhibits finds from a 1st-century shipwreck. The two modest rooms are presided over by an impressive reconstructed cross-section of the Roman vessel containing more than 200 amphorae.

You can arrange excursions around the islands with operators at Cala Mangiavolpe (east of the Cala Gavetta). **Oasis Charter** (333 590 97 50; www.oasischarter.it) runs cruises of the island in a beautiful 18m schooner. A day trip, with a lobster lunch thrown in, costs between €80 and €100 per person. There's also some excellent diving in the marine park – **Sea World Scuba Centre** (349 619 07 11; www.seaworldscuba.com; Piazza 23 Febbraio) can organise dives from about €40. Opening hours can be irregular, so phone ahead or email via their website.

Sleeping

Camping Abbatoggia (0789 73 91 73; www.campinga bbatoggia.it, in Italian; per person/tent €8/2; Jun-Sep) The facilities at this spartan campsite might not be the most luxurious but the location more than makes up, close to a couple of excellent beaches. You can arrange the hire of canoes and windsurfing equipment on site.

Hotel Arcipelago (0789 72 73 28; fax 0789 72 81 00; Via Indipendenza 2; s €45-55, d €60-80; P) This, the cheapest option in La Maddalena town, is a modest family-run *pensione* in an uninspiring residential street about 20 minutes' walk from the port. You won't want to hang around all day, but if you're just after a simple base, the homey, clean rooms will do fine.

Hotel Miralonga (0789 72 25 63; Strada Panoramica; www.miralonga.it; d €90-140, half board per person €55-105; P) A big modern affair west of the centre, the Miralonga is one of Maddalena's few year-round hotels. Its bright, airy rooms are functional more than inviting and the restaurant is popular with hungry coach parties.

Eating

Most of the good eating options are in La Maddalena town; elsewhere around the island there are slim pickings outside of the big hotels.

Trattoria Pizzeria L'Olimpico (0789 73 77 95; Via Principe Amedeo 45-47; pizzas €6, meals around €25; Wed-Mon) It's worth hunting down this popular local eatery in the bland streets east of the centre. The food is excellent – pizzas and the usual array of pastas, grilled meats

and seafood – and the friendly service a real pleasure in such a touristy town. The prices are pretty tasty too.

Osteria Enoteca da Liò (0789 73 75 07; Corso Vittorio Emanuele 2-6; sea/land lunch menus €15/18) Go through the pretty ivy-clad exterior to enter this historic *osteria* (wine bar serving some food), on the go since 1890. The food is as you'd expect in such a down-to-earth place, hearty and unpretentious, and the atmosphere is cheerfully laid back.

Trattoria La Grotta (0789 73 72 28; www.lagrotta .it; Via Principe di Napoli 3; meals €35-50; May-Sep) The tantalising displays of iced fish give the game away here. Tucked into a little side alley off Via Italia, this refined restaurant, with its wicker chairs and smart outdoor tables, specialises in seafood, which it cooks superbly.

Getting There & Away

See p177 for information on ferries to La Maddalena from the mainland. They arrive (and leave) at separate points along the waterfront.

Getting Around

Turmo Travel operates two island bus services, both departing from Via Amendola on the waterfront. One goes to the Compendio Garibaldi complex on Isola Caprera (opposite), and the other heads around the island, passing the Museo Archeologico Navale and several beaches, including Cala Spalmatore and Spiaggia Bassa Trinita.

To go it alone you can hire bikes and scooters from **Noleggio Vacanze** (0789 73 52 00; 3392655837; Via Mazzini 1; 9am-1pm & 3-7pm), just off the waterfront. Budget for about €10 per day for a bike and from €30 for a scooter.

ISOLA CAPRERA

The road east out of La Maddalena town takes you through desolate urban relics to the narrow causeway (first built towards the end of the 19th century) that spans the Passo della Moneta between Isola Maddalena and Isola Caprera. Unlike Maddalena, Caprera is covered in green pines, which look stunning against the ever-present seascape.

Sights

Giuseppe Garibaldi, professional revolutionary and all-round Italian hero, bought half of Caprera in 1855 (he got the rest 10 years later). He made it his home and refuge, the place he would return to after yet another daring campaign in the pursuit of liberty. You can visit his home, the **Compendio Garibaldi** (admission €2; ⌚ 9am-1.30pm & 4-6.30pm Tue-Sun Jun-Sep, 9am-1.30pm Tue-Sun Oct-May), an object of pilgrimage for many Italians. Entry is by guided visits (in Italian) only.

The red-shirted revolutionary first lived in a hut that still stands in the courtyard while building his main residence, the Casa Bianca. You enter the house proper by an atrium adorned with his portrait, a flag from the days of Peru's war of independence and a reclining wheelchair donated to him by the city of Milan when he became infirm a couple of years before his death. You then proceed through a series of bedrooms where he and family members slept. The kitchen had its own freshwater pump, a feat of high technology in such a place in the 1870s. In what was the main dining room are now displayed all sorts of odds and ends, from binoculars to the general's own red shirt. The last room contains his death bed, facing the window and the sea, across which he would look longingly, dreaming until the end that he might return to his native Nice.

Outside in the gardens are his rough-hewn granite tomb and those of several family members (he had seven children by his three wives and one by a governess).

Activities

Green, shady Caprera is ideal for walking, and there are plenty of trails through the pine forests. There's a stairway right up to the top of the island (212m) where you'll find the **Teialone** lookout tower.

The island is also dotted with several tempting beaches. Many people head south for the **Due Mari** beaches. You could, however, head north of the Compendio Garibaldi for about 1.5km and look for the walking trail that drops down to the steep and secluded **Cala Coticcio** beach. Marginally easier is **Cala Brigantina** (signposted), southeast of the Garibaldi complex.

In the early evening you might consider a horse ride among the fragrant *macchia* with **Cavalla Marsala** (☎ 347 235 90 64; Localita Stagnali, Isola di Caprera), or you could just lark around on water skis in the calm waters of the Passo della Moneta with **Sci Club Saint Tropez** (☎ 0789 72 77 68, 335 654 52 14; Via Giuseppe Mari 15), located

near the bridge over to Isola Caprera. Half an hour costs €70.

Eating

ourpick **Agriturismo Garibaldi** (☎ 0789 72 74 49; www .agriturismogaribaldi.net; meals €25-30) Housed in the buildings where Garibaldi's farmers used to live, this friendly *agriturismo* is a top spot to feast on traditional Sardinian food. The farm produces all its own honey, vegetables, lamb and pork, all of which appears on the delicious fixed menu. To get here follow the signs left after crossing the bridge over from Isola Maddalena.

OTHER ISLANDS

The five other main islands can only be reached by boat. Numerous excursions leave from Isola Maddalena, Palau and Santa Teresa di Gallura and approach the islands in various combinations. Alternatively, you can hire motorised dinghies and do it yourself.

Isola Santo Stefano is partly occupied by the military and so is mostly inaccessible. **Isola Spargi**, west of Isola Maddalena, is surrounded by little beaches and inlets. One of the better-known ones is **Cala Corsara**. To the north lies a trio of islands, **Isola Budelli**, **Isola Razzoli** and **Isola Santa Maria**. With your boat and time to paddle about you could explore all sorts of little coves and beaches. On tours you are likely to be taken to see **Cala Rosa** (Pink Cove, so-called because of the sand's unique crimson tinge) on Isola Budelli (since 1999 swimming at the environmentally threatened Cala Rosa has been banned), **Cala Lunga** on Isola Razzoli and the often-crowded **Cala Santa Maria** on the island of the same name. The beautiful stretch of water between the three islets is known as the **Porto della Madonna** and is on most waterborne itineraries through the archipelago.

NORTH COAST

North of Palau the wind-whipped coast rises and falls like a rocky sculpture, culminating in the lunarlike headland of Capo Testa. Fine beaches stretch out towards Vignola in the west and sunny Santa Teresa di Gallura in the east, the fashionable heart of the summer scene. The windy waters are a magnet for wind- and kitesurfers, and the annual Kitesurfing World

Cup is held here at the end of September. Many competitions also dash across the windy straits to Bonifacio in Corsica.

SANTA TERESA DI GALLURA
pop 4830

One of the main resorts on Gallura's northern coast, Santa Teresa di Gallura boasts a great seafront location and a young, laid-back summer scene. It gets extremely busy in high season yet somehow manages to retain a distinct local character, making it an agreeable alternative to the more soulless resorts on the Costa Smeralda.

The town was established by the Savoy rulers in 1808 to help combat smugglers, and its neat grid of streets was designed by an army officer. However, most of the modern town grew up as a result of the tourism boom since the early 1960s. Santa Teresa's history is caught up with Corsica as much as it is with Sardinia. Over the centuries plenty of Corsicans have settled here, and the local dialect is similar to that of southern Corsica. You'll find the town fills up on Thursday, when Corsicans make the short trip over for market day.

Orientation

Santa Teresa is a straightforward grid-plan town. At the northern end of town, the centre is on a rise, focused on Piazza Vittorio Emanuele. Further north, roads drop down to the Rena Bianca beach.

Information

Banca di Sassari (Via XX Settembre 21) Has an ATM.
Bar Sport (Via Mazzini 7; per hr €5; ⏱ 6am-midnight) For internet access.
Cartalibreria (☎ 0789 75 50 83; Piazza Vittorio Emanuele 30) A bookshop with guides and maps (mostly in Italian).
Farmacia Santa Teresa (Piazza San Vittorio 2; ⏱ 9am-1pm & 5-8pm Mon-Sat)
Post office (Via Eleonora d'Arborea; ⏱ 8am-1.15pm Mon-Sat)
Tourist office (☎ 0789 75 41 27; www.comunesantateresagallura.it; Piazza Vittorio Emanuele 24; ⏱ 9am-1pm & 5-9pm daily Jun-Sep, 9am-1pm & 4-6pm Mon-Sat, 9am-1pm Sun rest of year) Very helpful with loads of information.

Sights & Activities

When not on the beach, most people hang out in the centre, eyeing-up fellow holiday-makers, lounging on the cafe-lined piazza and admiring the pastel-coloured houses.

Otherwise, you can wander up to the 16th-century **Torre di Longonsardo** overlooking a natural deep port on one side and the entrance to the town's idyllic (but crowded) **Spiaggia Rena Bianca** on the other.

If you tire of navel gazing on the beach then head down to the tourist port, a small enclave of whitewashed villas set round a cloistered courtyard and crowded marina. Between May and October regular concerts are staged here among the boutiques and expensive cafes. While down here you can treat yourself to a sauna and massage at the **Centro Benessere di Terme del Porto** (☎ 0789 74 10 78; www.termedelporto.com; ⏱ 11am-8.30pm). Treatments range from a €35 facial massage to €65 mud wraps and seaweed scrubs.

At the bottom of Via del Porto you'll find operators running excursions to the Maddalena archipelago. The biggest outfit is the **Consorzio delle Bocche** (☎ 0789 75 51 12; www.consorziobocche.com; ⏱ 9am-1pm & 5pm-12.30am May-Sep), which also has an office at Piazza Vittorio Emanuele 16. It runs various excursions, including trips to the Maddalena islands and down the Costa Smeralda (summer only). These cost between €40 and €45 per person and include lunch.

If you want a boat to yourself, you'll have to dig deep into your wallet. **Capo Testa Yachting** (☎ 0789 74 10 60; www.capotestayachting.com; Localita Porto) charters a range of boats from €1800 to €5700 per week. It's located at the tourist port.

There's also excellent diving around Santa Teresa and the islands in the Bocche di Bonifacio. A reliable operator is the **Centro Sub Marina di Longone** (☎ 0789 74 10 59; www.marinadilongone.com; Viale Tibula 11), which charges from €35 for a dive.

Sleeping

There are plenty of hotels, although most open only from Easter to October. In August you'll probably have to pay *mezza pensione* (half board).

Camping La Liccia (☎/fax 0789 75 51 90; www.campinglaliccia.com; SP for Castelsardo km 59; per person/car €12.50/3, 4-person bungalows €55-105; ⏱ late Apr-Sep) This slick seaside camping ground is 9km west of town on the road towards Castelsardo.

Hotel Da Cecco (☎ 0789 75 42 20; hoteldacecco@tiscalinet.it; Via Po 3; s €42-72, d €66-107; P ⏱) Value

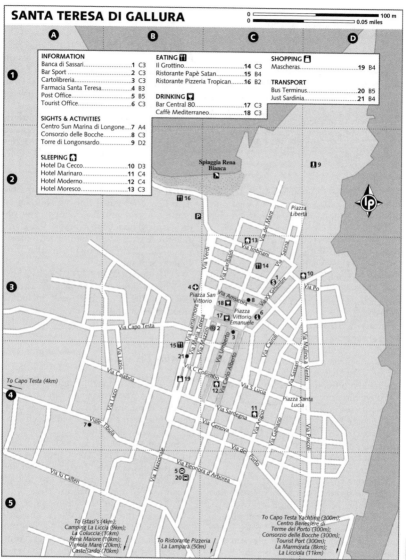

SANTA TERESA DI GALLURA

INFORMATION		
Banca di Sassari	**1**	C3
Bar Sport	**2**	C3
Cartolibreria	**3**	C3
Farmacia Santa Teresa	**4**	B3
Post Office	**5**	B5
Tourist Office	**6**	C3

SIGHTS & ACTIVITIES		
Centro Sun Marina di Longone	**7**	A4
Consorzio delle Bocche	**8**	C3
Torre di Longonsardo	**9**	D2

SLEEPING		
Hotel Da Cecco	**10**	D3
Hotel Marinaro	**11**	C4
Hotel Moderno	**12**	C4
Hotel Moresco	**13**	C3

EATING		
Il Grottino	**14**	C3
Ristorante Papè Satan	**15**	B4
Ristorante Pizzeria Tropican	**16**	B2

DRINKING		
Bar Central 80	**17**	C3
Caffè Mediterraneo	**18**	C3

SHOPPING		
Mascheras	**19**	B4

TRANSPORT		
Bus Terminus	**20**	B5
Just Sardinia	**21**	B4

for money is a commodity in these parts but you'll get it at this friendly, family-run hotel. Sporting a jolly pistachio-and-pink exterior and a summery interior, it offers comfortable rooms and a central location.

Hotel Moderno (☎ 0789 75 42 33, 0789 75 51 08; www.modernohotel.eu; Via Umberto 39; s €45-65, d €62-130; ✶ mid-Apr–Oct; ✷) This is a warm

and welcoming *pensione* near the central piazza. Rooms are bright and airy, with not much overt decor except some classic blue-and-white Gallurese bedspreads and tiny little balconies.

Hotel Marinaro (☎ 0789 75 41 12; www.hotel marinaro.it; Via Angioi 48; s €45-100, d €65-140, half board per person €50-90; ✶ closed Jan & Feb; ✷ ▢) Fresh, unfussy rooms and attractive rates make this evergreen hotel a popular choice. Staff are friendly and the location, a quick hop from the main square, makes it a good choice if you want to stay near the action.

Hotel Moresco (☎ 0789 75 41 88; www.moresc ohotel.it; Via Imbriani 16; d €104-176, half board per person €61-119; ❤ mid-Apr–Oct; **P** 🍽) Overlooking the sea, this is a refined three-star. Rooms are stylishly turned out with solid furniture and arched balconies, while the restaurant features colourful maiolica-tiled floors and a wooden ceiling.

Eating

Between May and September Santa Teresa's restaurants are open seven days a week and then close completely between December and March.

Il Grottino (☎ 0789 75 42 32; Via del Mare; pizzas from €5, meals around €30; ❤ closed Feb & Mar) Il Grottino sets a rustic picture with bare grey stone walls and warm, low lighting. In keeping with the look, the food is wholesome and hearty with no-nonsense pastas, fresh seafood and juicy grilled meats.

Ristorante Pizzeria La Lampara (☎ 0789 74 10 93; Via S Pertini pizzas €7, meals around €30; ❤ Wed-Mon) Down in a residential neighbourhood, this restaurant-pizzeria is frequented by locals and visitors alike. Sit down on the roadside terrace and tuck into fish dishes such as risotto *alla pescatore* (fisherman's risotto) or spaghetti *ai ricci* (with sea urchins).

Ristorante Papè Satan (☎ 0789 75 50 48; Via Lamarmora 20; pizzas €8; ❤ late Apr-Sep) Great wood-fired pizza is the main draw here. The internal courtyard is a pleasant place to linger, and the service is smiley and quick.

Ristorante Pizzeria Tropican (☎ 0789 75 55 69; Località Rena Bianca; meals around €30; ❤ May-Sep) Run by the same people as the Hotel Moresco, this restaurant is set beautifully on the beach. Justifiably popular, it's a great place to dig into grilled fish and meat while watching the tanned bodies splayed on the beach beneath you.

Drinking & Entertainment

Hanging around any of the cafe-bars on Piazza Vittorio Emanuele is a pleasant option.

Caffè Mediterraneo (☎ 0789 75 90 14; Via Amsicora 7; cocktails €6.50; ❤ 8am-midnight Mon-Thu, 7am-3.30am Fri-Sun) With its arched windows and polished-wood bar, this stylish cafe attracts a young, good-looking crowd. Join them for a lunchtime *panino* (€3.50) or a cool evening cocktail.

Bar Central 80 (☎ 0789 75 41 15; Piazza Vittorio Emanuele; ❤ 6am-2am) Right on the main square, this central hub swells with happy holidaymakers until the early hours. Grab an outside table and enjoy ringside views of the piazza with your drink.

Three kilometres south of town towards Palau is Santa Teresa's nightlife hub, centred on the noisy, outdoor club **Estasi's** (☎ 392 054 19 00; ❤ 10.30pm-late Fri & Sat summer only).

Shopping

Coral, some of it found locally, is the big item here, and you'll find no shortage of boutiques and jewellery shops. The pedestrianised Via Umberto and Via Carlo Alberto, leading south from Piazza Vittorio Emanuele, also host a nightly market from June to September.

At **Mascheras** (☎ 347 767 79 571; Via Maria Teresa 54), a small shop, you can pick up a traditional Sardinian carnival mask, including wooden *boes* and *merdules* masks from Ottana. Reckon on from €130. There's also a range of cheaper wooden knick-knacks.

Getting There & Around
BOAT

Santa Teresa is the main jumping-off point for Corsica. Two companies run car ferries on this 50-minute crossing to Bonifacio, although between November and March services are drastically reduced.

Saremar (☎ 0789 75 41 56; www.saremar.it), run by Tirrenia, has three daily departures each way (two at weekends between October and mid-March). A one-way adult fare in high season is €10 and a small car costs up to €37. Taxes add another €8 to the price.

Between the end of March and late September **Moby Lines** (☎ 199 30 30 40; www.moby lines.it) operates four daily crossings. Adult tickets cost €9 to €13.50, plus €4.20 tax; a car costs €22 to €63 plus €2.80 tax.

BUS

From the bus terminus on Via Eleonora d'Arborea, ARST buses run to/from Arzachena (€2.50, one hour, five daily), Olbia (€4.50, 1½ hours, five daily), Castelsardo (€4.50, 1¼ hours, two daily) and Sassari (€6.50, 2½ hours, three daily).

Turmo Travel (☎ 0789 2 14 87; www.gruppotu rmotravel.com) operates a daily service to/from Cagliari (€22.50, 6¼ hours) and a summer service to Olbia airport (1½ hours, six daily June to September) via Arzachena and Palau.

Other summer services are provided by **Caramelli** (☎ 079 67 06 13), which runs a daily bus to/from Porto Cervo (€4, 1¼ hours) via Palau and Baia Sardinia, and **Sardabus** (☎ 079 68 40 87), which operates five circle-line buses connecting Baia Santa Reparata, Capo Testa, Santa Teresa and La Marmorata. The run takes half an hour.

CAR & MOTORCYCLE

Santa Teresa di Gallura is at the northernmost end of the SS133b and on the SP90 which runs southwest to Castelsardo.

There are numerous rental agencies in town, including **Just Sardinia** (☎ 0789 7 54 34; www.justsar dinia.it; Via Maria Teresa 26), which has bikes (from €8 per day), scooters (€25) and cars (€50).

AROUND SANTA TERESA DI GALLURA

If you've got transport it's worth exploring the long sandy beaches around Santa Teresa. East of town is the Conca Verde, a wild stretch of coastline covered with bushy umbrella pines. Along here you can try **La Marmorata** (8km) or **La Licciola** (11km).

Head 10km in the other direction (west) and you'll arrive at the long, sandy **Rena Maiore**, backed by appealing, soft dunes. ARST buses to Castelsardo can drop you at the turnoff. Further on are the beaches of **Spiaggia Montirussu**, **Spiaggia Lu Littaroni** and **Spiaggia Naracu Nieddu**, none of them very busy even in high summer. Finally, you'll come to the little seaside resort of **Vignola Mare**, the heart of kitesurfing territory.

Of the resort hotels around here, the hip **La Coluccia** (☎ 0789 75 80 04; www.mobygest.it; Localita Conca Verde; d €260-580; ⚘ May-Sep; Ⓟ ⚹ ⚹) stands out. Just over the water from the Isola Spargi, part of the Maddalena archipelago, it's a vision of contemporary cool with soothing natural tones and textures of wood, marble and limestone.

Capo Testa

Four kilometres from Santa Teresa, this extraordinary granite headland seems more like a sculptural garden. Giant boulders lay strewn about the grassy slopes, their weird and won-

derful forms the result of centuries of wind erosion. The Romans quarried granite here, as did the Pisans centuries later.

The place also has a couple of beaches. **Rena di Levante** and **Rena di Ponente** lie either side of the narrow isthmus that leads out to the headland itself.

Right on Rena di Ponente you can rent surfing gear, beach umbrellas and sun loungers at **Nautica Rena di Ponente** (☎ 347 321 52 14; www.nauticarenadiponente.com).

THE INTERIOR

Away from the preening millionaires on the beach, Gallura's interior is remote and resolutely rural. In fact it was the area's fertile hinterland that attracted the waves of Corsican migrants who settled here to farm the cork forests and plant the extensive Vermentino vineyards. Cork has long been a mainstay of the local economy and still today it's harvested annually; see the boxed text, p52.

TEMPIO PAUSANIA

pop 14,100

Elevated above the hot Gallurese plain and surrounded by dense cork woods, Tempio Pausania is a lively and attractive town. Joint capital of the Olbia-Tempio province, it's an unpretentious spot with a rustic historic centre and a laid-back pace of life.

The town was founded by the Romans in the 2nd century BC, and was developed to become an administrative centre of the medieval Giudicato di Gallura. Tempio Pausania's heyday came under the Spanish and then the Savoys, when many of the churches that adorn the town's grey stone centre were constructed. These days there are few must-see sights for tourists, but it's a relaxed place to hang out and the surrounding countryside is perfect for touring. Nearby Monte Limbara provides numerous trekking opportunities.

Information

Banco Sanpaolo (Piazza Gallura 2) One of several central banks with an ATM.

Ospedale Civile (☎ 079 67 10 81; Via Grazia Deledda 19)

Post office (Largo A de Gasperi; ⚘ 8am-6.50pm Mon-Fri, to 1.15pm Sat)

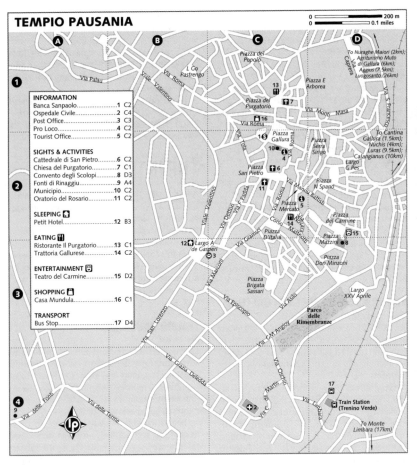

TEMPIO PAUSANIA

INFORMATION	
Banca Sanpaolo	..................1 C2
Ospedale Civile	.....................2 C4
Post Office	.........................3 C3
Pro Loco	...........................4 C2
Tourist Office	......................5 C2

SIGHTS & ACTIVITIES	
Cattedrale di San Pietro	.........6 C2
Chiesa del Purgatorio	............7 C1
Convento degli Scolopi	..........8 D3
Fonti di Rinaggiu	..................9 A4
Municipio	.........................10 C2
Oratorio del Rosario	............11 C2

SLEEPING	
Petit Hotel	..........................12 B3

EATING	
Ristorante Il Purgatorio	........13 C1
Trattoria Gallurese	..............14 C2

ENTERTAINMENT	
Teatro del Carmine	..............15 D2

SHOPPING	
Casa Mundula	.....................16 C1

TRANSPORT	
Bus Stop	............................17 D4

Pro Loco (☎ 079 63 12 73; Piazza Gallura 2; 10am-1pm & 4-7pm Mon-Fri, 10am-1pm Sat) An extremely friendly information office.

Tourist office (☎ 079 639 00 80; www.comune.te mpiopausania.ss.it, in Italian; Piazza Mercato 3; 9am-1pm & 4-7pm Mon-Fri, 10.30am-1pm Sun) Run by helpful, multilingual staff.

Sights

The town's imposing centrepiece is the granite **Cattedrale di San Pietro** (Piazza San Pietro; 8am-12.30pm & 3-8pm). All that remains of the 15th-century original is the bell tower and main entrance. Across the square, the **Oratorio del Rosario** dates to the time of Spanish domination of the island. Behind the cathedral, the town's main square, **Piazza**

Gallura, is fronted by the grave **Municipio** (town hall). A couple of cafes make good spots for people-watching. Nearby, Piazza del Purgatorio is presided over by the modest 17th-century **Chiesa del Purgatorio**. The story goes that a member of the noble Misorro family was found guilty of carrying out a massacre on this very spot. To expiate his sins, the pope ordered the man to fund the building of this church, where to this day it is the custom of townspeople to come and pray after a funeral.

Tempio is replete with churches, and an indication of the town's former importance lies in the presence of the 17th-century **Convento degli Scolopi** (Piazza Mazzini; closed for restoration). It's now a college, but you can peer through the gates to the leafy cloister from Piazza del Carmine.

Since Roman days Tempio has been known for its springs; the **Fonti di Rinaggiu** is a pleasant 1km walk southwest from the centre (take the shady Via San Lorenzo and follow the 'Alle Terme' signs). For liquid sustenance of a more alcoholic nature, head 1.5km east of town to the **Cantina Gallura** (☎ 079 63 12 41; www.cantinagallura.com; Via Val di Cossu; ☺ 9am-noon & 3.30-7pm) where you can stock up on the local DOCG Vermentino di Gallura.

Festivals & Events

Tempio has a whole host of festivals and events, from music concerts to folklore parades and key religious festivals.

Carnevale (in February) is big here, as is **Easter**. On Good Friday members of *confraternita* (religious brotherhoods) dress up in sinister-looking robes and hoods for the **Via Crucis** night procession. The musical **Festival d'Estate** runs from July to mid-August.

Sleeping & Eating

Petit Hotel (☎ 079 63 11 34; www.petit-hotel.it, in Italian; Largo A de Gasperi 9/11; s/d €58/85; ❄) A functional, modern affair on the fringes of the old town, the Petit is a favourite with travelling suits. Rooms are comfortable but rather bland with polished wood desks and forgettable floral fabrics. Still, staff are friendly and the location is good.

Trattoria Gallurese (☎ 079 67 10 48; Via Novara 2; set menu €15, meals €20-25; ☺ Sat-Thu) Venture upstairs to the simple homespun dining area for a warm welcome and some genuine Gallurese soul food. Dig into *lumache piccante* (spicy snails) or *pecora alla gallurese* (Gallurese-style lamb) to get with the traditions.

Ristorante Il Purgatorio (☎ 079 63 43 94; Piazza del Purgatorio 9; meals around €45; ☺ Wed-Mon) Generally considered one of the best restaurants in town, Il Purgatorio serves earthy seasonal fare and fresh seafood. Menu stalwarts include *cinghiale in umido* (wild boar stew) and *ravioli carciofi e bottarga* (ravioli with artichokes and mullet roe).

Entertainment

Teatro del Carmine (☎ 079 67 15 80; Piazza del Carmine) A variety of performances, from operetta to classical concerts, can be enjoyed here, especially during the summer Festival d'Estate.

Shopping

Cork is the big thing around here and you can buy safe in the knowledge that you're not harming the environment. Cork trees are not damaged when their bark is stripped off, and the local cork industry has a vested interest in looking after the area's forests.

Casa Mundula (☎ 079 63 40 23; www.casamundula.com; Via Roma 102) You'll find plenty of cork-based knick-knacks as well as wine, filigree jewellery and an impressive selection of knives.

Getting There & Away

From Olbia (€3, one hour 20 minutes) there are seven weekday ARST buses to Tempio and three on Sundays.

The train station, a tough downhill walk from the centre, comes to life for the summertime **trenino verde** (☎ 800 460 220; www.treninoverde.com, in Italian) to/from Sassari (€12.50, 2½ hours, one daily), Arzachena (€9.50, 70 minutes, two daily) and Palau (€11, 1¾ hours, two daily).

AROUND TEMPIO PAUSANIA

Two kilometres north of town on the SS133 road to Palau is the **Nuraghe Maiori** (admission €2.50; ☺ 9.30am-7pm), signposted off to the right and immersed in thick cork woods. As the name suggests (*maiori* means 'major'), it is a good deal bigger than many of the simple ruined towers you will repeatedly spot around the countryside here. Off the entrance corridor is a chamber on each side, and a ramp leads you to a third, open room at the back. Stairs to the left allow you to walk to the top.

On the other side of town, 4km along the road to Calangianus, is the small hamlet of **Nuchis**. Here in the neat grey *borgo* (village centre) you'll find the **Hotel il Melograno** (☎ 079 67 40 43; www.hotelilmelograno; Via Vittorio Emanuele; s €40-45, d €65-72; ❄), the airy, tiled rooms of which provide a good-value alternative to the more expensive accommodation up in Tempio.

Monte Limbara

Some 17km southeast of Tempio, the summit of Monte Limbara (1359m) dominates the gritty landscape. The easiest way to reach it is to drive. From Tempio, head south out of town past the train station and follow the SS392 road for Oschiri. After 8km you will hit the left turn-off for the mountain.

The initial stretch takes you through thick pine woods. As you emerge above the tree line, a couple of *punto panoramico* (viewing spots) are indicated, from where you have terrific views across all of northern Sardinia. One is marked by a statue of the Virgin Mary and child, near the simple **Chiesa di Santa Maria della Neve** church.

The road then flattens out to reach the viewing point of Punta Balistreri (1359m), where the RAI national TV network has stacked its relay and communication towers. The air is cool and refreshing, even on a mid-summer's day, and the views west towards Sassari and beyond and north to Corsica are breathtaking.

Monte Limbara is also a popular trekking spot. If you want a guide contact **Gallura Viaggio Avventura** (☎ 333 183800; c/o Pro Loco office), which organises trekking and mountain biking excursions on the mountain.

For places to visit south of here, see right.

Calangianus & Luras

Archaeology fans might want to make the short drive to Calangianus, Sardinia's cork capital, about 10km east of Tempio. Its **Tomba dei Giganti di Pascaredda** is among the best preserved in the area.

Nearby, the small town of Luras is also worth a quick stopover for its **Dolmen de Ladas** and small museum. The **Museo Etnografico Galluras** (☎ 079 64 72 81; www.galluras.it; Via Nazionale; ❧ by appointment) celebrates the area's rural traditions with a collection of agrarian tools and a reconstruction of a typical village house. Among the displays, look out for a gruesome hammer that was traditionally used to put the terminally sick out of their misery. For more on this practice of rural euthanasia see the Sa Femmina Accabadora boxed text, p37.

Aggius & Luogosanto

Eight kilometres to the northwest of Tempio, Aggius is a quiet village set amid granite walls and cork woods. It's famous for its choral music and carpets, the latter tradition dating back to the 1900s, when 4000 looms were said to have been busy in the area. You can view some excellent work at the **Museo Etnografico 'Olivia Carta Cannas'** (☎ 079 62 10 29; www.museomeoc .com; Via Monti di Lizu 6; ❧ 10am-1pm & 3-8.30pm daily mid-May–mid-Oct, 10am-1pm & 3.30-7pm Tue-Sun rest of year), which boasts comprehensive displays dedicated to local life and traditions.

A few kilometres northwest of Aggius towards Trinita d'Agultu, you come to the

---

---

strange boulder-strewn landscape of the **Valle della Luna**. The valley is a fantastic place for a cycle ride, and the road through here down to the coast is tremendously scenic.

From Aggius it's possible to loop round northwest onto the SS133 towards remote **Luogosanto** (Holy Place). It's a pretty place peppered with churches, the grandest of which is the **Basilica di Nostra Signora di Luogosanto**, built in 1228. Pope Onorio III gave it the title of basilica when he sanctioned its Holy Door. Like the Holy Door at St Peter's in Rome, this door is walled up and only opened every seven years. There's an even older church here, the **Chiesa di San Trano**, which was built to honour the 6th-century St Trano and is moulded into the granite rock.

Near Aggius you can stay at the **Agriturismo Muto di Gallura** (☎ 079 62 05 59; www.mutodigallura .com; Localita Fraiga; half board per person €84; P), a slick rural retreat in the rocky countryside. It offers lovely rooms renovated in true country style with wooden beams, stone fireplaces and wrought-iron beds. You can also organise horse rides and trekking here, and dine in fine style (menus €20 to €40).

LAGO DI COGHINAS, OSCHIRI & BERCHIDDA

Those with wheels could make another excursion south of Monte Limbara. Once down from the mountain, turn left on the SS392 and head for Oschiri. The road skirts the western side of the Limbara massif, tops the Passo del Limbara (646m) and then begins its descent. After about 12km the green gives way to scorched straw-coloured fields and the blue mirror of the artificial Lago di Coghinas comes into view.

Just before the bridge over the lake, a narrow asphalted road breaks off east towards Berchidda around the northern flank of Monte Acuto (493m), the woody hill where Eleonora d'Arborea hid out for a period in the 14th century. Berchidda is a fairly nondescript farming town with a strong wine tradition. You can find out about local wine-making and taste some of the area's Vermentino at the modern **Museo del Vino** (☎ 079 70 45 87; admission €3; ◷ 9am-1pm & 3-6pm Tue-Fri, to 7pm Sat & Sun) right at the top of town. The best time to visit is August, when Berchidda holds its big **Time in Jazz** (www.timeinjazz.it, in Italian) festival, a festive multicultural event showcasing anything from string quartets to Moroccan *gnaoua* (sub-Saharan reed pipe and percussion) music.

ourpick **Tenuta Lochiri** (☎ 3391197266; www .tenutalochiri.com; r per person €40-45, apt per week €600-700; P) Should you want to stay in the area, and it is a beautiful part of the island, you could do a lot worse than book a room here, a delightful *agriturismo* with sweeping views over Monte Acuto. At the end of a 3km dirt track off the Berchidda–Oschiri road, the main farmstead has been lovingly converted into a stylish restaurant with huge panoramic windows, four guestrooms and two apartments. Needless to say the food is home produced and absolutely divine (meals €35 to €40), and the location is perfect for escaping your everyday stresses.

A daily ARST bus passes through Berchidda en route from Nuoro (€6.50, 1¼ hours) to Olbia (€2.50, two hours).

Nuoro & the East

To get a feel for Sardinia's proud and ancient heart you need to visit this spectacular mountainous region. Often dubbed an island within an island, Nuoro and its provinces have been shaped by centuries of isolation. Uncompromising mountains have kept the world at bay, and small rural communities have learned to fend for themselves. As a result, local traditions have survived and the countryside has remained largely unspoilt.

Nowhere else in Sardinia is the landscape such an overpowering force. From the great, grey arena of the Gennargentu to the breathtaking coastline of the Golfo di Orosei and the vast, empty valleys of the Ogliastra, this is one of Sardinia's great untamed wildernesses. A paradise for outdoor enthusiasts, it boasts exhilarating trekking, cycling and climbing, as well as myriad water-borne possibilities.

Yet while the landscape thrills, the towns are often downright ugly. Cheap breeze-block housing and neglected roads suggest that the problems of poverty, unemployment and emigration have not all been consigned to the history books. But get behind the veneer and you'll discover a defiant spirit. Nuoro, not one of Sardinia's most beautiful cities, has produced a string of top authors, including Nobel Prize–winner Grazia Deledda, and hosts one of the island's most theatrical festivals. Orgosolo, once the kidnap capital of Sardinia, is reinventing itself as a tourist site thanks to its colourful murals, while the small Barbagia village of Gavoi stages an international literature festival.

Of the many archaeological sites, the prehistoric village of Tiscali is strange and wonderful, and the Fonte Sacra Su Tempiesu is magnificently located.

HIGHLIGHTS

- Plunge into Europe's Grand Canyon, the **Gola Su Gorruppu** (p210), and trek to **Tiscali** (p211), a poignant prehistoric village

- Sail down the **Golfo di Orosei's** imperious coastline, stopping off at secluded beaches and hidden coves (p212)

- Leave the world behind as you explore the weird highland plain of the **Altopiano del Golgo** (p217)

- Scale the hidden heights in the hills around **Ulassai** (p217)

- Get a glimpse into the life of Sardinia's most famous author at her childhood home, now resurrected as Nuoro's **Museo Deleddiano** (p193)

NUORO

pop 36,455

A scruffy and not immediately likeable town, Nuoro (Nugoro in the local dialect) does little to endear itself. Its nondescript suburbs are modern and ugly and there's little of immediate interest, even in the historic centre. But scratch beneath the surface and you'll discover a proud, hospitable city, sustained by long-held traditions and an ingrained culture. Literary heroine Grazia Deledda was born here, as was novelist Salvatore Satta and acclaimed poet Sebastiano Satta, and its museums, some of the island's best, open a fascinating window onto the rural identity of its mountainous environs.

HISTORY

Archaeologists have unearthed evidence of prehistoric nuraghic settlements in the Nuoro area. A popular theory maintains that the city was established when locals opposed to Roman rule grouped together around Monte Ortobene. The fact is, however, little is known of the city before the Middle Ages, when it was passed from one feudal family to another under the Aragonese and later Spain.

By the 18th century the town, by now under Piedmontese control, had a population of around 3000, mostly farmers and shepherds. A tough, often violent place, it rose in rebellion in 1868 when citizens burned down the town hall to protest attempts to privatise public land (and thus hand it to the rich landowners). This action, known as Su Connuttu, no doubt confirmed the new Italian nation's view of the whole Nuoro district as a 'crime zone', an attitude reflected in its treatment of the area, which only served to further alienate the Nuoresi and cement their mistrust of authority.

Nuoro was appointed a provincial capital in 1927. It quickly developed into a bustling administrative centre, attracting internal migrants from all over the province. Although the traditional problem of banditry has subsided and the town presents a cheerful enough visage, Nuoro remains troubled, as high unemployment forces many young people to leave in search of work.

ORIENTATION

The old centre is huddled into Nuoro's northeastern corner, on a high spur of land that juts eastward to become Monte Ortobene. The main street is Corso Garibaldi, which bisects a warren of tidy lanes, where you'll find several restaurants and popular cafes. Most of Nuoro's hotels are in the scruffy modern town that extends westwards of the *centro storico*. The train and bus stations are down Via Lamarmora, the extension of Corso Garibaldi, and the tourist office is on Piazza Italia, a big modern square above the historic centre.

INFORMATION

Banco di Sardegna (Corso Garibaldi 90) One of several banks with an ATM.
Libreria Mondadori (☎ 0784 3 41 61; Corso Garibaldi 147) A bookshop selling good maps, but little in English.
Main post office (Piazza F Crispi; ✆ 8am-6.50pm Mon-Fri, 8am-1pm Sat)
Ospedale Civile San Francesco (☎ 0784 24 02 37; Via Mannironi) The city's main hospital, west of the centre.
Police station (☎ 0784 3 21 00; Viale Europa)
Punto Informa (☎ 0784 3 87 77; Corso Garibaldi 155; ✆ 9am-1pm & 3.30-7pm Mon-Sat) A very helpful private tourist office.
Tourist office (☎ 0784 3 00 83; www.enteturismo .nuoro.it; Piazza Italia 19; ✆ 8.30am-1.30pm & 3-7pm daily Jun-Sep, same hours Mon-Fri Oct-May) Has plenty of useful information on Nuoro and environs, including an excellent archaeological map of the province, the *Carta Archeologica Illustrata*.

SIGHTS & ACTIVITIES

Nuoro's appeal lies in the historic centre. To put the area into geographical perspective, stop for a moment on Via Aspromonte, the road that twists along the *centro storico*'s eastern lip, to admire sweeping views over to Monte Ortobene. This panorama reminds the visitor that Nuoro was originally an isolated hilltop village. Indeed, the alleyways around Grazia Deledda's old house retain something of a rural atmosphere.

Museo della Vita e delle Tradizioni Sarde

The wonderful **Museo della Vita e delle Tradizioni Sarde** (☎ 0784 25 70 35; Via Antonio Mereu 56; adult/child €3/1; ✆ 9am-8pm daily Jun-Sep, 9am-1pm & 3-7pm daily Oct-May) provides a fascinating insight into Sardinian traditions, folklores, superstitions and celebrations. The museum's 8000-piece collection comprises filigree jewellery, carpets, tapestries, rich embroidery, musical instruments, weapons, household tools and

NUORO & THE EAST

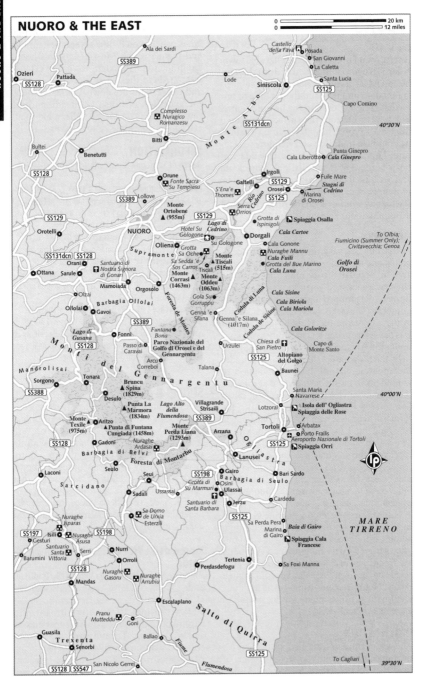

NUORO & THE EAST

0 — 20 km
0 — 12 miles

Ozieri
SS128
Pattada
Ala dei Sardi
SS389
Castello della Fava
Posada
San Giovanni
La Caletta
Santa Lucia
SS125
Lode
Siniscola
Capo Comino
Bultei
Complesso Nuragico Romanzesu
Monte Albo
SS131dcn
40°30'N
Benetutti
SS128
Bitti
Punta Ginepro
Cala Liberotto Cala Ginepro
SS389
Orune
Fonte Sacra Su Tempiesu
Galtelli
SS129
Irgoli
Fuile Mare
S'Ena'e Thomes
Orosei
Stagni di Cedrino
Lollove
SS389
Serra
Rio Cedrino
SS125
Marina di Orosei
SS129
Monte Ortobene (955m)
SS129
S'Orrios
Spiaggia Osalla
SS129
Orotelli
NUORO
Lago di Cedrino
Grotta di Ispinigoli
Cala Cartoe
To Olbia; Fiumicino (Summer Only); Civitavecchia; Genoa
Hotel Su Gologone
Dorgali
Su Gologone
Cala Gonone
SS131dcn SS128
Oliena
Grotta Sa Oche
Nuraghe Mannu
Cala Fuili
Supramonte
Sa Sedda 'e Sos Carros
Monte Tiscali (518m)
Grotta del Bue Marino
Cala Luna
Golfo di Orosei
Orani
Santuario di Nostra Signora di Gonari
Monte Corrasi (1463m)
Tiscali
Monte Oddeu (1063m)
Ottana
Sarule
Mamoiada
Olzai
Orgosolo
Gola Su Gorruppu
Cala Sisine
Cala Biriola
Cala Mariolu
Barbagia Ollolai
Foresta de Montes
Ollolai
Gavoi
Genna 'e Silana
Codula di Luna
Cala Goloritze
Lago di Gusana
Fonni
SS389
Funtana Bona
Parco Nazionale del Golfo di Orosei e del Gennargentu
(Genna e Silana (1017m))
Codula de Sisine
Capo di Monte Santo
Monti del
SS128
Passo del Caravai
Urzulei
Chiesa di San Pietro
Mandrolisai
Arcu Correboi
Talana
Altopiano del Golgo
Sorgono
Tonara
Bruncu Spina (1829m)
Baunei
SS388
Gennargentu
Santa Maria Navarrese
40°00'N
Desulo
Punta La Marmora (1834m)
Lago Alto della Flumendosa
Villagrande Strisaili
Lotzorai
Isola dell' Ogliastra
Spiaggia delle Rose
Monte Texile (975m)
Aritzo
Punta di Funtana Cungiada (1458m)
SS389
Monte Perda Liana (1293m)
Arzana
Tortoli
Arbatax
Porto Frailis
Aeroporto Nazionale di Tortoli
SS128
Gadoni
Nuraghe Ardasai
Ogliastra
SS125
Spiaggia Orri
Barbagia di Belvi
Foresta di Montarbu
Lanusei
Laconi
Seulo
Sarcidano
Seui
Sadali
Ussassai
SS198
Grotta di Su Marmuri
Gairo
Osini
Ulassai
Bari Sardo
Barbagia di Seulo
Santuario di Santa Barbara
Jerzu
Cardedu
SS125
Nuraghe Isparas
Sa Domo de Urxia
Esterzili
Sa Perda Pera
Baia di Gairo
SS197
Isili
SS198
Nuraghe Asusa
Marina di Gairo
Spiaggia Cala Francese
Gesturi
Serri
Nurri
Orroli
Santuario Santa Vittoria
Barumini
SS128
Tertenia
MARE TIRRENO
Mandas
Nuraghe Gasoru
Nuraghe Arrubiu
Perdasdefogu
Sa Foxi Manna
Escalaplano
Pranu Mutteddu
Goni
Salto di Quirra
Guasila
Trexenta
Ballao
Fiume
Senorbi
SS125
To Cagliari
39°30'N
SS128 SS547
San Nicolo Gerrei
Flumendosa

masks. The highlight, though, is the comprehensive display of traditional costumes.

In the central hall up to 80 costumed mannequins crowd onto a podium. The variety of styles, colours, patterns and materials speaks volumes about the people and their villages. The fiery red skirts belong to the fiercely independent mountain villages, while the dresses of Orgosolo and Desulo have an Armenian flavour, their red wool aprons finished with a blue-and-yellow silk border. Is it coincidence that the women's headdress of Orgosolo, Sardinia's most notorious town, includes a cloth to cover the face? Or that the bourgeois of Quartu Sant'Elena adorned themselves in velvets and lace, while the poor wives of the Iglesiente miners had to make do with a plain-Jane outfit of brown and black? And what of the burkalike headdresses of the ladies of Ittiri and Osilo?

Other rooms display life-size exhibits from the region's more unusual festivals. These include Mamoiada's sinister *mamuthones*, with their shaggy sheepskins and scowling masks, and Ottana's *boes*, with their tiny antelopelike masks, huge capes and furry boots.

A short wander up from the museum brings you to the quiet **Parco Colle Sant'Onofrio**. From the highest point you can see across to Monte Ortobene and, further south, to Oliena and Orgosolo. There are swings for kids and benches for the pooped.

Museo d'Arte (MAN)

Housed in a restored 19th-century townhouse, the **MAN** (☎ 0784 25 21 10; www.museoman .it; Via S Satta 15; adult/child €3/2; ☼ 10am-1pm & 4.30-8.30pm Tue-Sun) is the only serious contemporary art gallery in Sardinia. Its permanent collection boasts more than 200 works by the island's top 20th-century painters, including Antonio Ballero, Giovanni Ciusa-Romagna, Mario Delitalia and abstract artist Mauro Manca. Local sculptors Francesco Ciusa and Costantino Nivola are also represented. To see a bronze copy of Francesco Ciusa's *Madre dell'Ucciso* (Mother of the Killed), which won a prize at the Venice Biennale in 1907, you should visit the **Chiesa di San Carlo** (Piazza San Carlo).

The gallery also hosts more wide-ranging temporary exhibits, usually held on the ground and top floors.

Piazza Satta

From the MAN, a brief walk up Via Satta leads to Piazza Satta, a small square dedicated to the great poet Sebastiano Satta (1867–1914), who was born in a house here. To celebrate the centenary of his birth, the square was given a complete makeover by sculptor Costantino Nivola (1911–88) in 1967. Nivola whitewashed the surrounding houses to provide a blank backdrop for his curious work – a series of granite sculptures planted in the piazza like menhirs. Each sculpture has a carved niche containing a small bronze figurine (a clear wink at the prehistoric *bronzetti*) depicting a character from Satta's poems. It was an unusual idea and must originally have been an impressive sight, but now the menhirs do little to overcome the general air of neglect that surrounds the piazza.

Museo Deleddiano

Piazza Satta verges on the oldest part of town, the small hill where Nobel prize–winner Grazia Deledda (1871–1936) lived the first 29 years of her life. The house has now been transformed into a small museum, the **Museo Deleddiano** (☎ 0784 25 80 88; Via Grazia Deledda 53; adult/child €3/1; ☼ 9am-8pm Tue-Sun mid-Jun–Sep, 9am-1pm & 3-7pm Mon-Sat Oct–mid-Jun). It's been done very well, and the plain, white rooms contain all sorts of memorabilia relating to the writer – pens, letters, family snapshots and the like. Best of all is the material relating to her Nobel prize – a congratulatory telegram from the king of Italy and official pictures of the prize-giving ceremony which show her, proud and tiny, surrounded by a group of stiffly suited men.

Several rooms, including the author's bedroom, have been carefully restored to show what a well-to-do 19th-century Nuorese house actually looked like. There's a storeroom piled with sacks of wheat and legumes, an internal courtyard, and a large kitchen crammed with pots and pans.

Although she lived 36 of her 65 years in Rome, Deledda's life was consumed by Nuoro and its essential dramas. Fittingly, she was brought home to be buried in the plain granite church of the **Chiesa della Solitudine** (Viale della Solitudine). You will find her granite sarcophagus to the right of the altar. On the eve of 28 August, the religious high point of Nuoro's Festa del Redentore, a solemn torchlight parade starts here at 9pm and concludes at the cathedral.

Museo Archeologico Nazionale

The only other museum of interest in Nuoro is the **Museo Archeologico Nazionale** (☎ 0784 3 16 88; Via Mannu 1; www.museoarcheologiconuoro.it; admission free; ☷ 9am-1pm Tue-Sat & 3-5.30pm Tue-Thu), which showcases finds from the surrounding province. These range from ancient ceramics and fine *bronzetti* to a drilled skull from 1600 BC and Roman and early-medieval finds. Students of nuraghic culture will enjoy the reconstruction of a prehistoric temple and ancient bronze laboratory.

Cattedrale Santa Maria della Neve

A big, pink wedding cake of a church, the 19th-century **Cattedrale Santa Maria della Neve**, (Piazza Santa Maria Della Neve) is one of 300 or so Italian churches dedicated to the Madonna della Neve. The so-called Mary of the Snow earned her name after she supposedly appeared to Pope Liberius in a dream and told him to build a church on the site where it would snow the next morning. It promptly snowed the next day and the Pope commissioned what was to become the Basilica di Santa Maria Maggiore in Rome. The cathedral's facade is a big flouncing neoclassical spread, giving onto a single-nave interior. Of note inside is *Disputa de Gesù Fra i Dottori* (Jesus Arguing with the Doctors), a canvas attributed to the school of Luca Giordano and located between the first and second chapels on the right.

Monte Ortobene

About 7km northeast of Nuoro is the granite peak of **Monte Ortobene** (955m), capped by a 7m-high bronze statue of the Redentore (Christ the Redeemer) and covered in thick woods (full of ilex, pine, fir and poplar). A favourite picnic spot, the mountain is the focus of Nuoro's annual festival, the **Sagra del Redentore**. On 29 August, the brightly clothed faithful make a pilgrimage here from the cathedral, stopping off for mass at the **Chiesa di Nostra Signora del Monte**, and then again under the statue.

The statue was raised in 1901 in response to a call by Pope Leo XIII to raise 19 statues of Christ around Italy to represent the 19 centuries of Christianity. Since then the statue, which shows Christ trampling the devil underfoot, has been an object of devotion to pilgrims who attribute all manner of cures and interventions to it.

The views across the valley to Oliena and Monte Corrasi are at their most breathtaking from the road to the left shortly before you reach the top of the mountain.

To get to the summit by public transport take local bus 8 from Via A Manzoni (€1.10, twice daily Monday to Saturday mid-September to mid-June, 14 times daily Monday to Saturday mid-September to mid-June).

FESTIVALS & EVENTS

The Sagra del Redentore (Feast of Christ the Redeemer) in the last week of August is the main event in Nuoro, and one of Sardinia's most exuberant folkloristic festivals. First celebrated in 1901, it attracts costumed participants from across the island and involves much parading, music-making and dancing. On the evening of 28 August a torch-lit procession winds its way through the city.

SLEEPING

Accommodation in Nuoro is geared to the business market and there are few appealing hotels. If you've got your own car, there are a number of *agriturismi* (farm-stay accommodation) in the surrounding countryside which make a far more attractive bet.

Casa Solotti (☎ 0784 3 39 54; www.casasolotti.it; per person €26-35) This welcoming B&B is set in a rambling garden on Monte Ortobene, surrounded by woods and walking trails. The accommodation is suitably relaxed, with a friendly family atmosphere. Horse riding may be arranged, and the owners will happily supply you with packed lunches and evening meals.

Agriturismo Testone (☎ 0784 23 05 39; www.agriturismotestone.com; Via Giuseppe Verdi; r €38-50, half board per person €55-65, meals around €27; ℗) About 20km from Nuoro, deep in a forest of cork trees, this rustic farm-stay is housed in a beautiful stone farmhouse. The look is perfectly in theme, with exposed walls, heavy wooden furniture and hanging pots and pans. To get here from the SS131 take the SP389 exit towards Bitti and follow for about 10km until the fork for Benetutti; go left and after a further 3km turn right and follow the signs.

Hotel Grillo (☎ 0784 3 86 78; www.grillohotel.it, in Italian; Via Monsignor Melas 14; s/d €65/90; ☒) Housed in a big pink building, the Grillo is the most central of Nuoro's five officially listed hotels. It's not an especially thrilling choice, but it's central and the rooms are comfortable enough.

NUORO

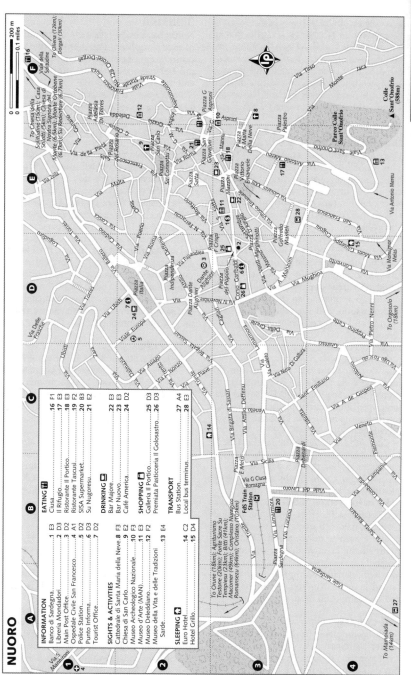

Euro Hotel (☎ 0784 3 40 71; www.eurohotelnuoro.it; Via Trieste 44; s €60-160, d €80-240; ⊠ ⌨) Better in than out, this large corporate hotel is about five minutes' walk from the tourist office. Pastel-coloured leather sofas brighten the pillared lobby, while upstairs, rooms feature modern parquet floors, firm beds and large bathrooms. There's free wi-fi and satellite TV.

EATING

Ristorante Tascusì (☎ 0784 3 72 87; Via Aspromonte 13; tourist menu €10, meals around €25; ☯ Mon-Sat) This humble trattoria is a good spot for a hearty meal of no-nonsense grub. Tables are set out in a sunny white dining room where you can tuck into bowls of tasty pasta and simply cooked meat dishes. Pizzas are also available.

Il Rifugio (☎ 0784 23 23 55; Via Antonio Mereu 28-36; meals around €30; ☯ Thu-Tue) One of Nuoro's most popular eateries, this jovial restaurant has won a faithful following for its creative brand of local cooking. Typical dishes include *risotto con verdura, coda di gambero e zafferano* (risotto with vegetables, prawns and saffron) and *pecora alla nuorese con cipolline* (Nuoro lamb with onions). And all at very reasonable prices.

Su Nugoresu (0784 25 80 17; Piazza San Giovanni 7; pizzas €7, meals around €30; ☯ Tue-Sun) Join the lunching suits at this modish trattoria on pretty Piazza San Giovanni. The square-side tables provide an atmospheric setting for a pleasant pasta lunch or a bubbling hot pizza (evenings only).

Ciusa (☎ 0784 25 70 52; Viale Francesco Ciusa 53; pizza €8, meals around €30; ☯ Wed-Mon) Just outside the *centro storico*, this is a popular trattoria specialising in earthy Sardinian fare. Expect plenty of meat and healthy portions.

Ristorante Il Portico (☎ 0784 25 50 62; Via Monsignor Bua 13; meals around €35; ☯ Thu-Tue) Despite its modest decor, Il Portico serves above-average food at above-average prices. Seafood features in many of the creative dishes, including an original take on lasagne – *lasagnetta con calamaretti, porcini e scampi all'oregano fresco* (small lasagne with squid, porcini mushrooms, scampi and fresh oregano).

Self-catering

Stock up on picnic provisions at **SISA supermarket** (Via Lamarmora 173; ☯ 8.30am-8.30pm Mon-Sat, 9am-1.30pm Sun) on the main road between the bus station and the historic centre.

DRINKING

Nuoro has a lively cafe scene with a number of excellent places dotted around the town centre. At most cafes you can pick up a light meal or *panini*, alongside coffees, aperitifs and wines.

Bar Majore (Corso Garibaldi 71; ☯ 7am-2.30pm & 3.30pm-midnight, closed Sun morning) Also called Caffè Tettamanzi, this is Nuoro's oldest cafe, and is much loved by the locals. It gets very busy at lunchtime as hungry office workers stop by the richly decorated interior for a quick bite to eat – the *panini* are delicious.

Bar Nuovo (Piazza Mazzini; ☯ 7am-midnight) Strategically placed on Piazza Mazzini, this is an excellent place to park yourself with a cool beer and watch the world go by. It's equally good for the morning paper and an evening aperitif.

Café America (☎ 0784 23 50 81; Piazza Italia 5; ☯ 7am-midnight, to 2am Sat) A busy coffee bar during the day, this cafe becomes a trendy hangout at night. Young locals come to sip drinks in the wooden alcoves and chill to a soft jazz soundtrack. Occasional live music adds to the atmosphere.

SHOPPING

Galleria Il Portico (☎ 0784 3 05 11; Piazza del Popolo 3; ☯ 10am-1pm & 5-8.30pm Mon-Sat) This good art gallery showcases works by contemporary artists such as Antonio Corriga, Vittorio Calvi and Franco Carenti. Oils and watercolours predominate, and prices range from a few hundred euros to several thousand.

Premiata Pasticceria Il Golosastro (☎ 0784 3 79 55; Corso Garibaldi 173-5; ☯ 7.30am-3pm & 4-8pm Mon-Sat) If you're after something sweet, this traditional pastry shop is the answer. Choose from a tantalising display of intricately crafted local cakes.

GETTING THERE & AWAY
Bus

ARST (☎ 0784 29 08 00; www.arst.sardegna.it, in Italian) buses run from the **bus station** on Viale Sardegna to destinations throughout the province and beyond. These include Dorgali (€3, 45 minutes, six daily), Orosei (€3, one hour, 10 daily), La Caletta (€4.50, one hour, seven daily), San Teodoro (€6.50, one hour 50 minutes, eight daily), Baunei (€6.50, two hours, four daily), Santa Maria Navarrese (€6.50, two hours 25 minutes, five daily) and Tortoli (€5.50, two hours 40 minutes, five daily). There are also regular buses to Oliena (€1, 20 minutes) and Orgosolo (€2, 35 minutes). Two daily nonstop buses connect with Cagliari (€14.50, 2½ hours to five hours).

From the same station, up to six FdS buses serve Oristano (€7.50, 2½ hours) and Sassari (€7.50 to €9.50, 2½ hours).

For Olbia, there's an ARST bus (€8.50), and **Deplano** (☎ 0784 29 50 30; www.deplanobus.it) also runs up to five daily buses to Olbia airport (€10, 1¾ hours) via Budoni (€3.50, one hour 5 minutes) and San Teodoro (€5, 1¼ hours).

For Alghero **Redentours** (☎ 0784 3 03 25; www .redentours.com) has three daily buses (€20, 2¼ hours), for which bookings are required.

Car & Motorcycle
The SS131dcn cross-country, dual-carriage highway between Olbia and Abbasanta (where it runs into the north–south SS131 Carlo Felice highway) skirts Nuoro to the north. Otherwise, the SS129 is the quickest road east to Orosei and Dorgali. Several roads head south for Oliena, Orgosolo and Mamoiada.

Train
The **FdS train station** is west of the town centre on the corner of Via Lamarmora and Via G Ciusa Romagna. FdS trains run from Nuoro to Macomer (€3.10, 1¼ hours, seven daily Monday to Saturday), where you can connect with mainline Trenitalia trains to Cagliari (from Macomer €8.75, 1¾ hours, 10 daily).

GETTING AROUND
Local **ATP** (☎ 0784 3 51 95; www.atpnuoro.it, in Italian) buses 2 and 3 can be useful for the train station, the ARST bus station (bus 3) and heading up to Monte Ortobene (€1.10, bus 8 from Via A Manzoni). Tickets for city routes cost €0.80 and are valid for 90 minutes.

You can call for a **taxi** (☎ 335 39 91 74) or try to grab one along Via Lamarmora.

NORTH OF NUORO

North of Nuoro, the forgotten and lonely countryside harbours a couple of wonderful archaeological sites. They're not easy to get to – even with a car you'll be wondering where on earth you're heading – but persevere and you'll be amply rewarded. Few

people make it out here and there are no better places to experience the mystery and isolation of Sardinia's silent interior.

FONTE SACRA SU TEMPIESU
Set in dramatic hill country near the dusty town of **Orune**, the **Fonte Sacra Su Tempiesu** (☎ 328 756 51 48; adult/child €3/2; ☯ 9am-7pm Jun-Sep, to 5pm Oct-May) is a sophisticated and elegant nuraghic well temple. Curiously, its name has nothing to do with the temple's prehistoric origins but is a reference to a farmer from Tempio who came across it in 1953.

The temple displays a strange keyhole-shaped entrance with stairs leading down to the well bottom, and it's oriented in such a way that on the day of the summer solstice sunlight shines directly down the well shaft. Water brims to the top of the stairs and trickles down a runnel to another small well, part of the original, more primitive temple that was built around 1600 BC. The newer temple, dating to about 1000 BC, is a (partially restored) masterpiece. Above the well and stairs rises an A-frame structure of carefully carved interlocking stones of basalt and trachyte (sealed watertight with lead). The stone was transported from as far away as Dorgali. No other such structure has been found in Sardinia, and this one, whose excavation began in 1981, was for centuries hidden by a landslide that had buried it back in the Iron Age.

Getting here is a problem if you don't have your own transport. Head for Orune, 18km northeast of Nuoro (turn off the SS131dcn highway at the Ponte Marreri exit for the 11km climb to the town). From Orune it is a 5km drive southeast down a sometimes precarious dirt track (signposted). Buses run only as far as Orune. From the ticket office you walk 800m downhill to the temple. You may be accompanied by a guide (in Italian).

BITTI & COMPLESSO NURAGICO ROMANZESU
From Orune the SS389 continues 12km on to the pastoral town of **Bitti**, made famous in recent years by its singing quartet, the Tenores de Bitti. This male-only vocal group is the most famous exponent of the island's traditional form of harmonic singing. To learn more, stop off at the **Museo Multimediale del Canto a Tenore** (☎ 0784 41 43 14; www.coopistelai .com, in Italian; Via Mameli 57; adult/concession €2.60/2.10; ☯ 9.30am-12.30pm & 2.30-5.30pm daily), where you

NUORO & THE EAST

can listen to recordings of various groups in action.

About 13km beyond Bitti – follow the road towards Budduso – is the **Complesso Nuragico Romanzesu** (☎ 0784 41 43 14; www .coopistelai.com, in Italian; admission €3.10, incl the Museo Multimediale del Canto a Tenore and Museo della Civiltà Contadina e Pastorale in Bitti €3.60; ⊗ 9am-1pm & 3-7pm Mon-Sat, 9.30am-1pm & 2.30-7pm Sun Apr-Oct, 8.30am-1pm & 2.30-6pm Mon-Sat, 9am-5pm Sun Nov-Mar). Spread over a seven-hectare site in a thick cork and oak wood, this 17th-century BC nuraghic sanctuary comprises several religious buildings and circular village huts. The highlight is the sacred well temple, covered by a typical tholos and connected to a semi-elliptic amphitheatre. To make sense of the ruins, there are up to six daily guided tours (in Italian).

Shortly before the site, there's a turn-off signposted for the **Agriturismo Romanzesu** (☎ 0784 41 57 16, 3471643238; Localita Romanzesu). You can't stay overnight here, unless you've got your own tent (€10 per night), but you can eat like a king. You'll need to book in advance, but do so and you'll soon be sitting down to a feast of genuine home-produced country cooking – the farmer-host produces all his own pasta, salami, *porceddu* (suckling pig) and lamb. All for the princely sum of €26.

SUPRAMONTE

Southeast of Nuoro rises the great limestone massif of the Supramonte, its sheer walls like an iron curtain just beyond Oliena. Despite its intimidating aspect, it's actually not that high – its peak, Monte Corrasi, only reaches 1463m – but it is impressively wild, the bare limestone plateau pitted with ravines and ragged defiles. It makes for a raw, uncompromising landscape, made all the more thrilling by its one-time notoriety as the heart of Sardinia's bandit country.

The Supramonte provides some magnificent hiking. However, as much of the walking is over limestone there are often few discernible tracks to follow, and in spring and autumn you should carefully check the weather conditions. Unless you are fully confident in your skills, engage a local guide at one of the cooperatives in Oliena or Dorgali.

OLIENA
pop 7525

From Nuoro you can see the multicoloured rooftops of Oliena cupped in the palm of Monte Corrasi. A good base for exploring the Supramonte, it is an atmospheric place with a grey-stone centre and a magnificent setting.

The village was probably founded in Roman times, although its name is a reference to the Ilienses people, descendants of a group of Trojans who supposedly escaped Troy and settled in the area. Unfortunately, history offers no proof of this. The arrival of the Jesuits in the 17th century was better documented and set the seeds for the village's modern fame. The eager fathers helped promote the local silk industry and encouraged farmers to cultivate the surrounding slopes. The lessons were learnt well, and now Oliena is famous for its beautiful silk embroidery – much on show during the peacock-coloured Easter parades – and its blood-red wine, Nepente di Oliena. Oliena is also the home town of Gianfranco Zola, English football's favourite Sardinian import, who was born here in 1966.

Orientation & Information

Follow the road up past the petrol station to Piazza Santa Maria, the village's focal piazza.

The best source of information in Oliena is **Tourpass** (☎ 0784 28 60 78; Corso Deledda 32; ⊗ 9.30am-1pm & 4-7pm), a private agency that can advise on activities in the area, as well as provide internet access, bike hire and an accommodation booking service. It also sells ferry tickets.

Sights & Activities

Piazza Santa Maria is the site of the Saturday market and the 13th-century **Chiesa di Santa Maria**. There are several other wonderful old churches here, including the blessedly simple 14th-century **Chiesa di San Lussorio** (Via Cavour).

ARCHAEOLOGICAL GEMS

Archaeology students won't want to miss the following sites.

- Fonte Sacra Su Tempiesu (p197)
- Tiscali (p211)
- Serra Orrios (p210)
- Nuraghe Mannu (p212)
- Santuario Santa Vittoria (p207)

SAFETY GUIDELINES FOR WALKING

Before embarking on a walking trip, consider the following points to ensure a safe and enjoyable experience:

- Routes are often poorly signposted, so consider hiring a local guide.
- Don't underestimate the terrain. Sardinia's mountains might not be the highest, but they're plenty tough.
- Do your homework. The website www.sardiniahikeandbike.com has maps (free to download) and descriptions of various routes.
- Pay any fees and possess any permits required by local authorities.
- Be sure you are healthy and feel comfortable walking for a sustained period.
- Obtain reliable information about physical and environmental conditions along your intended route (eg from park authorities).
- Be aware of local laws, regulations and etiquette about wildlife and the environment.
- Walk only in regions, and on tracks, within your realm of experience.
- Be aware that weather conditions and terrain can vary from one track to another. These differences will influence the way you dress and the equipment you carry.
- Ask before you set out about the environmental characteristics that can affect your walk and how local, experienced walkers deal with these considerations.
- Make sure your travel insurance covers trekking and hiking.

Once you've seen these and walked around the steep grey streets you've pretty much covered the village's sites. However, if you're lucky enough to be here during Easter week, you'll find the village a hive of festive activity. The culmination of the weeklong celebrations is the *S'Incontru* (The Meeting), a boisterous procession on Easter Sunday in which bearers carry a statue of Christ to meet a statue of the Virgin Mary in Piazza Santa Maria. Cultural events are also held in September and October as part of the Barbagia-wide initiative **Autunno in Barbagia** (Autumn in Barbagia). See the boxed text, p201.

The countryside surrounding Oliena provides some awesome trekking. Just 4km south of town in the woods of Maccione you'll find a track up to the highest peaks of the Supramonte. It's a hair-raising trail of vertigo-defying switchbacks called the **Scala 'e Pradu** (Steps of the Plateau) that culminates at the summit of **Punta sos Nidos** (Nests' Peak). To reach the trail, head for the trekking centre **Cooperativa Enis** (www.coopenis.it), which can also arrange guided treks and 4WD excursions; see Hotel Monte Maccione, right.

Sardegna Nascosta (☎ 0784 28 85 50; www.sardegnanascosta.it) and **Barbagia Insolita** (☎ 0784 28 60 05; www.barbagiainsolita.it; Corso Vittoria Emanuele 48) both organise a range of excursions, including trek-

king, canoeing, abseiling, climbing and riding. Prices depend on the size of the group; contact them directly for information.

Sleeping & Eating

Agriturismo Guthiddai (☎ 0784 28 60 17; www.agriturismoguthiddai.com; Nuoro-Dorgali bivio Su Gologone; half board per person €48-50) On the road to Su Gologone, this bucolic *agriturismo* is in a lovely white-washed farmstead, surrounded by fig, olive and fruit trees and backed by a looming 500m sheer rock face. Olive oil and wine are produced and home-grown fruit and veg ends up on the breakfast and dinner table. The rooms are exquisitely tiled in pale greens and cobalt blues.

Hotel Cikappa (☎ 0784 28 87 33; www.cikappa.com; Corso Martin Luther King; s/d €40/60, meals around €25; ☒) Near the village centre, this small hotel has seven tidy rooms above a popular local restaurant. They are simply decorated with pine furniture and bare white walls, and the best have balconies overlooking the town and its mountain backdrop. Food in the restaurant is pretty good, with the onus on hearty meat dishes such as *agnello in umido* (lamb stew).

Hotel Monte Maccione (☎ 0784 28 83 63; www.coopenis.it; s €36-45, d €60-74, half board per person €49.50-64; ℗) Run by the Cooperativa Enis, this place offers simple, rustic rooms and fine views from its hilltop location – deep in the woods of Monte Maccione (700m), 4km from Oliena up a nausea-inducing 21-bend road. You can also pitch a tent here (per tent €13.50 to €14.50) and eat at the tasty restaurant (€25 to €30).

ourpick **Hotel Su Gologone** (☎ 0784 28 75 12; www.sugologone.it; s €115-180, d €140-240, ste €340-440; P ✖ ♨) About 7km east of Oliena, this is a fabulous hacienda-style rural retreat. Cobbled paths lead to a series of whitewashed cottages decorated with olive-wood beams, embroidered linens, antique furniture and local handicrafts. There's a pool, a leisure centre, a huge wine cellar and plenty of walking in the surrounding countryside. The restaurant (meals €55), one of Sardinia's best, specialises in traditional Sardinian cooking, including a delicious *porceddu*.

Ristorante Masiloghi (☎ 0784 28 56 96; Via Galiani 68; meals around €30) Housed in a sunny Mediterranean villa on the main road into town, this smart restaurant showcases local art in its rustic dining hall and serves delicious food. Speciality of the house is the tasty local lamb.

Getting There & Away

ARST runs frequent buses from Via Roma to Nuoro (€1, 20 minutes, up to 12 Monday to Saturday, six Sunday).

LE BARBAGIE

Sardinia's geographic and spiritual heartland is a tough, mountainous area known as Le Barbagie (a plural collective noun indicating the several distinct zones that make up the region). The name is a derivation of the Latin term 'Barbaria' (itself derived from the Greek word *barbaros* (foreign person, barbarian), which the Romans gave the area after repeatedly failing to subdue it. The dramatic topography and tough locals kept the legionnaires out, just as they have since kept the outside world at arm's length. Even today the population maintains a fierce sense of inward-looking pride. Dialects of the Sardinian tongue are widely spoken in the Barbagia villages, and traditional festivities are celebrated with fervent passion. It's still common to see older women walking down the street wearing traditional black vestments.

At the region's heart are the bald, windswept peaks of the Gennargentu massif, the highest points on the island. This also represents the centre of the **Parco Nazionale del Golfo di Orosei e del Gennargentu**, Sardinia's largest national park, which takes in the Supramonte plateau and the Golfo di Orosei.

Orientation & Information

Dozens of distinct village communities dot the Barbagia region, which is divided into districts around the Gennargentu. To the north is Barbagia Ollolai, to the west Mandrolisai, to the southwest the Barbagia di Belvi, and in the south there's the Barbagia di Seulo.

It's a sparsely populated area and travel routes between the towns are usually limited to a single twisty road. The best sources of information are the tourist offices in Nuoro, Oliena and Dorgali. Useful maps include Belletti Editore's Parco del Gennargentu (1:100,000; €6) and Nuoro (1:200,000; €6.50), a map of the province of Nuoro published by Litografia Artistica Cartografica.

Getting There & Away

This is not an easy place to get around by public transport, so it's definitely worth hiring a car if you want to tour the area with any freedom.

ARST runs limited services between these mountain villages, usually only one or two per day and generally in the morning only. From Nuoro there are services to Mamoiada (€1.50, 20 minutes, five Monday to Saturday, one Sunday), Fonni (€2.50, 40 minutes, eight Monday to Saturday, two Sunday), Gavoi (€2.50, one hour 10 minutes, four Monday to Saturday, one Sunday), Desulo (€4, one hour 20 minutes, one Monday to Saturday) and Aritzo (€5.50, two hours, one daily).

BARBAGIA OLLOLAI
Orgosolo
pop 4515

Some 18km south of Nuoro, Orgosolo is Sardinia's most notorious town, its name long a byword for the banditry and violence that plighted this part of the island for so long. The violence has now largely dried up and the town is attempting, with some success, to reinvent itself as an alternative tourist attraction. Nowadays, it's not unusual to see

OPEN HOUSE

Autunno in Barbagia (Autumn in Barbagia) is a great way to gain an insight into how people still live in these small, apparently unsustainable, mountain villages. Throughout September and October each village takes it in turn to host a weekend of events, when residents open their doors to visitors and put on a feast of local fare. Events might include a cheese-making workshop, a show of paintings, costumes or furniture, or a demonstration of some sort of craftwork. It's also a great opportunity to buy local produce.

You should be able to pick up a leaflet detailing the schedule of events at any major tourist office and certainly at information points in Nuoro and Oliena. You can also get information on the Sardegna Turismo website (www.sardegnaturismo.it). Follow the links for Culture – Feasts, Festivals & Events – Autumn.

coachloads of visitors walking down the main strip photographing the vibrant graffiti-style murals that adorn the village's buildings. But once the day trippers have gone, the villagers come out to reclaim their streets – the old boys to sit staring at anyone they don't recognise and the lads with crew cuts to race up and down in their mud-splattered cars.

Orgosolo's history makes chilling reading. Between 1901 and 1950 the village was averaging a murder every two months as rival families feuded over a disputed inheritance. In her book *Colombi e sparvieri* (Doves and Hawks), Grazia Deledda describes an effort to defuse the enmities that saw the virtual extermination of these two families. In the postwar years, sheep rustling gave way to more lucrative kidnapping, led by the village's most infamous son, Graziano Mesina, otherwise known as the Scarlet Rose. He spent much of the 1960s earning himself a Robin Hood reputation by stealing from the rich and giving to the poor. Although captured in 1968 and imprisoned on the mainland, he had to be flown back to Sardinia in 1992 to help negotiate the release of eight-year-old Saudi Farouk Kassam, who had been abducted from the Costa Smeralda and was being held on Monte Albo, near Siniscola.

SIGHTS & ACTIVITIES

The majority of Orgosolo's **murals** line Corso Repubblica, the village's main thoroughfare. They were initiated by Professor Francesco del Casino in 1975 as a school project to celebrate the 30th anniversary of the Liberation of Italy. There are now over 150 murals, many of them executed by Casino and successive generations of Orgosolo students. Other notable artists include Pasquale Buesca and Vincenzo Floris.

The styles vary wildly according to artist: some are naturalistic, others are like cartoons, and some, such as those on the Fotostudio Kikinu, are wonderfully reminiscent of Picasso. Like satirical caricatures, they depict all the big political events of the 20th century and vividly document the struggle of the underdog in the face of a powerful, and sometimes corrupt, establishment. Italy's own political failings are writ large, including the shocking corruption of the Cassa del Mezzogiorno and Prime Minister Giulio Andreotti's trials for collusion with the Mafia, where speech bubbles mock his court refrain of 'I don't remember'. WWII, the creation of the atomic bomb, the miner's strikes of the Iglesiente, the evils of capitalism, women's liberation – you can find it all here. Even more interesting are the murals depicting recent events. On the corner of the *corso* (main street) and Via Monni you'll find portrayals of the destruction of the two World Trade Center towers (dated 28 September 2001) and the fall of Baghdad (dated 17 April 2003). Further along there's an incredibly moving series of three images – made to look like photographic stills – depicting the killing of 12-year-old Palestinian Mohammed el Dura as he hid behind his father during a Gaza shoot-out that was televised around the world on 30 September 2000.

If hunger strikes whilst you're wandering around, pop into the **Cortile del Formaggio** (Corso Repubblica 216; ☽ 10am-1pm & 3-8pm Mon-Fri), a tiny courtyard house where you can buy locally made cheeses.

Five kilometres to the south of the town, the SP48 local road heads up to the Montes heights. Another 13km south is the **Funtana Bona**, the spring at the source of the Cedrino river. On the way you pass through the tall oaks of the **Foresta de Montes**.

FESTIVALS

You'll catch Orgosolo at its best during the **Festa dell'Assunta** (Feast of the Assumption) on 15 August, when folk from all around the Barbagia converge on the town for one of the region's most colourful processions.

SLEEPING & EATING

If you need to overnight in Orgosolo, you'll find little choice.

Petit Hotel (☎ 0784 40 33 13; Via Mannu; s €26-29, d €37-39, half board per person €31) Just off the main drag, this is a welcoming, family-run two-star with clean, basic rooms and a decent restaurant. If you're travelling out of the summer season phone ahead to make sure it's open.

Hotel Sa 'e Jana (☎ /fax 0784 40 24 37; Via E Lussu; s €42-50, d €52-60) In a dusty lane at the western end of town, this is the larger of Orgosolo's two hotels. Its spacious, light-filled rooms are fairly run of the mill but the best offer magnificent views over the distant green peaks. There's a downstairs restaurant/pizzeria where breakfast is served for a rip-off €6.

Il Portico (☎ 0784 40 29 29; Via Giovanni XXIII; pizza €4.50, meals around €20; ⊙ daily in summer, Fri-Wed in winter) An excellent pizzeria-cum-restaurant serving fulsome, woody pizzas and superb local vegetables and meats. The airy dining room and friendly, smiley service add to the pleasure.

GETTING THERE & AWAY

Regular buses make the run to/from Nuoro (€2, 35 minutes, six Monday to Saturday, three Sunday).

Mamoiada

pop 2570

Just 14km south of Nuoro, the undistinguished village of Mamoiada stages Sardinia's most compelling carnival celebrations. These kick off with the **Festa di Sant'Antonio** on 16 and 17 January. According to myth, Sant'Antonio stole fire from hell to give to man, and to commemorate the fact bonfires are lit across the village. But more than the fireworks, it's the appearance of the *mamuthones*, the costumed characters for which the village is famous, that gives the festival its sinister edge. These monstrous figures reemerge on Shrove Tuesday and the pre-

ceding Sunday, for the main **Carnevale** celebrations. Up to 200 men don shaggy brown sheepskins and primitive wooden masks to take on the form of the *mamuthones*. Weighed down by up to 30kg of *campanacci* (cowbells), they make a frightening spectacle. Anthropologists believe that the *mamuthones* embodied all the untold horrors that rural man feared, and that the ritual parade is an attempt to exorcise these demons before the new spring. The *mamuthones* are walked on a long leash held by the *issokadores*, dressed in the guise of outmoded gendarmes, whose job it is to drive them out of town.

If you can't be here for Carnevale, you can get an idea of what it's all about at the **Museo delle Maschere Mediterranee** (☎ 0784 56 90 18; www.museodellemaschere.it; Piazza Europa 15; adult/child €4/2.60; ⊙ 9am-1pm & 3-7pm Tue-Sun, daily Jul & Aug). The exhibit includes a multimedia presentation (in Italian) and garbed mannequins wearing their famous shaggy sheepskins.

There are a couple of shops in the village selling the wooden masks worn by the *mamuthones*. Don't expect to pay less than €100 for a good one.

For a bite to eat, try **La Campagnola** (☎ 0784 5 60 75; Via Satta; pizzas €6, meals around €25; ⊙ Tue-Sun), a sunny eatery which offers more than 30 types of pizza and a limited range of pasta and main courses.

Infrequent ARST buses connect with Nuoro (€1.50, 20 minutes, five Monday to Saturday, one Sunday).

Orani & Ottana

A grey and uninspiring village, Orani offers little of interest except for the **Museo Nivola** (☎ 0784 73 00 63; www.museonivola.it; Via Gonare 2; adult/child €3/1.50; ⊙ 9am-1pm & 4-9pm Tue-Sun Jun-Sep, to 8pm Oct-May), just inside the southern entrance to the town. It celebrates the work of Costantino Nivola, the son of a local stonemason, who fled Fascist persecution in 1938 and spent most of his life working in America.

Five kilometres south of Orani, the village of Sarule sits at the foot of the 1083m Monte Gonare. The village itself doesn't really warrant a stop but a narrow side road east leads up to the 17th-century **Santuario di Nostra Signora di Gonare**, a grey buttressed church atop a lone conical hill. It's an important pilgrimage site, and every year between 5 and 8 September villagers celebrate

---

DEADLY SERIOUS JOCU DE SA MURRA

The scene is tense. Two pairs of men lean in towards one another in deadly earnest competition. Tempers can be short as they each launch hands at one another and scream out numbers in Sardinian in what appears for all the world like an excitable version of the rock, paper and scissors game.

The rules of the game, a pastime with centuries of colourful history in central Sardinia and especially in the Barbagia region of Nuoro, are not that complicated. Two or four men can participate – in the latter case it works a little like a tag-team match. One on each side stretches out a hand and shows some of his fingers. They both scream out numbers in an attempt to guess the total number of fingers shown by both players. The operation is repeated in rapid-fire manner until one side guesses correctly and so wins a point. At each successful guess (where four are playing) the winner of the round then continues with the loser's partner. The side to reach 16 points (sometimes 21) first with a two-point advantage wins. Where both teams are neck and neck at 16 (or 21), they pass to a sudden-death round, in which the first to five points wins.

The game is played with extraordinary passion and speed, and at the increasingly popular organised competitions the passions grow as wine bottles empty.

Traditionally, the game was an impromptu affair played on street corners or wherever idle men came together. The problem was that no one liked to lose, and accusations of cheating often flew. Frequently the game ended with knives drawn and used, so much so that for long periods the *murra* was banned. Since the late 1990s championships have been organised, especially in Urzulei and Gavoi but also on the Montiferru outside Seneghe in Oristano province. The competition takes place in the morning, followed by a long and boozy lunch, and impromptu bouts are held in the afternoon. To the outsider these postprandial bouts can seem more inflamed than the official morning sessions!

---

the Madonna di Gonare with horse races, singing and dancing.

More dramatic by far are the carnival celebrations held on Shrove Tuesday at **Ottana**, an otherwise lacklustre village considered the dead centre of Sardinia. Said to rival those of Mamoiada, festivities culminate in a parade of costumed *boes* (men masked as cattle) herded down the streets by their masters, the *merdules* (masked men symbolising our prehistoric ancestors).

Gavoi
pop 2855

Famous for its *fiore sardo* (*pecorino* cheese) and literature festival (see boxed text p204), Gavoi is one of the prettier villages in the Barbagia. It has a wonderfully maintained historic centre, with a small web of narrow lanes hemmed in by attractive stone houses. Three kilometres to the south, **Lago di Gusana** shimmers amidst thick woods of cork, ilex and oak trees.

Up in the village centre, the **Chiesa di San Gavino** was built in the 16th century to a Gothic-Catalan design, as evidenced by the plain red trachyte facade and splendid rose window. From the piazza outside the church,

cobbled alleyways lead up through the medieval *borgo* (village) that has remained almost totally free of modern intrusion.

A popular fishing spot, the lake and surrounding countryside provide plenty of sporting opportunities. You can hire canoes (€25 per day) with **Barbagia No Limits** (☎ 0784 52 90 16; www.barbagianolimits.it; Via Cagliari 85), a local operator who can organise a whole range of outdoor activities, including trekking, canyoning, caving and jeep tours.

If you want to overnight on the lake, and it is a lovely spot, try the **Hotel Sa Valasa** (☎ 0784 5 34 23; savalasa@tiscali.it; Localita Sa Valasa; s/d €25/50, half board per person €40-45; P), a big, rambling two-star set in its own lakeside grounds. The simple pine-furnished rooms and surrounding silence ensure a good night's sleep and the downstairs pizzeria/restaurant makes an attractive, laid-back dining option. Breakfast costs €5 extra.

Up in the village proper, the rustic **Ristorante Sante Rughe** (☎ 0784 5 37 74; Via Carlo Felice 2; meals around €30; ☽ Mon-Sat) serves fine local cooking. Speciality of the house is *lu su erbuzzu*, a heart-warming soup of bacon, sausage, cheese and beans flavoured with wild herbs. The cheese selection is a

---

BOOKS IN THE BARBAGIA

The small Barbagia village of Gavoi is the most unlikely place to bump into the likes of Jonathan Coe, Nick Hornby and Zadie Smith. But these best-selling British authors are just some of the big-name literary stars who have descended on the village for its annual literary festival.

A rare story of unmitigated success, **L'Isola delle Storie, Festival Letterario della Sardegna** has gone from strength to strength since it was inaugurated in 2003. The brainchild of Nuoro-born Marcello Fois and local girl Andreuccia Podda, it grew out of the latter's desire to break the monotony of long summer nights and the former's ambition to create an important literary event.

Now in its sixth year, the festival has become a major island event. For four days in early July, the village is transformed into an outdoor stage, hosting readings, concerts, theatrical performances, screenings and seminars.

For more information check out the festival's website, www.isoladellestorie.it.

---

further treat and the pizzas (evenings only) are excellent.

By bus, there are four weekday ARST connections from Nuoro (€2.50, one hour 10 minutes) and one on Sunday.

Fonni & Desulo

At 1000m Fonni is the highest town in Sardinia and is a sizeable rural community. It's also a popular base for hikers, who come to explore Sardinia's highest peaks – the Bruncu Spina (1829m) and the Punta La Marmora (1834m).

At the highest point of the village, just off Piazza Europa, is the imposing 17th-century **Basilica della Madonna dei Martiri**, one of the most important baroque churches in the Barbagia region. Surrounded by *cumbessias* (pilgrims' huts), it's famous for a revered image of the Madonna that's said to be made from the crushed bones of martyrs. In June it is the focus of Fonni's two main feast days, the **Festa della Madonna dei Martiri** on the Monday after the first Sunday in June and the **Festa di San Giovanni** on 24 June.

Outside the church a couple of trees have been curiously transformed by sculptors into religious scenes, notably one showing the crucified Christ and the two thieves.

Twenty-seven kilometres south of Fonni is **Desulo**, a long string of a town that was once three separate villages. There's nothing much to see, but like Fonni it provides a good base for hikers, given its proximity to the Gennargentu.

BRUNCU SPINA & PUNTA LA MARMORA

It's relatively easy to reach Sardinia's two highest peaks from either Fonni or Desulo. You'll find the turn-off for the **Bruncu Spina** trailhead

5km out of Fonni, on the road to Desulo. From here a 10km road winds through treeless territory to the base of an abandoned ski lift. One kilometre before the lift you'll see a steep dirt trail to the right, from where a 3km track leads right to the summit (1829m). From here you have broad, sweeping views across the island in all directions. For a view from 5m higher you need to march about 1½ hours south to **Punta La Marmora** (1834m). Although it looks easy enough from Bruncu Spina, you need a good walking map or a guide to avoid getting into any difficulty.

SLEEPING & EATING

The best hotel in Fonni, and one of the best in the Barbagia area, is **our pick** **Hotel Sa Orte** (☎ 0784 5 80 20; www.hotelsaorte.it; Via Roma 14; s €35-40, d €60-80, ste €90-100; ⓟ). A sombre granite facade opens onto a vibrant modern interior decorated with tangerine walls, parquet floors and blanched wood furniture. Downstairs, the restaurant serves delicious home-made pasta and local meat.

Down in the modern part of the village, the **Ristorante Albergo Il Cinghialetto** (☎ 0784 5 76 60; www.ilcinghialetto.it; Via Grazia Deledda 115; s/d €40/70, half board per person €55; ⓟ) is an excellent restaurant (meals €20 to €25) that doubles as a small hotel with seven clean, functional rooms.

In Desulo, **Hotel Lamarmora** (☎ 0784 61 70 15; www.hotellamarmora.com, in Italian; Via Lamarmora 147; s €31-42, d €37-57, half board per person €37-57), has modest rooms and a decent restaurant. It's at the northern end of town by the hairpin bend that leads to Fonni.

GETTING THERE & AWAY

From Nuoro, there are ARST buses to both Fonni (€2.50, 40 minutes, eight Monday to

Saturday, two Sunday) and Desulo (€4, one hour 20 minutes, one Monday to Saturday).

BARBAGIA DI BELVI
Aritzo
pop 1425

A vivacious mountain resort, Aritzo has been attracting visitors since the 19th century. Its cool climate and alpine character (its elevation is 796m) caught the imagination of the Piedmontese nobility, who came here to hunt boar in its forests.

But long before tourism took off, the village was flourishing thanks to the lucrative business of snow gathering. For some five centuries the village held a monopoly on snow collection and supplied the whole of Sardinia with ice. Snow farmers, known as *niargios*, collected the white stuff from **Punta di Funtana Cungiada** (1458m) and stored it in straw-lined wooden chests before sending it off to the high tables of Cagliari.

You can see some of the chests in the **Museo Etnografico** (☎ 0784 62 98 01; Via Guglielmo Marconi; admission incl Sa Bovida Prigione Spagnola €2; ⏱ 10am-1pm & 4-7pm Tue-Sun Jun-Sep, 9am-1pm & 3-6pm Oct-May), a small museum in the village elementary school. The museum also has a motley collection of traditional costumes and masks, as well as various farm implements and household objects.

The same ticket gets you into **Sa Bovida Prigione Spagnola** (⏱ same as Museo), a 16th-century prison just off the main drag on Via Scale Carceri. Built of dark grey schist stone, this chilling jail was used as a maximum-security facility right up until the 1940s.

A short hop away, the **Chiesa di San Michele Arcangelo** retains little of its early Gothic origins. Inside, you'll find an 18th-century *pietà* and a 17th-century portrait of San Cristoforo. Across the road from the church is a viewpoint from where you can see the oddly box-shaped **Monte Texile**, now a minor nature reserve.

There are plenty of marked walking trails around the village, most of which are fine to go alone.

Aritzo also holds two good foodie festivals. In mid-August at the **Festa de San Carapigna** you can try the village's famous lemon sorbet. On the last Sunday of October, people crowd the streets in search of chestnuts at the **Sagra delle Castagne**.

The town's hotels, each with its own restaurant, are clustered along the main road near the southern exit. The cheapest is the cheerful **Hotel Castello** (☎ 0784 62 92 66; Corso Umberto; s €24-26, d €36-41, half board per person €34-36), which has 19 ultra-spartan rooms spread over three floors. It's never going to win any design awards, but it's open year-round, many rooms have fine views, and there's occasional live music in the restaurant. A couple of kilometres outside of the village proper, **Hotel La Capannina** (☎ 0784 62 91 21; www.hotelcapannina.net; Via A Maxia 36; s/d €40/70, half board per person €60) is a smart Alpine-chalet affair with unfussy rooms bathed in white light.

BARBAGIA DI SEULO
To the south and east of Aritzo, the Barbagia di Seulo sidles up to the rocky heights of the Gennargentu national park. It's a lonesome area of small towns and snaking mountain roads.

From Aritzo the road southeast winds through the small towns of **Seulo** and **Seui**, the latter of which has a few traditional houses with wrought-iron balconies. Continue upwards towards Ussassai until after about 9km you come to a fork in the road at Cantoniera Arcueri. Follow for Montarbu and after another 9km or so you'll see Sardinia's largest *nuraghe* (ancient stone tower) the **Nuraghe Ardasai**, on your left. Built on a rocky outcrop

---

DETOUR: SORGONO

As much for the getting there as the being there, **Sorgono** rewards a detour. Deep in the heart of the Mandrolisai, the remote hilly area to the west of the Gennargentu, the village is surrounded by huge tracts of forest, full of ilex, cork, chestnut and hazel trees. In the vicinity, the **Biru 'e Concas** archaeological site boasts one of the largest collections of menhirs in Sardinia, while in town, the **Cantina del Mandrolisai** (☎ 0784 6 01 13; www.mandrolisai.com; Corso IV Novembre 20) is one of the area's most important wine producers, famous for its beefy reds.

By train you can reach Sorgono on the *trenino verde*. If you're driving it's a 25km twisty drive from Aritzo on the SS295.

OFF THE BEATEN TRACK

Want to get really lost in the Nuoro region? We spoke to Giancarlo, whose passion for the Sardinian countryside helps him in his work at a local tourist office. Born in Nuoro, he has spent his whole life exploring the area and is perfectly placed to recommend some off-track spots: 'What would my alternative tour be? Well, I really like the towns of the Flumendosa, starting at **Aritzo** and passing through **Gadoni**, **Seulo**, and **Seui** before finishing up in **Orroli**. The nature and archaeological sites around here are extraordinary, and everywhere you go you're met with wonderful hospitality. It really is a beautiful area.

'Near Seui, the **Montarbu** nature area is wonderful. Then, there's a fascinating archaeological site called **Sa Domo de Urxia** near Esterzili. It's amazing because you arrive at 1200m at Monte S Vittoria, and for kilometres around there's absolutely nothing but the wind and total solitude.

'Another stunning area is the **Usinava** zone (p170), near the sea at San Teodoro. It's not very well known and if you look at a map there's nothing there. From Budoni, head to Brunella and then up into the mountains. You'll find shepherds living in old *stazzi* (traditional stone houses), and if you're lucky you might see mouflon, boars and deer.'

dominating the deep Flumendosa River valley, it's worth a stop for the views. Six kilometres further on is a turn-off for the dense **Foresta di Montarbu**, towered over by the mountain of the same name (1304m). Several kilometres beyond this is the even more impressive **Monte Perda Liana**, at 1293m.

From here the road descends, leading eventually to the southern bank of the **Lago Alto della Flumendosa**, which the main road skirts eastward for about 10km before crossing over the *trenino verde* tourist train line a couple of times and reaching the main Nuoro–Lanusei road.

SARCIDANO

Southwest of Aritzo the mountains flatten out to the broad Sarcidano plain, littered with *nuraghi* and other mysterious prehistoric sites.

Laconi
pop 2170

Straddling the SS128 as it twists south, Laconi is a charming little town well worth a stopover. It boasts a number of genuine attractions, including a beautiful woodland park, the house where Sardinia's only saint was born, and a strange and wonderful archaeological museum.

Laconi is also one of the few towns in this area with a **tourist office** (☎ 0782 86 70 13; Piazza Marconi; ☼ 9am-1pm Mon-Fri). It's over the road from the neoclassical Municipio (Town Hall) on the central piazza. If it's closed you can get information from the helpful folk at the **Museo delle Statue Menhir** (☎ 0782 86 62 16; Via Amsicora; adult/child €3.50/2; ☼ 9am-1pm & 4-7pm Apr-Sep, 9am-1pm

& 4-6pm Oct-Mar, closed 1st Mon of month), a delightful museum exhibiting a collection of 40 menhirs. Taken from sites across the surrounding area, these stark anthropomorphic slabs are strangely compelling. Little is known of their function, but it's thought that they were connected with prehistoric funerary rites. In the backlit gloom they appear all the more mysterious, the shadows emphasising the faded sculptural relief that suggests whether they are 'male' or 'female'. The display is accompanied by well-presented explanations (in Italian). If you find this interesting you may want to detour to Pranu Mutteddu (opposite) further south, where you can see them in situ.

From the Municipio, cross the road and search out Via Sant'Ignazio, where you'll find the **Casa Natale di Sant'Ignazio** (Via Sant'Ignazio 58), a simple two-roomed house where St Ignatius is said to have been born (he died in 1781). The back room, with its low wood ceiling and stone walls, is a good example of what a poor village house must have looked like in the 18th century. There are no official opening hours but the house is almost always open; if it's not, ask at the tourist office.

Once in Via Sant'Ignazio again, continue past the saint's house and take the first left. This brings you to the **Parco Laconi** (☼ 8am-7pm), a smashing 22-hectare park full of exotic trees (including an impressive cedar of Lebanon and several eucalyptuses), springs, lakes, grottoes and the remains of an 11th-century castle, the **Castello Aymerich**. From here you have wonderful views across the park and the greenery surrounding Laconi.

To stay overnight in Laconi, head to the **Albergo Ristorante Sardegna** (☎ 0782 86 90 33; www.albergosardegna.it; s/d €36/65, half board per person €52), by the northern entrance to the village. Above the popular restaurant are six refined rooms, the best of which afford panoramic views over Sardinia's windswept interior.

Bus services to Laconi are fairly limited. There are connections with Isili (€1.50, 35 minutes one daily), Aritzo (€2, 40 minutes, three Monday to Saturday) and Barumini (€2, 35 minutes, two Monday to Saturday), but most run very early in the morning or in the late afternoon.

The FdS *trenino verde* calls in here on its way north from Mandas. The station is about 1km west of the town centre.

South of Laconi

About 20km south of Laconi, by the sports centre in Isili, the **Nuraghe Isparas** (☎ 0782 80 26 41; admission €3; ❧ 10am-1pm & 3.30pm-7pm), is notable for its tholos (cone) which, at 11.8m, is the highest in Sardinia.

However, this is just a taster for what lies 15km or so further up the road. Beyond the small village of Serri, the **Santuario Santa Vittoria** (☎ 388 049 24 51; adult/child €4/2, incl Nuraghe Arrubiu & Prano Mutteddu €9; ❧ 9am-7pm summer, to 5pm winter) is one of the most important nuraghic settlements in Sardinia. At the end of a scenic road – on one side you look over the Giara di Gesturi, on the other the land rises up towards the Gennargentu – the site was first studied in 1907 and later excavated in the 1960s. Still, only four of about 22 hectares have been fully uncovered.

What you see today is divided roughly into three zones. The central area, the **Recinto delle Riunioni** (Meeting Area), is a unique enclave thought to have been the seat of civil power. A grand oval space is ringed by a wall within which are towers and various rooms.

Beyond it is the religious area, which includes a **Tempietto a Pozzo** (Well Temple), a second temple, a structure thought to have been the **Capanna del Sacerdote** (Priest's Hut), defensive trenches, and a much later addition, the **Chiesa di Santa Vittoria**, a little country church after which the whole site is now named. Separated from both areas is the **Casa del Capo** (Chief's House), so-called perhaps because it is the most intact habitation, with walls still up to 3m high. Finally,

a separate area, made up of several circular dwellings, is thought to have been the main residential quarter.

Nuraghe Arrubiu

Rising out of the Sarcidano plain, about 10km south of Orroli, is the **Nuraghe Arrubiu** (adult/child €4/3, incl Santuario Santa Vittoria & Prano Mutteddu €9; ❧ 9am-1pm & 3-8.30pm daily Mar-Oct, to 5pm Nov-Feb), which takes its Sardinian name (meaning red) from the curious colour lent it by the trachyte stone. It is an impressive structure, centred on a robust tower, now about 16m high, which is thought to have reached 30m. Surrounding this is a five-tower defensive perimeter and, beyond that, the remains of an outer wall and settlement. The artefacts found on the site indicate that the Romans made good use of it.

Pranu Mutteddu

Near the village of Goni, **Pranu Mutteddu** (☎ 0782 84 72 69; admission €4/2, incl Nuraghe Arrubiu & Santuario Santa Vittoria €9; ❧ 9.30am-8.30pm summer, 9am-1pm & 2-6pm winter) is a unique funerary site dating to the neolithic Ozieri culture (between the 3rd and 4th millennia BC). The site is dominated by a series of *domus de janas* (literally 'fairy houses'; tombs cut into rock) and some 50 menhirs, 20 of them lined up east to west, presumably in symbolic reflection of the sun's trajectory. The scene is reminiscent of similar sites in Corsica and is quite unique in Sardinia.

To get here from the Nuraghe Arrubiu, follow the road south 11.5km to Escalaplano and from there 8km towards Ballao. Take the first turn west to Goni, which you hit after 9km. A few kilometres further on and you reach the site, just north of the road.

GOLFO DI OROSEI

This spectacular gulf forms the seaward section of the Parco Nazionale del Golfo di Orosei e del Gennargentu. Here the high mountains of the Gennargentu abruptly meet the sea, forming a crescent of dramatic cliffs riven by false inlets and lapped by crystalline waters. The area gets busy in high summer when Italian tourists flock to the secluded beaches, but there's enough room for everyone, especially in the rugged, elemental hinterland.

OROSEI

pop 6385

The main town on the gulf, Orosei sits at the gulf's northernmost point, amidst fruit orchards and marble quarries. A prosperous little place with a pretty historic centre, it was once an important Pisan port. However, the subsequent silting of the Rio Cedrino (Cedrino River), combined with Spanish neglect, malaria and pirate raids, ushered in a cycle of poverty, only recently broken by the arrival of tourism.

Once in town, follow signs for the *centro* to wind up in **Piazza del Popolo**, where you'll find the local **tourist office** (☎ 0784 99 83 67; Piazza del Popolo 13; ☯ 10am-12.30pm).

Overlooking the pretty tree-lined piazza is the **Cattedrale di San Giacomo**, a Spanish-style church with a blank neoclassical facade and a series of tiled domes. Across the square, the baroque yellow **Chiesa del Rosario** wouldn't look out of place in a spaghetti western. The lane leading up from its left-hand side takes you to Piazza Sas Animas and the **church** of the same name, a pleasant stone building with a vaguely Iberian feel about it. Opposite rises the empty hulk of the **Prigione Vecchia**, also known as the Castello, a tower left over from a medieval castle.

On the fringes of the historic centre, the **Chiesa di Sant'Antonio** dates largely from the 15th century, although it has been much altered over the centuries. The broad, uneven courtyard surrounding the church is lined with squat *cumbessias* and has a solitary Pisan watchtower.

Of Orosei's sleeping options, the best is **Su Barchile** (☎ 0784 9 88 79; www.subarchile.it; Via Mannu 5; s €50-80, d €80-120, half board per person €50-120; ☒), which is squeezed into a former dairy. Rooms differ, but the overall look is rural with rustic trappings and classic island fabrics. Downstairs, the restaurant (meals €40) has a good local reputation, specialising in traditional Sardinian fare.

Another good eating option is **La Taverna** (☎ 0784 99 83 30; Piazza G Marconi 6; meals €25-30; May-Oct), where you can sit down to seafood and earthy meats on a pleasant leafy square (just off Piazza Sas Animas). There are sometimes a few rooms to rent as well – it's worth a try.

Several daily buses run to Orosei from Nuoro (€3, about one hour, five daily services Monday to Saturday, three services

Sunday) and Dorgali (€1.50, 25 minutes, two Monday to Saturday, one Sunday).

Marina di Orosei

Orosei's beachfront satellite is 2.5km east of the town proper. The beach marks the northern end of the gulf, which from here you can see arched in all its magnificence to the south. A broad sandy strip runs 5km south and undergoes several name changes along the way: **Spiaggia Su Barone**, **Spiaggia Isporoddai** and **Spiaggia Osalla**. All are equally tempting and are mostly backed by pine stands, giving you the option of retreating to the shade for a picnic or even a barbecue (facilities are scattered about the pines).

Narrow roads run from Orosei and Marina di Orosei along the coast, giving you several access points along the way. The Marina di Orosei beach is closed off to the north by the Rio Cedrino and behind the beaches stretch the **Stagni di Cedrino** lagoons.

Past a big breakwater you can wander from Spiaggia Osalla around to **Caletta di Osalla**, the second stretch of sand after the main beach.

AROUND OROSEI
Galtelli

pop 2452

On the face of it, this nondescript one-horse town 8.5km inland from Orosei holds little of interest. However, stop a while and you'll discover a small but wonderfully pristine historic centre.

Information is available from the **tourist office** (☎ 0784 9 01 50; www.galtelli.com; Via Sassari 12; ☯ 9am-noon & 4-7pm Jun-Sep, 9am-1pm Tue-Sun Oct-May) up in the old town.

The town's main claim to fame is its mention in Grazia Deledda's most famous novel *Canne al Vento* (Reeds in the Wind). The tourist office can advise on Grazia Deledda itineraries which take in the **Chiesa di San Pietro**, a Romanesque-Pisan church near the town cemetery, and the 17th-century **Casa delle Dame Pintor**, the fictional home of the Nieddu sisters.

Housed in an 18th-century noble villa, the **Museo Etnografico Sa Domo 'e sos Marras** (☎ 0784 9 04 72; Via Garibaldi 12; admission €3; ☯ 9.30am-12.30pm & 4.30-7.30pm Tue-Sun) contains a fascinating collection of rural paraphernalia. There's a loom made out of juniper wood, a donkey-drawn millstone and a small display of children's toys. Upstairs, rooms have been decorated in their original 18th-century style.

Also up in the old town is the **our pick** **Antico Borgo** (☎ 0784 9 06 80; www.borgodigaltelli.it; Via Sassari; per person €30-40; ❄). Hidden behind a discreet entrance, this tranquil hotel has tasteful rooms set round a central courtyard and decked out with wooden ceilings, brick floors and wrought-iron beds. If there's no one around when you arrive, ask at **Il Ritrovo Restaurant** (☎ 0784 9 06 80; Via Nazionale), which is run by the same family.

Up to five daily buses connect Galtellì and Orosei (€1, 10 minutes).

DORGALI
pop 8380

Set amidst vineyards and olive groves on the slopes of Monte Bardia, Dorgali is a typical Sardinian mountain town. It's a dusty, bustling place that, while of little interest in itself, makes an excellent base for exploring the surrounding countryside. It's within easy reach of the Supramonte, Cala Gonone and the Gola Su Gorruppu, all of which can be explored independently or on a guided tour.

Information
The local **tourist office** (☎ 0784 9 62 43; www .dorgali.it, in Italian; Via Lamarmora 108/b; ❄ 9am-1pm & 3.30-7.30pm Mon-Fri, also Sat in Jul & Aug) can provide information on Dorgali and Cala Gonone, including contact details for local trekking outfits and accommodation lists.

You can get cash at the **Banca di Sassari** (Corso Umberto 48). If you need a good hiking map try at the **Cartolibreria La Scolastica** (Via Lamarmora 75).

Sights & Activities
In town, you can peruse the shops selling local craftwork – Dorgali is famous for its leather goods, ceramics, carpets and filigree jewellery – and examine a modest collection of archaeological finds at the **Museo Archeologico** (☎ 349 442 55 52; Via Vittorio Emanuele; adult/child €3/1.50; ❄ 9am-1pm & 4-7pm Jun-Aug, 9.30am-1pm & 3.30-6pm Sep-Oct, 9.30am-1pm & 2-4.30pm Nov-Dec, 9am-1pm & 3.30-6pm Jan-May). Once you've done that you've pretty much exhausted Dorgali's opportunities and can turn your attention to the area's great granite wilderness.

There are several outfits in Dorgali that organise 4WD excursions, hikes and caving expeditions. These include **Atlantikà** (☎ 328 972 97 19; www.atlantika.it; Via Lamarmora 195), a consortium of local guides offering everything from hiking day trips to canyoning and kayaking in the Gennargentu. A similar set up, the **Cooperative Ghivine** (☎ /fax 0784 9 67 21, 349 442 55 52; www.ghivine .com; Via Lamarmora 69/e) organises a huge range of expeditions, including a four-hour hike through the Gola Su Gorruppu (€35 per person) and a 3½-hour trek up to the prehistoric village of Tiscali (€40 per person).

Sleeping & Eating
If you have no luck finding accommodation in Dorgali, try contacting **Cala 'e Luna Bookings** (☎ 346 235 63 46; www.calaeluna.com; Via Lamarmora 4), a local accommodation booking service.

Hotel S'Adde (☎ 0784 9 44 12; hotelsadde-sardegna@ libero.it; Via Concordia 38; s €40-70, d €70-110, half board per person €60-80; P ❄) A short, signposted walk up from the main thoroughfare, this is a pink Alpine-chalet affair. Rooms are pine-clad with terraces and green views, and the owners are a welcoming bunch. The restaurant-pizzeria (meals €25 to €30) opens onto a 1st-floor terrace. Breakfast costs an extra €5.

Hotel Il Querceto (☎ 0784 9 65 09; www.ilquerceto .com; Via Lamarmora 4; s €40-100, d €50-190, half board per person €50-130; P ❄ ❅) An eco-friendly hotel using solar and geothermal energy, Il Querceto boasts nicely low-key rooms with lashings of cream linen and honey-coloured tiles. It's slightly out of town (just beyond the southwestern entrance), but the pools and garden should make up for any inconvenience. Breakfast is €7 extra.

Ristorante Colibrì (☎ 0784 9 60 54; Via Gramsci 14; meals around €30; ❄ Mon-Sat) Tucked away in an incongruous residential area (follow the numerous signs), this is the real McCoy for meat eaters with dishes like *cinghiale al rosmarino* (wild boar with rosemary) and *porceddu*. The pasta is also excellent, which is more than can be said for the drab decor.

Getting There & Away

ARST buses serve Nuoro (€3, 50 minutes, eight Monday to Saturday, four Sunday) and Olbia (€6.50, two hours 50 minutes, two Monday to Saturday, one Sunday). Up to seven (four on Sundays) shuttle back and forth between Dorgali and Cala Gonone (€1, 20 minutes). You can pick up buses at several stops along Via Lamarmora. Buy tickets at the bar at the junction of Via Lamarmora and Corso Umberto.

NORTH OF DORGALI
Grotta di Ispinigoli

A short drive north of Dorgali, the **Grotta di Ispinigoli** (adult/child €7.50/3.50; ☻ tours on the hr 9am-1pm & 3-7pm Aug, to 6pm Jul & Sep, 9am-noon & 3-5pm 5pm Mar-Jun, 10am-noon & 3-4pm Nov-Dec, 10am-noon Jan-Feb) is home to the world's second-tallest stalagmite (the highest is in Mexico and stands at 40m).

Unlike most caves of this type, which you enter from the side, here you descend 60m inside a giant 'well', at whose centre stands the magnificent 38m-high stalagmite.

Exploration of the caves began in earnest in the 1960s. In all, a deep network of 15km of caves with eight subterranean rivers has been found. Cavers can book tours of up to 8km through one of the various tour organisers in Dorgali or Cala Gonone. *Nuraghe* artefacts were discovered on the floor of the main well, and Phoenician jewellery on the floor of the second main 'well', another 40m below. On the standard tour you can just peer into the hole that leads into this second cavity, known also as the **Abbisso delle Vergini** (Abyss of the Virgins). The ancient jewellery found has led some to believe that the Phoenicians launched young girls into the pit in rites of human sacrifice.

If you want to hole up for the night, the **Hotel Ispinigoli** (☎ 0784 9 52 68; www.hotelispinigoli .com; s/d €72/98, half board per person €67) has warm, rustic rooms just below the entrance to the cave. Its restaurant is also well-known locally, specialising in earthy local food. You can eat à la carte or choose from a series of set menus (€25 to €37); there's even a kids' menu for €14.

Serra Orrios & S'Ena 'e Thomes

Eleven kilometres northwest of Dorgali (and 3km off the Dorgali–Oliena road) you'll find the ruins of **Serra Orrios** (adult/child €6/2.50; ☻ hourly tours 9am-noon year-round & 4-6pm Jul-Aug, 3-5pm Apr-Jun & Sep, 2-4pm Oct-Dec & Jan-Mar), a nuraghic village occupied between 1500 and 250 BC. The remains outline a cluster of 70 or so houses grouped around two temples: Tempietto A, thought to be used by visiting pilgrims, and Tempietto B, for the villagers. A third temple has also been discovered, leading experts to surmise that this may have been a significant religious centre. There's a diagram near the entrance, which helps you to understand the site, as the guided tours are in Italian only.

From here you could continue north to see a fine example of a *tomba di gigante* (literally 'giant's tomb'; ancient mass grave). Continue 3km north of the crossroads on the Nuoro–Orosei route and **S'Ena 'e Thomes** (admission free; ☻ dawn-dusk) is signposted to the right. The stone monument (16m long by 7m wide) is dominated by a central, oval-shaped stone stele (standing stone) that closes off an ancient burial chamber.

SOUTH OF DORGALI
Gola Su Gorruppu

The Grand Canyon of Europe, the Gola Su Gorruppu (Gorruppu Gorge) is a spectacular gorge flanked by vertical rock walls of up to 400m in height. There are two main approach routes.

The hardest – although also the most immediately apparent if approaching from the south on the SS125 – is from the Genna 'e Silana pass (difficult to miss, as a hotel and restaurant mark the spot on the eastern side of the SS125 at kilometre 183). The trail is signposted to the east of the road, although this is pretty much the last sign you'll see on this route. If you don't get lost, and it's a real possibility without a guide, you'll reach the gorge after about two hours' hiking. There is nothing to stop you from wandering a little either way along the Rio Fluminedda riverbed, but beyond that you will need harnesses and proper equipment.

The second and much easier route is via the Sa Barva bridge, about 15km from Dorgali. To get to the bridge, exit Dorgali and follow for Cala Gonone, but instead of taking the tunnel down to the sea, continue towards Tortoli. After another kilometre or so, you'll see a sign on the right for the Gola Su Gorruppu and Tiscali. Take this and continue until the asphalt finishes after about 20 minutes. Park here and cross the Sa Barva bridge, after which you'll see the trail for the Gola signposted off to the left. From here it's a two-hour hike down to the mouth of the gorge, beyond which you can go for a further 500m or so until the path is blocked by a series of huge boulders. To go any further you'll need a guide.

Although some people do go it alone, you'll be much safer with a guide. As well as the outfits in Dorgali (see p209), the **Cooperativa Gorropu** (☎ 0782 64 92 82, 333 850 71 57; www.gorropu .com; Via Sa Preda Lada 2, Urzulei) arranges all sorts of excursions. Some of the longer treks also include meals and accommodation.

Tiscali

Hidden in a mountain-top cave deep in the Valle Lanaittu, the nuraghic village of **Tiscali** (admission adult/child €5/2; ☉ 9am-7pm May-Sep, to 5pm Jan-Apr & Oct-Dec) is one of Sardinia's archaeological highlights. Dating to the 6th century BC and populated until Roman times, the village was discovered at the end of the 19th century. At the time it was relatively intact, but since then grave robbers have looted the place, stripping the conical stone and mud huts (originally capped by juniper wood roofs) down to the skeletal remains that you see today.

There are many companies in Oliena, Dorgali and Cala Gonone offering guided tours to Tiscali. Typically these cost from €35 per person and sometimes include lunch. If you want to explore the village independently there are two main routes: one relatively simple, the other much more difficult.

The easy route starts at the Sa Barva bridge, the same start point as the simpler route to the Gola Su Gorruppu (see opposite). The trail is signposted and takes about 1¾ hours.

The harder route, which is not well marked, is outlined here. The start of the walk is near the Hotel Su Gologone, signposted about 7km east of Oliena, just off the Oliena–Dorgali road. Pass the hotel entrance and shortly afterwards turn right as signposted for the Valle di Lanaittu. The road climbs before rounding a rocky shoulder to reveal the valley crowned by imposing limestone peaks. Descend towards the Sa Oche River, and when the road splits in two keep to the left until you reach another fork.

Turn right here and you'll find the **Grotta Sa Oche** (Cave of the Voice), which is named after the water that gurgles in its secret underground caverns. You'll also find the Rifugio Lanaittu here (closed). Three hundred metres north of the *rifugio* (mountain hut) is the five-hectare site of **Sa Sedda 'e Sos Carros** (admission €3; ☉ 9.30am-4.30pm), with the remains of some 150 *nuraghe* huts. The most interesting ruin, however, is the circular **Temple of the Sacred Well**, surrounded by stone spouts that would have fed spring water into a huge central basin.

To continue on to Tiscali, return to the fork and instead of turning right, turn left (southwest) up a steep dirt track. After about 20 minutes of hard climbing you'll come to a boulder with a painted arrow. Here you leave the dirt road and climb uphill to the left (east) into the forest, climbing the very steep slope until you come to the base of a rock face. To your left (north) is an impressive split in the mountain, which you climb into. After another short climb you'll come out of the fissure onto a wide ledge. The end of the ledge is high on the western edge of the enormous *dolina* (sinkhole) where you'll find the village, although you're unable to see it at this point. To enter the *dolina* you need to go round to the east – head north and to the right – where you'll find a passage down through the rocks. It's an eerie sight, jumbled ruins huddled in the twilight of the mountain. The inhabitants of Sa Sedda 'e Sos Carros used it as a hiding place, and its inaccessibility ensured that the Sards were able to hold out here until well into the 2nd century BC.

CALA GONONE

Cala Gonone's growing popularity as a resort has done nothing to diminish its spectacular setting. Backed by the grey peaks of **Monte Tului** (917m), **Monte Bardia** (882m) and **Monte Irveri** (616m), and flanked by imperious cliffs, it is quite magnificent. The village itself, a cluster of hotels, bars, restaurants, is touristy but not overpoweringly so.

Originally a remote fishing village, Cala Gonone tickled the fancy of 1930s Italian aristocrats and well-placed Fascists who rather liked it and used it as a privileged summer meeting place. Tourism didn't kick off until the mid-1950s, when the Grotta del Bue Marino first opened. Today a fleet of boats operates out of the small port, offering excursions to the magical coves and cliffs along the coast.

Information

You can find information at the very helpful **tourist office** (☎ 0784 9 36 96; www.calagonone.com; Viale Bue Marino 1/a; ☺ 9am-1pm & 3-5pm, longer opening in summer) in the small park off to the right as you enter town.

There's an ATM down at the port, and you can check your email at **Internet point** (Piazza Da Verrazzano 3; per hr €5; ☺ 8.30-12.30pm & 4-7.30pm Mon-Sat).

Sights & Activities

Beach lovers will be spoilt for choice along Cala Gonone's coast. **Spiaggia Centrale**, the small beach in town, is good for a quick dip, but the best beaches are further south. Further along the waterfront, **Spiaggia Palmasera** is a sequence of extremely narrow patches of sand interrupted by rocky stretches. For something better, walk 1km south to **Spiaggia Sos Dorroles**, backed by a striking yellow-orange rock wall. **Cala Fuili**, about 3.5km south of town (follow Via Bue Marino), is a small, rocky inlet backed by a deep green valley. From here you can hike over the cliff tops to the stunning **Cala Luna**, about two hours' (4km) away on foot.

To the north of town, **Cala Cartoe** is another excellent beach, a silky strip of fine white sand sandwiched between emerald waters and dense woodland. It gets predictably busy in August, but visit out of season and it will probably be all yours. To get there, and you'll need a car, take Via Marco Polo from behind the port and follow it to a T-junction; the cove is signposted to the right (north).

To get an eagle's-eye view over the whole coast, take the short detour up to the **Nuraghe Mannu** (adult/child €3/1.50; ☺ guided tours on the hr 9-11am & 5-7pm Jul & Aug, 9-11am & 4-6pm May, Jun & Sep, 9-11am & 3-5pm Apr, 10am-noon & 3-5pm Mar & Oct), signposted off the Cala Gonone–Dorgali road. After 3km the rocky track peters out at a wild headland where you can see nearly the entire curve of the gulf. The *nuraghe* itself is a modest ruin, but its location is terribly romantic, the silver-grey blocks strewn beneath the olive trees.

The best way of exploring the coast is by boat. You can either hire your own or jump on an excursion out of the port – see right for further details.

There's also a whole range of activities for those who have time or money or both; diving, snorkelling, hiking, rock climbing and moun-

tain biking are the most popular. **Argonauta** (☎ 0784 9 30 46, 347 530 40 97; www.argonauta.it; Via dei Lecci 10) offers a range of water-based activities, including snorkelling tours (€25, €15 for kids), dives (from €35) and canyoning excursions (€40).

Climbing hot spots include Cala Goloritze (accessible by boat only), Cala Fuili, and the Poltrona rock face above Cala Gonone's tennis courts. For climbing information and assistance contact **Prima Sardegna** (☎ 0784 9 33 67; www.primasardegna.com; Via Lungomare Palmasera 32), which also rents out bikes, scooters and kayaks. Bank on about €20 per day for a mountain bike.

Tours

A huge fleet of boats, from large high-speed dinghies to small cruisers and graceful sailing vessels, is on hand at Cala Gonone to whisk you along the beautiful coastline.

One such, the **Nuovo Consorzio Trasporti Marittimi Calagonone** (☎ 0784 9 33 05; www.calagononecrociere.it) offers a range of tours, including return trips to Cala Luna (€12), Cala Sisine (€18), Cala Mariolu (€26), Cala Gabbiani (€26), and Cala Goloritze (€30). A trip to Cala Luna and the Grotta Bue Marino costs €23, which includes entry to the cave.

Between April and October, **Cielomar** (☎ 0784 92 00 14; cielomar@tiscali.net) runs daylong tours, costing from €35 per person, as well as hiring out *gommone* (motorised dinghies) for €80 to €120 per day, excluding petrol which usually costs an extra €25 or so.

To sail in real style, book a berth on the **Dovesesto** (☎ 0784 9 37 37; www.dovesesto.com), a beautiful 1918 yacht. Daily cruises will set you back €62 to €67 per person, with an optional €35 for lunch. Groups with a minimum of four people can also charter the yacht for weekends and longer cruises. The price depends on the itinerary you agree on when chartering the boat.

Boats operate from March until about November – dates depend a lot on demand. Prices vary according to season with 'very high season' being around 11 to 25 August. You can get information at agencies around town or at the booths at the port.

To explore the rocky hinterland, there are a number of outfits that can help. At the roundabout before you enter Cala Gonone you'll find **Atlantikà** (☎ 328 972 97 19; www.atlantika.it; Localita Iscrittiore), a consortium of local guides. They can arrange excursions to Gola

THE BLUE CRESCENT

If you do nothing else in Sardinia, you should try to make an excursion along the 20km southern stretch of the Golfo di Orosei by boat. Intimidating limestone cliffs plunge headlong into the sea, interrupted periodically by pretty beaches, coves and grottoes. With an ever-changing palette of sand, rocks, pebbles, seashells and crystal-clear water, the unfathomable forces of nature have conspired to create sublime tastes of paradise. The colours are at their best until about 3pm, when the sun starts to drop behind the higher cliffs.

From the port of Cala Gonone you head south to the **Grotta del Bue Marino** (adult/child €8/4, ☑ tours on the hr 9am-noon & 3-5pm Aug, 10am, 11am & 3pm Jul & Sep, 11am & 3pm Mar-Jun & Oct-Nov), the last island refuge of the monk seal, although none have been seen for a long time. The watery gallery is certainly impressive, with shimmering light playing on the strange shapes within the cave. Guided visits take place up to seven times a day. In peak season you may need to book in advance.

The first beach after the cave is **Cala Luna**, a crescent-shaped strand closed off by high cliffs to the south. Thick vegetation covers the mountains that stretch back from the beach. The strand (part sand, part pebble) is lapped by rich turquoise and deep emerald-green waters close in, changing to a deep, dark blue further out.

Cala Sisine is the next beach of any size, also a mix of sand and pebbles and backed by a deep, verdant valley. **Cala Biriola** quickly follows, and then several enchanting spots where you can bob below the soaring cliffs – look out for the patches of celestial blue.

Cala Mariolu is arguably one of the most sublime spots on the coast. Split in two by a cluster of bright limestone rocks, there is virtually no sand here. Don't let the smooth, white pebbles put you off, though. The water that laps these beaches ranges from a kind of transparent white at water's edge through every shade of light and sky blue and on to a deep purplish hue.

The last beachette of the gulf, **Cala Goloritze**, rivals the best. At the southern end bizarre granite figures soar away from the cliffside. Among them is **Monte Caroddi**, a 100m-high pinnacle loved by climbers. Beyond the beach you can proceed in the shadow of the coast's stone walls towards **Capo di Monte Santo**, the cape that marks the end of the gulf.

Su Gorruppu (€35) and Tiscali (€35), as well as any number of canoeing, biking, caving, diving and canyoning activities. Another reliable operator is **Dolmen** (☎ 0784 9 32 60; www.sardegnadascoprire.it; Via Vasco da Gama 18) which runs 4WD tours into the Supramonte, and has bikes, scooters and dinghies for hire.

Sleeping

Cala Gonone is well served with hotels. Still, in July and August you will need to book ahead.

Camping Cala Gonone (☎ 0784 9 31 65; www.campingcalagonone.it; per person incl car & tent €15-19, 2-bed bungalow €48-103; ☑ Apr-Oct; ☑) By the entrance to town on the main road from Dorgali, this shady campsite has excellent facilities including a tennis court, barbecue area, pizzeria and swimming pool. Book ahead for August.

ourpick Agriturismo Nuraghe Mannu (☎ 0784 9 32 64; www.agriturismonuraghemannu.com; off the SP 26 Dorgali-Cala Gonone road; d €48-80, half board per person €40-48) Immersed in greenery and with blissful sea views, this is the real McCoy, an authentic working farm with four simple rooms and a restaurant open to all. The fixed €23 menu is a feast of home-produced cheese, salami, pork, lamb, and wine. Bookings are essential. There are also five tent pitches available for €8 to €10 per person.

Pop Hotel (☎ 0784 9 31 85; www.hotelpop.it; s €42-68, d €54-106; ☑) This is a cheerful year-round hotel yards from the port. Rooms are spacious and sunny and the roadside restaurant is a good place to eat. There's a huge menu including a number of interesting fusion dishes. Set menus range from €16-28, otherwise you're looking at around €30 for a meal.

Hotel Cala Luna (☎ 0784 9 31 33; www.hotelcalaluna.com; Lungomare Palmasera 6; s €45-95, d €72-140; ☑ Easter-October; ☑ ☑) A modern hotel in the centre of the village, the Cala Luna offers clean, unfussy rooms ideally suited to hot summer days. The white and pearl-grey colour scheme and the sea views – not all rooms have them – are wonderfully relaxing.

Hotel Costa Dorada (☎ 0784 9 33 32; www.hotelcostadorada.it; Lungomare Palmasera 45; s €73-118, d

€106-186; ✆ Apr-Oct) The best-looking hotel in town, the flower-clad Costa Dorada offers luxurious sea views and tasteful rooms decorated with local handicrafts. It's at the southern end of the *lungomare* (promenade), just over the road from the beach.

Eating

Most hotels offer restaurants, including the Agriturismo Nuraghe Mannu and Pop Hotel as listed above. Otherwise there are plenty of eateries on or near the waterfront. Most of these close over winter and get very busy in summer.

Ristorante Acquarius (☎ 0784 9 34 28; Lungomare Palmasera 34; pizza €6-8, meals around €30; ✆ Apr-Sep) One of a number of restaurants on the *lungomare*, this bustling, laid-back restaurant serves a typical menu of wood-fired pizza, pasta and seafood. Dishes to look out for include *spaghetti al ragu di seppia* (spaghetti with cuttlefish sauce) and *gamberoni e scampi al forno* (roasted prawns and scampi).

Hotel Bue Marino (☎ 0784 92 00 78; www.hotelbuemarino.it; Via Vespucci 8; set menus €18/22, meals around €30) The fashionable seafront bar of this smart hotel attracts a good-looking early evening crowd, and its 4th-floor restaurant dishes up surprisingly unpretentious food at very reasonable prices.

Il Pescatore (☎ 0784 9 31 74; Via Acqua Dolce 7; meals around €35; ✆ Apr-Sep) A bit pricier than average, this serious restaurant is all about fresh fish. And with the sea breeze cooling your tan, the wine on ice and the smell of the sea wafting in on the warm air, it's a pretty good spot for a seafood supper.

Getting There & Away

Buses run to Cala Gonone from Dorgali (€1, 20 minutes, seven Monday to Saturday, four Sunday) and Nuoro (€3, 70 minutes, six Monday to Saturday, three Sunday). Buy tickets at **Bar La Pineta** (Viale C Colombo).

OGLIASTRA

Wedged in between the much larger provinces of Nuoro and Cagliari, Ogliastra boasts some of the island's most spectacular scenery. Inland, it's a dramatic, vertical land of vast, unspoilt valleys, silent woods and windswept rock faces, while the coastal stretches

become increasingly dramatic the nearer you get to the Golfo di Orosei.

There are various approaches to the province, the most obvious being a ferry to the port of Arbatax, near the provincial capital of Tortoli. If approaching from the north, the SS125 wends its way south from Dorgali through the mountainous terrain of the Parco Nazionale del Golfo di Orosei e del Gennargentu. The 18km stretch south to the **Genna 'e Silana** pass (1017m) is the most breathtaking. To the west your eyes sweep across a broad valley to a high chain of mountains, including the 1063m **Monte Oddeu** and, behind it, the impressive Supramonte.

Getting round the area is fairly slow, particularly inland. Distances are not great, but the mountainous landscape means roads are steep and often very twisty. You can get round the area by bus, but you'd really be advised to hire a car if you want to get to the more out-of-the-way corners.

TORTOLI & ARBATAX
pop 10,310

Your impressions of Tortoli, Ogliastra's bustling provincial capital, depend on where you've arrived from. If you've just disembarked from the mainland you might be disappointed with the town's mundane, modern appearance. If, however, you've just emerged from the heavy silences of the interior you might find the cheery souvenir shops and large roadside hotels a welcome change.

Ferries from Cagliari arrive at Arbatax port, and you can also arrange boat tours up the coast to the Golfo di Orosei from here. In summer you can catch the *trenino verde* from the station in Arbatax.

Orientation & Information

Tortoli is the main town while Arbatax, about 4km away down Viale Monsignor Virgilio, is little more than a port fronted by a few bars and restaurants. Local buses 1 and 2 run from Arbatax to Tortoli and, in the case of the latter service, to the beach and hotels at nearby Porto Frailis.

At the time of writing the tourist office in Tortoli was closed indefinitely. At Arbatax you can get information from a summer-only **tourist office** (☎ 0782 66 76 90; Via Lungomare 21) by the *trenino verde* terminus.

In Tortoli, there are various banks with ATMs, including the **Banca di Sassari** (Via Monsignor

Virgilio 54) on the main strip. **Frailis Viaggi** (☎ 0782 62 00 21; www.frailisviaggi.it; Via Roma 12, Tortoli, ⊙ 9am-1pm & 4.30-8pm Mon-Fri) is a useful travel agency where you can book ferry and plane tickets, as well as organise boat excursions (€50 per person) and hire a car (€70 per day).

Sights & Activities

Tortoli and Arbatax are resort towns and have no real sights in themselves. If you have a moment in Arbatax, head across the road from the port and behind the petrol station to the **rocce rosse** (red rocks). These bizarre, weather-beaten rock formations dropping into the sea are well worth a camera shot or two. In the distance your gaze is attracted by the imperious cliffs of the southern Ogliastra and Golfo di Orosei.

At the port you can arrange **boat excursions** up the coast to the beaches and grottoes of the Golfo di Orosei. Costs vary but are typically around €40 to €50 per person.

Near the port, you'll find the terminus for the **trenino verde**, the summer tourist train to Mandas. The route between Arbatax and Mandas is the most scenic on the island, taking an exhausting five hours to chug along a gravity-defying track through some of Sardinia's least accessible mountain terrain. It stops at a multitude of towns in between, making it impossible to do the return journey in one day. Tickets (one-way €17) are available from the Arbatax tourist office. Departures are twice daily (7.50am and 2.35pm) between mid-June and mid-September.

Other than that you can head out to the beaches on either side of Arbatax. You'll find the better beaches of **Spiaggia Orri**, **Spiaggia Musculedda** and **Spiaggia Is Scogliu Arrubius** about 4km south of Porto Frailis (the location of a number of hotels). If you're really determined you can continue even further south to the near-pristine beach of **Spiaggia Cala Francese** at Marina di Gairo.

The province of Ogliastra produces some of Sardinia's finest red wine, namely the ruby-red Cannonau from Jerzu (p217). You can stock up at the **L'Enoteca del Cannonau** (☎ 0782 62 60 27; Via Monsignor Virgilio 74; ⊙ 9am-1.30pm & 3.30-8pm daily), in Tortoli.

Sleeping & Eating

There's no shortage of accommodation around these parts, although most tend to be big resort-style hotels. For beachside accommodation, head for Porto Frailis, near Arbatax.

Hotel Splendour (☎ 0782 62 30 37; www.hotelsplendor.com; Viale Arbatax; s €35-50, d €50-70; **P**) Halfway between Tortoli and Arbatax, this is a welcoming two-star decorated with colourful oil paintings and family knick-knacks. Rooms are small and unpretentious but do offer balconies overlooking a jolly back garden.

La Bitta (☎ 0782 66 70 80; www.hotellabitta.it; Localita Porto Frailis; s €60-190, d €93-290; **P** 🍴 🖥 🏊) This big four-star resort hotel is right on the beach in Porto Frailis. It's a luxurious affair with palatial vaulted rooms (sea views cost extra), a seafront pool, and a fine restaurant (closed between November and mid-February; meals €55) serving excellent seafood.

Star 2 (☎ 0782 66 75 03; Via Lungomare, Arbatax; pizzas €6, meals around €25) Near the port in Arbatax, Star 2 is a bustling, laid-back pizzeria-cum-restaurant. The menu caters to most tastes with a selection of pizzas, pastas and mains, but it's the tasty wood-fired pizzas that stand out. If possible go for one of the outdoor tables on the terrace.

Getting There & Away

AIR

The tiny Arbatax–Tortoli **airstrip** (☎ 0782 62 43 00; www.aeroportotortoliarbatax.it, in Italian) is about 1.5km south of Tortoli. It's served by summer-only charter flights from mainland Italian destinations including Rome and Albenga in Liguria. Most arrivals come on a package with transport arranged.

BOAT

Tirrenia (☎ 892 123; www.tirrenia.it) is the main ferry company serving Arbatax. Ferries sail to/from Genoa (€57, 18 hours, twice weekly), Civitavecchia (€47, 10½ hours, twice weekly) and, from late July to August, Fiumicino (€60, 4½ hours, twice weekly). There are also connections with Cagliari (€33, 5¼ hours, twice weekly) and Olbia (€31.50, 4½ hours, twice weekly). Get tickets and information from Tirrenia's ticket agency, **Torchiani & Co** (☎ 0782 66 78 41; Via Venezia 10) at the port.

BUS

ARST buses connect Tortoli with Santa Maria Navarrese (€1, 15 minutes, 11 daily Monday to Saturday, two Sunday), Dorgali (€4.50, one hour 50 minutes, one daily Monday to

Saturday), and Nuoro (€5.50, 2½ to three hours, four daily Monday to Saturday), as well as many inland villages.

TRAIN

The **trenino verde** (☎ 800 460 220; www.treninoverde .com, in Italian) runs between Arbatax and Mandas (€17, five hours) twice daily between mid-June and mid-September. Stops include Lanusei, Arzana, Ussassai and Seui.

NORTH OF TORTOLI & ARBATAX
Lotzorai
pop 2150

About 6km north of Tortoli, Lotzorai is not of enormous interest in itself but it sits behind some glorious pine-backed beaches, such as **Spiaggia delle Rose**. To find the beach, follow the signs to the three camping grounds that are clustered just behind it.

If you fancy a bite to eat in Lotzorai, make for **L'Isolotto** (☎ 0782 6 69 43; Via Ariosto 4; meals around €30; ⏲ Tue-Sun), down a side street off Via Dante. It might look pretty unprepossessing, but the home-made pasta and fresh fish make for a fine lunch.

Santa Maria Navarrese

At the southern end of the Golfo di Orosei, the unpretentious and attractive small town of Santa Maria Navarrese is a popular beach resort. Shipwrecked Basque sailors built a small church here in 1052, dedicated to Santa Maria di Navarra, on the orders of the Princess of Navarre, who happened to be one of the survivors. The church was built in the shade of a grand olive tree that is still standing – some say it's nearly 2000 years old.

Information

Information on the town and environs is available from the helpful **Tourpass office** (☎ 0782 61 53 30; www.turinforma.it; Piazza Principessa di Navarra 19; ⏲ 9am-1pm & 4-6pm Mon-Sat, extended hours Jun-Aug), hidden behind the Banco di Sardegna in the town centre. It also sells climbing and trekking maps for €3.

Sights & Activities

Lofty pines and eucalyptus trees back the lovely beach lapped by transparent water (with more sandy stretches to the south). Offshore are several islets, including the **Isolotto di Ogliastra**, a giant hunk of pink porphyritic rock rising 47m out of the water. The leafy northern end

of the beach is topped by a watchtower built to look out for raiding Saracens.

About 500m further north is the small pleasure port, where various operators run cruises up the increasingly wild coastline. The **Consorzio Marittimo Ogliastra** (☎ 0782 61 51 73; www.mareogliastra.com) is one such, charging between €30 and €35 per person, for tours that take in seacaves and several stunning swimming spots, such as Cala Goloritze, Cala Mariolu, and Cala Sisine. If you prefer your thrills under the blue stuff, **Nautica Centro Sub** (☎ 0782 61 55 22; www.nauticasub.com) organises dives, costing from €35, to some wonderful underwater spots (see the boxed text, p213).

Sleeping & Eating

our pick **Ostello Bellavista** (☎ 0782 61 40 39; www .ostelloinogliastra.com; Via Pedra Longa; s €32-65, d €44-100; ☒) The name says its all – Hostel Beautiful View. This wonderful hostel – in fact, more a hotel than a hostel – offers superb views from its hilltop location. Its plainly decorated rooms, some with balconies (€12 extra), are in a series of buildings rising up the hill, so the higher you go the better the view. The restaurant serves cracking local food at affordable prices (meals around €25).

Hotel Agugliastra (☎ 0782 61 50 05; www.hote laguglastra.it, in Italian; Piazza Principessa di Navarra 27; d €52-100, half board per person €40-77; ⏲ Apr-Oct; ☒) Above a cafe on the central piazza, rooms at this cordial three-star are modern and rather sterile. But the convenient location and panoramic sun terrace more than make up for any shortcomings in decor. A meal in the restaurant will set you back about €25.

You'll find several eateries and a handful of bars dotted about within quick strolling distance of the centre. **Bar L'Olivastro** (☎ 0782 61 55 13; Via Lungomare Montesanto 1) has tables and chairs set up on shady terraces below the weird and wonderful branches of the town's famous olive tree.

Getting There & Around

A handful of ARST buses link Santa Maria Navarrese with Tortoli (€1, 15 minutes, 11 daily Monday to Saturday, two Sunday), Dorgali (€4.50, 1½ hours, two daily), Nuoro (€6.50, 2½ hours, four daily Monday to Saturday, two on Sundays) and Cagliari (€9.50, four hours, four daily Monday to Saturday).

BAUNEI & THE ALTOPIANO DEL GOLGO
pop 3845

Continuing north along the coast, after about 9km you come to the uninspiring shepherd's town of Baunei. There's little reason to stop off here, but what is seriously worth your while is the 10km detour up to the **Altopiano del Golgo**, a strange, other-worldy plateau where goats and donkeys graze in the *macchia* (shrub) and dusty woodland. From the town a signpost sends you up a 2km climb of impossibly steep switchbacks to the plateau. Head north and, after 8km, follow the **Su Sterru** (Il Golgo) sign (for less than 1km), leave your vehicle and head for this remarkable feat of nature – a 270m abyss just 40m wide at its base. Its funnellike opening is now fenced off but, knowing the size of the drop, just peering into the dark opening is enough to bring on the vertigo.

Opposite the turn-off for Su Sterru is a signpost for the **Ristorante Golgo** (☎ 337 81 18 28; Localita Golgo; meals €25-30; ☷ Apr-Sep), a quaint stone restaurant specialising in local spit-roasted meats. It's run by the **Cooperativa Turistica Golgo** (www.golgotrekking.com), which also organises treks in the surrounding area.

Further along, the **Locanda Il Rifugio** (☎ 0782 61 05 99, mobile 368 702 89 80; www.coopgoloritze.com, in Italian; s/d €45/55, half board €100; ☷ Apr-Oct) is a similar outfit, offering hearty food and basic rooms in a converted farmstead. Managed by the **Cooperativa Goloritzè** (www.coopgoloritze .com), the refuge makes an excellent trekking base, organising a number of excursions ranging from trekking and horse riding (€15 per hour) to 4WD jeep trips. Many treks involve a descent from the plateau through dramatic *codula* (canyons), such as the Codula di Luna or the Codula de Sisine, to the beautiful beaches of the Golfo di Orosei. Staff at the refuge also organise guides and logistical support for walkers attempting the infamous Selvaggio Blu, Sardinia's toughest trek – see the boxed text, p139. If you're interested in attempting this uber-trek, make sure to plan well in advance.

Prices for the excursions vary depending on the itinerary – which you can agree on beforehand – and how many people are in the group.

Just beyond the refuge's stables is the late 16th-century **Chiesa di San Pietro**, a humble construction flanked to one side by some even humbler *cumbessias* – rough, largely open stone affairs which are not at all comfortable for the passing pilgrims who traditionally sleep here to celebrate the saint's day.

INLAND OGLIASTRA

Jerzu
pop 3295

Known as the *Citta del Vino* (Wine Town), Jerzu is famous for its Cannonau red wine. The town is set precariously on the side of a vertiginous mountainside, its steeply stacked buildings surrounded by imposing limestone towers, known locally as *tacchi* (heels) and some 800 hectares of vineyards. Each year about 50,000 quintals of grapes are harvested and transformed into two million bottles of wine at the **Antichi Poderi di Jerzu** (☎ 0782 7 00 28; www.jerzuantichipoderi.it; Via Umberto 1; ☷ 8.30am-1pm & 3-6pm Mon-Fri), the town's modern cantina.

Ulassai & Osini
pop 1585

Heading north from Jerzu you're in for some scenic treats as the road licks a tortuous path around the titanic mountains to Ulassai, dwarfed by the rocky pinnacles of Bruncu Pranedda and Bruncu Matzei. Although nothing special in itself, this small village is surrounded by some of Sardinia's most thrilling and impenetrable countryside, a vast natural playground for outdoor enthusiasts with superb rock climbing and trekking. Climbers in particular will have a high time of it. The sheer rock faces of the Bruncu Pranedda canyon provide 45 routes, including a number of pretty tough ascents. Experts will find further challenges on the Lecori cliffs, where there are an additional 34 recognised climbs. Trekkers can walk the canyon or head 7km southwest to view the dramatic waterfall **Cascata Lequarci** before picnicking in the idyllic environs of the **Santuario di Santa Barbara**. The www.ulassai.net site is a useful resource.

High above the village, the huge **Grotta di Su Marmuri** (☎ 0782 7 98 59; admission €7; tours ☷ 11am, 1pm, 3pm, 5pm & 6.30pm Aug, 11am, 2pm, 4pm & 6pm May, Jun, Jul & Sep, 11am, 2.30pm & 5pm Apr, 11am & 2.30pm Oct) is a 40m-high cave complex. Visits are by guided tour only (minimum of four people are required), which take you on a one-hour, 1km walk through an underground wonderland festooned with stalactites and stalagmites. By the car park at the cave ticket office is a fine trattoria, the **Su Bullicciu** (☎ 0782 7 98 59) where you can

NUORO & THE EAST

lunch on delicious roast meats for about €20 per person.

A short way to the north, and accessible from the village of Osini, is the **Scala di San Giorgio**. This vertical gully takes its name from the 12th-century saint who is said to have divided the rock as he walked through the area proselytising in 1117. From the top you get vast views over the valley to the abandoned villages of Osini Vecchio and Gairo Vecchio, both destroyed by landslides in 1951.

Also worth visiting are the extensive ruins of the **Complesso Nuragico di Serbissi**, a complex site with an unusual underground cave once used to store foodstuffs.

You can explore the area on your own, but with a guide you'll learn far more. Operating out of the nearby village of Osini, **Archeo Taccu** (☎ 329 764 33 43; Via Eleonora D'Arborea, Osini) is a small local cooperative running guided tours.

Before you leave, take a moment to head up to the **Su Marmuri Cooperative Tessile Artigiana** (☎ 0782 7 90 76; Via Dante; ⊗ 8am-7pm daily Jul-Sep, 8am-noon & 2-6pm Mon-Fri Oct-Jun) where a group of dedicated ladies is keeping alive traditional hand-looming techniques. Here you can see the noisy looms in action and browse a selection of towels, curtains and bedspreads bearing designs by local artist Maria Lai. Prices start at around €20 for a hand towel.

Accommodation in the village is provided by the irrepressible Tonino Lai and his wife at the **Hotel Su Marmuri** (☎ 0782 7 90 03; Corso Vittorio Emanuele 20; s/d €30/60). A well-known village institution, it offers simple, neat rooms and stupendous views. Tonino can offer you all the advice you need about the surrounding area, and delights in showing visitors its hidden corners.

Directory

CONTENTS

ACCOMMODATION

First the bad news: accommodation in Sardinia can be hideously expensive. The Costa Smeralda and Santa Margherita di Pula resorts have such a constellation of star ratings and sky-high prices that unless you're a Russian oligarch you probably can't afford to stay there. In summer, at least.

Now the good news: Sardinia has plenty of good-value accommodation. There are many reasonably priced resorts, as well as a range of modest hotels and a growing number of B&Bs. Inland, you'll find *agriturismi* (farm-stay accommodation) dotted around the island, many of which offer real value for money.

As a general rule, accommodation gets cheaper the further you are from the sea, so staying even as little as 5km inland can often represent a saving. You will also be pleasantly surprised by the drop in rates outside of the July and August high season and the Easter peak – in some cases by as much as half.

In this book accommodation is divided into budget (under €80 for a high season double), midrange (€80 to €140) and top end (€140 and up). All rooms have private bathrooms unless otherwise stated. During the high, high season (August, or part of August) many places only offer half board (room, breakfast and dinner) and in this case we have listed low- and high-season prices per person. Otherwise we have quoted minimum and maximum high-season rates. Unless otherwise stated, breakfast is also included.

It is essential to book in advance during peak periods (mid-June to the end of August). Prices rise 5% to 10% annually and drop between 30% and 40% in low season.

In winter (November to Easter) many places, particularly on the coast, almost completely shut down. In the cities and larger towns, accommodation tends to remain open all year. The relative lack of visitors to the island in these down periods means you should have little trouble getting a room in the places that stay open.

Unlike in the rest of Italy, you will seldom be asked for a letter or fax to confirm a reservation in a regular hotel. For popular resort hotels, however, you will need to confirm your booking by fax or email. In many cases you'll also be required to leave a credit card number or pay a deposit.

Sardegna Turismo (www.sardegnaturismo.it) has accommodation listings for the whole island.

BOOK YOUR STAY ONLINE

For more accommodation reviews and recommendations by Lonely Planet authors, check out the online booking service at www.lonelyplanet.com/hotels. You'll find the true, insider lowdown on the best places to stay. Reviews are thorough and independent. Best of all, you can book online.

Agriturismi & B&Bs

Staying at an *agriturismo* (farm stay) is an excellent way of experiencing the Sardinian countryside. Traditionally, an *agriturismo* was a working farm with one or two guest rooms and although some still are (by Sardinian regional law an *agriturismo* must produce most of the food it serves), many have developed into more sophisticated rural retreats. In general, *agriturismi* are ideal for families with small kids (most have plenty of garden space), gourmets (many offer lunch and/or dinner) and those wishing to get off the beaten path (many *agriturismi* are immersed in greenery at the end of long dirt tracks). The only catch is that you'll almost certainly need your own wheels to get to them.

Useful websites include www.agriturismo disardegna.it, which has lists and up-to-date prices; www.sardiniapoint.it; tuttoagritur ismo.net; and www.sardegnaturismo.it.

Another popular option, especially in Cagliari, Sassari and Alghero, is bed and breakfast. Like the country *agriturismi,* B&Bs often offer good value for money, particularly when compared with the prices of local hotels. There is no island-wide umbrella group for these, but tourist offices can usually provide contact details. In Cagliari, **Domus Karalitanae** (www.domuskaralitanae.it) offers a comprehensive listing of the city's B&Bs. Online listings are available at www.bed-and-breakfast.it.

On average, budget for about €25 to €40 per person per night in a B&B.

Camping

With seaside hotels at a premium and expensive in July and August, camping is a viable alternative – campers are well catered for in Sardinia. Most camping grounds are serious complexes offering tent pitches, bungalows, swimming pools, restaurants and supermarkets.

Prices at even the most basic camping grounds can be surprisingly expensive during peak months and especially in August. Rates range from around €10 to €20 per adult, with additional charges for tent space, parking, showers and electricity. Rates quoted in this book are high-season prices.

At most grounds there is no need to book for a caravan or camping space. If you want a bungalow, treat them like hotel rooms and book in advance for July and August. A two-person bungalow generally works out between €60 and €100 per night.

Most camping grounds operate only in season, which means roughly April to October (in some cases June to September only).

Independent camping is generally not permitted. However, out of the main summer season, and away from the main resorts, you can often get away with overnighting in the country, providing that you keep the noise down and don't light fires. Always get permission from the landowner if you want to camp on private property.

The Touring Club Italiano (TCI) publishes an annual camping guide, *Campeggi e Villaggi*

Turistici (€20), and the Istituto Geografico de Agostini produces the annual *Guida ai Campeggi in Europa,* sold with *Guida ai Campeggi in Italia* (€21). Otherwise, you can get lists of camping grounds from local tourist offices or online at www.campeggi.com, www .camping.it or www.touringclub.it.

Hostels

Ostelli per la gioventù (youth hostels), of which there are only five in Sardinia, are run by the **Italian Youth Hostel Association** (Associazione Italiana Alberghi per la Gioventù; ☎ 06 487 11 52; www .ostellionline.org, www.aighostels.com; Via Cavour 44, Rome), affiliated with **Hostelling International** (HI; www .hihostels.com). You'll need to have an HI card (€18) to stay at these hostels, but if you're only travelling in Sardinia, it's probably not worth becoming a member.

Dorm rates range from €13 to €18, including breakfast. All the hostels also have beds in private rooms, typically costing around €20 per person. A meal usually costs €10.

Hostels usually have a lock-out period between 10am and 3.30pm. Check-in is from 6pm to 10.30pm, although some hostels will allow you a morning check-in before they close for the day (confirm beforehand). It is usually necessary to pay before 9am on the day of your departure, otherwise you could be charged for another night.

Hotels & Guest Houses

There is often no difference between a *pensione* (guest house) and an *albergo* (hotel). However, a *pensione* will generally be of one-to three-star standard and is often a family-run operation, while an *albergo* can be awarded up to five stars. A relatively recent innovation, an *albergo diffuso* is a hotel spread over several refurbished *palazzi* in a town's historic centre.

Quality varies enormously, and the official star system gives only limited clues. One-star hotels/*pensioni* tend to be very basic and usually have only a few rooms with private bathrooms. Standards at two-star places are often only slightly better, but rooms will generally have a private bathroom. At three-star places you can usually assume reasonable standards. Four- and five-star hotels offer facilities such as room service, laundry, parking and internet.

For guaranteed character and comfort look out for the Charme e Relax sign. This Italian association specialises in small to mid-sized hotels, usually in unique buildings (monasteries, castles, old inns and so on) or special locations, and it offers an excellent standard of accommodation combined with professional service.

Hotels in Sardinia are generally unexciting. Until the 1960s there were not too many around, so the chances of staying in a charming old hotel are few and far between. If you're looking for character, try to book an *albergo diffuso,* otherwise most hotels are imaginative modern affairs, whose main appeal is based on position (near the sea) and facilities. Fortunately, though, serious dives are as rare as the glittering jewels.

Tourist offices have booklets listing all local accommodation, including prices.

Rental Accommodation

Finding rental accommodation can be difficult and time-consuming. About the only way to locate *affittacamere* (local rooms for rent) is through tourist offices, although a handful are listed in provincial hotel guides. They are more common in the north than elsewhere.

Tourist offices can provide lists of apartments and villas for rent in popular centres like Santa Teresa di Gallura, Stintino and Alghero. Otherwise, there are hundreds of agencies offering apartment and villa rentals. Reliable operators include the following:

Costa Smeralda Holidays (www.costasmeralda-hol idays.com) Offers upmarket villas on the Costa Smeralda.

Cottages to Castles (www.cottagestocastles.com) Has properties on the Costa Rei.

GULP (www.gulpimmobiliare.it, in Italian) An Italian outfit with properties in the northeast.

Long Travel (www.long-travel.co.uk) For self-catering apartments in the north.

Voyages Ilena (www.voyagesilena.co.uk) Lists 53 properties across the island.

Resorts

Some of the best spots on Sardinia's coastline are dominated by resort-style villages, usually in the four- to five-star category. These places can be huge – the Forte Village on the southwest coast boasts seven hotels on its 25,000-hectare site – and usually include restaurants, pools, shopping malls, sports facilities and, on the Costa Smeralda, marinas.

Prices are as stunning as the facilities. At the Forte Village and Is Morus on the southwest coast and the big Starwood hotels on the

Costa Smeralda, you can easily pay €1500 per night for a standard double room.

Interspersed between these bastions of luxury are other more affordable resorts, particularly around Villasimius on the southeast coast, Cannigione and Baia Sardinia in the northeast, and Pula and Chia on the southwest coast. With all the activities on offer and an impressive array of facilities, they are particularly well suited to families.

ACTIVITIES

Sardinia is a dream island for sports fans. The interior provides superb hiking, biking and climbing while the coast attracts surfers, sailors and scuba divers. For an indepth look at the island's activities, see p137.

BUSINESS HOURS

Shops generally open from 9am to 1pm and 4pm to 8pm Monday to Saturday. In many of the touristy areas, shops tend to stay open later in summer, sometimes till around 11pm. The length of the midday break can range from three hours to as many as five.

In the big towns, most major department stores and some supermarkets are open continuously from 9am (sometimes 10am) to 7.30pm Monday to Saturday. Some also open on Sunday mornings, typically from 9am to 1pm. Food shops are often closed on Thursday afternoons; some other shops remain shut on Monday mornings.

Banks tend to open from 8.30am to 1.30pm and then from 2.45pm to 4.30pm Monday to Friday. Most banks have ATMs that accept foreign credit and debit cards.

Major post offices open from 8am to 6.50pm Monday to Friday, and also from 8am to 1.15pm on Saturday. Smaller post offices generally open from 8.30am to 1.15pm Monday to Friday, and to 11.50am on Saturday. All post offices close at least two hours earlier than normal on the last business day of each month (not including Saturday).

Farmacie (pharmacies) open 9am to 1pm and 4pm to 7.30pm Monday to Friday, and on Saturday morning. Outside of these hours, pharmacies open on a rotation basis. All are required to post a list of places open in the vicinity.

Bars (in the Italian sense; that is, coffee-and-cornetto joints) and cafes generally open from 7.30am to 8pm. Those with a nocturnal vocation open until about 1am during the week and as late as 2am on Friday and Saturday. *Discoteche* (clubs) might open around 10pm (or earlier if there's a restaurant on the premises), but there'll rarely be much action until after midnight. Chucking-out time can be as late as 5am.

Restaurants open from about noon to 3pm and 7.30pm to 11pm, although the kitchen often shuts an hour earlier than final closing time. In summer (June to September) most restaurants open seven days for lunch and dinner. Conversely, many restaurants in coastal resorts close their shutters for several months in the off-season. Those that stay open usually close one day a week.

The opening hours of museums, galleries and archaeological sites vary enormously. As a rule museums close on Monday, but from June to September many are open daily. Outside the high season, hours tend to reduce drastically, and more out-of-the-way sights frequently close altogether. Where winter hours apply, they are usually in force between November and late March/early April.

CHILDREN

Like all Italians, Sardinians adore children and they are welcome just about everywhere. Facilities in coastal resorts are often geared towards families, and kids are well catered to. However, in less touristy area like the major cities and inland in the Gennargentu you will find few special amenities, and travel will require some planning.

Practicalities

Discounts are available for children on public transport and for admission to sights. On trains and ferries children under four generally travel for free although without right to a seat or cabin berth; for children between four and 12, discounts of 50% are usually applied. Sardinian trains are seldom very busy, but in high season it's advisable to book seats. You'll also need to book car seats if you're planning to hire a car.

You can buy baby formula in powder or liquid form, as well as sterilising solutions such as Milton, at *farmacie*. Disposable nappies (diapers) are widely available at *farmacie* and supermarkets, where you'll find a wider selection. Remember that shop opening hours may differ from your home country, so run out of nappies on a Saturday evening and you could be in for a messy Sunday.

Fresh cow's milk is sold in litre and half-litre cartons in supermarkets, *alimentari* (food shops) and in some bars. If it is essential that you have milk, you should carry an emergency carton of *lungo conservazione* (UHT), since most bars close at 8pm.

When planning your trip, Lonely Planet's *Travel with Children* is packed with practical tips, and *Italy with Kids,* published by Open Road, has tons of useful information. The website www.travelwithyourkids.com provides plenty of general advice, although nothing specific to Sardinia. **Tots Too** (www.totstoo.com) is an online agency specialising in upmarket, kid-friendly properties.

Sights & Activities

Successful travel with children usually requires special effort. Don't try to overdo things, and plan activities that include the kids – older children could help you here. Remember also to factor in time for the kids to play; taking a toddler to a playground for an hour or so can make an amazing difference to their tolerance for sightseeing in the afternoon.

On the coast, the beach is always a winner. Sardinia boasts some of the Mediterranean's longest sandy beaches and warm, limpid seas. Older kids wanting to try water sports will find plenty of opportunities, particularly around Porto Pollo (p178) and the family-orientated resorts of Cannigione (p176) and Cala Gonone (p211). As long as seasickness is not a problem, kids will enjoy boat trips along the coast, the most popular of which visit spectacular sea caves such as the Grotta di Nettuno (p161) near Alghero, or the Grotta del Bue Marino (see the boxed text, p213) at Cala Gonone.

Away from the coast, horse riding in the province of Oristano (see p116 and p109) is a good option. Little 'uns might also like a trip on the *trenino verde* (see p72), a tiny tourist train, which chugs through some of Sardinia's most spectacular and inaccessible countryside and towns.

Many resort-style hotels have excellent facilities for children, including kids' clubs and babysitting so you can get out in the evening.

Eating out with Children

Eating out with the kids is pretty stress-free in Sardinia, particularly in the coastal resorts where kids are made to feel very welcome in hotel restaurants. There are few taboos about taking children to restaurants, even if locals with little ones in tow tend to stick to the more popular trattorias – you'll seldom see children in an expensive restaurant. You're unlikely to come across a children's menu, but most places will cheerfully tailor a dish to serve young taste buds and serve a *mezzo porzione* (child's portion). Some restaurants have *seggioloni* (high chairs), although it's best to check in advance.

CLIMATE CHARTS

Sardinia has a mild Mediterranean climate, defined by hot, dry summers followed by mild winters with light rainfall. However, climatic conditions vary across the island. The finest weather is usually found around the coast. The southern and western coasts are hotter due to their exposed aspect and proximity to North Africa. The eastern coast is shielded by

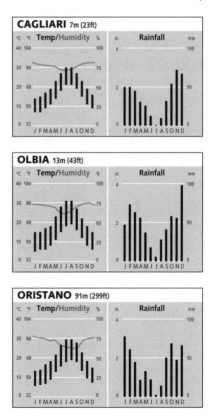

the Gennargentu mountains and the weather there can be changeable.

Sardinia's interior presents a different story. Summer days are dry and hot, although at higher altitudes the air is surprisingly fresh and it's even cold in the evenings. On the highest mountains there is substantial snowfall, usually in January. Rain falls mainly in spring and autumn.

See p13 for information on the best times to visit Sardinia.

CUSTOMS & REGULATIONS

Entering Italy from another EU country you can bring, duty-free: 10L spirits, 90L wine and 800 cigarettes. If you're arriving from a non-EU country the limits are 1L spirits, 2L wine, 50mL perfume, 250mL eau de toilette, 200 cigarettes and other goods up to a total of €175.50; anything over this limit must be declared on arrival and duty paid. On leaving the EU, non-EU citizens can reclaim any value-added tax on expensive purchases (see www.globalrefund.com to learn how). You can bring up to €10,000 cash into Italy.

DANGERS & ANNOYANCES

Despite past notoriety as a centre of banditry and kidnapping, Sardinia is a peaceful island, and you will seldom be subject to the more unsavoury cons or petty crime that are prevalent in many mainland Italian cities. Muggings, moped-assisted bag-snatching and overcharging in hotels are almost unheard of, and your stay should be trouble free.

Theft

Although theft is not a big problem in Sardinia, you should still use your common sense. A money belt with your essentials (passport, cash, credit cards) is a good idea. However, to avoid delving into it in public, carry a wallet with a day's cash. If you're carrying a bag or camera, wear the strap across your body and away from the road. Be careful when you sit down at a streetside table – never drape your bag over an empty chair by the road or put it where you can't see it.

Don't leave valuables lying around your hotel room. And *never* leave valuables visible in your car – in fact, try not to leave anything in the car and certainly not overnight. It's worth paying extra to leave your car in supervised car parks.

In case of theft or loss, always report the incident at the *questura* (municipal police station) within 24 hours and ask for a statement, otherwise your travel insurance company won't pay out. Emergency numbers are listed throughout this book.

Traffic

In July and August traffic on minor roads can be a pain, as can parking. In the bigger towns you'll need to keep a keen eye on what's going on around you, especially when slowing down to check street names or to look for a parking spot. On the whole, though, driving in Sardinia isn't nearly as intimidating as it is in the rest of Italy, and islanders generally observe the road rules. As a pedestrian you'd still be advised to keep your wits about you.

DISCOUNT CARDS
Senior Cards

Senior citizens will find that they are not entitled to many discounts around Sardinia, although admission to some of the sites is reduced for those aged 65 (sometimes 60) and over. To claim the discount, you'll need proof of your age, ideally an ID card or passport.

Student & Youth Cards

Discounts (usually half the normal fee) are available for some sights to EU citizens aged between 18 and 25. As proof of age the **International Student Identity Card** (ISIC; www.isic.org) is not always sufficient as discounts are often based on age, so a passport, driving licence (with photo attached) or **Euro<26** (www.euro26 .org) card is preferable.

An ISIC card does, however, entitle you to various shopping, accommodation and museum discounts in Cagliari, Sassari and Nuoro. Similar cards are available to teachers, the International Teacher Identity Card (ITIC), and to nonstudents under 26, the International Youth Travel Card (IYTC).

Student cards are issued by student unions, hostelling organisations and some youth travel agencies. In Cagliari, the **Centro Turistico Studentesco e Giovanile** (www.cts.it, in Italian) youth travel agency can issue ISIC, ITIC and Euro<26 cards.

EMBASSIES & CONSULATES

It's important to realise what your embassy can and can't do for you. Generally speaking, it won't be much help in emergencies if the trouble you're in is remotely your own fault. Remember that you're bound by the laws of the country you're in. Your embassy will not be sympathetic if you end up in jail after committing a crime locally, even if such actions are legal in your own country.

In genuine emergencies you might get some assistance, but only if other channels have been exhausted. For example, if you need to get home urgently, a free ticket home is exceedingly unlikely as the embassy would expect you to have insurance. If you have all your money and documents stolen, it might assist with getting a new passport, but a loan for onward travel is almost always out of the question. In genuine emergencies, however, your consulate can help in several ways. Most importantly it can (a) issue an emergency passport (b) help get a message to friends or family and (c) offer advice on money transfers. In exceptional circumstances it might provide a loan for a ticket home.

Most countries have an embassy in Rome, and several also maintain an honorary consulate in Cagliari. Passport inquiries should be addressed to the Rome-based offices:

Australia Rome (☎ 06 85 27 21, emergencies 800 87 77 90; www.italy.embassy.gov.au; Via Antonio Bosio 5; ☼ 8.30am-5pm Mon-Fri)

Canada Rome (☎ 06 85 44 41; www.international .gc.ca/canada-europa/italy; Via Salaria 243)

France Rome (☎ 06 68 60 11; www.ambafrance-it.org; Piazza Farnese 67)

Germany Cagliari (Map p58; ☎ 070 30 72 29; Via Rafa Garzia 9); Rome (☎ 06 49 21 31; www.rom.diplo.de; Via San Martino della Battaglia 4; ☼ 8.30-11.30am Mon-Fri)

Ireland Rome (☎ 06 697 91 21; www.ambasciata -irlanda.it; Piazza Campitelli 3; ☼ 10am-12.30pm, 3-4.30pm Mon-Fri)

Netherlands Cagliari (Map p58; ☎ 070 30 38 73; Viale Diaz 76; ☼ 8.30am-1pm Mon-Fri); Rome (☎ 06 322 86 001; www.olanda.it; Via Michele Mercati 8; ☼ 9am-noon Mon, Tue, Thu & Fri)

New Zealand Rome (☎ 06 853 75 01; www.nzembassy .com; Via Clitunno 44; ☼ 8.30am-12.45pm & 1.45-5pm Mon-Fri)

Spain Rome (☎ 06 684 04 01; www.mae.es/embaj adas/roma/es/home; Palazzo Borghese, Largo Fontanella Borghese 19)

UK Cagliari (☎ 070 82 86 28; Viale Colombo 160, Quartu Sant'Elena; ☼ 9am-12.30pm Tue-Thu); Rome (☎ 06 422 00 001; www.britishembassy.gov.uk/italy; Via XX Settembre 80a; ☼ 9am-5pm Mon-Fri)

USA Rome (☎ 06 4 67 41; www.usis.it; Via Vittorio Veneto 119a; ☼ 8.30am-12.30pm Mon-Fri)

FESTIVALS & EVENTS

Sardinians celebrate their traditions with spectacular brio. Grotesque animal costumes, anarchic horse races and passionate parades all feature in the island's festival calendar.

The island's most important festivals predate Christianity and are linked to the farming calendar. However, as elsewhere in the Christian world, these feast days were gradually appropriated by the Church, which simply imposed a Christian saint as the focus of the original pagan ritual.

For a full festival calendar, turn to p17.

FOOD & DRINK

In this book we have used the term 'budget' to describe places where you can get a meal for less than €25. For a full, midrange restaurant meal you should reckon on €25 to €40 per person. The most expensive meals will set you back anything from €40 upwards. A standard meal consists of a *primo piatto*, a *secondo* and a dessert. Within each section, restaurants are listed in budget order.

In touristy areas like the northeast coast, Alghero and the Golfo di Orosei, you may well find places offering three-course tourist menus for around €15. You'll generally save money eating one of these, but you'll usually find the choice limited to one or two pasta options and a couple of main courses. Top-end restaurants also offer fixed menus, which generally include all courses but no wine. These usually hover around €40 to €50 per head.

For more on food and drink in Sardinia see p40. For info on eating out with children, see p223.

Where to Eat & Drink

The most basic sit-down eatery is a *tavola calda* (literally 'hot table'), which offers canteen-style food. Pizzerias, the best of which have a *forno a legna* (wood-fired oven), serve the obvious but often a full menu as well. For takeaway, a *rosticceria* sells cooked meats and a *pizza al taglio*, pizza by the slice. Most bars/cafes serve *brioches* (breakfast pastries), *cornetti* (croissants), *tramezzini* (sandwiches), *panini* (bread rolls with simple fillings), and *spuntini* (snacks), alongside coffees, soft drinks and alcoholic drinks. A cheaper lunch alternative is to go to an *alimentari* (food shop) and ask them to make a *panino* with the filling of your choice. At a *pasticceria* you can buy pastries, cakes and biscuits, and a *gelateria* is the place to go for gelato – a crowd outside usually heralds good things inside.

For a full meal you'll want a trattoria or a *ristorante*. Traditionally, *trattorie* were family-run places that served a basic menu of local dishes at affordable prices and, thankfully, a few still are. *Ristoranti* offer more choice and smarter service.

After a meal, a coffee is traditional, although light sleepers should be wary about drinking a caffeine-charged espresso after a late dinner. The espresso is the standard coffee drink in Sardinia and is what you get if you ask for *un caffè*. *Doppio espresso* is a double shot and a *caffè americano* is a watered-down version. If you prefer your coffee with milk there are various options. A *caffè latte,* regarded by locals as a breakfast drink, is coffee with a reasonable amount of milk. A *caffè macchiato* is an espresso with a dash of milk and a *latte macchiato* is a glass of hot milk with a dash of coffee. The cappuccino is a frothy version of the *caffè latte*. For coffee with a little bite, there's a *corretto,* an espresso 'corrected' with a dash of grappa or some other spirit. Some locals have it as a heart starter.

After lunch and dinner it wouldn't occur to Italians to order a *caffè latte* or cappuccino, although there's absolutely no reason why you shouldn't ask for one if that's what you want.

Tea is not a Sardinian speciality and is usually served with lemon rather than milk. The island's tap water (*acqua naturale* or *acqua dal rubinetto*) is perfectly drinkable. *Acqua minerale* (mineral water) is available *frizzante* (sparkling) or *naturale* (still).

On a restaurant/trattoria bill expect to be charged for *pane e coperto* (bread and a cover charge). This is standard and is added even if you don't ask for or eat the bread. Typically it ranges from €1 to €4. *Servizio* (service charge) of 10% to 15% may or may not be included; if it's not, tourists are expected to round up the bill or leave 10%.

All eating establishments in Sardinia are officially nonsmoking.

Vegetarians & Vegans

Vegetarians will have a tough time of it in Sardinia, a robustly meat-eating island. Vegetarian restaurants are almost unheard of, and even apparently meat-free food such as risotto or soup is often prepared with meat stock. Vegans will find it even harder as so many dishes feature some sort of animal product, be it dairy, eggs or animal stock. The good news is that vegetables are of a universally high standard and appear in many *antipasti* (starters) and *contorni* (side dishes).

GAY & LESBIAN TRAVELLERS

Discretion is the key. Although homosexuality is legal (the age of consent is 16), Sardinia is no Mykonos and attitudes remain largely conservative. There is practically no open gay scene on the island and overt displays of affection could attract unpleasant attention, especially in the rural interior. The only places where attitudes towards homosexuality are really changing are the island's two largest cities, Sassari and Cagliari.

The island's most high-profile gay activist organisation is the Sassari-based **Movimento Omosessuale Sardo** (079 21 90 24; www.movimentomosessualesardo.org, in Italian; Via Rockfeller 16/c). In Cagliari the main organisation is the **Associazione Arc** (Via Leopardi 3). The national gay organisation **Arcigay** (www.arcigay.it/Sardegna) is also a useful point of reference.

Online, www.gayfriendlyitaly.com is an excellent resource with background information on gay life in Italy, links, and listings of gay-friendly B&Bs and beaches in Sardinia.

HOLIDAYS

Most Italians take their annual holiday in August, deserting the cities for the coast or cool mountain resorts. And with Sardinia ranked as one of the Mediterranean's top beach destinations, the island gets pretty busy. Over July and August, hundreds of thousands of Italians and foreigners flock to the island, while city-dwelling Sardinians head out to holiday homes on the coast. As a consequence, many city businesses and shops close for a couple of weeks, typically in the period around Ferragosto (Feast of the Assumption) on 15 August. Settimana Santa (Easter Week) is another busy holiday time for Italians.

Italian schools close for three months in summer, from mid-June to mid-September; for three weeks over Christmas, generally the last two weeks of December and the first of January; and for a week at Easter.

Individual towns have public holidays to celebrate the feasts of their patron saints (see p17). National holidays include the following:

Capodanno (New Year's Day) 1 January
Epifania (Epiphany) 6 January
Pasqua (Easter Sunday) March/April
Pasquetta (Easter Monday) March/April
Giorno della Liberazione (Liberation Day) 25 April
Festa del Lavoro (Labour Day) 1 May
Festa della Repubblica (Republic Day) 2 June
Ferragosto (Feast of the Assumption) 15 August
Ognissanti (All Saints' Day) 1 November
Immacolata Concezione (Feast of the Immaculate
Conception) 8 December
Natale (Christmas Day) 25 December
Festa di Santo Stefano (Boxing Day) 26 December

INSURANCE

Travel insurance to cover theft, loss and medical problems is highly recommended. It may also cover you for cancellation of and delays in your travel arrangements. Paying for your ticket with a credit card can often provide limited travel accident insurance, and you may be able to reclaim the payment if the operator doesn't deliver.

There are hundreds of policies out there, so make sure you get one tailored to your needs. Factors to consider include the following:

- Does the policy have lower and higher medical expense options? If you're from a country with high medical expenses (such as the USA) go for the latter.
- Are 'dangerous activities' (scuba diving, motorcycling and, for some policies, trekking) covered? Some policies might not cover you if you're riding a motorbike with a locally acquired motorcycle licence.
- Does it cover ambulance service or an emergency flight home?

You may prefer a policy that pays doctors or hospitals directly rather than you having to pay on the spot and claim later. If you have to claim later make sure you keep all documentation. (Similarly, if you have to claim for a theft make sure you've got a statement from the local police.) Some medical policies ask you to call (reverse charges) a centre in your home country where an immediate assessment of your problem is made.

Worldwide travel insurance is available at www.lonelyplanet.com/travel_services. You can buy, extend and claim online anytime – even if you're already on the road.

For information on car and motorcycle insurance, see p242.

INTERNET ACCESS

Given that Sardinia's regional governor is the founder of the internet service provider Tiscali, you would expect Sardinia to be better connected. As it is, the easiest way to access the internet is at an internet cafe, which you'll find in all the major holiday centres and dotted sporadically around the island (and listed in this book). You certainly can't rely on finding an internet cafe in small towns and villages. Access is expensive, typically costing around €5 an hour. Note also that whenever you use an internet cafe you're legally obliged to show an ID card or passport.

Many hotels offer internet access, and an increasing number are providing wi-fi.

If you're bringing your own laptop or palmtop, you'll find that many midrange and top-end hotels now have dataports for customer use. But remember that if you have to plug your computer into a power socket you might need a power transformer (to convert from 110V to 220V if your notebook isn't set up for dual voltage), an RJ-11 telephone jack that works with your modem, and a plug adaptor.

Italy's phone companies **Telecom Italia** (www .tim.it, in Italian) and **Wind** (www.wind.it, in Italian) both offer wireless connection packages which allow you to connect through the mobile telephone network. They're not especially cheap though, costing about €25 per month with a 12-month minimum.

LEGAL MATTERS

Unless you have something nicked and need to report it for your insurance claim, you're unlikely to have much to do with the Sardinian police.

The police is divided into three main bodies – the *polizia* who wear navy-blue jackets; the *carabinieri*, in a black uniform with a red stripe; and the grey-clad *guardia di finanza*, responsible for fighting tax evasion and drug smuggling. If you run into trouble you're most likely to end up dealing with the *polizia* or *carabinieri*. That is, unless you're on the receiving end of a parking ticket, in which case you'll be cursing the *vigili urbani*, the local traffic police.

If you are detained, for any alleged offence, you should be given verbal and written notice of the charges laid against you within 24 hours. You have no right to a phone call upon arrest, but you can choose not to respond to questions without the presence of a lawyer.

For serious crimes, it is possible to be held without trial for up to two years.

In February 2006 the Italian parliament approved tough antidrugs laws that abolished the distinction between hard and soft drugs, effectively putting cannabis on the same legal footing as cocaine, heroin and ecstasy. If caught with what the police deem to be a dealable quantity, you risk fines of up to €260,000 or prison sentences of between six and 20 years.

The legal limit for a driver's blood-alcohol reading is 0.05%. Following a spate of road fatalities in 2007, authorities began to stamp down hard on drink-driving. Random roadblocks are not uncommon, and at the time of writing the Italian police were experimenting with drugs tests at roadblocks.

MAPS

The best road maps of Sardinia are produced by Michelin (1:200,000; €7) and the Touring Club Italiano (1:200,000; €7). The Istituto Geografico de Agostini also produces a regional map (1:130,000; €7.50) as do Belletti Editore (1:300,000; €6) and Litografia Artistica Cartografica (1:250,000; €7.50).

The city maps in this book, combined with tourist-office maps, are generally adequate, although you can buy more detailed maps in bookshops in Cagliari, Olbia and Alghero. The best large-scale maps are produced by Litografia Artistica Cartografica, which has maps of Cagliari, Nuoro, Oristano and Sassari. Belletti Editore sells maps of Alghero (1:5000; €6) and the Costa Smeralda & Olbia (1:8000; €6), as does Studio FMB Bologna, which also produces a road map of Nord Sardegna (North Sardinia; 1:170,000; €7).

MONEY

Sardinia's unit of currency is the euro (€), which is divided into 100 cents. Coin denominations are one, two, five, 10, 20 and 50 cents and €1 and €2. The seven euro notes come in denominations of €5, €10, €20, €50, €100, €200 and €500.

Exchange rates are given on the inside front cover of this book. For the latest rates log on to www.oanda.com. See p14 for more on costs.

Money can be exchanged in banks, post offices and exchange offices. Banks generally offer the best rates, but shop around, as rates fluctuate considerably.

ATMs

ATMs (known in Italian as *bancomat*) are widely available in Sardinia and are undoubtedly the simplest (and safest) way to access your money while travelling. Most will accept cards tied into the Visa, MasterCard, Cirrus or Maestro systems. As a precaution, though, check that the appropriate logo is displayed on the ATM before inserting your card. The daily limit for cash withdrawal is €250.

When you withdraw money from an ATM, the amounts are converted and dispensed in euros. However, there will be fees. Typically, you'll be charged a withdrawal fee (usually around 1.5%) as well as a conversion charge; if you're using a credit card you might also be hit by interest on the cash withdrawn.

Note also that you'll need to have a four-digit PIN to be able to use your card in a Sardinian ATM.

Cash

Cash is readily available in ATMs, so there's little point in bringing large quantities with you. That said, it's not a bad idea to bring a small amount to tide you over until you get to an exchange facility or ATM. When travelling the island, you'll need cash for many day-to-day transactions, as credit cards are not always accepted, especially in many B&Bs and cheap trattorias.

Credit & Debit Cards

Carrying plastic is the simplest way to organise your holiday funds. You don't have large amounts of cash to lose, you can get money after hours and the exchange rate is often better.

Major cards such as Visa, MasterCard, Eurocard, Cirrus and Eurocheque are accepted in Sardinia. Check charges with your bank, but most banks now build a fee of around 3% into every foreign transaction, as well as a charge of around 1.5% for ATM withdrawals.

If your card is lost, stolen or swallowed by an ATM, telephone one of the following toll-free numbers to block it:

Amex (☎ 800 914 912)
MasterCard (☎ 800 870 866)
Visa (☎ 800 81 90 14)

Tipping

You're not expected to tip on top of restaurant service charges, but if you think the service warrants it, feel free to round up the bill or leave a little extra – 10% is fine. In bars, Italians often leave small change (€0.10/€0.20) as a tip. Tipping taxi drivers is not common practice, but you should tip the porter at top-end hotels.

Travellers Cheques

Largely outmoded by plastic, travellers cheques are useful as a form of back-up, especially as you can claim a refund if they're stolen (provided that you've kept a separate record of their numbers).

American Express, Visa and Travelex cheques are the most widely available, particularly if in euros. Cashing them outside of the main tourist centres can be tricky, though, as exchange offices are thin on the ground and ever fewer banks are prepared to accept them. Those that do tend to charge hefty commissions, even on cheques denominated in euros. Always take your passport as ID when cashing in travellers cheques.

For lost or stolen cheques, call one of these numbers:

Amex (☎ 800 914 912)
MasterCard (☎ 800 870 866)
Travelex (☎ 800 87 20 50)
Visa (☎ 800 874 155)

POST

Italy's, and by association Sardinia's, postal system **Poste** (☎ 803 160; www.poste.it) is not the world's most efficient, although it has improved in recent years. Unfortunately, Sardinia's distance from the mainland doesn't help matters.

Stamps (*francobolli*) are available at post offices and tobacconists (*tabacchi*) – look for the official sign, a big white 'T' against a black background. Since letters often need to be weighed, what you get at the tobacconist's for international airmail will occasionally be an approximation of the proper rate.

Using the standard *posta prioritaria* service, it costs €0.65 to send a normal 20g letter to a European country (zone 1), €0.85 to the States (zone 2), and €1 to Australia and New Zealand (zone 3). The slightly quicker *posta raccomandata* (registered mail) costs €3.45/3.65/3.80 to the respective zones. To insure your post you'll need *posta assicurato* (insured post). For €18.45 you can insure a letter up to a value of €3000.

SHOPPING

Although Sardinia has a rich craft heritage, shopping on the island isn't terribly exciting. The most interesting craft shops and delis cluster around the tourist resorts, but these can be very expensive.

To be sure of reasonable prices and quality, head for the local Istituto Sardo Organizzazione Lavoro Artigiano (ISOLA) shop. As the official promoter of traditional crafts, it authenticates all the pieces it sells. It has shops in several cities and towns, some of which are indicated in this guide.

Particular regions are known for specific crafts. In the north, around Castelsardo, women still make traditional baskets from asphodel, rush, willow and dwarf palm leaves. Aggius and Tempio Pausania have a strong cottage industry in wool carpets, decorated with traditional geometric designs. Cork is used to make any number of souvenir-style products, especially in the northern Gallura region, and festival masks haunt many shops in the Nuoro area.

Sardinia has a strong history of ceramics, which tend to use simple patterns and colour combinations (often just blue and white, giving the pots a Greek flavour). As most tourists frequent the northwest and northeast of the island, you'll find the better shops along the Costa Smeralda and in towns such as Santa Teresa di Gallura and Alghero.

Both Alghero and Santa Teresa di Gallura also have a long tradition of coral jewellery. The best-quality coral is harvested off Alghero's Riviera del Corallo (Coral Riviera) and is tightly controlled. In many cases coral is combined with exquisite *filigrana* (filigree work), for which the whole island is justifiably famous. If you catch a local festival you will see Sardinian women decked out in some extraordinary pieces. The best places to purchase *filigrana* are Cagliari and Alghero.

A Sardinian man will undoubtedly say that the island's greatest craft is the handmade pocket knife, notably produced in Pattada and Arbus. The knives are real works of art, prepared by a handful of remaining master craftsmen. For more information, see the boxed text, p134.

SOLO TRAVELLERS

Women will find it more difficult to travel alone than men, especially in the interior. There's no particular danger – in fact, you'll

DIRECTORY

invariably be treated with duty-bound courtesy – but local attitudes are largely based on old-fashioned norms of gender division. In practical terms, this means that you won't see many local women in bars and cafes in rural areas, and that lone women travellers will often attract uncomfortable stares. Fortunately, though, it usually stops there, and unpleasant comments and heavy harassment are rare.

Apart from this, the greatest problem facing solo travellers is the dearth of single rooms in popular tourist spots like the northeast coast, along the Golfo di Orosei, and in and around Alghero. In these places you will probably find yourself paying pretty much a double-room rate, and in high summer the single supplement can be very expensive. If you are on a budget you should seek out B&Bs and *agriturismi*, where the rates are much more reasonable and many places charge per person rather than per room. That said, these places don't often have specific single rooms and when demand is high in summer, owners prefer to give rooms to couples rather than solo travellers.

Backpacking is virtually unheard of, and visiting bars and restaurants on your own will earn you a few incredulous stares, as well as the occasional 'Sorry, we have no tables for one, we're fully booked'. Sardinian culture is also quite tight-knit, so you may find yourself feeling a little lonely at times, although contrary to the stereotype Sardinians are actually very friendly and helpful.

Other than that, normal common-sense rules apply. Avoid unlit streets and parks in Cagliari and Sassari at night, and ensure your valuables are safely stored.

TELEPHONE
Mobile Phones
Italy is one of the most mobile-saturated countries in the world and Sardinia is no exception. Even lonesome shepherds often carry a mobile to keep in touch with the distant farmstead.

Phones operate on the GSM 900/1800 network, which is compatible with the rest of Europe and Australia but not with the North American GSM 1900 or the Japanese system (although some GSM 1900/900 phones do work here).

If you have a GSM, dual- or tri-band phone that you can unlock (check with your service provider), you can activate a *prepagato* (prepaid) SIM card in Italy. **TIM** (www.tim.it),

Wind (www.wind.it) and **Vodafone** (www.vodafone.it) all offer SIM cards and all have retail outlets across the island. To recharge a card, simply pop into the nearest outlet or buy a *ricarica* (charge card) from a *tabacchi*. Call rates vary according to the call plan you activate but are typically around €0.20 per minute to Italian fixed phones and from €0.50 to €3 per minute to Europe and the US.

When you buy a card, make sure you have your passport with you.

Payphones & Phonecards
In the face of competition from the all-conquering *cellulare* (mobile), Telecom Italia's public payphones are a dying breed. You can still find them around train stations and in some bars – they're silver in colour – but they're not as widespread as they once were. The most common payphones accept only *schede telefoniche* (telephone cards), although you will still find some that accept both cards and coins. Some also accept credit cards.

You can buy phonecards (usually at a fixed euro rate of €2.50, €5 or €10) at tobacconists and news stands. Remember to snap off the perforated corner before using them.

As an alternative, you'll usually save a bit of money by calling from a cut-price call centre, which you'll find in some of Sardinia's main cities, often doubling as internet points.

For directory inquiries, call ☎ 12 54.

Phone Codes
The country code for Italy is ☎ 39. Mobile-phone numbers begin with a three-digit prefix such as 330 or 339; toll-free (free-phone) numbers are known as *numeri verdi* and usually start with 800; national call rate numbers start with 848 or 199.

Area codes are an integral part of all Italian phone numbers, meaning that you must always use them, even when calling locally.

Direct international calls can easily be made from public telephones or cut-price call centres. Dial ☎ 00 to get out of Italy, then the relevant country and area codes, followed by the telephone number.

TIME
Sardinian time is one hour ahead of GMT/UTC. Daylight-saving time, when clocks move forward one hour, starts on the last Sunday in March. Clocks are put back an hour on the last Sunday in October.

Italy operates on a 24-hour clock, so 6pm is written as 18.00.

TOURIST INFORMATION

Tourist information is widely available in Sardinia, although the quality varies enormously. Some offices are managed by enthusiastic, patient staff, happy to answer your questions and inundate you with useful lists; others are run by indifferent bureaucrats who are either unwilling or unable to help. On the whole, offices in important tourist centres such as Alghero, Cala Gonone, Santa Teresa di Gallura and Villasimius are efficient and helpful with English-speaking staff.

Alongside the 'official' tourist offices there are a plethora of private agencies advertising tourist information, alongside tours and accommodation. In some cases, these places are more useful than the official sources. Where this is the case we've listed them in this book.

Like all aspects of regional organisation, Sardinia's tourist information infrastructure is highly political. For the sake of simplicity we refer to 'tourist offices' in this guide, although in reality these offices have much more elaborate titles depending on which umbrella organisation they belong to and who funds them – the region, province or, at the lowest level, the local council.

On the ground you may come across an Azienda Autonoma di Soggiorno e Turismo (AAST) office with town-specific information on things like bus routes and museum opening times, or an office of the Azienda di Promozione Turistica (APT) or Ente Provinciale per il Turismo (EPT), which can provide information on the town you're in and the surrounding province. In small towns and villages the only tourist office is usually the Pro Loco, which is run by the local council and has limited local information.

Tourist offices are generally open 9am to 12.30pm or 1pm and then from 4pm to 6pm Monday to Friday. However, hours are usually extended in summer, when some offices also open on Saturday and Sunday. Most offices will respond to written and telephone requests for information.

Online information is available at the excellent www.sardegnaturismo.it and on the website of the **Italian State Tourist Board** (ENIT; www.enit.it).

TRAVELLERS WITH DISABILITIES

Sardinia has little infrastructure to ease the way for disabled travellers, and few museums and monuments have wheelchair access. A notable exception is Cagliari's Museo Archeologico Nazionale.

Under European law, airports are obliged to provide assistance to passengers with disabilities, so if you need help en route to Sardinia, or on arrival, tell your airline when you book your ticket and they should inform the airport. Information on services available at Rome's two airports is available online at www.adrassistance.it.

If you need assistance travelling by train, Trenitalia runs a dedicated telephone line on ☎ 199 30 30 60. It's active daily between 7am and 9pm.

The Italian State Tourist Office in your country may be able to provide advice on Italian associations for the disabled and information on what help is available in the country.

Some useful organisations include the following:

Accessible Italy (☎ 378 94 11 11; www.accessibleitaly .com) A San Marino–based company that specialises in holiday services for the disabled, including tours and the hiring of adapted transport.

Associazione Italiana Assistenza Spastici (☎ 070 37 9101; www.aiasnazionale.it, in Italian; Viale Poetto 312, Cagliari) The Italian Spastics Assistance Association has a branch in Cagliari.

Disability World (www.disabilityworld.com) A UK website with hotel listings across the world. At the time of research it had three hotels in Sardinia.

Holiday Care Service (☎ in the UK 0845 124 99 71; www.holidaycare.org.uk) Produces an information pack on Italy (£3.50) for the physically disabled and others with special needs. The website also has a useful FAQs section.

Lonely Planet (www.lonelyplanet.com) The Thorn Tree forum has a section dedicated to travellers with disabilities.

Royal Association for Disability & Rehabilitation (RADAR; ☎ in the UK 020 7250 32 22; www.radar.org.uk) A British-based organisation that can advise on all aspects of travelling.

VISAS

EU citizens do not need a visa to enter Italy. Nationals of some other countries, including Australia, Brazil, Canada, Israel, Japan, New Zealand, Switzerland and the USA do not need visas for stays of up to 90 days in Italy, or the 15 Schengen countries currently implementing common visa provisions.

At the time of research, 30 European countries had signed the Schengen Convention, an agreement whereby participating countries abolished customs checks at common borders, but only 15 were implementing the provisions. These were: Austria, Belgium, Denmark, Finland, France, Germany, Greece, Iceland, Italy, Luxembourg, the Netherlands, Norway, Portugal, Spain and Sweden.

The standard tourist visa for a Schengen country is valid for up to 90 days. As a rule, a Schengen visa issued by one Schengen country is valid for travel in other Schengen countries, although it's always worth checking as individual countries may impose additional restrictions on certain nationalities. You must apply for a Schengen visa in your country of residence and you can apply for no more than two in any 12-month period. They are not renewable inside Italy.

For further information on Schengen visas and to download an application form, go to www.schengenvisa.cc.

Technically all foreign visitors to Sardinia are supposed to register with the local police within eight days of arrival. However, if you're staying in a hotel you don't need to bother as the hotel does this for you – this is why they always take your passport details.

Up-to-date visa information is available on www.lonelyplanet.com – follow links through to the Italy destination guide.

Permesso di Soggiorno

A *permesso di soggiorno* (permit to stay) is required by all non-EU nationals who stay in Sardinia longer than three months. You should apply for one within eight days of arriving in Italy but few people do. EU citizens don't require a *permesso di soggiorno*.

To get one you'll need a valid passport, containing a stamp with your date of entry into Italy (ask for this as it's not automatic); a photocopy of your passport; a study visa if necessary; four passport-style photographs; proof of your ability to support yourself financially (ideally a letter from an employer or school/university); and a €14.92 official stamp (known as a *marca da bollo*).

Although correct at the time of writing, the documentation requirements change periodically so always check before you join the inevitable queue. Up-to-date information is available on the website of the **Polizia di Stato** (www.poiziadistato.it, in Italian).

Kits containing application forms are available from main post offices.

Study Visas

Non-EU citizens who want to study in Sardinia must have a study visa. These can be obtained at your nearest Italian embassy or consulate. You will normally require confirmation of your enrolment, proof of payment of fees and proof that you can support yourself financially. The visa covers only the period of the enrolment. This type of visa is renewable within Italy but, again, only with confirmation of ongoing enrolment and that you are still financially self-supporting (bank statements are preferred).

Work Visas

To work in Italy all non-EU citizens require a work visa. Apply to your nearest Italian embassy or consulate. You'll need a valid passport, proof of health insurance and a *permesso di lavoro* (work permit). If your employer is an Italian company, they will obtain the *permesso* in Italy and then forward it to you prior to your visa application. In other cases, you'll have to organise it yourself through the Italian consulate in your country.

WOMEN TRAVELLERS

Sardinians are almost universally polite to women (see p229 for information for female solo travellers), and it is unlikely that you will suffer the sort of harassment that you might in parts of mainland Italy. If you do find yourself the recipient of unwanted male attention, it's best to ignore it. If that doesn't work, politely tell your would-be companion that you are waiting for your *marito* (husband) or *fidanzato* (boyfriend) and, if necessary, walk away. Avoid becoming aggressive as this may result in a confrontation. If all else fails, approach the nearest member of the police or *carabinieri*.

As always, common sense is the best protection for women travellers. Avoid walking alone in deserted and dark streets, and look for hotels that are central and within easy walking distance of places where you can eat at night. Women should also avoid hitchhiking alone.

It is wise – and polite – to dress modestly in inland Sardinia. Communities here are very conservative, and you will still see older women wearing the traditional long, pleated skirts and shawls. Skimpy clothing is both shocking and inconsiderate. Take your cue from Sardinian women on this one.

Transport

CONTENTS

GETTING THERE & AWAY

The easiest and fastest way to get to Sardinia is by air. The boom in budget air travel has done much to open Sardinia's skies, and if you're coming from Europe you should have no problem finding a direct flight. If you're travelling from outside Europe, you'll have to pick up a connecting flight on the Italian mainland. A slower, cheaper alternative is to catch a ferry from Genoa, Livorno, Civitavecchia or Naples.

Flights, tours and rail tickets can be booked online at www.lonelyplanet.com/travel-services.

ENTERING THE REGION

If you're coming to Sardinia from outside Europe you'll have to pick up a connecting flight (and change airlines) on the Italian mainland. There are flights to Sardinia from most Italian airports but most frequently from Rome and Milan. All customs and immigration formalities will take place there, and the Sardinian leg of your journey will be considered an internal flight.

Boarding a ferry to Sardinia is as easy as getting on a bus. Book your passage if you're travelling in high season. You don't need to show your passport on these internal routes, but it is a good idea to keep some ID handy.

Passports

Citizens of EU member states can travel to Italy with their national identity cards. People from countries that do not issue ID cards must carry a valid passport. All non-EU nationals must have a full valid passport.

You're likely to have your passport stamped when you arrive by air but not if you're coming from another Schengen country (see p231). Non-EU nationals planning to stay in Italy for an extended period should always ask for the entry stamp. Without it you could encounter problems when trying to get a *permesso di soggiorno* (permit to stay; see opposite).

AIR

High season in Sardinia is June to September. Holidays such as Easter also see a huge jump in prices.

Airports & Airlines

Flights from Italian and European cities serve Sardinia's three main airports: **Elmas** (CAG; ☎ 070 211 211; www.sogaer.it) in Cagliari; Alghero's **Fertilia** (AHO; ☎ 079 93 52 82; www.algheroairport.it) in the northwest; and the **Aeroporto Olbia Costa Smeralda** (OLB; ☎ 0789 56 34 44; www.geasar.it) in Olbia in the northeast. Flight schedules are available on the websites of all three airports.

The tiny Arbatax-Tortoli **airstrip** (☎ 0782 62 43 00; www.aeroportotortoliarbatax.it, in Italian), 1.5km south of Tortoli on the southern Nuoro coast, opens in summer only for specialist charter flights.

THINGS CHANGE...

The information in this chapter is particularly vulnerable to change. Check directly with the airline or a travel agent to make sure you understand how a fare (and ticket you may buy) works and be aware of the security requirements for international travel. Shop carefully. The details given in this chapter should be regarded as pointers and are not a substitute for your own careful, up-to-date research.

TRANSPORT

AIRLINES FLYING TO/FROM SARDINIA

The number of airlines flying into Sardinia has risen, and you can now easily pick up flights from cities across Europe, including Amsterdam, Barcelona, Brussels, Birmingham, Dublin, Hamburg, London, Madrid, Manchester, Paris, Prague, Stuttgart and Vienna.

International and national airlines flying to/from Sardinia include the following:

Air Berlin (AB; ☎ 199 400 737; www.airberlin.com)
Air Dolomiti (EN; ☎ 045 288 61 40; www.airdolomiti.it)
Air One (AP; ☎ 199 20 70 80; www.flyairone.it)
Alitalia (code AZ; ☎ 06 22 22; www.alitalia.it)
Austrian Airlines (OS; ☎ 02 896 34 296; www.aua.com)
British Airways (BA; ☎ 199 712 266; www.britishair ways.com)
easyJet (U2; ☎ 899 234 589; www.easyjet.com)
Iberia (IB; ☎ 199 10 11 91; www.iberia.com)
Lufthansa (LH; ☎ 199 400 044; www.lufthansa.com)
Meridiana (IG; ☎ 89 29 28; www.meridiana.it)
MyAir (8I; ☎ 848 868 120; www.myair.com)
Ryanair (FR; ☎ 899 678 910; www.ryanair.com)
Transavia (HV; ☎ 899 009 901; www.transavia.com)
TUIfly (X3; ☎ 199 192 692; www.tuifly.com)

Tickets

The best place to buy airline tickets for Sardinia is on the web with one of the (low-cost) airlines listed above.

Students and people aged under 26 (under 30 in some countries) coming from outside Europe have access to discounted fares with valid ID such as an International Student Identity Card (ISIC). Discounted tickets are also released to selected travel agents and specialist discount agencies.

The alternative to booking direct with a low-cost airline on the internet is to surf online agents:

Booking Buddy (www.bookingbuddy.com)
Cheap Tickets (www.cheaptickets.com)
Discount-Tickets (www.discount-tickets.com)
Ebookers (www.ebookers.com)
Expedia (www.expedia.com)
Kayak (www.kayak.com)
Orbitz (www.orbitz.com)
Priceline (www.priceline.com)
Travelcuts (www.travelcuts.com)
Travelocity (www.travelocity.com)

Australia

Flights from Australia to mainland Italy generally go via Southeast Asian capitals. **Qantas** (www.qantas.com.au) and Alitalia offer the only direct flights from Melbourne and Sydney to Rome. Also try **Malaysian Airlines** (www.malaysianairlines.com) and the **Star Alliance carriers** (www.staralliance.com), such as **Thai Airways International**

CLIMATE CHANGE & TRAVEL

Climate change is a serious threat to the ecosystems that humans rely upon, and air travel is the fastest-growing contributor to the problem. Lonely Planet regards travel, overall, as a global benefit, but believes we all have a responsibility to limit our personal impact on global warming.

Flying & Climate Change

Pretty much every form of motor travel generates CO_2 (the main cause of human-induced climate change), but planes are far and away the worst offenders, not just because of the sheer distances they allow us to travel but because they release greenhouse gases high into the atmosphere. The statistics are frightening: two people taking a return flight between Europe and the US will contribute as much to climate change as an average household's gas and electricity consumption over a whole year.

Carbon Offset Schemes

Climatecare.org and other websites use 'carbon calculators' that allow jet-setters to offset the greenhouse gases they are responsible for with contributions to energy-saving projects and other climate-friendly initiatives in the developing world – including projects in India, Honduras, Kazakhstan and Uganda.

Lonely Planet, together with Rough Guides and other concerned partners in the travel industry, supports the carbon offset scheme run by climatecare.org. Lonely Planet offsets all of its staff and author travel.

For more information check out our website: lonelyplanet.com (www.thaiair.com), **Singapore Airlines** (www.singapore .com) and **Air China** (www.airchina.com). From Sydney you'll be looking at airfares upwards of A$2200. Flights from Perth are generally a few hundred dollars cheaper.

Canada

For airfares from the Canadian east/west coast, reckon on around C$750/820.

Alitalia currently has daily flights to Rome from Toronto. In summer, **Air Transat** (www .airtransat.com) flies nonstop from Montreal to Rome. **Air Canada** (www.aircanada.com) flies daily from Toronto to Rome direct and via Montreal and Frankfurt, and to Milan via Frankfurt, Munich or Zurich.

Continental Europe

There are plenty of flights from continental Europe direct to Sardinia, although services drop off considerably in winter, particularly to Alghero and Olbia. In Spain, Ryanair operates flights to Cagliari from Barcelona Girona and Madrid, and to Alghero from Madrid. In addition, Iberia runs seasonal flights to Olbia from Madrid and Barcelona.

From Paris, Meridiana operates flights to Cagliari and, in summer, to Olbia.

If you're travelling from Germany you shouldn't find it difficult to pick up a flight to Sardinia. TUIfly flies to Cagliari from Stuttgart, Cologne and Munich, and to Olbia from Hamburg. In summer, Ryanair operates flights to Alghero from Dusseldorf and Frankfurt, and easyJet flies to Olbia from Berlin.

If you want to travel via the Italian mainland, all national European carriers fly to Italy. The largest of these, Air France, Iberia, Lufthansa and KLM, have representatives in all major European cities.

Italy

Domestic flights from the Italian mainland are operated by a number of international companies, including Ryanair and easyJet, and Italy's big three domestic airlines: Alitalia, Meridiana and Air One. At the time of writing, Alitalia's future was looking uncertain. In late 2008, after months of political and industrial turmoil, Alitalia was saved from bankruptcy by a consortium of Italian investors who bought the company from the Italian government.

For the internal leg of the journey, return fares cost approximately €70 to €160

from Rome and between €130 and €180 from Milan.

You can also pick up flights to Sardinia from Bergamo, Bologna, Brescia, Florence, Naples, Palermo, Parma, Perugia, Pisa, Rimini, Trieste, Turin, Venice and Verona.

New Zealand

Singapore Airlines flies from Auckland through Singapore to Rome's Fiumicino airport, sometimes with more than one stop. **Air New Zealand** (www.airnewzealand.com) flies to Rome from Auckland via Hong Kong or Los Angeles and then London. Otherwise, Qantas or Alitalia flights from Australia are the most direct way to get to Italy and then Sardinia.

UK & Ireland

From the UK you're looking at around £70 for a direct flight to Sardinia with a lowcost airline such as Ryanair or easyJet.

Between the end of March and the end of October Ryanair flies twice weekly to Alghero from East Midlands Airport and Dublin. Then from mid-April there are two weekly flights from Liverpool to Alghero. EasyJet operates daily flights to Cagliari from London's Luton Airport and, between June and October, twice-weekly flights to Olbia from London Gatwick.

Over spring and summer, British Airways gets in on the act with weekly flights between April and October from Gatwick to Cagliari. From May to October, **British Midland** (www.flybmi.com) flies weekly from Manchester to Olbia.

Alitalia and **Aer Lingus** (www.aerlingus.com) both have regular daily flights from Dublin to Rome.

USA

The North Atlantic is the world's busiest longhaul air corridor and the flight options are bewildering. There are no direct flights from the USA to Sardinia, so you'll have to fly via Rome or Milan.

From the east/west coast of the United States fares start at about US$600/750.

Alitalia, **Delta Airlines** (www.delta.com) and **American Airlines** (www.aa.com) have regular flights from New York's JFK to Malpensa in Milan and Rome's Fiumicino airport. The latter also flies from Chicago O'Hare to Rome. **Continental Airlines** (www.continental.com) operates from Newark to Rome and Milan, while

TRANSPORT

TRANSPORT

United Airlines (www.united.com) has a service from Washington to Rome. Standard fares can be expensive, but you can usually find something cheaper if you shop around.

Standby fares are often sold at 60% of the normal price for one-way tickets. **Airhitch** (www .airhitch.org) is an online specialist. You give a general idea of where and when you need to go, and a few days before your departure you will be presented with a choice of two or three flights.

Courier Travel (☎ 303 570 7586; www.couriertravel .org) is a comprehensive search engine for courier and standby flights. You can also check out the **International Association of Air Travel Couriers** (IAATC; ☎ 308 632 3273; www.courier.org).

LAND

Sardinia is the most isolated island in the Mediterranean, some 200km from the nearest land mass, so any overland trip will include a ferry leg; see opposite for details. The shortest ferry route is from Civitavecchia, north of Rome, to Olbia on the northeast coast of Sardinia, although there are various alternatives. The other main points of departure are Genoa, Livorno and Naples. In summer there are a couple of ferries from Marseille in France.

Travelling to Sardinia this way can either be an enormous drain on your time and money (ferry tickets are not cheap) or, if you have plenty of time to spare, a bit of a European adventure.

If you are travelling by bus, train or car to Italy, check whether you require visas to the countries you intend to pass through.

Border Crossings

The main points of entry into Italy are the Mt Blanc tunnel from France at Chamonix, which connects with the A5 for Turin and Milan; the Grand St Bernard tunnel from Switzerland (SS27), which also connects with the A5; the Gotthard tunnel, also from Switzerland; the Swiss Lötschberg Base tunnel that connects with the century-old Simplon tunnel into Italy; and the Brenner Pass from Austria (A13), which links up with the A22 to Bologna. All are open year-round.

Mountain passes in the Alps are often closed in winter and sometimes even in autumn and spring, making the tunnels a less scenic but more reliable option. Make sure you have snow chains in winter.

Continental Europe
BUS

A consortium of 32 European coach companies, **Eurolines** (☎ 055 35 70 59; www.eurolines .com) operates across Europe with offices in all major European cities. Italy-bound buses head to Ancona, Florence, Rome, Siena and Venice. Its multilanguage website gives details of prices, passes and travel agencies where you can book tickets.

CAR & MOTORCYCLE

Most people travelling overland to Sardinia will be bringing their own wheels. This is a perfectly sensible idea, as the island's public-transport network is not the best, and car hire is relatively expensive.

As with the bus or train, you'll need to make your way to the most convenient port. For many this will be Genoa, although you could add a few hours' driving time and continue down as far as Livorno, from where the sea crossing is shorter. Drivers coming from the UK, Spain or France may prefer to time their trip with vessels leaving from Marseille.

A useful website with plenty of practical information on driving in Europe is www .ideamerge.com (click on the Moto Europa Guidebook link in the left-hand column). For route planning try www.viamichelin .com, which provides printable maps and driving directions.

TRAIN

Although more expensive than the bus, travel by rail is infinitely more comfortable and can be quicker, too. As with the bus, your options will be determined by your choice of embarkation point, which for many will mean either Marseille or Genoa.

For overnight journeys you can choose between sleepers, compartments with up to three fold-down beds, or more rudimentary couchettes with up to six bunks. On average sleepers cost between €25 and €50 per person per night on top of the regular time price; couchettes are cheaper at around €15. It is advisable, and sometimes compulsory, to book seats on international trains to and from Italy. Some of the main international services include transport for private cars – an option that'll save wear and tear on your vehicle before it arrives in Italy.

The *Thomas Cook European Timetable* is the trainophile's bible, giving a complete listing of train schedules. It is updated monthly and is available from Thomas Cook offices and agents worldwide.

UK

CAR & MOTORCYCLE

From the UK you can take your car across to France by ferry or on the Channel Tunnel car train, **Eurotunnel** (☎ 0870 535 3535; www.eurotunnel .com). The latter runs 24 hours, with up to four crossings (35 minutes) each hour between Folkestone and Calais in the high season. You pay for the vehicle only, and fares vary according to the time of day and season, but a standard return fare could be as much as £300 (valid for one year).

UK drivers holding the old-style green driving licence will need to obtain an International Driving Permit (IDP) before they can drive on the continent. For breakdown assistance both the **AA** (☎ 0870 600 03 71; www.theaa.co.uk) and the **RAC** (☎ 0870 010 63 82; www.rac.co.uk) offer comprehensive cover in Europe.

TRAIN

Regular trains on two lines connect Italy with main cities in Austria and on into Germany, France or Eastern Europe. Those crossing the frontier at the Brenner Pass go to Innsbruck, Stuttgart and Munich. Those crossing at Tarvisio proceed to Vienna, Salzburg and Prague. Trains from Milan head for Switzerland and on into France, and the Netherlands. The main international train line to Slovenia crosses near Trieste.

The passenger-train **Eurostar** (☎ 0870 518 6186; www.eurostar.com) travels from St Pancras International station in London to Paris Gare du Nord, Lille, Brussels and Avignon. At the time of writing one-way fares cost £154.50 to Paris and £135 to Lille. Strangely, the return fares on the same routes start at £59 for Paris and £55 to Lille. Alternatively, you can get a train ticket that includes the Channel crossing by ferry, SeaCat or hovercraft.

The simplest way of taking the train to Sardinia is to travel to Marseille where you can pick up a summer ferry to Porto Torres. To get to Marseille from London, take the Eurostar to Lille and change onto one of the regular **TGV** (www.sncf-voyages.com) services to Marseille. Alternatively, you could get the Eurostar to Paris and pick up a TGV

service to Marseille. Return fares, which are strangely often cheaper than one-way fares, from London to Marseille start at about £109. Note, however, that if you take the Paris route you'll have to get yourself and your luggage from Gare du Nord to Gare de Lyon from where the southbound TGVs depart.

For Genoa, you can travel via Paris and Milan or via Paris and Nice. On the Milan route you'll need to catch the overnight Stendhal train from Paris Gare de Bercy to Milan and then an Intercity train from Milan to Genoa, from where you can pick up ferries to Olbia, Arbatax and Porto Torres. Fares from Paris to Milan cost from £30 to £81 in a six-berth couchette; from Milan to Genoa is about €16.

Alternatively, catch the overnight Train Bleu from Paris Gare d'Austerlitz to Nice, where you can pick up a EuroCity train to Genoa. Paris to Nice in a six-person couchette costs anything from £30 to £95; Nice to Genoa will set you back around €20.

For the latest fare information on journeys to Italy, including Eurostar, contact the **Rail Europe Travel Centre** (☎ 08448 484 064; www .raileurope.co.uk) or **Rail Choice** (☎ 0870 165 73 00; www.railchoice.com).

For advice, information and handy rail tips check out the encyclopaedic www.seat61.com. There is almost nothing this website can't tell you about travelling in Europe, or indeed the entire world, by train.

SEA

The island is accessible by ferry from the Italian ports of Genoa, Savona, La Spezia, Livorno, Piombino, Civitavecchia, Fiumicino and Naples, and from Palermo and Trapani in Sicily.

Ferries also run from Bonifacio and Porto Vecchio in Corsica. French ferries running from Marseilles and Toulon sometimes call in at the Corsican ports of Ajaccio and Propriano en route for Sardinia.

The arrival points in Sardinia are Olbia, Golfo Aranci, Palau, Santa Teresa di Gallura and Porto Torres in the north; Arbatax on the east coast; and Cagliari in the south.

Numerous ferry companies ply these routes (see p238 for details), and services are most frequent from mid-June to mid-September, when it is advisable to book well ahead.

TRANSPORT

Ferry prices are determined by the season and are at their highest between June and September. You can book tickets at travel agents throughout Italy or directly on the internet. Offices and telephone numbers for the ferry companies are listed in the Getting There & Away sections for the relevant cities.

A useful online booking service is www .traghettionline.net, covering all the ferry companies in the Mediterranean. The similarly named www.traghettionline.com lists all the routes into Sardinia and has links to the ferry companies operating them.

Corsica

There are links between Santa Teresa di Gallura and Bonifacio, in Corsica. **Saremar** (☎ 892 123; www.saremar.it), run by Tirrenia, has three daily departures each way (two at weekends between October and mid-March). A one-way adult fare in high season is €10 and a small car costs up to €37. Taxes add another €8 to the price. The trip takes one hour.

Between the end of March and late September **Moby Lines** (☎ 199 30 30 40; www.moby lines.it) operates four daily crossings. Adult tickets cost €9 to €13.50, plus €4.20 tax; a car costs €22 to €63 plus €2.80 tax. **Sardinia Ferries** (☎ 199 400 500; www.sardiniaferries.com) sail three times daily between April and September, less in the rest of the year. Adults pay €10 plus €4.10 tax; to transport a car costs €37 with an extra €2.50 tax.

SNCM (☎ France 08 91 70 18 01, in Sardinia ☎ 079 51 44 77; www.sncm.fr) ferries between Porto Torres and the French mainland call at Propriano or, less frequently, Ajaccio en route to Marseille and Toulon. The adult one-way fare for Propriano is €32.30 or €73.90 with a small car; for Ajaccio €33.70 per adult, €79 with a car.

France

SNCM (☎ France 0825 88 80 88; www.sncm.fr) and **CMN La Méridionale** (☎ France 0810 20 13 20; www.cmn.fr) together operate ferries from Marseille to Porto Torres (via Corsica). There are two to four sailings weekly, but in July and August some leave from Toulon instead. Crossing time is 15 to 17 hours (12½ hours from Toulon). A reclinable seat costs €78 and a small car €148.

For tickets and information in Porto Torres, go to **Agenzia Paglietti** (☎ 079 51 44 77; fax 079 51 40 63; Corso Vittorio Emanuele 19).

Italy

Several companies run ferries of varying types and speeds from a number of Italian ports to Sardinia.

For route and operator details see the boxed text, p240. The prices quoted in the table are for standard high-season one-way fares in a *poltrona* (reclinable seat) for adults – children aged four to 12 generally pay around half price; those under four go free – and small cars. Depending on the service you take, you can also get cabins, the price of which varies according to the number of occupants (generally one to four) and position (with or without window). Most companies offer discounts on return trips and other deals – it's always worth asking. You might want to consider taking a sleeping berth for overnight trips, which will cost as much as double.

GETTING AROUND

If at all possible it is preferable to have your own car in Sardinia. Getting around the island on public transport is difficult and time-consuming but not impossible. In most cases buses are preferable to trains, which are nearly always slower and often involve lengthy changes.

The website www.getaroundsardinia.com has some useful advice about navigating the island without a car.

AIR

Sardinia is so small that you don't really need internal flights. However, **Meridiana** (☎ 89 29 28; www.meridiana.it) operates a daily flight between Cagliari and Olbia – which is, admittedly, a long grind overland. The flight takes 35 minutes and costs from €30 to €90.

BICYCLE

Sardinia lends itself well to cycling. The roads are rarely busy outside of high summer, the scenery is magnificent and it doesn't rain much. That said, it's pretty tough going and the hilly (sometimes mountainous) terrain will take it out of you and your bike.

Transporting your bike to Sardinia poses no special problems. Different airlines apply different rules, but most will require that you pack it in a bike bag or box, turn the pedals and handlebars flush with the frame, and deflate the tyres. There'll then be an additional charge, typically between €25 to €40. You can also carry bikes with you on ferries to Sardinia for a small fee, usually from €3 to €10.

Bikes are available for hire in most major towns and resorts, including Alghero, Santa Teresa di Gallura, La Maddalena, Palau and Olbia. Rates range from around €10 per day to as much as €25 for mountain bikes. See Getting Around under the relevant cities in this guide for more information.

There are no special road rules for cyclists. Helmets and lights are not obligatory, but you would be wise to equip yourself with both. You cannot cycle on the highway. Make sure you include a few tools, spare parts and a very solid bike lock.

If cycling in summer make sure you have plenty of water and sunblock as the heat can be exhausting.

Bikes can be taken on almost all trains in Sardinia. They are put in a separate wagon and the cost (€5) is the same regardless of the destination.

In the UK **Cyclists' Touring Club** (☎ 0844 736 84 50; www.ctc.org.uk) can help you plan your own bike tour or organise guided tours. Membership costs £35.

BOAT

Local ferry companies **Enermar** (☎ 899 200 001; www.enermar.it) and **Saremar** (☎ 892 123; www.saremar.it) connect Palau with the Isola di La Maddalena. In summer services run every 15 minutes and cost €5 for the 20-minute crossing. A car fare is €13.

In the southwest, Saremar has up to 17 sailings per day from Portovesme to Carloforte on the Isola di San Pietro. The trip takes about 30 minutes and costs €5.90/9.80 per person/car. Saremar also links Carloforte with Calasetta on Isola di Sant'Antioco. In summer there are nine daily crossings between 7.35am and 8.20pm. Tickets for the 30-minute crossing cost €5.30/8.40 per person/car. Nightly crossings are operated by **Delcomar** (☎ 0781 85 71 23; www.delcomar.it) for €5/15 per person/car.

Services are cut back considerably over the winter months so always check ahead. If taking a car in summer, try to arrive in good time as boats fill up quickly.

In summer it is possible to join boat tours from various points around the coast. This is an excellent way to see Sardinia's more inaccessible highlights. The most popular tours include trips out of Cala Gonone and Santa Maria Navarrese along the majestic Golfo di Orosei. Close behind is a trip around the islands of the Maddalena archipelago. Boats frequently head out of Porto San Paolo (p169), south of Olbia, for trips around Isola Tavolara and the nearby coast. Others sail out of Alghero and from the Sinis Peninsula. Most trips are by motorboats or small tour ferries, but a handful of sailing vessels are also on hand. For more information, see the relevant destination chapters.

BUS

Bus services within Sardinia are provided by a variety of private companies and vary from local routes linking small villages to intercity connections. By using the local services, it is possible to get to just about anywhere on the island, although you'll need to be patient to do so. Often there is only one service a day to out-of-the-way places. That said, buses are usually more reliable and faster than trains, which are limited to the island's very restricted rail network.

Sardinia's main bus company is **Azienda Regionale Sarda Trasporti**; (ARST; ☎ 800 865 042; www.arst.sardegna.it, in Italian), which runs the majority of local and long-distance services.

The other major bus companies are **Ferrovie Meridionali Sarde** (FMS; ☎ 800 044 553; www.ferroviemeridionalisarde.it, in Italian) and **Ferrovie della Sardegna** (FdS; ☎ 070 34 31 12; www.ferroviesardegna.it, in Italian), which also operates a limited network of private narrow-gauge railways, most notably the *trenino verde* (see p243).

At the time of research, the island's bus network was about to be reorganised, so some minor services might be affected. All the island's big towns have an ARST bus station, which is usually centrally located. Other companies also sometimes use these stations but by no means always. Generally, bus companies merely have a stop (and sometimes a ticket office) elsewhere in town. In smaller towns and villages there will simply be a *fermata* for intercity buses, not always in an immediately apparent location.

ARST and FdS tickets must be bought prior to boarding at stations or designated bars, *tabacchi* (tobacconists) and newspaper stands near the stop. With other companies you

TRANSPORT

FERRIES TO SARDINIA

The following is a rundown of the main ferry routes to Sardinia, the companies that operate them and the route details. Prices quoted are high-season fares for a 2nd-class *poltrona* (reclinable seat). Children aged four to 12 generally pay around half price; children under four go free.

From	To	Company	Fare	Car	Duration (hr)	Frequency
Civitavecchia	Arbatax	Tirrenia	€47	€94	10½	2 weekly
Civitavecchia	Cagliari	Tirrenia	€56	€102	14½	daily
Civitavecchia	Olbia	Moby	€60	€111	4½–10	4 weekly mid-Mar–May, daily Jun-Sep
Civitavecchia	Olbia	SNAV	€56	€116	7½	daily
Civitavecchia	Olbia	Tirrenia	€41	€100	7	daily
Civitavecchia	Golfo Aranci	Sardinia F	€52.50	incl	6¾	3 weekly mid-Mar–May, daily Jun-Sep
Civitavecchia	Golfo Aranci+	Sardinia F	€76.50	€133	3½	3 weekly mid-Mar–May, daily Jun-Sep
Fiumicino	Arbatax+	Tirrenia	€60	€107	4½	2 weekly late Jul-Aug
Fiumicino	Golfo Aranci+	Tirrenia	€60	€107	4	daily late Jul-Aug
Genoa	Arbatax	Tirrenia	€57	€104	18	2 weekly
Genoa	Olbia	GNV	€92.50	€155	8–10	daily mid-May–mid-Sep
Genoa	Olbia	Moby	€86	€132	10	daily mid-May–mid-Oct
Genoa	Olbia	Tirrenia	€59	€106	13¼	3 weekly, 5 weekly Jul-Aug
Genoa	Palau	Enermar	€70.50	€118.50	11	5 weekly Jun-Sep
Genoa	Porto Torres	GNV	€89	€152	11	4 weekly, daily mid-May–mid-Sep
Genoa	Porto Torres	Moby	€86	€132	10	6 weekly mid-May–Sep
Genoa	Porto Torres+	Tirrenia	€105	€179	10	daily
Livorno	Golfo Aranci	Sardinia F	€51.50	incl	10	daily Mar-Oct
Livorno	Golfo Aranci+	Sardinia F	€73.50	€131	6	daily Mar-Oct
Livorno	Olbia	Moby	€66	€120	7–9	daily
Naples	Cagliari	Tirrenia	€52	€91	16¼	1 weekly, 2 Aug
Palermo	Cagliari	Tirrenia	€50	€90	14½	1 weekly
Piombino	Olbia	Moby	€65	€118	6½	6 weekly, daily mid-May–Sep
Trapani	Cagliari	Tirrenia	€50	€92.50	11	1 weekly

+ indicates a high-speed service

Ferry Operators

Enermar (☎ 899 20 00 01; www.enermar.it) To Palau from Genoa.

Grandi Navi Veloci (☎ 010 209 45 91; www.gnv.it) To Olbiaand Porto Torres from Genoa.

Moby Lines (☎ 199 30 30 40; www.mobylines.it) To Olbia from Civitavecchia, Genoa, Livorno & Piombino; to Porto Torres from Genoa.

Sardinia Ferries (☎ 199 400 500; www.sardiniaferries.com) To Golfo Aranci from Civitavecchia & Livorno.

SNAV (☎ 081 428 55 55; www.snav.it) To Olbia from Civitavecchia.

Tirrenia (☎ 892 123; www.tirrenia.it) To Cagliari from Civitavecchia, Naples, Palermo & Trapani; to Olbia from Civitavecchia and Genoa; to Arbatax from Civitavecchia, Fiumicino & Genoa; to Golfo Aranci from Fiumicino; to Porto Torres from Genoa.

generally buy the ticket on board. Timetables are sometimes posted next to the stop, but don't hold your breath. Tourist offices in bigger towns can usually provide timetable information for their area. In smaller locations you would do well to ask wherever you buy tickets.

Note also that services might be frequent on weekdays but are cut back drastically on Sundays and holidays – runs between smaller towns often fall to one or none. Keep this in mind if you depend on buses, as it is easy to get stuck in smaller places, especially at weekends.

CAR & MOTORCYCLE

Driving in Sardinia is fairly stress free. Away from the main towns (Cagliari, Sassari and Olbia, in particular) and outside of high summer, traffic is rarely a problem and local drivers tend to be courteous. In some of inland rural towns you might find youths revving it up on Saturday nights, but other than that the main hazards are flocks of sheep and the stunning scenery.

Main roads are generally good, although to really explore the island, you'll need to use the system of provincial roads, *strade provinciali*, marked as P or SP on maps. These are sometimes little more than country lanes, but they provide access to some of the more beautiful scenery and the many small towns and villages. Many of the more spectacular beaches are only accessible by dirt tracks.

Motorcycle fever has not yet made it out to Sardinia, although the island is very popular with German and Austrian bikers who enjoy racing around the island's scenic roads and hairpin bends. With a bike you rarely have to book for ferries and can enter restricted traffic areas in cities. Crash helmets are compulsory. Unless you're touring it's probably easier to rent a bike once you have reached Sardinia.

Automobile Associations

Italy's motoring organisation **Automobile Club d'Italia** (ACI; www.aci.it) is an excellent source of information and provides 24-hour roadside assistance – call ☎ 803 116 or ☎ 800 116 800 if calling from a non-Italian mobile phone. Foreigners do not have to join but instead pay a fee in case of breakdown assistance (€100 to €120, 20% more on weekends and holidays). In the UK, both the **AA** (☎ 0870 600 03 71; www .theaa.co.uk) and the **RAC** (☎ 0870 010 63 82; www.rac .co.uk) offer breakdown cover in Europe.

If you are hiring a car from a reputable company they will usually give you an emergency number of their own to call in the case of breakdown.

Bring Your Own Vehicle

Cars entering Italy from abroad need a valid national licence plate and an accompanying registration card. You should always carry proof of ownership of a private vehicle. A warning triangle is compulsory in Italy as is a fluorescent orange or yellow safety vest to be worn if you have to get out of your car in the event of a breakdown. A first-aid kit, a spare-bulb kit and a fire extinguisher are also recommended.

Driving Licence

All EU driving licences are recognised in Sardinia. Holders of non-EU licences must get an International Driving Permit (IDP) to accompany their national licence. Your national automobile association can issue this, and it is valid for 12 months.

Fuel

Fuel is pretty expensive in Sardinia and you'll pay around €1.15 per litre for *benzina senza piombo* (unleaded petrol) and about €1 per litre for *gasolio* (diesel). There are plenty of fuel stations in and around towns and on the main road networks.

Hire

With so many budget airlines flying into Sardinia's airports, the rise of the fly/drive package now provides some reasonably priced car rental. It is *always* better to arrange car hire before you arrive. Major car-hire outlets have offices at the airports, where you usually pick up your car and deposit it at the end of your stay. The most competitive national and multinational car-hire agencies are

Avis (☎ 06 452 10 83 91; www.avis.com)
Budget (☎ 800 283 438; www.budgetautonoleggio.it)
Europcar (☎ 199 30 70 30; www.europcar.com)
Hertz (☎ 199 11 22 11; www.hertz.com)
Italy by Car (☎ 091 639 31 20; www.italybycar.it)
Maggiore (☎ 199 151 120; www.maggiore.com)

If you only want to hire a car for a couple of days, or decide to hire one after you have arrived, you will find car-hire outfits in most of the coastal resorts, although the big international companies only have offices in a handful of big cities. Age restrictions vary from agency to agency but generally you'll need to be 21 or over. Also, if you're under 25 you'll probably have to pay a young-driver's supplement on top of the usual rates. Pricewise you'll be looking at between €55 and €65 for a Fiat Punto or equivalent. You'll need a credit card.

No matter where you hire your car, make sure you understand what is included in the price (unlimited kilometres, tax, insurance, collision damage waiver and so on) and what your liabilities are. It is also a very good idea

Road Distances (km)

	Alghero	Bosa	Cagliari	Iglesias	Nuoro	Olbia	Oristano	Porto Torres	Santa Teresa di Gallura	Sant'Antioco	Sassari
Bosa	45										
Cagliari	247	180									
Iglesias	255	192	58								
Nuoro	155	86	180	193							
Olbia	138	143	265	285	105						
Oristano	155	88	94	110	90	173					
Porto Torres	39	117	230	250	137	120	135				
Santa Teresa di Gallura	196	208	335	345	162	62	243	101			
Sant'Antioco	288	220	84	38	219	315	132	268	375		
Sassari	37	94	217	220	123	106	126	20	100	256	
Tempio Pausania	110	128	256	260	146	46	157	75	58	290	68

to get fully comprehensive insurance to cover any untoward bumps or scrapes.

In the popular tourist hot spots (like Santa Teresa di Gallura and Alghero) you'll usually find a few rental outlets offering motorcycles and scooters. As a rough guide reckon on around €60 a day for a 600cc motorbike. Scooters cost around €25 to €35 per day.

Most agencies will not hire out motorcycles to people under 18. Note that many places require a sizeable deposit and that you could be responsible for reimbursing part of the cost of the bike if it is stolen.

Insurance

Third-party motor insurance is a minimum requirement in Italy. To drive your own vehicle in Sardinia you'll also need to carry an International Insurance Certificate, known as a Carta Verde (Green Card), available from your car insurer. While you're at it ask your insurer for a European Accident Statement form, which can simplify matters in the event of an accident. Similarly, a European breakdown-assistance policy will make your life a whole lot easier if you break down.

Road Conditions

Sardinia's road network is dictated by the island's hilly geography. Much of the mountainous interior is untarnished by tarmac, and as a general rule it's easier to travel north to south (or vice versa) than east–west.

The island's principal artery, the mostly dual-carriageway SS131 Carlo Felice highway, runs from Cagliari to Sassari (and on to Porto Torres) via Oristano and Macomer. Branching off it at Abbasanta, the SS131dcn runs up to Olbia by way of Nuoro.

Another strip, the SS130, runs west from Cagliari to Iglesias, and dual-carriageway stretches reach from Sassari part of the way to Alghero, and from Porto Torres to the SS291 Sassari–Alghero road.

Along the north coast, the SS200 bypasses Castelsardo en route from Porto Torres to Santa Teresa di Gallura. From nearby Palau, the SS125, or Orientale Sarda, is another key artery, running down the eastern side of the island to Cagliari in the south.

These and many roads in the more touristy coastal areas are well maintained but can be narrow and curvy. In summer, when the island fills with visitors, it is virtually impossible not to get caught in traffic jams along many of them. The area between Olbia and Santa Teresa di Gallura is particularly bad. You may find your patience wears thin in the midsummer heat, and you won't be the only one executing dodgy overtaking manoeuvres. Further inland, the quality of roads is uneven. Main roads are mostly good but narrow and winding, while many secondary routes are potholed and in pretty poor shape.

Getting into and out of the cities, notably Cagliari and Sassari, can be a test of nerves as traffic chokes approaches and exits.

You will also be surprised by the number of unpaved roads on the island – a cause of worry as you bounce down mountain terrain in that expensive rental car. Still, you'll find many a good *agriturismo* (farm-stay accommodation), prehistoric site or fine country restaurant at the end of a dirt track.

Road Rules

In Sardinia, as in the rest of continental Europe, drive on the right-hand side of the road and overtake on the left. Unless otherwise indicated, you must always give way to cars entering an intersection from the right. It is compulsory to wear front seat belts, as well as rear seat belts if the car is fitted with them. If you are caught not wearing a seatbelt you will be required to pay an on-the-spot fine.

Random breath-tests take place. If you're involved in an accident while under the influence of alcohol, the penalties can be severe. The blood-alcohol limit is 0.05%.

Speed limits on main highways (there are no *autostrade* in Sardinia) are 110km/h, on secondary highways 90km/h and in built-up areas 50km/h. Speeding fines follow EU standards and are proportionate with the number of kilometres that you are caught driving over the speed limit, reaching up to €1433 with possible suspension of your licence. Since 2002 drivers are obliged to keep headlights switched on day and night on all dual carriageways.

You don't need a licence to ride a moped under 50cc, but you should be aged 14 or over and you can't carry passengers or ride on highways. The speed limit for a moped is 40km/h. To ride a motorcycle or scooter up to 125cc, you must be aged 16 or over and have a licence (a car licence will do). For motorcycles over 125cc you will need a motorcycle licence. Helmets are compulsory on all mopeds, scooters and motorbikes.

On a motorcycle you will be able to enter restricted traffic areas in cities and towns without any problems, and traffic police generally turn a blind eye to motorcycles or scooters parked on footpaths. There is no lights-on requirement for motorcycles during the day.

HITCHING

Hitching is never entirely safe in any country in the world, and we don't recommend it. Travellers who decide to hitch should understand that they are taking a small but potentially serious risk.

Furthermore, hitchhiking is extremely uncommon in Sardinia. Sardinians can be wary of picking up strangers, which makes getting around this way a frustrating business. Never hitch where drivers can't stop in good time or without causing an obstruction. Look presentable, carry as little luggage as possible and hold a sign in Italian indicating your destination. Do not use the normal thumbs-up signal, as this can offend (it means 'up yours'!). Women travelling on their own would be extremely ill-advised to hitch.

LOCAL TRANSPORT

Bus

All the major towns have a reasonable local bus service. Generally, you won't need to use them, as the towns are compact, with sights, hotels, restaurants and bus/train stations within walking distance of each other. Tickets (around €1) must be purchased from newspaper stands or *tabacchi* outlets and stamped on the bus.

All three airports are linked by local bus services to their respective town centres.

Train

Travelling by train in Sardinia may be slow, but it's straightforward and cheap. **Trenitalia** (☎ 89 20 21; www.trenitalia.com) is the state train system that runs the bulk of the limited network in Sardinia. You will find the *orario* (timetable) posted on station noticeboards. *Partenze* (departures) and *arrivi* (arrivals) are clearly indicated. Note, however, that there are all sorts of permutations on schedules, with services much reduced on Sundays. Handy indicators to look out for are *feriale* (Monday to Saturday) and *festivo* (Sunday and holidays only).

Sardinia's main Trenitalia line runs from Cagliari to Oristano and on to Chilivano-Ozieri, where it divides into two branches. One line heads northwest to Sassari and Porto Torres; the other goes northeast to Olbia and Golfo Aranci. Macomer is another important hub with connections to Nuoro.

Private railway **FdS** (☎ 070 34 31 12; www.fer roviesardegna.it, in Italian) offers limited services. The trains are not the most modern and often consist of a mere handful of clunky carriages. The lines are Sassari–Alghero, Sassari–Nulvi, Sassari–Sorso, Macomer–Nuoro and Monserrato–Isili.

Between mid-June and early September, FdS operates a tourist train service known as the **trenino verde** (☎ 800 460 220; www.tren inoverde.com, in Italian). This operates four lines:

TRANSPORT

Arbatax to Mandas (which connects with the Mandas–Cagliari rail/metro service); Isili to Sorgono; Bosa Marina to Macomer (which links with the Macomer–Nuoro line); and Palau to Nulvi (where you can connect with a regular service to Sassari) via Tempio Pausania. As a means of public transport the *trenino verde* is of limited use – it's extremely slow and covers few likely destinations – but it's an excellent way of experiencing the island's most dramatic and inaccessible countryside, countryside that you would otherwise probably never see. The Mandas–Arbatax route is particularly impressive.

For more detailed information on prices and frequency, see the Getting There & Away sections in the relevant destination chapters.

There is only one class of service in Sardinia, the basic *regionale*. Most of these trains are chuggers that stop at every village on the way, so you won't get anywhere fast by train.

Some trains offer 1st and 2nd class, but there's no big difference between them, other than few people opt to pay extra for 1st class.

As a rough guide, the following fares will give you an idea of costs: Cagliari to Sassari (€13.65), Oristano (€5.15) and Olbia (€14.60); Olbia to Sassari (€6.35); and Sassari to Alghero (€2.20).

It is not worth buying a Eurail or InterRail pass if you are only travelling in Sardinia.

TOURS

A superb destination for outdoor lovers, Sardinia offers no end of possibilities for keen sports fans and armchair sailors. Throughout the island local operators offer all manner of guided excursions and tours. These include:

Archeo Tours (☎ 329 764 33 43; Via Eleanora D'Arborea, Osini) This small association leads archaeological and nature tours through the countryside around Osini and Ulassai.

Atlantikà (☎ 328 972 97 19; www.atlantika.it; Via Lamarmora 195, Dorgali) A consortium of guides in Dorgali, offering everything from hiking day trips to canyoning and kayaking in the Gennargentu.

Barbagia No Limits (☎ 0784 5 29 06; www.barbag ianolimits.it; Via Cagliari 85, Gavoi) This adventure sports outfit organises all sorts of outdoor activities, including caving trips, jeep tours and survival courses.

Esedra Sardegna (☎ 0785 37 42 58; www.esedrasar degna.it; Corso Vittorio Emanuele 64; Bosa) Esedra arranges excursions in and around Bosa, and across the whole island.

Gallura Viaggi Avventura (☎ 079 63 12 73; c/o Pro Loco Tourist Office, Piazza Gallura 2, Tempio Pausania) A small local group that organises biking and hiking tours of Monte Limbara.

Mare e Natura (☎ 393 985 04 35; www.marenatura.it; Via Sassari 77, Stintino) Organises tours of the Parco Nazionale dell'Asinara, a tiny island off the northwest coast.

Sardinia Hike and Bike (☎ 070 924 32 329; www.sa rdiniahikeandbike.com; Loc Pixina Manna, Pula) Based on the south coast, this outfit runs hiking and cycling tours for all levels, from easy half-day outings to weeklong marathons.

As well as these specialist organisations, you'll find hundreds of outfits running boat trips along Sardinia's coastal waters. Popular spots include Alghero, Cala Gonone, Stintino, Santa Maria Navarese and Porto San Paolo.

Health

CONTENTS

BEFORE YOU GO

While Sardinia has good health care, prevention is the key to staying healthy while abroad. A little planning before departure, particularly for preexisting illnesses, will save trouble later. Bring medications in their original, clearly labelled containers. A signed and dated letter from your physician describing your medical conditions and medications, including their generic names, is also a good idea. If carrying syringes or needles, be sure to have a physician's letter documenting their medical necessity. If you are embarking on a long trip, make sure your teeth are OK (dental treatment is expensive in Italy) and take your optical prescription with you.

INSURANCE

If you're an EU citizen, a European Health Insurance Card (EHIC), available from health centres or, in the UK, post offices, covers you for most medical care. It will not cover you for nonemergencies or emergency repatriation.

Citizens from other countries should find out if there is a reciprocal arrangement for free medical care between their country and Italy; Australia, for instance, has such an agreement. If you do need health insurance, make sure you get a policy that covers you for the worst possible scenario, such as an accident requiring an emergency flight home. Find out in advance if your insurance plan will make payments directly to providers or reimburse you later for overseas health expenditures.

RECOMMENDED VACCINATIONS

No jabs are required to travel to Sardinia. The World Health Organization (WHO), however, recommends that all travellers should be covered for diphtheria, tetanus, measles, mumps, rubella and polio, as well as hepatitis B.

INTERNET RESOURCES

The WHO's publication *International Travel and Health* is revised annually and is available online at www.who.int/ith. Other useful websites include www.mdtravelhealth.com (travel-health recommendations for every country; updated daily), www.fitfortravel .scot.nhs.uk (general travel advice for the layman), www.ageconcern.org.uk (advice on travel for the elderly) and www.marie stopes.org.uk (information on women's health and contraception).

IN TRANSIT

DEEP VEIN THROMBOSIS (DVT)

Blood clots may form in the legs during plane flights, chiefly because of prolonged immobility (the longer the flight, the greater the risk). The chief symptom of DVT is swelling or pain of the foot, ankle or calf, usually but not always on just one side. When a blood clot travels to the lungs, it may cause chest pain and breathing difficulties. Travellers with any of these symptoms should immediately seek medical attention. To prevent the development of DVT on long flights you should walk about the cabin of the plane, contract the leg muscles while sitting down, drink plenty of fluids, and avoid alcohol and tobacco.

JET LAG

To avoid jet lag try drinking plenty of non-alcoholic fluids and eating light meals. Upon arrival, get exposure to natural sunlight and readjust your schedule (for meals, sleep etc) as soon as possible.

IN SARDINIA

AVAILABILITY & COST OF HEALTH CARE

If you need an ambulance anywhere in Sardinia call ☎ 118. For emergency treatment, go straight to the *pronto soccorso* (casualty) section of a public hospital, where you can also get emergency dental treatment.

Excellent health care is readily available throughout Sardinia, but standards can vary. Pharmacists can give valuable advice and sell over-the-counter medication for minor illnesses. They can also advise when more specialised help is required and point you in the right direction.

The Guardia Medica is an on-call medical service that offers assistance throughout the night (8pm to 8am), at weekends and on public holidays. They do not provide emergency care (for that go to the *pronto soccorso* department at the nearest hospital), although they will make home visits when absolutely necessary. The service is available in most major towns.

Italian hospitals charge flat, all-inclusive rates (itemised bills are not provided), which cover all assistance, bed and board. Many hospitals will agree to bill you after discharge, but not all accept credit cards. Private hospitals, which charge more and rarely offer emergency treatment, will insist on payment before discharge.

TRAVELLERS' DIARRHOEA

If you develop diarrhoea, be sure to drink plenty of fluids, preferably in the form of an oral rehydration solution such as Dioralyte. If diarrhoea is bloody, persists for more than 72 hours or is accompanied by fever, shaking, chills or severe abdominal pain, you should seek medical attention.

ENVIRONMENTAL HAZARDS
Heatstroke

Heatstroke occurs following excessive fluid loss with inadequate replacement of fluids and salt. Symptoms include headache, dizziness and tiredness. Dehydration is already happening by the time you feel thirsty – aim to drink sufficient water to produce pale, diluted urine. To treat heatstroke drink water and/or fruit juice, and cool the body with cold water and fans.

Hypothermia

Hypothermia occurs when the body loses heat faster than it can produce it. As ever, proper preparation will reduce the risks of getting it. Even on a hot day in the mountains the weather can change rapidly, so carry waterproof garments, warm layers and a hat, and inform others of your route. Hypothermia starts with shivering, loss of judgment and clumsiness. Unless rewarming occurs, the sufferer deteriorates into apathy, confusion and coma. Prevent further heat loss by seeking shelter, warm dry clothing, hot sweet drinks and shared bodily warmth.

Bites, Stings & Insect-Borne Diseases

Throughout the centuries Sardinia was devastated by malaria, with nearly 60% of the population affected in 1945. After the war, however, the malarial mosquito was eradicated by an American health program, which cleared the island in 1951.

Mosquitoes are still a real problem around low-lying marshy areas such as Cabras and Olbia; you should be particularly wary if you are considering camping. If travelling in summer you should pack mosquito repellent as a matter of course.

Sardinian beaches are occasionally inundated with jellyfish. Their stings are painful but not dangerous. Dousing in vinegar will deactivate any stingers that have not fired. Calamine lotion, antihistamines and analgesics may reduce the reaction and relieve pain. On dry land, you'll be much safer as Sardinia has absolutely no poisonous snakes.

Always check all over your body if you have been walking through a potentially tick-infested area as ticks can cause skin infections and other more serious diseases such as Lyme disease and tick-borne encephalitis. If a tick is found attached, press down around the tick's head with tweezers, grab the head and gently pull upwards. Avoid pulling the rear of the body as this may squeeze the tick's gut contents through the attached mouth parts into the skin, increasing the risk of infection and disease. Lyme disease begins with the spreading of a rash at the site of the bite, accompanied by fever, headache, extreme fatigue, aching joints and muscles, and severe neck stiffness. If untreated, symptoms usually disappear, but disorders of the nervous system, heart and joints can develop later. Treatment works best early in the illness – medical help should be sought. Symptoms of tick-borne encephalitis include blotches around the bite, which is sometimes pale in the middle, and headaches, stiffness and other flulike symptoms (as well as extreme tiredness) appearing a week or two after the bite. Again, medical help must be sought.

Leishmaniasis is a group of parasitic diseases transmitted by sandflies and found in coastal parts of Italy. Cutaneous leishmaniasis affects the skin tissue and causes ulceration and disfigurement; visceral leishmaniasis affects the internal organs. Avoiding sandfly bites by covering up and using repellent is the best precaution against this disease.

TRAVELLING WITH CHILDREN

Make sure children are up to date with routine vaccinations, and discuss possible travel vaccines well before departure as some vaccines are not suitable for children aged under a year. Lonely Planet's *Travel with Children* includes travel-health advice for younger children.

WOMEN'S HEALTH

Emotional stress, exhaustion and travelling through different time zones can all contribute to an upset in the menstrual pattern.

If using oral contraceptives, remember that some antibiotics, as well as diarrhoea and vomiting, can interfere with the effectiveness of the pill. Time zones, gastrointestinal upsets and antibiotics do not affect injectable contraception.

Travelling during pregnancy is usually possible, but always consult your doctor before planning your trip. The most risky times for travel are during the first 12 weeks of pregnancy and after 30 weeks.

SEXUAL HEALTH

Condoms are readily available in Sardinia, but emergency contraception is not, so take the necessary precautions.

HEALTH

Language

CONTENTS

Tourism has brought the outside world to Sardinia but Sardinians with a fluent command of foreign languages remain fairly thin on the ground. Staff working in tourist offices, hotels and restaurants in the main coastal resorts will often have a smattering of English, and maybe German, but inland, you can't rely on finding English-speakers. If you can learn a little Italian, you'll find it both useful and culturally rewarding.

Many Sardinians are bilingual, switching from Sardinian to Italian with equal ease, although a growing proportion of the population, especially those in the cities and bigger towns, are losing command of the island tongue (which itself divides into several dialects). A 16th century version of Catalan is still spoken in Alghero, although locals differ in opinion on how widely it is used.

ITALIAN

Italian is a Romance language related to French, Spanish, Portuguese and Romanian. The Romance languages belong to the Indo-European group of languages, which includes English. Indeed, as English and Italian share common roots in Latin, you will recognise many Italian words.

Although it's commonly accepted that modern standard Italian developed from the Tuscan dialect, history shows that Tuscany's status as the political, cultural and financial power base of the nation ensured that the region's dialect would ultimately be installed as the national tongue.

The Italian of today is something of a composite. What you hear on the radio and TV, in educated discourse and indeed in the everyday language of many people is the result of centuries of cross-fertilisation between the dialects, greatly accelerated in the postwar decades by the modern media.

If you have more than the most fundamental grasp of the Italian language, you need to be aware that many Sardinians still expect to be addressed in the third person formal (*lei* instead of *tu*). Also, it isn't polite to use the greeting *ciao* when addressing strangers unless they use it first; it's better to say *buongiorno* (or *buona sera*, as the case may be) and *arrivederci* (or the more polite form, *arrivederla*). This is the case in most parts of Italy, but in Sardinia use of the informal can be considered gravely impolite – and in some cases downright insulting – especially when talking to an older person.

We've used the formal mode of address for most of the phrases in this guide. Use of the informal address is indicated by 'inf' in brackets. Italian also has both masculine and feminine forms (usually ending in 'o' and 'a' respectively). Where both forms are given in this guide, they are separated by a slash, the masculine form first.

If you'd like a more comprehensive guide to the language, pick up a copy of Lonely Planet's pocket-sized but comprehensive *Italian Phrasebook*.

PRONUNCIATION

Sardinians' pronunciation of standard Italian is refreshingly clear and easy to understand, even if you have only a limited command of the language.

Italian pronunciation isn't very difficult to master once you learn a few easy rules. Although some of the more clipped vowels

SARDINIAN – A LATIN LANGUAGE & ITS DIALECTS

Speakers of Italian will not be long in noticing the oddness of Sardinian. Signs, family and place names and traditional menus will soon have you wondering about all the 'uddus' and other strange sounds and suffixes. Another giveaway are the definite articles, *su, sa, sus, sos, sas* etc, in place of the Italian *il, lo, la, i, gli* and *le*.

Sardinia has seen colonists, occupiers, pirates, foreign viceroys and kings come and go since Rome managed to occupy the island more than 2000 years ago. Many Sardinians reacted by retreating into themselves and their island and it is probably largely due to this passive defiance that they've managed to preserve a key to their own identity – their language.

Sardinians will tell you with a sort of contrary pride that their language is much closer to its mother tongue, Latin, than any of its other offshoots, Italian and all its dialects included. Simple words confirm the claim – while in Italian the word for house is *casa*, the Sardinians have stuck with the Latin *domus* (the Italian equivalent, *duomo* has come to mean 'cathedral').

The 'purest' form of Sardinian is supposedly Logudorese, the dialect of the Logudoro area in the north of the island, although it is probably more a question of quantity (of speakers) than quality. Also considered important is the southern Campidanese. Other dialectal variants thrive across the island.

Nowadays, Sardinian (Sardo) is experiencing the same problems other minority regional languages face in the fight for survival against imposed national tongues. Since Italian unity in the 19th century, the erosion of Sardinian in the cities and towns has accelerated. While many Sardinians still understand the language, city folk tend not to speak it. You're more likely to hear it in the small towns and villages of the interior.

No language is impermeable and the centuries of Catalan and Spanish rule inevitably had an effect on Sardinian. In particular, Catalan words managed to slip through. In Catalonia and Sardinia a river is generally called a *riu* (often rendered in the Spanish *rio* in Sardinia now), while glasses are *ulleres* in the former and *oglieras* in the latter. The spelling may be different but the pronunciation is virtually the same.

On the subject of Catalan, some residents of Alghero, long an independent Catalan settlement, even today speak a dated version of Catalan, snubbing both Sardinian and Italian.

and stress on double letters require careful practice for English speakers, it's easy enough to make yourself understood.

Vowels

Vowels sounds are generally shorter than English equivalents:

a   as in 'art', eg *caro* (dear); sometimes short, eg *amico/a* (friend)
e   short, as in 'let', eg *mettere* (to put); long, as in 'there', eg *mela* (apple)
i   short, as in 'it', eg *inizio* (start); long, as in 'marine', eg *vino* (wine)
o   short, as in 'dot', eg *donna* (woman); long, as in 'port', eg *ora* (hour)
u   as the 'oo' in 'book', eg *puro* (pure)

Consonants

The pronunciation of most Italian consonants is similar to that of their English counterparts. Pronunciation of some consonants depends on certain rules:

c   as the 'k' in 'kit' before **a**, **o** and **u**; as the 'ch' in 'choose' before **e** and **i**
ch   as the 'k' in 'kit'
g   as the 'g' in 'get' before **a**, **o**, **u** and **h**; as the 'j' in 'jet' before **e** and **i**
gli   as the 'lli' in 'million'
gn   as the 'ny' in 'canyon'
h   always silent
r   a rolled 'rr' sound
sc   as the 'sh' in 'sheep' before **e** and **i**; as 'sk' before **a**, **o**, **u** and **h**
z   at the beginning of a word, as the 'dz' in 'adze'; elsewhere as the 'ts' in 'its'

Note that when **ci**, **gi** and **sci** are followed by **a**, **o** or **u**, the 'i' is not pronounced unless the accent falls on the 'i'. Thus the name 'Giovanni' is pronounced jo-*va*-nee.

A double consonant is pronounced as a longer, more forceful sound than a single consonant. This can directly affect the meaning of a word, eg *sono* (I am), *sonno* (sleep), but the context of a sentence will usually get the message across.

Word Stress

Stress is indicated in our pronunciation guide by italics. Word stress generally falls on the second-last syllable, as in spa-*ghet*-ti, but when a word has an accent, the stress falls on that syllable, as in cit-*tà* (city).

ACCOMMODATION

I'm looking for a ...	Cerco ...	*cher*-ko ...
guesthouse	una pensione	*oo*-na pen-*syo*-ne
hotel	un albergo	oon al-*ber*-go
youth hostel	un ostello per la gioventù	oon os-*te*-lo per la jo-ven-*too*

Where is a cheap hotel?
Dov'è un albergo   do-*ve* oon al-*ber*-go
a buon prezzo?   a bwon *pre*-tso
What is the address?
Qual'è l'indirizzo?   kwa-*le* leen-dee-*ree*-tso
Could you write the address, please?
Può scrivere l'indirizzo,   pwo *skree*-ve-re leen-dee-*ree*-tso
per favore?   per fa-*vo*-re
Do you have any rooms available?
Avete camere libere?   a-*ve*-te *ka*-me-re *lee*-be-re

MAKING A RESERVATION
(for inclusion in letters, faxes and emails)

To ...	A ...
From ...	Da ...
Date	Data
I'd like to book ...	Vorrei prenotare ... (see the list on this page for bed/room options)
in the name of ...	nel nome di ...
for the night/s of ...	per la notte/le notti di ...
credit card ...	carta di credito ...
number	numero
expiry date	data di scadenza
Please confirm availability and price.	Vi prego di confirmare disponibilità e prezzo.

I'd like (a) ...	Vorrei ...	vo-*ray* ...
bed	un letto	oon *le*-to
single room	una camera singola	oo-na *ka*-me-ra *seen*-go-la
double room	una camera matrimoniale	oo-na *ka*-me-ra ma-tree-mo-*nya*-le

room with two beds	una camera doppia	oo-na *ka*-me-ra *do*-pya
room with a bathroom	una camera con bagno	oo-na *ka*-me-ra kon *ba*-nyo
to share a dorm	un letto in dormitorio	oon *le*-to een dor-mee-*to*-ryo

How much is it ...? Quanto costa ...?   *kwan*-to *ko*-sta ...

per night	per la notte	per la *no*-te
per person	per persona	per per-*so*-na

May I see it?
Posso vederla?   *po*-so ve-*der*-la
Where is the bathroom?
Dov'è il bagno?   do-*ve* eel *ba*-nyo
I'm/We're leaving today.
Parto/Partiamo oggi.   *par*-to/par-*tya*-mo *o*-jee

CONVERSATION & ESSENTIALS

Hello.	Buongiorno.	bwon-*jor*-no
	Ciao. (inf)	chow
Goodbye.	Arrivederci.	a-ree-ve-*der*-chee
	Ciao. (inf)	chow
Yes.	Sì.	see
No.	No.	no
Please.	Per favore/	per fa-*vo*-re/
	Per piacere.	per pya-*chay*-re
Thank you (very much).	Grazie (mille).	*gra*-tsye (*mee*-le)
You're welcome.	Prego.	*pre*-go
Excuse me. (for attention)	Mi scusi.	mee *skoo*-zee
Excuse me. (when going past)	Permesso.	per *me*-so
I'm sorry.	Mi dispiace/	mee dees-*pya*-che/
	Mi perdoni.	mee per-*do*-nee

What's your name?
Come si chiama?   *ko*-me see *kya*-ma
Come ti chiami? (inf)   *ko*-me tee *kya*-mee
My name is ...
Mi chiamo ...   mee *kya*-mo ...
Where are you from?
Da dove viene?   da *do*-ve *vye*-ne
Di dove sei? (inf)   dee *do*-ve *se*-ee
I'm from ...
Vengo da ...   *ven*-go da ...
Do you like ...?
Ti piace ...?   tee *pya*-che ...
I (don't) like ...
(Non) Mi piace ...   (non) mee *pya*-che ...
Just a minute.
Un momento.   oon mo-*men*-to

DIRECTIONS

Where is ...?
Dov'è ...? do·ve ...
Go straight ahead.
Si va sempre diritto. see va sem·pre dee·ree·to
Vai sempre diritto. (inf) va·ee sem·pre dee·ree·to
Turn left.
Giri a sinistra. jee·ree a see·nee·stra
Turn right.
Giri a destra. jee·ree a de·stra
at the next corner
al prossimo angolo al pro·see·mo an·go·lo
at the traffic lights
al semaforo al se·ma·fo·ro

SIGNS

Ingresso/Entrata	Entrance
Uscita	Exit
Informazione	Information
Aperto	Open
Chiuso	Closed
Proibito/Vietato	Prohibited
Camere Libere	Rooms Available
Completo	Full/No Vacancies
Polizia/Carabinieri	Police
Questura	Police Station
Gabinetti/Bagni	Toilets
Uomini	Men
Donne	Women

behind	dietro	dye·tro
in front of	davanti	da·van·tee
far (from)	lontano (da)	lon·ta·no (da)
near (to)	vicino (di)	vee·chee·no (dee)
opposite	di fronte a	dee fron·te a
beach	la spiaggia	la spya·ja
bridge	il ponte	eel pon·te
castle	il castello	eel kas·te·lo
cathedral	il duomo	eel dwo·mo
island	l'isola	lee·so·la
(main) square	la piazza (principale)	la pya·tsa (preen·chee·pa·le)
market	il mercato	eel mer·ka·to
old city	il centro storico	eel chen·tro sto·ree·ko
palace	il palazzo	eel pa·la·tso
ruins	le rovine	le ro·vee·ne
sea	il mare	eel ma·re
tower	la torre	la to·re

EMERGENCIES

Help!
Aiuto! a·yoo·to
There's been an accident!
C'è stato un incidente! che sta·to oon een·chee·den·te
I'm lost.
Mi sono perso/a. mee so·no per·so/a
Go away!
Lasciami in pace! la·sha·mi een pa·che
Vai via! (inf) va·ee vee·a

Call ...!	Chiami ...!	kee·ya·mee ...
a doctor	un dottore/ un medico	oon do·to·re/ oon me·dee·ko
the police	la polizia	la po·lee·tsee·ya

HEALTH

I'm ill. Mi sento male. mee sen·to ma·le
It hurts here. Mi fa male qui. mee fa ma·le kwee

I'm ...	Sono ...	so·no ...
asthmatic	asmatico/a	az·ma·tee·ko/a
diabetic	diabetico/a	dee·a·be·tee·ko/a
epileptic	epilettico/a	e·pee·le·tee·ko/a

I'm allergic ...	Sono allergico/a ...	so·no a·ler·jee·ko/a ...
to antibiotics	agli antibiotici	a·lyee an·tee·bee·o·tee·chee
to aspirin	all'aspirina	a·la·spe·ree·na
to penicillin	alla penicillina	a·la pe·nee·see·lee·na
to nuts	ai noci	a·ee no·chee

antiseptic	antisettico	an·tee·se·tee·ko
aspirin	aspirina	as·pee·ree·na
condoms	preservativi	pre·zer·va·tee·vee
contraceptive	contraccetivo	kon·tra·che·tee·vo
diarrhoea	diarrea	dee·a·re·a
medicine	medicina	me·dee·chee·na
sunblock cream	crema solare	kre·ma so·la·re
tampons	tamponi	tam·po·nee

LANGUAGE DIFFICULTIES

Do you speak English?
Parla inglese? par·la een·gle·ze
Does anyone here speak English?
C'è qualcuno che parla inglese? che kwal·koo·no ke par·la een·gle·ze
How do you say ... in Italian?
Come si dice ... in italiano? ko·me see dee·che ... een ee·ta·lya·no

What does ... mean?
Che vuol dire ...? ke vwol *dee*·re ...
I (don't) understand.
(Non) capisco. (non) ka·*pee*·sko
Please write it down.
Può scriverlo, per favore? pwo *skree*·ver·lo per fa·*vo*·re
Can you show me (on the map)?
Può mostrarmelo pwo mos·*trar*·me·lo
(sulla pianta)? (soo·la *pyan*·ta)

NUMBERS

0	zero	dze·ro
1	uno	oo·no
2	due	doo·e
3	tre	tre
4	quattro	kwa·tro
5	cinque	cheen·kwe
6	sei	say
7	sette	se·te
8	otto	o·to
9	nove	no·ve
10	dieci	dye·chee
11	undici	oon·dee·chee
12	dodici	do·dee·chee
13	tredici	tre·dee·chee
14	quattordici	kwa·tor·dee·chee
15	quindici	kween·dee·chee
16	sedici	se·dee·chee
17	diciassette	dee·cha·se·te
18	diciotto	dee·cho·to
19	diciannove	dee·cha·no·ve
20	venti	ven·tee
21	ventuno	ven·too·no
22	ventidue	ven·tee·doo·e
30	trenta	tren·ta
40	quaranta	kwa·ran·ta
50	cinquanta	cheen·kwan·ta
60	sessanta	se·san·ta
70	settanta	se·tan·ta
80	ottanta	o·tan·ta
90	novanta	no·van·ta
100	cento	chen·to
1000	mille	mee·le
2000	due mila	doo·e mee·la

PAPERWORK

name	nome	no·me
nationality	nazionalità	na·tsyo·na·lee·ta
date/place of	data/luogo di	da·ta/lwo·go dee
birth	nascita	na·shee·ta
sex (gender)	sesso	se·so
passport	passaporto	pa·sa·por·to
visa	visto	vee·sto

QUESTION WORDS

Who?	Chi?	kee
What?	Che?	ke
When?	Quando?	kwan·do
Where?	Dove?	do·ve
How?	Come?	ko·me

SHOPPING & SERVICES

I'd like to buy ...
Vorrei comprare ... vo·ray kom·*pra*·re ...
How much is it?
Quanto costa? kwan·to ko·sta
I don't like it.
Non mi piace. non mee pya·che
May I look at it?
Posso dare po·so da·re
un'occhiata? oo·no·kya·ta
I'm just looking.
Sto solo guardando. sto so·lo gwar·dan·do
It's cheap.
Non è caro/cara. non e ka·ro/ka·ra
It's too expensive.
È troppo caro/a. e tro·po ka·ro/ka·ra
I'll take it.
Lo/La compro. lo/la kom·pro

Do you accept	Accettate carte	a·che·ta·te kar·te
credit cards?	di credito?	dee kre·dee·to

I want to	Voglio	vo·lyo
change ...	cambiare ...	kam·bya·re ...
money	del denaro	del de·na·ro
travellers	assegni di	a·se·nyee dee
cheques	viaggio	vee·a·jo

more	più	pyoo
less	meno	me·no
smaller	più piccolo/a	pyoo pee·ko·lo/la
bigger	più grande	pyoo gran·de

I'm looking for ...	Cerco ...	cher·ko ...
a bank	un banco	oon ban·ko
the church	la chiesa	la kye·za
the city centre	il centro	eel chen·tro
the ... embassy	l'ambasciata	lam·ba·sha·ta
	di ...	dee ...
the market	il mercato	eel mer·ka·to
the museum	il museo	eel moo·ze·o
the post office	la posta	la po·sta
a public toilet	un gabinetto	oon ga·bee·ne·to
the telephone	il centro	eel chen·tro
centre	telefonico	te·le·fo·nee·ko
the tourist	l'ufficio	loo·fee·cho
office	di turismo	dee too·reez·mo

TIME & DATES

What time is it?	Che ore sono?	ke o·re so·no
It's (8 o'clock).	Sono (le otto).	so·no (le o·to)

in the morning	di mattina	dee ma·tee·na
in the afternoon	di pomeriggio	dee po·me·ree·jo
in the evening	di sera	dee se·ra
When?	Quando?	kwan·do
today	oggi	o·jee
tomorrow	domani	do·ma·nee
yesterday	ieri	ye·ree

Monday	lunedì	loo·ne·dee
Tuesday	martedì	mar·te·dee
Wednesday	mercoledì	mer·ko·le·dee
Thursday	giovedì	jo·ve·dee
Friday	venerdì	ve·ner·dee
Saturday	sabato	sa·ba·to
Sunday	domenica	do·me·nee·ka

January	gennaio	je·na·yo
February	febbraio	fe·bra·yo
March	marzo	mar·tso
April	aprile	a·pree·le
May	maggio	ma·jo
June	giugno	joo·nyo
July	luglio	loo·lyo
August	agosto	a·gos·to
September	settembre	se·tem·bre
October	ottobre	o·to·bre
November	novembre	no·vem·bre
December	dicembre	dee·chem·bre

TRANSPORT
Public Transport

When does the	A che ora parte/	a ke o·ra par·te/
... leave/arrive?	arriva ...?	a·ree·va ...
boat	la nave	la na·ve
(city) bus	l'autobus	low·to·boos
(intercity) bus	il pullman	eel pool·man
plane	l'aereo	la·e·re·o
train	il treno	eel tre·no

I'd like a ...	Vorrei un	vo·ray oon
ticket.	biglietto ...	bee·lye·to ...
one way	di solo andata	dee so·lo an·da·ta
return	di andata e	dee an·da·ta e
	ritorno	ree·toor·no
1st class	di prima classe	dee pree·ma kla·se
2nd class	di seconda	dee se·kon·da
	classe	kla·se

I want to go to ...
Voglio andare a ...   vo·lyo an·da·re a ...

The train has been cancelled/delayed.
Il treno è soppresso/   eel tre·no e so·pre·so/
in ritardo.   een ree·tar·do

the first	il primo	eel pree·mo
the last	l'ultimo	lool·tee·mo
platform (two)	binario (due)	bee·na·ryo (doo·e)
ticket office	biglietteria	bee·lye·te·ree·a
timetable	orario	o·ra·ryo
train station	stazione	sta·tsyo·ne

Private Transport

I'd like to hire	Vorrei	vo·ray
a/an ...	noleggiare ...	no·le·ja·re ...
car	una macchina	oo·na ma·kee·na
4WD	un fuoristrada	oon fwo·ree·
		stra·da
motorbike	una moto	oo·na mo·to
bicycle	una bici(cletta)	oo·na bee·chee·
		(kle·ta)

ROAD SIGNS

Dare la Precedenza	Give Way
Deviazione	Detour
Divieto di Accesso	No Entry
Divieto di Sorpasso	No Overtaking
Divieto di Sosta	No Parking
Entrata	Entrance
Passo Carrabile	Keep Clear
Pericolo	Danger
Rallentare	Slow Down
Senso Unico	One Way
Uscita	Exit

Is this the road to ...?
Questa strada porta   kwe·sta stra·da por·ta
a ...?   a ...

Where's a service station?
Dov'è una stazione   do·ve oo·na sta·tsyo·ne
di servizio?   dee ser·vee·tsyo

Please fill it up.
Il pieno, per favore.   eel pye·no per fa·vo·re

I'd like (30) litres.
Vorrei (trenta) litri.   vo·ray (tren·ta) lee·tree

diesel	gasolio/diesel	ga·zo·lyo/dee·zel
leaded petrol	benzina con	ben·dzee·na kon
	piombo	pyom·bo
unleaded petrol	benzina senza	ben·dzee·na
	piombo	sen·dza pyom·bo

(How long) Can I park here?
(Per quanto tempo)   (per kwan·to tem·po)
Posso parcheggiare qui?   po·so par·ke·ja·re kwee

Where do I pay?
Dove si paga?   *do*·ve see *pa*·ga
I need a mechanic.
Ho bisogno di un   o bee·*zo*·nyo dee oon
  meccanico.   me·*ka*·nee·ko
The car/motorbike has broken down (at ...).
La macchina/moto   la *ma*·kee·na/*mo*·to
  si è guastata (a ...).   see e gwas·*ta*·ta (a ...)
The car/motorbike won't start.
La macchina/moto   la *ma*·kee·na/*mo*·to
  non parte.   non *par*·te
I have a flat tyre.
Ho una gomma bucata.   o oo·na *go*·ma boo·*ka*·ta
I've run out of petrol.
Ho esaurito la benzina.   o e·zo·*ree*·to la ben·*dzee*·na
I've had an accident.
Ho avuto un incidente.   o a·*voo*·to oon een·chee·*den*·te

TRAVEL WITH CHILDREN

Is there a/an ...?   *C'è ...?*   che ...
I need a/an ...   *Ho bisogno di ...*   o bee·*zo*·nyo dee ...
  baby change   *un bagno con*   oon *ba*·nyo kon
    room   *fasciatoio*   fa·sha·*to*·yo

car baby seat	*un seggiolino*	oon se·jo·*lee*·no
	per bambini	per bam·*bee*·nee
child-minding	*un servizio*	oon ser·*vee*·tsyo
service	*di babysitter*	dee be·bee·*see*·ter
children's menu	*un menù per*	oon me·*noo* per
	bambini	bam·*bee*·nee
(disposable)	*pannolini*	pa·no·*lee*·nee
nappies/diapers	*(usa e getta)*	(*oo*·sa e *je*·ta)
formula (milk)	*latte in polvere*	*la*·te in *pol*·ve·re
(English-	*un/una*	oon/oo·na
speaking)	*babysitter (che*	be·bee·*see*·ter
babysitter	*parli inglese)*	(ke *par*·lee
		een·*gle*·ze)
highchair	*un seggiolone*	oon se·jo·*lo*·ne
potty	*un vasino*	oon va·*zee*·no
stroller	*un passeggino*	oon pa·se·*jee*·no

Do you mind if I breastfeed here?
Le dispiace se allatto il/la bimbo/a qui?
le dees·*pya*·che se a·*la*·to eel/la *beem*·bo/a kwee
Are children allowed?
I bambini sono ammessi?
ee bam·*bee*·nee so·no a·*me*·see

LANGUAGE

Glossary

AAST – Azienda Autonoma di Soggiorno e Turismo (tourist office)
ACI – Automobile Club d'Italia, the Italian automobile club
agriturismo – farm-stay accommodation
albergo – hotel (up to five stars)
albergo diffuso – hotel spread over more than one site, typically in the historic centre of a town
alto – high
anfiteatro – amphitheatre
aperitivo – aperitif
ARST – Azienda Regionale Sarda Transporti (state bus company)
assicurato/a – insured

bancomat – ATM
benzina – petrol
benzina senza piombo – unleaded petrol
borgo – ancient town or village

camera – room
campanile – bell tower
cappella – chapel
carabinieri – military police (see *polizia*)
Carnevale – carnival period between Epiphany and Lent
castello – castle
cattedrale – cathedral
cena – evening meal
centro – centre
centro storico – literally 'historical centre'; old town
chiesa – church
chiostro – cloister; covered walkway, enclosed by columns, around a quadrangle
colazione – breakfast
comune – equivalent to a municipality or county; town or city council
coperto – cover charge
corso – main street, avenue
cortile – courtyard
CTS – Centro Turistico Studentesco e Giovanile, the student/youth travel agency
cumbessias – pilgrims' lodgings found in courtyards around churches, traditionally the scene of religious festivities (of up to nine days' duration) in honour of a particular saint
cupola – dome

digestivo – after-dinner liqueur
dolci –sweets

domus de janas – literally 'fairy house'; ancient tomb cut into rock
duomo – cathedral

ENIT – Ente Nazionale Italiano per il Turismo, the Italian state tourist office
enoteca – wine bar or wine shop

farmacia – pharmacy
festa – festival
fiume – (main) river
fontana – fountain
fregola – a large couscouslike grain

gasolio – diesel
giudicato – province; in medieval times Sardinia was divided into the Giudicato of Cagliari, Giudicato of Logudoro, Giudicato of Gallura and Giudicato of Arborea
golfo – gulf
grotta – cave
guardia medica – emergency call-out doctor service

isola – island

lago – lake
largo – (small) square
lavanderia – laundrette
libreria – bookshop
lido – managed section of beach
lungomare – seafront road; promenade

macchia – Mediterranean scrub
mare – sea
mattanza – literally 'slaughter'; the annual tuna catch in southwest Sardinia
mezza pensione – half board
monte – mountain, mount
municipio – town hall
muristenes – see *cumbessias*
murra – a popular game in the Barbagia region, in which participants try to guess what numbers their opponents will form with their fingers

Natale – Christmas
numero verde – toll-free telephone number
nuraghe – Bronze Age stone towers and fortified settlements

oggetti smarriti – lost property
oratorio – oratory

ospedale – hospital
ostello per la gioventù – youth hostel

palazzo – palace; a large building of any type, including an apartment block
parco – park
Pasqua – Easter
passeggiata – traditional evening stroll
pasticceria – shop selling cakes, pastries and biscuits
pensione – small hotel, often with board
piazza – square
pietà – literally 'pity or compassion'; sculpture, drawing or painting of the dead Christ supported by the Madonna
pinacoteca – art gallery
polizia – police
poltrona – literally 'armchair'; airline-type chair on a ferry
ponte – bridge
porto – port
pronto soccorso – first aid, casualty ward

questura – police station

rio – secondary river
riserva naturale – nature reserve
rocca – fortress

sagra – festival, usually dedicated to one culinary item, such as *funghi* (mushrooms), wine etc

saline – saltpans
santuario – sanctuary, often with a country chapel
scalette – 'little stairs' (as in Scalette di Santa Chiara, a steep stairway up into Cagliari's Il Castello district)
servizio – service fee
spiaggia – beach
stagno – lagoon
stazione marittima – ferry terminal
stazzo/u – farmstead in the Gallura region
strada – street, road

teatro – theatre
tempio – temple
terme – thermal baths
tholos – name used to describe the conical shape of many *nuraghe*
tomba di gigante – literally 'giant's tomb'; ancient mass grave
tonnara – tuna-processing plant
tophet – sacred Phoenician or Carthaginian burial ground for children and babies
torre – tower
tramezzini – sandwiches
treno – train

via – street, road
viale – avenue
vicolo – alley, alleyway

The Author

DUNCAN GARWOOD

With this book Duncan completes a full Italian cycle. He's written guides to Rome, Piedmont, and Naples and the Amalfi Coast, and has contributed to the past three editions of Lonely Planet's *Italy* guide. Born and brought up in southern England, he got his first taste of journalism on a newspaper in Slough before landing a job on the in-house paper of a big utilities company. The thrill of writing about sewage and the benefits of tap water soon paled, and when he got the chance to move to Italy in 1999 he jumped at it. Duncan currently lives in a small town outside Rome with his wife and two kids, dividing his time between Wiggles DVDs, writing and the occasional translation.

My Sardinia

Travelling around Sardinia I could never escape the feeling of being on Italian soil, yet being somewhere quite different. I've explored most of Italy but I've never come across such a rich and varied landscape, so still and silent, and so incredibly beautiful. The coastline around Cala Gonone (p211) and the forested valleys around Tempio Pausania (p185), the Sinis Peninsula (p109) and the wild Costa Verde beaches (p84) – these were all highlights. Everywhere I went I was met with unfailing politeness; in some out-of-the-way villages I even found myself being greeted by women in traditional dress as I walked down the streets.

258

Behind the Scenes

THIS BOOK

The 3rd edition of Sardinia was researched and written by Duncan Garwood. The previous edition of this book was researched and updated by Paula Hardy. This guidebook was commissioned in Lonely Planet's London office, and produced by the following:

Commissioning Editor Paula Hardy
Coordinating Editor Jessica Crouch
Coordinating Cartographer Jolyon Philcox
Coordinating Layout Designer Nicholas Colicchia
Managing Editor Imogen Bannister
Managing Cartographers Mark Griffiths, Herman So
Managing Layout Designer Sally Darmody
Assisting Editors Rebecca Chau, Charlotte Orr
Cover Designer Brendan Dempsey
Project Managers Rachel Imeson, Chris Love
Language Content Coordinator Quentin Frayne

Thanks to Lucy Birchley, Jessica Boland, Michala Green, Paul Iacono, Carol Jackson, Laura Jane, Yvonne Kirk, John Mazzocchi, Lauren Meiklejohn, Clara Monitto, Trent Paton, Jacqui Saunders, Lyahna Spencer, Laura Stansfeld, Branislava Vladisavljevic

THANKS
DUNCAN GARWOOD

Sardinia can be a lonesome place, but wherever I went I was met with hospitality and kindness. I owe a lot of thanks. In Cagliari, *grazie* to Simone Scalas, Maria Antonietta Goddi and Giulia Fonnesu for their time and valuable insights. In Nuoro, Giancarlo went out of his way to help, as did Tonino Lai in Ulassai and Zizzu Pirisi in Galtelli; the Marogna family updated me on the jewellery scene in Alghero, and Paola and Andrea advised on Oristano and the Sinis beaches. Thanks also to tourist office staff, in particular to Adriana in Tempio Pausania, Mariangela Pepetto in Carloforte, Emanuela at the Tourpass office in Santa Maria Navarrese, Francesco and Valeria at Cala Gonone, and the teams at Alghero, Nuoro and Dorgali. Travellers were also happy to share their tips, so good on you Alan Paddison, Alice Grigg, Hema Mistry, Samantha Prymaka, Roberto Milia, Luca Antonelli and Stefania Masella.

At Lonely Planet heaps of thanks to Paula Hardy for the commission, Michala Green for the brief and Mark Griffiths for the maps. It's been a long haul and there's no way I could have got through it without the support of my in-laws, Nello and Nicla Salvati, my long-suffering wife, Lidia, and our two little boys, Ben and Nick.

OUR READERS

Many thanks to the travellers who used the last edition and wrote to us with helpful hints, useful advice and interesting anecdotes:

THE LONELY PLANET STORY

Fresh from an epic journey across Europe, Asia and Australia in 1972, Tony and Maureen Wheeler sat at their kitchen table stapling together notes. The first Lonely Planet guidebook, *Across Asia on the Cheap,* was born.

Travellers snapped up the guides. Inspired by their success, the Wheelers began publishing books to Southeast Asia, India and beyond. Demand was prodigious, and the Wheelers expanded the business rapidly to keep up. Over the years, Lonely Planet extended its coverage to every country and into the virtual world via lonelyplanet.com and the Thorn Tree message board.

As Lonely Planet became a globally loved brand, Tony and Maureen received several offers for the company. But it wasn't until 2007 that they found a partner whom they trusted to remain true to the company's principles of travelling widely, treading lightly and giving sustainably. In October of that year, BBC Worldwide acquired a 75% share in the company, pledging to uphold Lonely Planet's commitment to independent travel, trustworthy advice and editorial independence.

Today, Lonely Planet has offices in Melbourne, London and Oakland, with over 500 staff members and 300 authors. Tony and Maureen are still actively involved with Lonely Planet. They're travelling more often than ever, and they're devoting their spare time to charitable projects. And the company is still driven by the philosophy of *Across Asia on the Cheap*: 'All you've got to do is decide to go and the hardest part is over. So go!'

BEHIND THE SCENES

SEND US YOUR FEEDBACK

We love to hear from travellers – your comments keep us on our toes and help make our books better. Our well-travelled team reads every word on what you loved or loathed about this book. Although we cannot reply individually to postal submissions, we always guarantee that your feedback goes straight to the appropriate authors, in time for the next edition. Each person who sends us information is thanked in the next edition – and the most useful submissions are rewarded with a free book.

To send us your updates – and find out about Lonely Planet events, newsletters and travel news – visit our award-winning website: **lonelyplanet.com/contact**.

Note: we may edit, reproduce and incorporate your comments in Lonely Planet products such as guidebooks, websites and digital products, so let us know if you don't want your comments reproduced or your name acknowledged. For a copy of our privacy policy visit lonelyplanet.com/privacy.

Pia Aeschlimann, Monica Altmann, Simone Assor, Flavia Attardi, Hans-Peter Baertschi, Anne Bartholomew, Anthony Blaschetto, Jan Bryla, Steve Chamberlain, Hanne Kingo Christensen, Marta Coll, E Diengani, Malcolm Dillon, Sandra Duggan, Iris Elliott, Brian Gottesman, Rocio Hernandez Viciana, Peter Herold, John Hurley, Andy Hurst, Christian Huss, Colin Jones, Christoffel Klimbie, Yuri Lipkov, Jenny Lunn, Simonetta Macellari, Helena Mah, Rob Montanari, Serhat Narsap, Marina Nogué Pich, Jess Owens, Gordon Parker, Joe Parlavecchio, Liz Paxton, Mark Poole, David Porter, Crispin Roberts, Mike Rouweler, Laurent Schinckus, Ilene Sterns, GM Stoffel, Jon Turner, José Vieira, Don Weston

ACKNOWLEDGMENTS
Many thanks to the following for the use of their content:

Globe on title page ©Mountain High Maps 1993 Digital Wisdom, Inc.

265

Index

INDEX

INDEX

GreenDex

An unfortunate fact of much coastal tourism in Sardinia is that the large-scale resorts that so ably part you from your money contribute little to the local environment. In an effort to promote sustainable travel, we've highlighted the following sites, activities, accommodation options, shops, and festivals that make a real effort to maintain rural traditions, minimise environmental impact and benefit the local economy. They range from *agriturismi* farm stays and *alberghi diffusi* hotels in refurbished *palazzi*, to local markets, food festivals and archaeological sites.

We want to keep developing our sustainable travel content so if you think we've left someone or something out, contact us at www.lonelyplanet.com/feedback and set us straight for next time.

For more information about sustainable travel, check out our website at www.lonelyplanet .com/responsibletravel.

LEGEND

ROUTES

Tollway · Walking Path
Freeway · Unsealed Road
Primary Road · Pedestrian Street
Secondary Road · Stepped Street
Tertiary Road · Tunnel
Lane · One Way Street
Walking Tour · Walking Tour Detour

TRANSPORT

Ferry · Rail
Metro · Rail (Underground)
Monorail · Tram

HYDROGRAPHY

River, Creek · Lake (Salt)
Intermittent River · Mudflats
Canal · Reef
Glacier · Swamp
Lake (Dry) · Water

BOUNDARIES

International · Ancient Wall
State, Provincial · Cliff
Regional, Suburb · Marine Park

POPULATION

CAPITAL (NATIONAL) · CAPITAL (STATE)
Large City · Medium City
Small City · Town, Village

AREA FEATURES

Area of Interest · Land
Beach, Desert · Mall
Building · Market
Cemetery, Christian · Park
Cemetery, Other · Sports
Forest · Urban

SYMBOLS

SIGHTS/ACTIVITIES	INFORMATION	SHOPPING
Beach	Bank, ATM	Shopping
Buddhist	Embassy/Consulate	**TRANSPORT**
Castle, Fortress	Hospital, Medical	Airport, Airfield
Christian	Information	Border Crossing
Confucian	Internet Facilities	Bus Station
Diving, Snorkeling	Parking Area	Cycling, Bicycle Path
Hindu	Petrol Station	General Transport
Islamic	Police Station	Taxi Rank
Jain	Post Office, GPO	Trail Head
Jewish	Telephone	**GEOGRAPHIC**
Monument	Toilets	Hazard
Museum, Gallery	**SLEEPING**	Lighthouse
Picnic Area	Sleeping	Lookout
Point of Interest	Camping	Mountain, Volcano
Ruin	**EATING**	National Park
Shinto	Eating	Oasis
Sikh	**DRINKING**	Pass, Canyon
Skiing	Drinking	River Flow
Taoist	Café	Shelter, Hut
Winery, Vineyard	**ENTERTAINMENT**	Spot Height
Zoo, Bird Sanctuary	Entertainment	Waterfall

NOTE: Not all symbols displayed above appear in this guide.

LONELY PLANET OFFICES

Australia

Head Office
Locked Bag 1, Footscray, Victoria 3011
☎ 03 8379 8000, fax 03 8379 8111
talk2us@lonelyplanet.com.au

USA

150 Linden St, Oakland, CA 94607
☎ 510 250 6400, toll free 800 275 8555
fax 510 893 8572
info@lonelyplanet.com

UK

2nd fl, 186 City Rd,
London EC1V 2NT
☎ 020 7106 2100, fax 020 7106 2101
go@lonelyplanet.co.uk

Published by Lonely Planet Publications Pty Ltd

ABN 36 005 607 983

Mixed Sources
Product group from well-managed forests and other controlled sources
www.fsc.org Cert no. SGS-COC-005002
© 1996 Forest Stewardship Council

Although the authors and Lonely Planet have taken all reasonable care in preparing this book, we make no warranty about the accuracy or completeness of its content and, to the maximum extent permitted, disclaim all liability arising from its use.